920.7209 GRE
Cameron, Elspeth,
Great dames /
282175

GREAT DAMES

MI NOV 00
AR MAR 12

SU JUN 2014

Great Dames is a collection of biographical sketches, memoirs, and essays about twentieth-century Canadian women from all walks of life. While attempting to capture the meaning of the ordinary lives of extraordinary women, it also explores the possibility of challenging, even subverting, the traditional view of life writing as an endeavour to 'summarize and fix in time the public careers of public men.' The fifteen essays represent a variety of alternative approaches to feminist biography, including chronological narrative, thematic exploration, multiple biography, conversations between biographer and subject, interviews, diaries, and even fictional accounts.

In selecting their subjects, from Mennonite refugee women to an Ojibwa ethnologist, the contributors were asked to consider women who would be unlikely candidates for longer biographies; in the course of their research, however, it became clear that the lives of at least two of the chosen subjects warranted book-length examination. The selection also attempts to address perceived gaps in regional, class, racial, and disciplinary representation in life writing.

Together, the essays reveal that the content, form, and perspective of biography are now bound only by the creativity, research energy, and taste of the biographer.

ELSPETH CAMERON is a professor of English at the University of Toronto, and the author and editor of many Canadian literary biographies. JANICE DICKIN is an associate professor in the Faculty of General Studies at the University of Calgary, and the editor of *Suitable for the Wilds*.

D1017633

Edited by Elspeth Cameron and Janice Dickin

Great Dames

UNIVERSITY OF TORONTO PRESS
Toronto Buffalo London

© University of Toronto Press Incorporated 1997
Toronto Buffalo London
Printed in Canada

ISBN 0-8020-0422-9 (cloth)
ISBN 0-8020-7215-1 (paper)

Printed on acid-free paper

Canadian Cataloguing in Publication Data

Main entry under title:

Great Dames

Includes index.
ISBN 0-8020-0422-9 (bound)   ISBN 0-8020-7215-1 (pbk.)

1. Women – Canada – Biography.   I. Cameron, Elspeth,
1943–   . II. Dickin, Janice.

FC26.W6G73 1997   920.72'0971   C96-932371-9
F1005.G73 1997

University of Toronto Press acknowledges the assistance to its publishing
program of the Canada Council and the Ontario Arts Council.

For Doris McCarthy,
and for all the other great dames
whose lives make a difference

Contents

Giving Voice

GREAT DAMES

Introduction

Until fairly recently, writing lives has largely, though certainly not exclusively, been an endeavour to describe, interpret, and thereby fix in time the public careers of public men. The theme of Plutarch's *Lives*,[1] the first writings acknowledged as biographical, was the acquisition and husbanding of political power by Greek and Roman men. The enduring connection between biography and nationalism has been thoughtfully explored by Anna Makolkin in *Name, Hero, Icon* (1992).[2] To some readers, this is still what biography is for. As citizens affected by the decisions of leaders and lawmakers, they crave comfort from confirmation of a national ideology and security from familiarity with the who, why, and how of government. Inevitably, however, such an approach privileges the 'extraordinary' man over the 'ordinary' person. In similar fashion, it privileges men over women and the public over the private.

Great Dames specifically sets out to explore possibilities in challenging – even subverting – this approach. The project, as originally suggested to us by Gerry Hallowell, was to produce a collection of biographies of ordinary Canadian women. Many of our contributors have been known to us personally for years. Familiar with their areas of scholarship, we presented the opportunity to participate in this collection to them as the perfect chance to write up a woman they had come into contact with, either in their research or their private lives. Such a woman was to be one whose story would not easily find expression through any other publishing project. In particular, we stipulated that these women not be obvious candidates for longer biographies.

From our core of contributors, we worked to fill what we perceived as gaps in regional, class, racial, and disciplinary representation in life writing. We do not count ourselves as entirely successful in our efforts to be representative. Books are limited in terms of length; editors are limited in terms of contacts; not all would-be writers can afford to write. The subject of one of our prospective contributors died before the research could be finished, and a family feud resulted in the withdrawal of necessary documentation at the last minute. Another 'lost' contributor had her own life changed and her responsibilities multiplied by the election of a Liberal government to Ottawa. As we prepare the final manuscript for publication, the shortcomings glare. We seek comfort from a hope that this collection will offer a sense of possibility for further explorations of the greatness of ordinary women's lives.

We hope that this sense of possibility extends not simply to the type of subject appropriate to biographical treatment but the sort of approach taken to biography itself. Susan Mann Trofimenkoff raised some of the problems associated with writing women's lives in 'Feminist Biography' (1985). Noting 'something decidedly odd' about biographies of women, she speculated that 'the political commitment of feminist scholarship' might well 'challenge literary and historical stereotypes.'[3] That this challenge would probably take biographers in the direction of writing lives of ordinary women was posited by Elspeth Cameron in 'Biography and Feminism' (1990).[4] Certainly, it became apparent to us and to our contributors that conventional biography alone was not going to serve us well in consideration of our great dames. An obvious problem was one of sources: ordinary people don't usually have archival material stored away waiting for the researcher. Creation of material through interviewing is not only time consuming and often (because of the travel involved) expensive, it carries with it a personal obligation on the part of the researcher that simply digging through archived documents does not. There is absolutely no way on earth for the interviewer not to interject herself into such an interview, and for this she must bear responsibility. As has been cogently argued by Kristina Minister in 'A Feminist Frame for the Oral History Interview,' 'interviewers who validate women by using women's communication are the midwives for women's words.'[5]

However, more than one of our contributors could not bring herself to conduct personal interviews, something many scholars find themselves apprehensive about and untrained for. Such people necessarily limit themselves to subjects that can be researched through documents. Another contributor (Afua Cooper) stuck straight to an interview format, presenting her results with little interpretation other than that implicit in the questions asked in the interview itself. We asked each contributor to write a hypothetical letter to her subject, saying whatever she wished about her experience of writing. Marlene Kadar's letter is included at the end of her chapter as a self-reflective device identifying issues and feelings that arose for her in deciding how to present the information she had. These musings offer much insight into the complex process of life writing.

Many of our contributors found their objectivity further complicated by the fact that they had some personal connection with their subjects, were therefore privy to information a stranger would not likely have been able to access, and consequently were presented with a special ethical dilemma. Many contributors found themselves caught in a balancing act, one that manifested itself most obviously in a delicate struggle to decide what to *call* their subjects. Calling a subject by her first name seemed to some disrespectful; calling her by her last name to others seemed cold. We have ended up with a series of curious compromises: double names throughout, honorifics such as Professor or Dr or Mrs sprinkled about, first name for a child replaced by last name at adulthood, and so on. This dilemma was further complicated by the evolution of custom through which women, who not long ago would automatically have assumed their husbands' names at marriage, began to retain the same name throughout life, despite marriage. One of our contributors confronted this problem by starkly listing her subject's four successive names right at the outset of her article!

These and other approaches settled upon by our contributors may challenge the techniques of ordinary biography, but they are made necessary by the inadequacy of conventional techniques to serve the lives of women – or, for that matter, most men. Granted, it is possible to produce biographies of women that look a great deal like biographies of men. However, the names of two recent examples – *Heroines* (1993)[6] and *The Encyclopedia of Amazons* (1991)[7] – demonstrate graphically the limitations of trying to stick to the Plutarch's *Lives* model. In order to utilize the usual life-as-adventure-or-achievement model, one must look for women whose lives have aped conventional male notions of adventure and achievement. This, by definition, means first of all that one must overlook most women. Second of all, it would seem that when one *does* find a woman with a 'male enough' life to qualify her for the standard male treatment, one must apologize, dissemble, and cringe to ensure she still qualifies as well as a female.

The world of Canadian letters boasts a hilarious example of what can result when one gets courtliness confused with biography. Henry James

Morgan makes it clear in his introduction to *Types of Canadian Women and of Women Who Are or Have Been Connected with Canada* (1903) that the women represented are meant to be 'types' whose lives exemplify 'the rare deserts [*sic*] of many Canadian women.'[8] To his credit, he states as one of his reasons for writing the book a desire to demonstrate the good results of educating women. There can, however, be no doubt that his subjects were chosen because of the status of 'the predominant partner'[9] or some other prominent male in their lives. While Madame Albani and Sara Jeannette Duncan each get an entry, they are outnumbered by 'wives of' and 'daughters of.' Moreover, it is unclear what it is about education for women that Morgan values. One young woman, Mrs Clifford Cory (née Jane Anne Gordon of Hamilton), for example, is said to practise the piano four hours a day, to have been praised by Paderewski, and to devote a further two hours a day to producing 'exquisite' embroidery.[10] If he sees her as an example of education well spent, we see her as a candidate for impending madness.

Still, there is something about Morgan and his work that niggles. First, he has a good grasp of how hard it is to do biographical research on women. He offers us some embroidery of his own in his description of persevering against the odds: 'Arduous though the research (which involved the writing of thousands of letters) has necessarily been, I never for a moment had reason to rue my undertaking. If it sometimes caused weariness of the flesh, the languor was dispelled by refreshings of the patriotic heart as ever new surprises disclosed the wealth of the mine which it was my happy lot to have opened to the world ... I felt like a convert from whose eyes the scales had fallen.'[11] Second, while what he hopes will come from consideration of his types is a national ideology and Who's Who à la Plutarch, he shares with us the hope that these stories will mean something beyond the confines of the lives they describe.

Our ideology is, however, feminist, and as feminists we are interested in examining what has been described as the 'dailiness' of women's lives. Women's lives have been described as episodic, fragmented, dispersed,[12] and as distinguished by marginality, discontinuity, and improvisation.[13] By definition, this means that the classic 'and their times' approach to biography can be only marginally effective with women. 'Against their times,' though not the recommended approach, must be carefully considered, as well as 'apart from their times.' All three modes can be found in this collection. Since our contributors were free to approach their subjects in whatever way seemed appropriate, some still relied on the 'and their times' method, especially where their subjects defined themselves in the male hierarchy. For others a mixed approach involving 'against their times' and 'apart from their times' seemed most true to their subjects.

An earlier version of *Great Dames* is Mary Quayle Innis's *The Clear Spirit* (1966). Her inability to abandon the 'and their times' approach is made clear by her use of the phrase in the subtitle. Produced for the Canadian Federation of University Women, the book set out to celebrate 'women whose work has been of national significance.'[14] (We note that she also struggled with the question of regionalism.) Published at a time when feminists were looking for a position in society which current feminists now question the value of, the book bears the markings of a transitional period, not least of all in the fact that it deals with the naming problem in terms of its contributors by dubbing them, to choose an example, both Clara Thomas and Mrs Morley Thomas.

Innis and her work were too early to profit from all the wonderful feminist output since the sixties. Feminist scholars now take for granted things scholars of women thirty years ago did not even suspect. One among these is that biography does not presuppose fame.[15] Another is that biography is a dialogue between author and subject, not an objective chronicling of fact.[16] Yet another is that subjects are not to be trusted as authorities on their own lives; the autobiographies we draw upon as sources, even when we have no reason to doubt their sincerity and goodwill, have to be read within a relationship that includes writer, text, and reader.[17] Carolyn Heilbrun, a feminist scholar who has not only produced biographies and biographical theory but has adopted the pseudonym of Amanda Cross to write mysteries featuring the fictional detective Kate Fansler, hastens to assure us that our inability to pin down real life doesn't matter anyway, since it is stories, not lives, that serve as models.[18]

This of course loops back to *Heroines* and *Amazons* and even to Morgan – women as types, lives as lessons, but also biographers as creators. Most of our contributors seized the challenge to experiment with the standard paradigm of life writing, hoping to capture the essence of their subjects. The submissions we received varied enormously. It is as if our authors acknowledged that the life of an ordinary woman could not be communicated by the usual methods and techniques of ordinary biography alone.

The result is a spectrum of life writings that make widely different assumptions about what constitutes 'truth' and, indeed, about what constitutes 'life.' At one end of the spectrum is Afua Cooper's unedited interview with Stephanie Martin and Makeda Silvera. By refusing to interpret the interview, Cooper draws attention to the important issue of appropriation of voice. To interpret is to subsume and colonize. This stance on one of the ethical issues life writers face corresponds with her insistence that phrases in what Canadians might call Jamaican dialect, or Creole, in her subjects' responses *not* be put in italics. *All* language is dialect, she maintains, and to designate specific terms as such is a form of cultural denigration. Despite this deliberate honouring of voice and language, this contribution also demonstrates that even the raw data of life writing are shaped by the presence, interests, and biases of the interviewer. At the other end of the spectrum is Aritha van Herk's fusion of self with subject. In a tour de force of identification with her subject, van Herk projects her own emotions, personality, and literary style onto the few known facts about her subject. In between lies a range of objective, intellectual, intuitional, emotional, and imaginative approaches called into play by the nature of subject, life writer, and the assumed relationships between them.

Techniques reinforcing the authority of the biographer include an assumed objectivity, heavy factual documentation, the forging of strong links between the subject and society, and a linear narrative based on the successful quest story. These techniques depend on the availability of extensive source materials, inevitably separate private life from public career, and demote the private realm to the role of backdrop. This approach also compartmentalizes and conceals the emotional stances and intellectual biases of biographers towards their subjects so that readers more readily accept what are inescapably slanted portraits as absolute truth. Treating the subject as representative of society – an Aeneas overcoming one obstacle after another on behalf of his nation state – artificially augments the subject's (and the biographer's) importance and placates readers with heroic nationalistic myth. Modelling biographical narrative on the linear successful quest story conveys the power of the individual to imprint life and change the world. The result of these standard methods and techniques is life writing that resembles an encyclopedia entry or obituary writ large.

We must conclude from such mainstream biographies that doing is more important that being; that life can be shaped rationally by a 'great' or wilful individual. The possibility that the reverse might be true – that life shapes us in illogical ways – has been obscured by these methods and assumptions. Certainly, such approaches proved unsuitable for many of the writers in this volume. They were, ironically, too 'life-less.' Ruth Landes, an anthropologist whose work with the Ojibwa is recorded in this volume, offered as justification for her largely intuitive and highly personal methods that 'I wanted the whole life [of each Ojibwa woman] – its warm breath, its traditional forms.' This too has been our aim in the biographical pieces in this volume.

Because many of our contributors shamelessly acknowledge their partiality, feelings, and hunches about their subjects – some, in fact, basing their accounts on close, long-standing friendships with the women about whom they write – the lives of our great dames often emerge as complex, inconsistent, transitional, and perplexing. Still, the heroic-male-public paradigm at times peeks through. It is not flatly backgrounded – as lovers, wives, and children often are in standard biographies of great men – but serves as a foil, often an influential one, in the life of a great dame. The life of Henrietta Ball Banting, for example, is intertwined with that of the famous man to whom she was briefly married. Her extended role as the professional widow of a man preoccupied with 'big things' contrasts with her own life choices in a tangle of complexity.

Judging from the biographical contributions to this collection, the lives of women are much more likely to be tangled than purposeful. They are typically many-layered or compartmentalized rather than lucid and lock-step. There is much evidence here to substantiate Carol Gilligan's findings with regard to the differences in the way women and men approach moral and other problems. The heroic-male-public paradigm of mainstream biography, with its linear step-by-step problem-solving 'progress' towards 'success,' does indeed resemble climbing a ladder, the image Gilligan uses in *In a Different Voice* for the typically male approach.[19] Her image for women's sense of connection between problem and context is the web, an image largely validated by the findings of our contributors.

A striking example in terms of this collection of how difficult it is to disentangle women from the web and get them onto the ladder is the fact that – despite our invitation to write about one woman – many contributors found it impossible to isolate the life of one great dame from the lives of others around her. Partially the problem was one of sources. Faced with limited personal narratives and little other information, Helen Buss produced a consideration of two settler women so as to give a more complete idea of a settler woman's 'life.' Marlene Epp offered a similar consideration of five Mennonite refugees, using pseudonyms to preserve anonymity. Carolyn Strange, unable to document 'fleshy narratives that flow seamlessly from women's childhood to death,' instead took what she calls 'fleeting glances' at a number of women in the shadow of the law.

The only author who chose directly to portray a twosome was Afua Cooper, who interviewed the co-founders of Sister Vision Press. Theirs is a lesbian relationship and a direct collaboration. A different kind of collaboration between women is illustrated by Sally Cole in her treatment of the American anthropologist Ruth Landes and the Ojibwa Maggie Wilson. In addition, three of the pieces involve women who shared their lives over a long term with a close female companion: Wendy Mitchinson's Marion Hilliard (Opal Boynton), Janice Dickin's Henrietta Ball Banting (Cecilia Long), and Alison Prentice's Elizabeth Allin (Dorothy Forward). And Patricia Smart's Thérèse Renaud only makes sense in the context of the *Refus global* women with whom she shared part of her destiny.

In addition, many of our authors found it impossible to separate their own lives from the lives of their subjects. Alison Prentice knew Elizabeth Allin. Marlene Kadar feels a strong affinity with Ibolya Szalai Grossman. In Gwethalyn Graham, Elspeth Cameron finds an important Canadian writer who has been unjustly marginalized and left to languish unbiographied. Marianne Gosztonyi Ainley has been Mabel McIntosh's friend for twenty-five years. Donna Smyth's presentation of Evelyn Garbary is intimate; Anna Koivu reminds Beverly Rasporich of her own Finnish grandmother. There can be no doubt that these women matter as persons to these writers. This is not the objectivity of mainstream biography. And Aritha van Herk goes completely over the top in terms of subjectivity, candidly admitting her identification with a subject she could not have known personally and melding the imaginative with the factual in order to propose a different kind of truth than that usually associated with life writing.

It is not only in life writing that Canadian feminist scholars have broken with the mainstream. In the literary realm, such works as *Inventory of Research in Canadian and Quebec Literatures* (1983),[20] *In the Feminine: Women and Words/Les Femmes et les mots* (1985),[21] *Sub/version* (1986),[22] *Gynocritics = Gynocritiques: Feminist Approaches to Canadian and Quebec Women's Writing* (1987),[23] and *Language in Her Eye: Writing and Gender* (1990)[24] laid the theoretical and critical groundwork for reconsiderations of the Canadian canon from a feminist perspective. Such studies tended to conclude, as American critic Susan Winnett observed in 1990, that 'we [women] have been taught to read in drag and must begin to question seriously the determinants that govern the mechanics of our narratives, the notion of history as a sense-making operation, and the enormous investment the patriarchy has in maintaining them.'[25]

Likewise, Canadian women's history has come under attack for its doggedly personal approach to women, for insisting that topics previously considered marginal, if not outright unthinkable, be given serious consideration. The fact that historical examination of women could not help but threaten mainstream historiography was foreshadowed in the title of an early discussion of archives and women's history, Veronica Strong-Boag's 'Raising Clio's Consciousness.'[26] That article is now nearly two decades old and marks the emergence of women's history in the 1970s as a distinct field.

It is difficult to re-imagine that world from this long remove. The sparseness of material is astounding, compared with the current wealth. Perhaps our greatest mark of success is a general history, *Canadian Women* (1988).[27] This is paired with *Quebec Women: A History* (1987).[28] General texts such as these cannot exist until a massive amount of research and a large scholarly output has taken place. Before one can talk in generalities, the specifics have to be uncovered, sorted through, thought out, and put together. Monographs such as *The New Day Recalled* (1988)[29] and *Making and Breaking the Rules* (1994)[30] also depend heavily on preliminary work done by a large number of scholars.

We not only have scholars, but students, as is evidenced by the fact that we have both books of readings[31] and books of essays featuring work by graduate students and newly minted PhDs.[32] And we have over the years learned to work in interesting ways with sources. For example, sources written against us can be turned into useful information on us, as Wendy Mitchinson shows with medical writings on women in *The Nature of Their Bodies* (1991).[33] We've entered interdisciplinarity with such special journal issues as Women in Canadian Society,[34] which covers topics from politics to photography, from royal commissions to life writing.

Another special journal issue concentrates on 'Dionnology,' indicating that we are now in an era when we're not just digging out the basic facts but can sit back and consider a fairly broad historiography on a very narrow topic. The Dionne Quintuplets: The Birth of an Industry[35] includes articles from scholars in public administration, sociology, history, women's studies, and education. Male authors are represented, as well as female. The power that used to be granted by the male gaze (gee, this must be important if the guys are interested) now lies firmly in female hands (golly, why not let the guys try their hand).

We've even got something more recent than women's studies – gender studies. Joy Parr's recent article and book[36] serve as a nice bookend to Veronica Strong-Boag's earlier article. Gender studies indicates an advance in theory, and in theorizing. Just when women's history seemed to some to be a safe enough little sidelight because it could be trapped into treating only the history of women – that is, dealing only with matters perpetrated by or suffered by women – gender history came along to insist that *all* history be treated as gendered, no matter *who* the major players are. The appearance of this point of view indicates clearly the degree to which women scholars and scholars of women have quit cringing and apologizing: it clearly demands that mainstream history not only take to its bosom 'women's way of knowing,'[37] but also apply it broadly. It insists that the web be valued equally with the ladder, a revolutionary idea.

This seems particularly fitting in that both the women's movement and women's history are themselves going through revolutionary times. We have come to question the applicability of some of the values we have worked so hard for during the last three decades. In short, we have had to get our own selves off the ladder and onto the web. Only in this way have we become 'womanist' in a broader sense, not simply feminist in the political sense. We have realized that we need to examine women's experience across a wider spectrum in order to understand the sense of women's lives. In women's history, this has been termed the 'Riley paradox.' Denise Riley pointed out in 1988 that it was impossible to understand the continuity of women's lives without recognizing their diversity.[38] We too have tried to arrive at continuity through diversity and also by attempting to order our contributions to form at least the vague outline of a web. To our surprise and gratification, we could glimpse faint traces of other connections.

We found that our contributions sought their own sort of rough order. The six sections we created to organize this order take us through problems of research, problems of writing, specific types of lives, ending with two very personal pieces where the great dames involved have a great deal of control over what is said about them.

'Just the Facts?' is meant to be an ironic title. Ibolya Szalai Grossman is instructed by her imprisoned husband to 'write down everything just as you know it,' which is something she tries to do. Honouring her subject's principle, Marlene Kadar attempts the same thing but shows just how evocative such minimalism can be. Marlene Epp is caught in a situation where she had promised anonymity to women interviewed earlier. She turns what might be in less imaginative hands a disadvantage into a chance to treat these women as a conglomerate, exploring the life of such women rather than the life of one. 'Just the Facts?' ends with Aritha van Herk's semi-abandonment of the facts after careful research: she knows from the documentation 'what happened,' but she refuses to accept this as 'truth,' making it clear that, for her, her own impressions of her subject must be consciously written into the story.

'Creating Facts' deals with women who have been written about by others. In Sally Cole's story of the friendship and colleagueship of Ruth Landes and Maggie Wilson, she must deal with the fact that Ruth sought out Maggie as a source of information, as an amanuensis for the stories of her culture. While both Maggie and Ruth are, in the end, ethnographers, they come at the facts from different perspectives and for different reasons. Carolyn Strange faces another problem. How, as a late-twentieth-century feminist, does one use sources written not only about women, but against women, to come to a less biased understanding of the meaning of their lives? Wanting to write on women criminals, Strange must use official records and newspaper reports that cannot be termed exactly user-friendly.

In 'Struggle to Create,' we encounter women who have decided to create lives for themselves out of the ordinary and against the odds. Patricia Smart deals with one woman working within a revolutionary cultural movement who must stage her own psychological revolution before she can break free of the gendered expectations of her. Thérèse Renaud will seem familiar to all women whose professional life has had to dance to the tune of the personal. Elspeth Cameron's Gwethalyn Graham is a brave soul who, despite success, never achieves fame. Despite circumstantial advantages and vitality, she never truly gains control of her own life because both domestic and professional systems discriminate against women.

In '"Traditional" Lives,' we look at women who have filled 'ordinary' (in the sense of gender-ordered) lives with extraordinary verve and meaning. Helen Buss's two settler women have chosen to tell their own stories as a way of speaking against the choices made for them by the 'predominant partners' in their lives. They may not have been in charge of their lives, but Buss shows that they are in charge of their stories, obfuscation aside. Beverly Rasporich's self-named 'log-cabin granny' (Anna Koivu) is indeed just that, but she's also a savvy bagwoman (as opposed to baglady) for one of Canada's most influential politicians, C.D. Howe. As a speaker and writer for her Northern Ontario Finnish community, she has an indisputable influence that makes her choice of moniker seem cheeky. Lastly, Marianne Ainley gives us a portrait of Mabel McIntosh, a woman who, after a crushing divorce in middle age, finds a surprising and important focus for her abilities. Her new-found hobby of bird watching turns to obsession and then into a volunteer career firmly anchored in the conservation movement.

Women 'Breaking into "Men's Professions"' is the subject of the next three authors. Wendy Mitchinson gives us a quick sketch of the larger-than-life Marion Hilliard, a doctor who wrote advice books for other women. Janice Dickin writes about Henrietta Ball Banting, a protégée of Hilliard who carried on her own successful medical career but whose life was always overshadowed by that of her late husband, the discoverer of insulin. Alison Prentice's Elizabeth Allin is a woman who establishes a career as a female exception within the physics department of the University of Toronto. All three of these women found channels through which to realize their professional ambitions but were also to some extent 'channelled' themselves because of their gender.

The last two papers we have entitled 'Giving Voice' because both involve women who have not only found a way to express themselves but have fashioned modes of expressions for others. Afua Cooper's interview with Makeda Silvera and Stephanie Martin, the founders of Sister Vision Press, is a celebration of commitment to providing publishing opportunities for women otherwised silenced. Donna Smyth's highly personal piece on Evelyn Garbary deals with the determination to bring drama to the people of Nova Scotia.

This is the superstructure of our web. We were able to ascertain several supporting threads. One of these is the theme of fragmentation and discontinuity in women's lives.

Against this fragmentation are at least two themes of connection. One of these is marriage. It is hard to think of marriage as turning out to be an inadvertent theme in a book of short mainstream biographies on men, but it shows up in almost every one of our chapters. There is both tragic marriage (Kadar, Rasporich, Dickin, Epp) and troubled marriage (Cole, Smart, Cameron, Smyth, Ainley). Florence Lassandro's husband (in Aritha van Herk's chapter) seems to be of no importance to the story, but that in itself is reason for comment. At least two of the women never married (Mitchinson, Prentice), also reason for comment. One of Helen Buss's women allows herself finally to be married off, the other hints at her dissatisfaction with her husband. Carolyn Strange's 'criminals' are single women in a society in which failure to marry could bring disastrous results. Ironically, in some ways the women who seem most 'married' are Makeda Silvera and Stephanie Martin, with their 'baby' (a box of files for their press) beside the bed.

A related and equally unexpected theme that developed across the papers is women's friendships. This has been discussed above in terms of the difficulty some of our contributors found in trying to deal with their great dame solely as an individual. What we mean here is something slightly different. There has been little written on close female relationships, not only in Canada but elsewhere. The classic is still Lillian Faderman's *Surpassing the Love of Men* (1981).[39] It is interesting to note that three out of the four keys under which the Library of Congress catalogues Faderman's book are 'Lesbianism – History,' 'Lesbians – Psychology,' and 'Lesbianism in literature – History.' This is in fact misleading and serves to roll the book into the literature of lesbianism, a field much more developed than that on friendship. Faderman in fact writes about women whose sex lives are largely if not entirely blank to us. What we *do* know is that they were committed, for life, to other women.

Three of our great dames – Marion Hilliard, Henrietta Ball Banting, and Elizabeth Allin – lived for years with other women. None of these women identified themselves as lesbian, nor do we have anything else to go on to justify our putting them arbitrarily into that category, other than our own era's tendency to see commitment and passion between women as necessarily having a sexual element. Faderman was not willing to make this leap in her careful study, and neither are we. The truth is that we cannot know what we cannot know, and we are better advised to work with what we do know – that these women were committed to female partners – than to slot them into categories that can only serve to package further research in this area. A theme we see as needing urgently to be developed is that of woman-to-woman commitment, whether it be sexual or not. This is a part of the web that badly needs filling in.

Perhaps it is only now that this theme can be developed. We are acutely aware that in writing this introduction we are women writing about women (our contributors) writing about women (their subjects). In one instance (Cole), the subjects themselves have written about women. This extends backwards to cover four generations. Surely we are the first generation of women who can make such a claim.

We have learned much from compiling this collection. One of the things we learned was that at least three of our great dames – Graham, Landes, and Hilliard – warrant longer biographies. And of course we relearned how much we are dependent on our female colleagues to spin the web.

A final word – about our title. Reaction to it has been bipolar. While we respect the fears of those who react badly to it, we have decided to keep it. The term *Dame* is an honorific. It has been distorted by ill-wishers who fear the power of women and desire to denigrate us. We are reclaiming the word – positively.

NOTES

1 *Plutarch's Lives*, trans. Bernadotte Perrin, 11 vols. (Cambridge: Harvard University Press, 1986). Various paperback editions are available.
2 Anna Makolkin, *Name, Hero, Icon: A Semiotics of Nationalism through Heroic Biography* (Berlin: Mouton de Gruyter, 1992)
3 Susan Mann Trofimenkoff, 'Feminist Biography,' *Atlantis* 10, no. 2 (Spring 1985): 1–9
4 Elspeth Cameron, 'Feminism and Biography' in *Language in Her Eye: Writing and Gender, Views by Canadian Women Writing in English*, ed. Libby Scheier, Sarah Sheard, and Eleanor Wachtel (Toronto: Coach House Press, 1990), 72–82
5 Kristina Minister, 'A Feminist Frame for the Oral History Interview' in *Women's Words: The Feminist Practice of Oral History*, ed. Sherna Berger Gluck and Daphne Patai (New York and London: Routledge, 1991), 27–41
6 Norma Lorre Goodrich, *Heroines: Demigoddess, Prima Donna, Movie Star* (New York: HarperCollins, 1993)
7 Jessica Amanda Salmonson, *The Encyclopedia of Amazons: Women Warriors from Antiquity to the Modern Era* (New York: Paragon House, 1991)
8 Henry James Morgan, ed., *Types of Canadian Women and of Women Who Are or Have Been Connected with Canada* (Toronto: William Briggs, 1903), v
9 Ibid., vi
10 Ibid., 61
11 Ibid., v–vi
12 See the chapter on 'The Dailiness of Women's Lives' in Bettina Aptheker, *Tapestries of Life: Women's Work, Women's Consciousness, and the Meaning of Daily Experience* (Amherst: University of Massachusetts Press, 1989), 39–74.
13 See the introductory chapter 'Emergent Visions' in Mary Catherine Bateson, *Composing a Life* (Harmondsworth: Penguin, 1989), 1–18.
14 Mary Quayle Innis, ed., *The Clear Spirit: Twenty Canadian Women and Their Times* (Toronto: University of Toronto Press, 1966), ix

15 Innis's title is from Milton, *Lycidas*: 'Fame is the spur that the clear spirit doth raise ... / To scorn delights and live laborious days.'
16 See Carol Ascher, Louise De Salvo, and Sara Ruddick, eds., *Between Women: Biographers, Novelists, Critics, Teachers and Artists Write about Their Work on Women* (Boston: Beacon Press, 1984; reprint, New York: Routledge, 1993), for intimate descriptions of these dialogues. See especially, Carol Ascher, 'On "Clearing the Air": My Letter to Simone de Beauvoir,' 85–103 (page citations are to the reprint edition).
17 See Helen M. Buss, *Mapping Ourselves: Canadian Women's Autobiography in English* (Montreal and Kingston: McGill-Queen's University Press, 1993).
18 Carolyn G. Heilbrun, *Writing a Woman's Life* (New York: W.W. Norton, 1988), 37
19 Carol Gilligan, *In a Different Voice: Psychological Theory and Women's Development* (Cambridge: Harvard University Press, 1982, reprint 1993)
20 Barbara Godard, with Heliane C. Daziron, *Inventory of Research in Canadian and Quebec Literatures* (Downsview: York University, 1983)
21 Ann Dybikowski, Victoria Freeman, Daphne Marlatt, Barbara Pulling, and Betsy Warland, eds., *In the Feminine: Women and Words/Les femmes et les mots* (Edmonton: Longspoon Press, 1985)
22 Lorna Irvine, *Sub/version* (Toronto: ECW Press, 1986)
23 Barbara Godard, *Gynocritics = Gynocritiques: Feminist Approaches to Canadian and Quebec Women's Writing* (Toronto: ECW Press, 1987)
24 Sheier, Sheard, and Wachtel, eds., *Language in Her Eye*
25 Susan Winnett, 'Coming Unstrung: Women, Men, Narrative, and Principles of Pleasure,' *PMLA* 105 (May 1990): 516
26 Veronica Strong-Boag, 'Raising Clio's Consciousness: Women's History and Archives in Canada,' *Archivaria* 6 (Summer 1978): 70–82
27 Alison Prentice, Paula Bourne, Gail Cuthbert Brandt, Beth Light, Wendy Mitchinson, and Naomi Black, *Canadian Women: A History*, 2nd ed. (Toronto: Harcourt Brace, 1996). First published in 1988
28 Micheline Dumont, Michèle Jean, Marie Lavigne, and Jennifer Stoddart, *Quebec Women: A History* (Toronto: Women's Press, 1987). Originally published as *L'Histoire des femmes au Québec depuis quatre siècles*
29 Veronica Strong-Boag, *The New Day Recalled: Lives of Girls and Women in English Canada, 1919–1939* (Toronto: Copp Clark Pitman, 1988)
30 Andrée Lévesque, *Making and Breaking the Rules: Women in Quebec, 1919–1939* (Toronto: McClelland and Stewart, 1994). Originally published as *La Norme et les déviantes: des femmes au Québec pendant l'entre-deux-guerres*
31 Veronica Strong-Boag and Anita Clair Fellman, eds., *Rethinking Canada: The Promise of Women's History*, 2nd ed. (Toronto: Copp Clark Pitman, 1991)
32 See, for example, Franca Iacovetta and Mariana Valverde, eds., *Gender*

Conflicts: New Essays in Women's History (Toronto: University of Toronto Press, 1992).

33 Wendy Mitchinson, *The Nature of Their Bodies: Women and Their Doctors in Victorian Canada* (Toronto: University of Toronto Press, 1991)

34 *International Journal of Canadian Studies* 11 (Spring 1995), Special Issue, Women in Canadian Society

35 *Journal of Canadian Studies* 29 (Winter 1994–95), Special Issue, The Dionne Quintuplets: The Birth of an Industry

36 Joy Parr, 'Gender History and Historical Practice,' *Canadian Historical Review* 76 (Sept. 1995): 354–76; Joy Parr and Mark Rosenfeld, eds., *Gender and History in Canada* (Toronto: Copp Clark, 1996)

37 Mary Field Belenky, B.M. Clinchy, N.R. Goldberger, and J.M. Tarule, *Women's Way of Knowing: The Development of Self, Voice, and Mind* (New York: Basic Books, 1986)

38 Denise Riley, *'Am I That Name?' Feminism and the Category of 'Women' in History* (Minneapolis: University of Minnesota Press, 1988), 4, 98

39 Lillian Faderman, *Surpassing the Love of Men: Romantic Friendship and Love between Women from the Renaissance to the Present* (New York: Quill, 1981)

JUST THE FACTS?

'Write Down Everything Just as You Know It': A Portrait of Ibolya Szalai Grossman

MARLENE KADAR

We suffered so much, but I know others suffered more. Much, much more.

Ibolya Grossman, *An Ordinary Woman in Extraordinary Times*

I

The Life, a Chronology

10 December 1916   Ibolya was born in Pécs in the southwest part of Hungary to Ignacz Szalai and his second wife, Laura Fisher. She was the second-born of three daughters. She also had two half-sisters who were born to her father's first wife. Ignacz was a tinsmith; Laura kept a kosher house and blessed the children on Friday nights because the father, whose duty it would normally be to bless the family, was not very religious. Ibolya says that although there was always enough food on the table, the family was poor.

c. 1921–5   Ibolya went to a Hebrew elementary school, *Zsido Elemi Iskola*, but was not happy there. The students were well-off and mocked Ibolya because she was poor.

c. 1926–33   Ibolya went to a public school, *Varosi Polgari Iskola*. Her best friend was Ilona Czeininger, a Roman Catholic girl.

c. 1931   Ibolya joined the Hungarian Zionist youth movement; her Zionist name was Dvora. She met Zoltan Rechnitzer (referred to affectionately as Zolti) at the movement's farewell campfire. Ibi knew she was perceived as a radical by the local police, who kept records of the youth members.

1933   Ibolya moved to Budapest to live with her older sister, Aranka. To support herself, Ibi worked in the *Fonal Kikeszítő* thread factory for a few months.

1936   The Rechnitzer family moved to Budapest from the city of Pápa, located in the western part of the country. Henrik Rechnitzer made his living as a podiatrist; Janka Rechnitzer, his wife, practised Judaism faithfully, even later during the communist era, when it was disadvantageous to do so. Ibi saw Zolti again, and they began a courtship.

17 September 1939   Happily, Ibi married Zolti in Budapest, although Ibi had worried that Zolti's parents had wanted their only son to marry 'a rich Jewish girl,' and Ibi was by no means rich.

1940–4   'Although the Hungarian Jewish community ... was subjected to grave injustices, it survived the first four and a half years of World War II relatively intact. While their brethren in Nazi-dominated Europe were being eliminated under the Final Solution program, the Hungarian Jews continued to enjoy the physical protection of the aristocratic-conservative government of Miklós Kállay.'[1]

1941   Ibi became pregnant and, though generally optimistic, harboured some fear for the safety of her family. Her Jewish friends said, 'Are you crazy?' Zolti said, 'We need that baby. You will see.' Ibi's emotions vacillated between the fear she felt in the particular circumstance, and the optimism she said she inherited from her father.

16 July 1942   Andras (Andy) was born in a hospital in Budapest. It was during his delivery that Ibi experienced and witnessed anti-Semitism first-hand, but she still felt optimistic about her own circumstances. There appeared to be no bed for her in the hospital; she was instructed to deliver her baby on the floor. Later she heard a nurse refer to a new baby who was spitting up blood as a 'Jewish bastard,' for whom a doctor needn't hurry.

According to Maria Kovacs, institutions of public health were particularly virulent in their anti-Semitism. 'As early as 1919, a strong, right-

Mrs Ibolya Grossman

wing anti-Semitic doctors' association was formed.'[2] Kovacs compares physicians to lawyers: the proportion of Jewish lawyers declined only very slowly throughout the interwar period, from 51 per cent in 1920 to 40 per cent in 1938, whereas the proportion of Jews among physicians 'declined sharply.'[3]

25 November 1942   First notice posted: All Jewish men between the ages of eighteen and fifty must report to army headquarters for service. Zolti reported for army duty. 'A unique feature of the Hungarian policy toward Jews was the inclusion of Jewish men in the Hungarian army as forced labour. At its height, there were 80,000 workers in this program, many of whom worked side by side with German soldiers at the front.'[4]

Thus, Zolti was given a Hungarian soldier's army cap, but no uniform. He wore a yellow armband. Soldiers who were half-Jewish wore white armbands. Zoltan was taken to the Felvidék (a territory made up of the Upper Province, the highlands of Slovakia, re-annexed in 1938, and Ukraine)[5] for service. Ibi lived with her in-laws at 16 Népszínház Street.[6] Zolti visited once for two weeks, and then occasionally for a day at a time. He said that the conditions of his life were not so bad because his *keretlegeny* (army leader), George, was a good man. Things got worse when George was replaced by a sadistic fellow.

19 March 1944   German forces occupy Hungary. The leaders of Hungarian Jewry were ordered by the Eichmann-Sonderkommando to form a Jewish Council to manage the ghettos. Zolti began to write to Ibi in code, signing his name 'Radai, Zoltan' instead of 'Rechnizer.'

9 May 1944   Zolti was taken to a forced labour camp, the addresses of which were K.M.Sz\M 866/B, or K.M.Sz\B 499. This was the last time Ibi saw Zolti.

4 July 1944   The Jewish population of Pécs and its environs was taken to Auschwitz in cattle wagons. Ibi's parents and two half-sisters were among them. This Ibi knows from reading a Budapest newspaper much later in 1945, after she was liberated from the ghetto.

'Between May 15 and July 9, 1944, 437,402 Jews were deported from Hungary.'[7]

July 1944   Of the 800,000 Jews in Hungary, 440,000 were deported to Auschwitz. This was the swiftest of the Final Solution programs in Europe.

3 August 1944   Ibi received her ninth communication (out of sixteen) from Zolti, a postcard in which he instructs her to write down everything that she knows (about the present situation of the Jews in Hungary, Ibi and I assume). These words are underlined by Zolti.

17 August 1944   Western Allies accepted the so-called Horthy offer concerning the emigration of several thousand Hungarian Jews.[8] President Roosevelt agreed to admit 987 'carefully screened' refugees. Canada, however, 'failed to reply.'[9]

3 (?) October 1944   Ibi received a last communication from Zolti. She refers to this communication as her husband's farewell card because it is written as if he knew it was his last.

15 October 1944   Regent Admiral Miklos Horthy announced that Hungary was not going to war, and that 'nobody had to worry.' Ibi thought this meant she could tear the yellow star off her chest. Later that day Ferencz Szalasi and the Arrow Cross Party took over the government and promised that 'he would help the Germans to exterminate the Jews.'[10]

16 October 1944   Police and fascists announced: 'Every Jew down to the yard or [we] shoot!'[11] First the Jews living at 16 Népszínház Street were robbed, but Ibi was determined to keep her wedding ring. She hid it in Andy's coat pocket. Civilian spectators lined the sidewalks and harassed the poor people as they walked. They also beat Ibi's father-in-law. An ordinary citizen grabbed Andy's blanket out of Ibi's hands. Ibi and her family were led to the Tattersal racetrack where they were kept without major incident for two days. All of a sudden, Szalasi's voice bellowed on the loudspeaker at 3 AM that the captured Jews could all go home now, but as the terrified victims exited the racetrack, German guards shot at them at random. This was a popular form of entertainment among members of the SS. 'Many were wounded and killed, but somehow we got home.'[12]

c. November 1944   Ibi and Andy hid at the Red Cross Home on Columbus Street for two weeks. But Andy became ill, so Ibi returned home to Janka to help him recover. Just before the next round-up of Jews at Népszínház, Ibi, Janka, and Andy went back to the Red Cross Home. 'The lucky ones were taken to the Columbus Street [house].'[13] One or two police officers escorted Ibi, Janka, a few other parents, and approximately twenty children to the home, which was a twenty-minute walk from Népszínház Street.

3 December 1944   The Jews hiding in the home were captured and taken to a football stadium for 'sorting.' By chance, Ibi survived the sorting and was sent to the ghetto with the 'older' women and Andy. The younger women were sent to concentration camps. Some very young children were taken to the ghetto by their relatives and other adults. Andy was two and a half years old at the time.[14]

The non-Jewish population was evicted from the area designated 'the ghetto.' Those evicted had their choice of houses abandoned by Jews elsewhere in the city. Ibi, Janka, and Andy were taken to 45 Akácfa Street, Budapest Ghetto District 10. *Akácfa* is the Hungarian word for the acacia tree, beautiful and fragrant. Because it produced pink and white blooms, the acacia was considered sacred by the Egyptians. In Hermetic doctrine, it symbolized the testament of Hiram, which teaches that 'one must know how to die in order to live again in eternity.'[15]

'The relocation of the Jews began toward the end of November and was virtually completed by December 2.'[16]

20 December 1944   The gates of the ghetto were shut. Only the hearse was allowed in and out. Food became very scarce.

25 December 1944   The Soviet Army encircled Budapest. The closer it came, the more virulent the attacks on the remaining Jews.

16 January 1945   The Swedish diplomat Raoul Wallenberg intervened on behalf of the Jewish population in Hungary. He somehow succeeded in botching a Nazi plan to wipe out the ghetto 'by mines or machine guns.'[17]

18 January 1945   Ibi saw the first Russian soldier in the ghetto yard at *Akácfa* Street.

30 January 1945   Ibi did as Zolti had instructed: she wrote down what she knew while it was fresh in her memory. This writing took the form of a letter to Zoltan, never delivered, but saved till this day.

18 February 1945   Zolti, who was very ill with typhus, was shot to death by Germans. He would have been thirty-one years old in March.

Ibolya Szalai Reti (to disguise the Jewishness of his name and therefore protect his family, Henrik changed it from Rechnitzer to Reti) was one of the 293,000 Jewish survivors of the Holocaust in Hungary. This means that approximately 502,500 Jewish men, women, and children were killed or died in Hungary during the Final Solution in 1944–5.[18]

October 1949   Ibi and Andy Reti attempted their first escape. However, they were betrayed by the Hungarian peasant woman who was meant to help them. They were detained by Czechoslovakian border guards and jailed in a border detention centre. Eventually Janka arrived at the detention centre to take Andy home with her to Budapest. Ibi was transported to a jail at Miskolc in the far north of the country with other political prisoners, largely women dissidents.

21 December 1950   Stalin's birthday. Political prisoners, including Ibi, were released in celebration.

23 October 1956   The Hungarian Revolution began, and so did anti-Semitic postering. Ibi swore 'never again,' and, in order to persuade him to leave his homeland, explained to Andy, who was fourteen years of age, that 'all those things happened to us because we are Jews.'[19] 'All those things' included Zolti's forced labour service and subsequent death.

27 December 1956   Ibi and Andy successfully escaped from Hungary. They set sail for Canada from Vienna aboard the ship *Berlin*.

8 January 1957   They arrived in Halifax. Helped by Jewish Family Services and the Jewish Congress, Ibi and Andy settled in Winnipeg where Ibi was able to get work in the textile factories. Ibi also studied English.

Summer 1958   Ibi and Andy moved to Toronto to be reunited with her sister Aranka and her family, who had also immigrated to Canada. Ibi got a job as a cleaning lady in the Toronto Western Hospital (now called the Toronto Hospital).

14 December 1958   Ibi married Émil Grossman in Toronto, and the period of her long migration from Hungary to Canada ended.
    Emil had been in a forced labour servicemen's camp in Hungary during the war. He was forty-six years old and 'very hard-working. He is honest, clean and a handsome person'[20] from a small village in the north of Hungary, Meszes.

1990   Ibi writes her life and, true to her modest self, calls the book *An Ordinary Woman in Extraordinary Times*. Ibi becomes a writer. Ibi must write down what she remembers, as instructed by Zolti so many years ago.

II

A Night in 1944

Ibolya Szalai Grossman wrote a letter to her husband, Zoltan Rechnitzer, on 30 January 1945 from her home in Budapest. Thereafter Zolti
had 'no real address.' He had been taken to a forced labour camp on
25 November 1942. From this place and others like it, he had sent Ibi at
least sixteen postcards. Each card had a return 'K.M.Sz.' number:
K.M.Sz. stands for *Katonai Munka Szolgálat* (Soldiers' Work Camp). For
the most part, Zolti's number was K.M.Sz.\M 866/B. Sometimes it was
K.M.Sz.\B499. To this day Ibi Grossman does not know where M866/B
or B499 were located.

Ibolya's letter to Zolti remained undelivered. She wrote it because he
had instructed her, somewhat obliquely, in one of his cards to 'write
down everything just as you know it.' Ibolya did what he told her to do.
In particular, she wanted to record that horrible day when she was
taken to the huge football field. Because she has no interest in sports,
Ibolya does not know the name of this field, nor does she know where
exactly it was located in Budapest. It was at the football field, however,
that Ibi knew, in her own words, 'life hanged on a thread.' As a consequence, Ibi Grossman says her sleep is still disturbed on two counts.

The First Count: 'Life Hanged on a Thread'

On 3 December 1944, Ibolya, Ibi's son Andy, and her mother-in-law,
Janka Reti, were found out in their hiding place, the Red Cross Home on
Columbus Street, certain that they 'had been denounced by our fellow
Hungarians.' The home was encircled by 'Hungarian Arrow Cross
bandits who called themselves soldiers.'[21] By 1944 the majority of the
Jewish people in the home were women and children, including
orphaned girls and boys. They were taken to a football field to be sorted
into two groups: according to Ibi, the young women to be sent to the
camps; the older women, and mothers with babies under one year of
age were 'allowed' to go to the ghetto. But older children had to be left
behind on the field, and Ibi does not really know what happened to
them. Initially Ibolya and Andy were separated. She can still hear Andy
screaming for her not to leave him. Ibi Grossman says her sleep is still
disturbed by the sound of the screams of the little ones and of the
mothers from whom they were taken.

Thankfully for Ibi, Janka knew one of the Hungarian policeman on duty in the football field. He redirected Ibi to 'the ghetto group' where she was reunited with Andy and her mother-in-law. She then wrapped a black kerchief around her head so that she would look more mature. She was only twenty-seven years old at the time, but to be sorted into the ghetto group, you had to be forty. Ibi covered her face and her son's face with a blanket as she marched on to the ghetto. The ghetto was familiar: it was located in downtown Pest (the eastern segment of Budapest), the 7th 'Jewish' District of the capital. Altogether it consisted of about ten streets, bounded by Király Street and Dóhany Street, Károly körút and Nagyatadi Szabo Street. This area was composed of 162 Yellow Star buildings, approximately 0.3 square kilometres, a fraction of the city's 207 square kilometres. Like the Warsaw ghetto, it was surrounded by a tall wooden fence; as in Warsaw, the fence was built at Jewish expense and with Jewish hands.[22] Early in December the ghetto contained approximately 33,000 Jews; by the end of the month the population had increased to 55,000. In January 1945, just before Ibi's 'liberation,' the ghetto contained nearly 70,000 Jews.[23] Many of these were elderly people, and lone girls and boys.

The Second Count

Ibi's sleep is also disturbed by the thought of the horrors that her beloved Zolti endured at the hands of the German *Schutzstaffel* (SS) and their Hungarian comrades, the Arrow Cross.[24] Nothing seems more final than this; nothing more gruesome. Ibi's memories of atrocities are the pain of a woman who has called herself ordinary.

III

About the Ordinary Woman

The truth is that most of the world's women are ordinary; they are not celebrities in the conventional sense, though their integrity and bravery are to be celebrated. What Ibi Grossman accomplished and surmounted in her life is testimony to her extraordinariness.

It wasn't until the seventeenth century that the adjective *ordinary* got a bad name, when it came to mean 'not singular or exceptional.' Better for those engaged in the reclamation of all women's voices that ordinariness, too, be reclaimed. The ordinary woman's identity is not only produced by her gender: most importantly, the ordinary woman creates knowledge out of her history as much as any other person who tells her or his story.[25]

For the sake of this 'portrait' of Ibi, an ordinary woman is a woman whose history is not validated by the ideology and norms of a dominant educated and classed culture, but whose character is singular in its strength and vision, and constructed persuasively in its own story. Key to this ordinariness is modesty; this modesty is disclosed in a lack of pretension in the life and in the life narrative constructed by the self-portraitist – in this case, Ibi Grossman's *An Ordinary Woman in Extraordinary Times*.

Ibi Grossman's contribution to our present-day world has to do with four life facts: first, she survived numerous attempts to end her life in her home country, Hungary; second, she withstood horrendous mental and physical suffering during the Holocaust in Hungary, especially between 1942 and 1944, and during her escape to the West; third, she overcame the obstacles faced by all Central European Jewish immigrants and made a new home in Canada in a new language and a new, predominantly Christian culture; and fourth, she did all of this after her husband, her parents, and two of her sisters died in death camps during the implementation of the Final Solution in Hungary, leaving her to raise a baby boy alone.

Ibolya's life stands now as a symbol of human dignity, intelligence, and forbearance. Who is to say what an ordinary woman is?

IV

Conclusion: Letter to Ibi, the Writer

30 January 1995

Dear Ibi,

I have been asked by my editors to write you a letter in order to help them generate some ideas for the introduction to *Great Dames*, the book in which my 'portrait' of you will appear. The editors want to get at the 'essence' of my experience of writing the 'portrait' inasmuch as is possible. Why have I written this portrait about you, and why have I written it in this fashion. I suspect that what I write, you will already know; it is for their sake, then (ostensibly), that I write this letter.

I think you know that in the first place it is my admiration of you that has inspired me to write about you. I admire you in two time frames: in the present, as the extraordinary woman you have become; and in the past, as the extraordinary woman who endured and negotiated her way through lies, torment, and homelessness.

Inspired by my admiration for you, I think you know that I also have my own political and theoretical reasons for attempting this portrait. These reasons are played out in my concerns about the relationships that form (unevenly) between cultures and politics, and about literary genres and intellectual expressions of pretension in and through nations. Thus, I am concerned about what I interpret as a rise in the number of expressions of 'racial,' cultural, and religious intolerance in Canada, including anti-Semitism, and also about the academic rubber stamping of ideas and generic types that reify already existing norms about who is bad and what is good. This political agenda I have is an opportunity to admire you 'in the past.' Thus, I saw your 'ordinary' life story as a permanent challenge to dualistic assumptions, and also as an unintentional deconstruction of pretentious intellectualism and hard-heartedness. Because I suspect that intolerance may be the political and social equivalent of intellectual pretentiousness, your 'life in the past' became a beacon for me, illuminating your 'life in the present.' But it also illuminated present trends in representation and expressions of prejudice, alongside stark events in the past, and necessary but wanting interpretations of genocidal policies and actions.

In addition to my admiration for you and my political agenda, it was a challenge, theoretically, to write *about* someone else, precisely because I had not included 'biography' (in its purest modern form) in my definition of life writing.[26] I wanted to tackle this portrait of you precisely because of my intellectual suspicions about biography as a totalizing genre that has, in the past, looked to great men's lives (also Visweswaran's 'unique and autonomous subjects'[27]) for great stories of legitimation.[28] Moreover, biography is based on the third-person recording and interpreting of 'personal' details of a life, details that are already always entrenched, entangled, contested,[29] and, too often, unforgiven and resented by the one living the life. Thus the genre requires, to my mind, that the biographer make claims and moral judgments about a life that is already complicated and pained, but also a life that belongs to someone else, and in that sense can never be known. I am uncomfortable about making these claims, and yet I know I make judgments about lives all the time.

I had to then write up your life somehow while allowing my discomfort with biographical writing to guide me – it, in fact, became a strategic opportunity (not to write biographically), not a bane. I also had to confront my battle with pretentiousness, and write up a life that was extraordinary to me, but 'ordinary' to you. Already I had set myself up as the expert on something I had no real part in, and in the midst of this contradiction, I was committed to writing as best I could. I decided to try and 'factualize' your life in a way that would prevent a reader from feeling sorry for you, even though facts and dates are not what usually move us. I remember Hannah Arendt's cautionary words. She suggests that pity actually 'endorses' suffering: 'Without the presence of misfortune, pity could not exist, and it therefore has just as much vested interest in the existence of the unhappy as thirst for power has a vested interest in the existence of the weak. Moreover, by virtue of being a sentiment, pity can be enjoyed for its own sake, and this will almost automatically lead to a glorification of its cause, which is the suffering of others.'[30]

In recording facts and dates, then, I felt I was countering the desire to feel pity, and in my own way I was also authorizing the Canadian survivor's ability to remember accurately (so many years later) by quoting you in my factualizing, and then referring to Hungarian and North American 'scientific' authorities. Shocking even to me was how often their story was corroborated by you, right down to the incident at the Red Cross house.

My own political goal here was to also further reclaim the genre of life writing, which includes oral testimony, and women's personal experience as expressed in it – fifty or more years later. As Meese writes, 'By means of oral testimony, we generate both the unwritten historical and the literary records, and ... we broaden the standard of comparison for women's written tradition.'[31] In addition, I had a literary goal to write a story that made sense without over-explaining the horror. I wanted a story that made an imaginative gesture towards the meaning of your life from the time of Zolti's death until now. That meaning was illuminated for me soon after you showed me the postcards – you were meant to write everything down just as it was. For me, that meant two things. You were meant to give the evidence to me. And you were meant to become a writer.

Respectfully,

Marlene Kadar

NOTES

I want to acknowledge ideas that I have used to construct this portrait that have been stimulated by conversations I have had with Elspeth Cameron, Ferne Cristall, Susan Ehrlich, Debbie Field, Marianne Grek, Emma Kadar Penner, Judith Kalman, Michael Kaufman, Gary Norman, and Christl Verduyn. In addition to the references cited in these notes, this portrait drew on interviews I conducted with Ibolya Grossman in Toronto, 25 October and 2 November 1994.

1 Randolph L. Braham, ed., *Studies on the Holocaust in Hungary* (Boulder: Social Science Monographs; New York: Csengeri Institute for Holocaust Studies of the Graduate School and University Center of the City University of New York, 1990), v
2 Mária Kovács, 'Lawyers against the Current Anti-Semitism and Liberal Response in Interwar Hungary' in *A Social and Economic History of Central European Jewry*, ed. Yehuda Don and Victor Karady (New Brunswick, NJ, and London: Transaction, 1990), 250
3 Ibid., 251, 250
4 Dieter Vaupel, 'The Hessisch Lichtenau Sub-Camp of the Buchenwald Concentration Camp, 1944–45' in *Studies on the Holocaust*, 199
5 Tamás Majsai, 'The Deportation of Jews from Csíkszereda and Margit Slachta's Intervention on Their Behalf' in *Studies on the Holocaust*, 114
6 Described in Ibolya Grossman, 'A Mother's Kiss from the Grave,' *Canadian Woman Studies* 14, no. 1 (Fall 1993): 25–6.
7 Vaupel, 'Hessisch Lichtenau Sub-Camp,' 200
8 Randolph L. Braham, *The Politics of Genocide: The Holocaust in Hungary* (New York: Columbia University Press, 1981), 2:1215
9 Ibid., 1116–17
10 Ibolya Grossman, *An Ordinary Woman in Extraordinary Times* (Toronto: Multicultural History Society of Ontario, 1990), 37
11 Ibid.
12 Ibid., 38
13 Braham, *Politics of Genocide*, 2:954; Jeno Lévai, *A Pesti gettó története* (Official History of the [Buda]Pest Ghetto) (Budapest: Officina nyomda, n.d.)
14 Grossman, *An Ordinary Woman*, 41
15 J.E. Cirlot, *A Dictionary of Symbols*, trans. Jack Sage (New York: Philosophical Library, 1962), 3
16 Braham, *Politics of Genocide*, 2:853
17 Grossman, *An Ordinary Woman*, 45

18 László Varga, 'The Losses of Hungarian Jewry: A Contribution to the Statistical Overview' in *Studies on the Holocaust*, 261–2

19 Grossman, *An Ordinary Woman*, 78

20 Ibid., 99

21 Ibid., 41

22 Braham, *Politics of Genocide*, 2:854

23 Ibid.

24 To be exact, the SS was the Élite Corps of the Nationalsocialistische Deutsche Arbeiterpartei (NSDAP), the National Socialist German Workers' (Nazi) Party. The Arrow Cross Party, or Nyilaskeresztes Párt, was the Hungarian Nazi Party, headed by Ferenc Szálasi, who was executed for war crimes in 1946.

25 Cf. Arun Mukherjee, 'Introduction' in *Sharing Our Experience* (Ottawa: Canadian Advisory Council on the Status of Women, 1993), 1–20

26 As articulated by Marlene Kadar in *Essays on Life Writing: From Genre to Critical Practice*, ed. Marlene Kadar (Toronto: University of Toronto Press, 1992), 3–12.

27 Kamala Visweswaran, *Fictions of Feminist Ethnography* (Minneapolis and London: University of Minnesota Press, 1994), 7

28 Jean-François Lyotard, *The Postmodern Condition: A Report on Knowledge*, trans. Geoff Bennington and Brian Massumi, Theory and History of Literature, vol. 10 (Minneapolis: University of Minnesota Press, 1984), 27–41

29 Paul Smith, *Discerning the Subject*, Theory and History of Literature, vol. 55 (Minneapolis: University of Minnesota Press, 1988)

30 Hannah Arendt, *On Revolution* (New York: Viking, 1965), 84

31 Elizabeth Meese, 'The Languages of Oral Testimony and Women's Literature' in *Women's Personal Narratives: Essays in Criticism and Pedagogy*, ed. Leonore Hoffman and Margo Culley (New York: Modern Language Association of America, 1985), 26

Victims of the Times, Heroes of Their Lives: Five Mennonite Refugee Women

MARLENE EPP

Observers and analysts of contemporary world events, such as social scientists and newsmakers, frequently cite the statistic that 80 per cent of the world's refugees are women and children.[1] Given this fact, anthropologist Doreen Indra has called for the study of gender as central to the refugee experience, pointing out that most research concerning refugees is primarily a 'male paradigm.'[2] Historical writing on immigration to Canada has also, until recently, been dominated by interpretation that has 'assumed (heterosexual) male behaviour and male-dominated public activity to define the immigrant experience.'[3] While research into the female experience of migration is increasing, the stories of refugee women in the past remain largely unexplored.[4]

Unlike other immigrant women, who may have their eyes turned to future opportunities in their new chosen homeland, refugee women are frequently looking back over their shoulders, reluctantly leaving their homes and, often, family members behind. Since the refugee identity usually arises in a context of war or persecution, these women will have been victims of violence, deprivation, and untold other physical and emotional hardships. While swept along by merciless forces of history, refugee women nevertheless devise strategies of survival that see them through impossible situations and bring them to new lives and often prosperity in a new land. As one analyst of contemporary displaced women has observed, 'The women refugees who have endured the horrors of war, dislocation, loss of loved ones, hunger, humiliation, and still opted for life and safety of their children are not weak women.'[5]

The five women whose stories are told here are part of a larger narrative recounting the migration to Canada of approximately 8,000 Mennonites in the decade following the Second World War. These five refugee women were victims of social and political events that caused tragedy and loss in their lives. Their families were torn apart, they experienced violence and hunger, and they lost opportunities for education and professional development. However, in a context in which they had limited choices, all of the women developed strategies for survival and accomplishment. Interpreting their lives within frameworks of either victimization or agency does not suffice to explain the complexities of the decisions they made and actions they took within equally complex situations.

As women living within family units that had no adult males, they took on roles that were traditionally allocated to the opposite sex – from driving a team of horses and fixing broken wagon wheels, to negotiating with or bribing border guards and immigration officials, to working for wages to provide for themselves and their children. Although they exhibited a pride of accomplishment in successfully filling male shoes, like the 'gold rush widows' of the American Midwest described by Linda Peavy and Ursula Smith, they interpreted their roles as head of the household, as 'something to be endured, not relished.'[6] For Mennonite refugee women, conclusions that ascribe to widowhood either liberating or debilitating outcomes are too simplistic. Women without husbands or fathers had to negotiate through a community terrain in which roles were strictly stratified by gender and a personal terrain of independence and self-sufficiency that derived from their experience of being women without men.

The stories of these five 'great dames' are constructed from conversations that I had with each of them in the early 1990s. In gathering their stories for the purposes of a larger research project, I promised anonymity to all the women and therefore I have chosen pseudonyms in writing this collective biography. Other identifying information has also been changed.[7] The life stories of the women are simultaneously unique and representative. Each of their individual stories as well as their combined story offer insight into the history of other groups of which they were part, such as postwar refugees in Canada or the Soviet Mennonites, and thus are representative of a wider experience. At the same time, each of the women's lives demonstrates singular responses to events and circumstances.

Their stories are both individual life histories and also microcosms of the communal story of which they were part. As Betty Bergland has argued, the 'I' of each woman's oral autobiography reveals the culture and ideology within which she lived at a given time.[8] At times certain

Exodus II. Oil painting by Agatha Schmidt depicting the trek of Mennonite
refugee women from the Ukraine in the winter of 1943–4

events and choices in their lives diverge from the master immigrant
narrative, and these incongruities are revealed in patterns ranging from
defiance to repression. The lives of the five women have marked
similarities in terms of event and chronology, but differ on the basis of
personality, choices made, and outcomes. Their life stories are also
mediated by their identification with a small, ethno-religious community, the Mennonites, and by their experience of being female in a patriarchal social and religious order.

Lena, Justina, Katie, Gertrude, and Anna were all born in the Mennonite colonies of Chortitza and Molotschna in the eastern Ukraine of the
former Soviet Union. They grew up during what was probably the most
difficult era of history for Mennonites living in Russia. Revolution, civil
war, famine, collectivization, the suppression of minorities, and the ter-
ror of the Stalin era all were forces that shaped their lives as children and
young women. Although Mennonites had dwelt in southern Russia for
150 years and had prospered economically and culturally, their community institutions eroded, especially during the 1930s, under a political
program that was diametrically opposed to the Christian values, German culture, and capitalist economy of the Mennonite 'commonwealth.'[9]

Beginning in the late 1920s and throughout the next decade, Mennonites and others considered subversive by the Soviet state were subject to arrest, imprisonment, and exile to labour camps in the northern and eastern regions of the country. The fate of those who were taken – a minority were released – was often death due to starvation or exposure, but most families never received any word from members who were taken. The majority of the disappeared were men, so, by the end of the 1930s, estimates suggest that about 50 per cent of Mennonite families were without a father.[10] The male population was further depleted during the early years of the war as the Soviet army evacuated German colonists eastward and later in the war as men, young and old, were conscripted into the German army.

Katie, who was born in the Ukraine in 1932, correlates the onset of unhappiness in her life with the arrest of her father in 1937. He was falsely accused of poisoning the horses in his care on the collective farm. The night before his arrest, Katie's nine-year-old sister had died of scarlet fever. Her mother, left with Katie and her infant brother, then went out to work in the vineyards of the collective. Katie recalled that after her father left, there was nothing but 'eating, and working, and crying' in her home.

Like Katie and other women whose fathers were taken when they were children, Anna held her father in high regard, expressing almost reverence for his abilities as a talented engineer and accomplished flautist. He also was taken in 1937, and so Anna's mother went to work cooking for the tractor operators of the collective in order to support her three young daughters. Anna said: 'How my mother managed I don't know. She sold my father's clothes, she sold his drafting tools, she sold them and she somehow managed to get us a little house.' To supplement wages earned on the collective farm, Anna's mother obtained a knitting machine on which she learned to make stockings, and also constructed house slippers from fabric and with glue made of flour and water.

Justina, born in 1926, was the middle of three daughters when both parents were drafted for the Soviet labour army in 1941 and sent to the war front to dig trenches to stall advancing German tanks. Although the family was fortunate in that both parents returned after several months, for a period of time the population of Justina's village was a curious mix of seniors and children.

Lena and Gertrude both became young widows during the same time period. Gertrude's husband was spared during the widespread arrests and disappearances of the 1930s, but was exiled to the east in 1941 as Germany declared war on the Soviet Union. Gertrude was left with three children under the age of five, her firstborn having died in infancy in 1936. Lena, whose husband was the son of a Christian preacher, spent the first years of her married life as a fugitive, moving frequently and occasionally living in hiding in order to avoid arrest and exile. In 1938, when officials came and searched their home, Lena fully expected that her husband would be taken. However, her father was taken instead, while her husband and two brothers remained at home until they were sent east with the village's machinery and livestock in August 1941. Lena was left with the care of two small children, her mother, and teen-aged sister.

The German occupation of the Ukraine brought a sense of stability to the Mennonite colonies for a two-year period (1941–3). Although one historian's assessment that the occupation represented 'years of grace for the Mennonite church in the fullest sense of that word'[11] is probably an exaggerated idealization of what was still a wartime environment, nevertheless under the administration of German authorities, some things did improve from the perspective of Soviet Mennonites. Public religious practice was resumed, German educational institutions were opened, and a move was made towards privatizing agriculture. Among German colonists, there were strong hopes that Germany would win the war and that exiled family members might return home.

For Mennonite women, the German occupation presented a variety of new job opportunities, especially as translators and interpreters. Lena became a translator for the German army, housing several German officers at the same time. Anna's mother moved with her three daughters to the city of Dnjepropetrovsk to take advantage of such work, and Anna was able to attend school while her two older sisters worked for occupation authorities. In Justina's case, the German occupation coincided with a severe illness that put her in the hospital for several weeks; the Rumanian soldiers accommodated in their home had brought with them lice, which resulted in typhus for Justina and many others in her village. For Katie, the German occupation meant a new family formation. Her mother, now a young 'widow' – although her first husband was not officially known to be dead – was courted by a German officer at the agricultural training station where she had obtained work as a cook. Despite condemnation from many of her Mennonite relatives and neighbours, given the fact that her first husband was not officially known to be dead, Katie's mother married the officer and had a child with him. The happiness in having a father once again was, for Katie, short-lived, when her stepfather was killed in action towards the end of the war.

The hopes that a German occupation might mean the reunification of families declined along with Germany's diminishing fortune on the warfront, and, when German forces began their westward retreat from the Ukraine in the fall of 1943, they took with them approximately 350,000 Soviet Germans, of which about 10 per cent were Mennonites. The five women whose stories are told here were among those who left their homes and fled westward.

The 1943 trek from the Ukraine has been mythologized through depictions in film, painting, photography, and numerous autobiographical narratives.[12] The images that arise from these portrayals liken the trek to the biblical exodus of the Israelites. Wagon caravans, several miles long, with thousands of people burdened both materially and psychologically, wended their way westward as winter approached. Deep mud and bone-chilling cold are recurring images in the narratives of all five women. After several days of travel, the continuous rain and over-burdened wagons made travel treacherous, and most families had to dispose of their heavier belongings, thus leaving sewing machines, butter churns, chests, and even sacks of dried fruit by the roadside. Many deaths occurred along the way, most from illness, but there were also violent deaths after attacks by partisan groups in the Ukrainian countryside. There were also births in and under wagons, often prematurely induced by the hardships of travel. Food was increasingly scarce as the trek progressed, and many families sent their children to beg in nearby villages, or furtively stole leftover produce from farmers' fields. Gertrude's daughter asked at one point why the corpses lying by the roadside were so fat (they were bloated) when she was so hungry. After a westward trek by horse and wagon and train, the refugees were resettled in that part of Poland that was under German control.

Soviet Mennonites who remained in Poland or the eastern territories of Germany were faced with another westward flight as the Soviet army advanced rapidly towards Berlin in the winter of 1944–5. Those who were overcome by Soviet forces or remained in the Russian occupied zone at war's end were faced with some of the most tragic and difficult experiences of the war. As persons who were born in the Soviet Union, the Mennonite refugees faced repatriation according to a postwar agreement between the Allied nations. As ethnic Germans, they faced retribution from Soviet soldiers as wartime enemies. What German women feared most was rape by individual or groups of Soviet soldiers. One estimate states that as many as two million women were raped in the aftermath of the war, 12 per cent of whom died as a result.[13]

Many Mennonite women were raped, although rarely are such experiences spoken of directly or with any detail in autobiographical accounts, oral or written.[14] Katie, at the age of thirteen, escaped rape only because her mother hid her under a pile of coal when their house was taken over by Soviet troops. Both her mother and grandmother were raped, as were two schoolfriends, who both died as a result of infections following the rapes. She recalled that day vividly: 'We were all hiding in the basement. The tanks drove over everything, the orchards, everything. The worst thing was molesting women and girls. My mother hid me under coal and she herself had to suffer. The grandparents had a very big house right beside a fresh water lake. Very beautiful area. How women and girls ran into the lake, drowning themselves. Yes. Bodies were just coming to the shore. I saw all that. It was ... I could almost think hell.' It was this experience that made Katie's mother resolve to flee to the Allied zone. The family, which at this point included an invalid aunt and an uncle, together with Katie, her mother, and two younger brothers, made a dangerous night-time escape across the border. When they were first stopped by a Soviet patrol, they were given leeway to pass if they left Katie with the soldiers. The offer of a watch and a wedding band from Katie's mother assuaged them, while a bribe of several whisky bottles was enough to get them past the next group of soldiers who threatened them. With that they were able to cross a muddy river through the fog to arrive in the American zone. Katie recalled, 'I had my first slice of baloney that night.'

Those who fled ahead of the advancing Soviet army in the winter of 1944–5 found themselves in the midst of total chaos. Attempting to board a westbound train in Poland, Anna was overwhelmed by the hordes of panicked people also trying to find a place. 'There was no way that three of us – my shy mama, my sister Mary, who had been quite ill, and I just a schoolgirl – had a chance to get on that train. We must have looked like chickens in the rain.' They were eventually assisted by an unknown soldier who lifted and pushed each one of them through a train window. Having lost their own protector in the form of husband and father, they looked to another man to take that role. Like other German women caught in the war, they displayed a psychological ambiguity between their need to be 'strong, brave and tough' and take on unconventional leadership and management roles, and their need for warmth and security, often epitomized in a 'male saviour figure.'[15]

Justina became separated from her family for two and a half years towards the end of the war. Justina had just returned to school in Poland after saying good-bye to her father, who had been drafted into the German Volkssturm, when the rapid Soviet advance forced the evacuation of the school. Justina began the flight west with two other schoolgirls and two of their teachers, but was quickly abandoned by their Polish wagon driver and the teachers. The three teenaged girls attempted to continue on through the January cold in hopes of reaching the city of Pozen, where their families lived. Their horses soon collapsed, and, with sounds of bombing coming ever closer, they simply started to run, leaving all their possessions on the wagon. Justina arrived in Pozen only two hours after her mother and two sisters had fled, and so Justina with one of her schoolmates caught the last train to leave the city, after which the tracks would be bombed. The train was severely overcrowded with refugees and soldiers, and the two girls had to hang onto the outside of the train, almost freezing as a result. Ironically, and miraculously, Justina discovered later that her mother had been on the same train.

Upon arriving in Berlin, Justina and her friend Hilda, who was an ethnic German from Volhynia, were placed as labourers on a German farm where they were treated well and had plenty to eat. When the Soviets came in she recalled that many girls were raped and molested, including the farmer's daughter as well as another twelve-year-old labourer on the farm where she worked, although Justina denies being raped herself. At night, she and the farmer's daughter hid in a concealed closet in the horse barn. During the day, the young girls and women put on kerchiefs and attempted to disguise themselves as boys or old women while working in the fields. On one occasion, Justina hid under a pile of hay while Soviet soldiers poked around with their bayonets. Even after they left, she remained hidden for hours, fearful that perhaps her employers had been bribed and would give her up. Eventually, she came out but was so shaken that she remained in bed and couldn't eat for several days.

Although she was initially inclined to join those refugees who were not resistant to repatriation, and who held hopes of being reunited with family members in the Soviet Union, Justina decided instead to escape to the west. She considers her border crossing a miraculous event, with her Soviet passport stashed in her shoe, and herself so tongue-tied that the border officials grew impatient with her and waved her across. The next miracle was her reunion with her mother and sisters and their later discovery of her father, who was a POW in France.

Gertrude also found herself living under Soviet occupation at war's end, a situation that for her meant difficult choices and even more difficult consequences. Gertrude, together with a friend and their seven children, joined the westward flight from Poland, her only destination being the train's last stop. This happened to be a town near Berlin where they found refuge in a horse stable at a racetrack. Later Gertrude and her friend Elizabeth were both assigned work cooking and housecleaning for Soviet officers and were given the basement of a house as accommodation for themselves and their children. Although they had work, the women struggled to bring home adequate food and, like many German families, were severely malnourished, if not on the brink of starvation.[16]

Smuggling or stealing food was common, particularly for refugees in the Soviet zone where food shortages were severe immediately after the war. Gertrude and Elizabeth received their noon meal free, while their seven children survived on the watery soup made of ground-up grain, potato peels, or any other scraps that their mothers could smuggle home past the guards. In one instance, Gertrude hid a small roast in a pail full of water that had been used for washing the floor. When relating this story, she laughed when recalling how, to her horror, the roast floated to the top as she was exiting past the guard and she quickly thew a dirty rag over the meat to conceal it. For Gertrude's family, the meal that resulted was an unheard of treat. In the same manner, the two women smuggled out pieces of coal, potato peelings, and anything else that would supplement their meagre existence. In recalling her family's strategies of survival, Gertrude's daughter said, 'Some people would likely say, "you were stealing" ... sure it's stealing, [but] we would never do it under ordinary circumstances. Mom didn't become a thief because of it.'

Stealing food wasn't the only strategy that Gertrude adopted in order to sustain herself and her children. Like some other German women, Gertrude entered into a sexual relationship with a Soviet officer, in part to avoid becoming vulnerable to rapes by many different soldiers. She said, 'If you had a friend, then the others would leave you alone.' Historian Annemarie Troeger has analysed the postwar situation for German women, caught between 'rape and prostitution,' pointing to the difficult ethical choices that women made in a context where options were limited.[17] Recognizing that her willingness to enter into such a liaison represented a moral problem, given her upbringing in a Mennonite home, Gertrude nevertheless pointed to the protection that she and her children received from the officer, arguing that 'it was better that way.' Her rationale for committing what was, in her mind, sin was simple. Motivated by a desire to keep her children alive, she recalled that she would have submitted to almost any sin to prevent them from starving. The outcome for Gertrude was a daughter, born in 1949. Gertrude and her three older children loved the new baby in their family and considered her a gift of hope in a time of tragedy. The circumstances of the child's conception followed her to Canada, where she was compelled to seek forgiveness from a Mennonite minister, and where on at least one occasion the daughter's own sexual innocence was challenged in light of her history.

Gertrude made choices that favoured life, while many other refugees and Germans chose suicide to avoid rape or chose abortion in the aftermath of rape. Gertrude's friend Elizabeth almost bled to death after receiving an abortion from a back alley butcher. In addition to rape, hunger, and other forms of mistreatment by Soviet soldiers, Gertrude feared discovery as a Soviet citizen. Much of her energy went into hiding the fact that she understood the Russian language.

Although fortuitous circumstance had saved the family from repatriation on earlier occasions, Gertrude began to make plans to escape to the west. Numerous times she had crossed into the American zone of Berlin, where she obtained food and clothing from a refugee depot. When she realized she was being watched, she made one last trip with her two daughters, sending her two sons on an earlier train, each carrying only small bundles. From Berlin the family was airlifted to Hamburg, after signing a declaration that they would not return.

Of the 35,000 Mennonites who had left the Ukraine in 1943, approximately 23,000 went missing in the war or were repatriated to the Soviet Union in accordance with the terms of the Yalta agreement. In the five years following war's end, the remaining 12,000 Mennonite refugees scattered throughout Europe found their way to Displaced Person camps or otherwise connected with relief and immigration agencies operating in the Allied zones.[18] Most of the Mennonite refugees that succeeded in reaching the west made contact with Mennonite Central Committee (MCC), a North American agency that was providing relief and immigration assistance to refugees in Europe. Through MCC, the refugees investigated possibilities of emigration from Europe. Canada was the preferred destination, but in the years immediately after the war, Canadian immigration policy was restrictive, and, in an effort to expedite the migration of Mennonites who were faced with repatriation,

MCC arranged the settlement of approximately 5,000 Mennonite refugees in Paraguay.[19]

Medical criteria were one aspect of Canadian immigration regulations that posed problems for refugees, many of whom suffered health problems related to starvation, exposure, and exhaustion. Katie's mother, who had bad varicose veins and lower labour potential as a result, decided independently to take a forward step in ensuring that her family would have a future in Canada. Her act of hope turned into a tragedy when she died from infection after surgery on her legs, leaving her three children orphans. Katie, at sixteen years old, had already lost her father and stepfather, and now became a mother of sorts to her two younger brothers. Lena's mother continued to have 'problems with her nerves' after suffering a nervous breakdown when her husband was arrested in 1938, while Lena herself developed stomach problems, which she attributed to poor diet, stress, and overwork. In Germany, Lena had undergone a folk treatment in which hot glasses were placed on one's back to draw out illness. The glasses had burned marks on her back, which proved awkward when she went before Canadian immigration doctors. In Canada, her stomach continued to be 'loose in the body,' and she had several operations to sew it up.

The first priority for all the women on arrival in Canada was to find a home and secure employment in order to pay off travel debts owed to relatives or sponsors. When Katie arrived in Manitoba, she resisted attempts on the part of individuals in the Mennonite community to adopt her two younger brothers, then aged thirteen and six. She did agree for them to be temporary boarders when she found a live-in position working in the laundry at a hospital in north Winnipeg. Her wages were fifty dollars per month, all but two dollars of which she sent punctually to her grandmother's cousin in British Columbia who had advanced money for their transportation. After Katie had repaid all but $100 of their $440 debt, the cousin waived the remainder. Much of her $2 in spending money was used to buy street car tickets that took her to night school where she was learning English.

Justina was similarly single-minded and notably upwardly mobile, as she was always seeking a new position that would bring her wages up. During her first year in Canada, Justina held various positions as domestic help in rural Manitoba and experienced one of the main dangers of being live-in help. At one placement, where she helped out before and after the arrival of a new baby, Justina was repeatedly molested by her male employer. 'With my milk pails full of milk he pressed me to the wall and squeezed me and even gave me a kiss. I was so very ashamed. He always did that. [His wife] was so good to me. I felt so guilty ... I couldn't look her in the eyes ... I didn't like it when his body came to mine always in such a corner. I was very uncomfortable. But I had to stay there. They gave me $45 a month.' Like many immigrant domestics, Justina was caught between a distasteful situation – more so because her employers were distant relatives – and her need to earn money to repay her debts and send money to family members who had been left behind for health reasons in a refugee camp in Germany. When released from this position, she spurned further domestic work and moved to Winnipeg, sharing an apartment with other immigrant women, and pursuing higher earning power from one factory job to the next.

After stopping in Ontario to meet some of her relatives, Gertrude and her four children continued on to southern Alberta, where they lived in a small house on the farm of other relatives, hoeing sugar beets and helping with the chores. Their living costs were minimal, since rent was free, and milk, eggs, and garden produce were plentiful on the farm. Gertrude's daughter recalls that they had sardines for lunch every day because they were cheap.

Many Mennonite refugees were sponsored and employed by near or distant relatives in Canada. While this relationship often gave new immigrants an immediate sense of being at home and created community bonds that were absent for those newcomers with no connections in the new land, the existence of blood ties between employer and employee could also make a bad situation that much worse. This was evident in Justina's encounter with sexual misconduct on the part of her employer. Some refugee immigrants were exploited by their employers, whether they were relatives or not, and many were demeaned or otherwise made to feel inferior. Justina recalled that the cousin sponsoring her and her sister was 'very mean,' fearing that her sons would become interested in the 'Russian girls.' The cousin also refused to buy the young women sanitary napkins, forcing them to revert to the old practice of using rags during their menstrual periods.

When Lena arrived in Canada in 1948 with her two young children and sickly mother, she was given a job at her cousin's cafe in Saskatoon, where she worked from 6:30 AM until one o'clock in the morning. 'There was not much time to think,' she said. 'I did not expect it to be so hard.' After six months they moved to British Columbia where they lived in an unheated cabin on her uncle's farm and picked raspberries, strawberries, and hops. Eventually, Lena was able to purchase her own house with two acres of berries, which generated a small amount of income. She found it difficult to obtain a well-paying steady job because she also had to care for her mother, who was at home and unwell, and so she was limited to part-time and flexible work cleaning houses. Later she moved to Vancouver where wages for housework were even better.

Like many other female-headed refugee families of this era, these women established themselves economically with minimal outside help. Rather, the labour resources of themselves and their children, combined with well-practised strategies of frugal living, allowed them to pay their debts, buy or build houses, and feed and clothe their families. Although all of the five women associated themselves with Mennonite churches in Canada, material help was less forthcoming than spiritual nurture and rehabilitation, which was viewed by the church as a priority in addressing the needs of the refugees. Lena, caring for two young children and her elderly mother, said they received assistance neither from the church nor the government. 'I didn't want any welfare. We managed,' she said. She did accept the newly instituted family allowance cheque from the government, which some Mennonite churches in Canada cautioned their members against.

Besides making a living, integrating themselves into Mennonite communities, and making a recovery from years of tragedy, refugee women also had to accommodate to Canadian society. Although the term 'displaced person' was an official United Nations designation for certain categories of war refugees, the label 'DP' was frequently used in a derisive manner to refer to new postwar immigrants. Anna viewed language as one of the greatest barriers facing her as a new immigrant to Canada in 1948. Mainly, it prevented her from taking what she considered to be 'important jobs.' While her mother and sister sewed men's shirts in a factory, Anna worked in an industrial laundry, where language wasn't as important. Even within Mennonite communities, where all of the women had near or distant relatives, refugees were often set apart and looked down upon because of their limited religious training, lack of formal education, and initial poverty. Justina felt that she and her sister were always thought of as 'the Russian girls.' Katie felt inferior because she was an orphan and was particularly jealous of other families that had fathers.

For women whose families had been torn apart by the Soviet purges of the 1930s and by death and disappearance during the war, the re-creation of a family life that was 'normal' by Canadian Mennonite standards was a main goal. The 'grab bag' family that characterized many refugee families was in stark contrast to the patriarchal nuclear family exalted by Mennonite religious discourse and also the 'happy united family' that was normative for postwar Canadian society generally.[20] For refugee 'widows' in Canada, restoring 'normalcy' to their families might mean remarrying, with or without confirmation of their first spouse's death, or struggling against all odds to be reunited with family members far away. Young single women usually married shortly after settling in Canada, and often at a relatively young age, perhaps to begin creating for themselves a certain kind of family life that they had never experienced.

Katie married in 1951, at the age of nineteen, partly to recover a father-figure in her life, a motive she readily admitted. 'I got married so young partly I think out of security. I felt vulnerable all my life since I was five [the year her father was arrested]. And here was a gentleman very much like what I used to know, my Dad. Who I could trust.' Justina also married young – to a man she had originally met in a DP camp in Germany – two years after arriving with her sister in Canada. She proudly described her wedding, which she had financed completely on her own. Her wedding dress of lace and pearls cost a week's wages at $15.50, while the cake alone cost $3.50. She also purchased bridesmaid dresses for three of her friends. The bouquet was store-bought and was couriered by bus to the southern Manitoba town where the wedding was held. In Justina's words: 'I did the whole wedding. I invited the whole church. I think there were 250 people. We had cookies, cheese, buns. I arranged everything. I even gave the ladies in the kitchen some money for all they did. They were very impressed with how far an orphan had come.' Happily married for over forty years, with seven children born in nine years, Justina's memories of marriage are positively correlated with the end of her refugee identity. Anna's memories of marriage, by contrast, are so negative that they are almost completely repressed in her personal narrative.

Anna was married already in Germany and in fact arrived in Canada with her husband, separately from her mother and sisters. However, her account of travel and arrival in Canada contains anecdotes that include her mother and sisters, with no reference to her husband at all. Further conversation revealed that she divorced her husband after an abusive and unhappy marriage, and thus her oral life history, while highly personal on many other topics, initially eliminated what was for her the most painful part of her life. Although she moved with her husband to western Canada, and had a daughter there, she began to fear for her life and returned to the community where her mother and sisters had settled. 'It didn't work out. I was too unhappy. I couldn't manage. I tried my best. There was no way out. After he tried to kill me one night ... there was no way out ... [F]or me to save my child and me, we had to leave.' In leaving her former husband out of the main text of her narrative, Anna was repressing not only that which was especially painful for her, but she was also removing an episode in her life that did not fit the culture of her community. In the 1950s, domestic violence was unspoken of in Mennonite communities, while divorce was proscribed by the church altogether. Although Anna was quietly allowed to remain in the Mennonite Church, despite her divorce, her experience marginalized her within that group. As theorists of memory and personal narrative have argued, individuals frequently eliminate from their life story elements that are at variance with the 'social memory' of their communities.[21]

Anna's life was problematized even further when her widowed mother, who had remarried in Canada, experienced a similar pattern of abuse. Anna's mother, whose first husband had disappeared in 1938, at age seventy married a man who came from the same village in the Soviet Union. According to Anna: 'It turned out very sad. He was everything we girls had feared. He didn't look after her ... All he wanted was a housekeeper.' When it became apparent that the mother's health was in danger, her daughters retrieved their mother from British Columbia and took legal action to prevent her second husband from trying to take her back.

Like Anna's mother, Gertrude also remarried after she received a letter confirming her first husband's death in the Soviet Union. The man was also a postwar immigrant, although a bachelor, and people in their community discouraged him from marrying Gertrude, saying, 'What do you want with her and all her four children? He should find someone younger who could bear his children.' As historians of widowhood have demonstrated, and as the experience of Gertrude and others like her revealed, the widow with children was viewed as a financial and emotional burden and in fact a threat to the patriarchal social order.[22]

Lena's restoration of her fragmented family came about in a very different manner. As a young woman, Lena had many opportunities to remarry in Canada, but chose not to, given that she never received confirmation whether her first husband was dead or alive. Although Canadian legal stipulations, as well as guidelines established within the Mennonite Church, allowed for remarriage after seven years of hearing no word from one's spouse, Lena felt she simply could not take this step. After fifteen years of hearing no word from her husband, Jacob, one Easter morning Lena received news that he was still living in the Soviet Union. Fortunately, Jacob had not remarried either, and the two began corresponding. Lena began a sixteen-year campaign, lobbying the Canadian government and writing endless appeals to have him emigrate. After several occasions in which Jacob's permit to leave the Soviet Union was denied at the last minute, Lena refused to place any more trust in promises. Ironically, the final telegram of confirmation never reached Lena, and so one night in the early 1970s she was awoken with a telephone call that announced Jacob's arrival at the Vancouver airport. They were reunited after a separation of over thirty years.

Although some couples reunited in this manner found that, after such a long separation, they were no longer compatible, Lena insists that she and Jacob simply resumed what had been a very happy marriage. Undoubtedly there were adjustments to make, especially in the area of gender roles, which had been altered when Lena became head of the family in Jacob's absence. Lena continued to do all the business because her husband spoke no English and she was thirty years ahead of him in assimilating to Canadian society. Within the household, she frequently found herself doing 'male' tasks, such as hammering a nail, when he would step in and say, 'What am I here for?'

Life in Canada, despite its hardships and obstacles, represented stability and prosperity, in sharp contrast to the years of war. Even though the prewar years in the Ukraine and the decade following as war refugees represented a much smaller portion of their lives than their residence in Canada, the era of the war took a central place in the memories of the five women as told in their oral narratives. Pamela Klassen, who has chronicled the life histories of two Mennonite refugee women, noted that the autobiography of one woman ended before her immigration to Canada at the age of twenty-four, indicating the 'overwhelming importance' of the war and prewar years to her self-identity.[23] Katie became closely involved in the Canadian Mennonite community, but always felt that her war experiences created a vast gap in understanding. Her 'horrible' memories had a debilitating effect for the remainder of her life. 'I would probably not have wanted to talk about [the horrible experiences] much because I cried a lot more than I ate. My hands are not steady. The doctor saw it and asked, what is the matter with you. I said that's a long story. I can't help this. I have very bad handwriting.'

All of the five women periodically referred to themselves as

Fluechtlinge (refugees) in their narratives, thus maintaining a strong identification with the dramatic early decades of their lives. Even in the midst of their hesitancy to talk about the horrible experiences, the detail in chronicling the years surrounding the war is in sharp contrast to the lesser time and space devoted to their lives as immigrant women in Canada. This allocation of narrative space may be due to the greater societal merit attributed to their heroic deeds in the public arena of war than to their lives as householp, factory workers, and mothers, wives, or widows in the new land.

Even while describing in lesser detail their lives as Canadians, the five women nevertheless exuded an understated pride over their success in coming through the refugee sojourn. While their anonymity here reduces their visibility as heroic women, it also allowed their voices to speak more candidly at a personal level and perhaps allowed their stories to depart at times from the master immigrant narrative that is common in published life histories. The collective biography of these five women thus becomes at the same time a possible glimpse into the lives of refugee women around the world, past and present.

NOTES

1 Susan Forbes Martin, *Refugee Women* (London: Zed Books, 1992), 5. Also, Ellen Cole, Oliva M. Espin, and Esther D. Rothblum, *Refugee Women and Their Mental Health: Shattered Societies, Shattered Lives* (Binghamton, NY: Haworth Press, 1992), xii. Several authors have noted the predominance of women and children in refugee movements from Cuba, Cambodia, and Vietnam, for instance. See Silvia Pedraza, 'Women and Migration: The Social Consequences of Gender,' *Annual Review of Sociology* 17 (1991): 303–25.

2 Doreen Indra, 'Gender: A Key Dimension of the Refugee Experience,' *Refuge* 6 (Feb. 1987): 3–4

3 Franca Iacovetta, 'Manly Militants, Cohesive Communities, and Defiant Domestics: Writing about Immigrants in Canadian Historical Scholarship,' *Labour/Le Travail* 36 (Fall 1995): 217–52

4 An important exception to the paucity of historical literature on refugee women is Janice Potter-MacKinnon, *While the Women Only Wept: Loyalist Refugee Women in Eastern Ontario* (Montreal and Kingston: McGill-Queen's University Press, 1993). See also Isabel Kaprielian, 'Creating and Sustaining an Ethnocultural Heritage in Ontario: The Case of Armenian Women Refugees' in *Looking into My Sister's Eyes: An Exploration in Women's History*, ed. Jean Burnet (Toronto: Multicultural History Society of Ontario, 1986),

139–53; Milda Danys, *DP: Lithuanian Immigration to Canada after the Second World War* (Toronto: Multicultural History Society of Ontario, 1986).

5 Sultana Parvanta, 'The Balancing Act: Plight of Afghan Women Refugees' in *Refugee Women*, 127

6 Linda Peavy and Ursula Smith, *The Gold Rush Widows of Little Falls: A Story Drawn from the Letters of Pamelia and James Fergus* (St Paul: Minnesota Historical Society, 1990), 55

7 Between 1992 and 1994 I conducted interviews, several hours each, with Mennonites who had immigrated to Canada after the Second World War. These interviews took place in Ontario, Manitoba, Alberta, and British Columbia and were gathered as research material for my doctoral dissertation, 'Women Without Men: Mennonite Immigration to Canada and Paraguay after the Second World War' (University of Toronto, 1996). All references to the stories of the five women are from these interviews, the tapes of which are currently in my possession.

8 Betty Bergland, 'Ideology, Ethnicity, and the Gendered Subject: Reading Immigrant Women's Autobiographies' in *Seeking Common Ground: Multidisciplinary Studies of Immigrant Women in the United States*, ed. Donna Gabaccia (Westport, CT: Praeger, 1992), 101–21

9 Studies that examine developments within the Mennonite colonies under the Soviet régime include John B. Toews, *Czars, Soviets, and Mennonites* (Newton, KS: Faith and Life Press, 1982), chaps. 11–12; John B. Toews, 'Early Communism and Russian Mennonite Peoplehood' in *Mennonites in Russia, 1788– 1988: Essays in Honour of Gerhard Lohrenz*, ed. John Friesen (Winnipeg: CMBC Publications, 1989), 265–87; Victor G. Doerksen, 'Survival and Identity in the Soviet Era' in *Mennonites in Russia*, 289–98; the other chapters in this collection provide useful background to Mennonites in the Russian empire. The experience of the Mennonites is similar to that of other German colonists in the Soviet Union. Useful for a broader perspective is Ingeborg Fleischhauer and Benjamin Pinkus, eds., *The Soviet Germans: Past and Present* (London: Hurst, 1986).

10 The 1930 population of Soviet Mennonites was about 100,000. 'World War II,' *Mennonite Encyclopedia*, 5:941–2; George K. Epp, 'Mennonite Immigration to Canada after World War II,' *Journal of Mennonite Studies* 5 (1987): 110. My own tabulations from village reports conducted by German occupation forces in 1942–43 have similar results and further show that in some areas the ratio of women to men was quite drastic. For instance, in the village of Tiege, in the colony Sagradowka, in February 1942 there were 127 families, 96 of which were without a father. See 'Tiege' in Captured German War Documents, from Library of Congress (Washington, DC), Conrad Grebel College Archives.

11 Epp, 'Mennonite Immigration to Canada,' 112
12 The film, *The Great Trek* (1992), was produced by Otto Klassen, a former refugee who obtained film footage from German government archives that provides graphic visual images of the hardships of the trek. (The film was sponsored by Faith and Life Communications of the Conference of Mennonites in Manitoba.) Kitchener artist Agatha Schmidt, also a postwar immigrant, has produced a number of oil paintings portraying the departure of men from the Ukraine and the trek. Autobiographies include Katie Friesen, *Into the Unknown* (1986, Author); Susanna Toews, *Trek to Freedom: The Escape of Two Sisters from South Russian during World War II*, trans. Helen Megli (Winkler, MB: Heritage Valley Publications, 1976); Jacob A. Neufeld, *Tiefenwege: Erfahrungen und Erlebnisse von Russland-Mennoniten in Zwei Jahrezehnten bis 1949* (Virgil, ON: Niagara Press, nd).
13 Barbara Johr, 'Die Ereignisse in Zahlen' in *BeFreier und Befreite: Krieg, Vergewaltigungen, Kinder*, ed. Helke Sander and Barbara Johr (Munich: Verlag Antje Kunstmann, 1992), 59
14 I have discussed the way in which wartime rape experiences are processed in memory in my paper 'The Memory of Violence: Mennonite Refugees and Rape in the Second World War,' *Journal of Women's History* (Spring 1997).
15 Annemarie Troeger, 'German Women's Memories of World War II' in Margaret Randolph Higonnet et al., *Behind the Lines: Gender and the Two World Wars* (New Haven: Yale University Press, 1987), 293–4
16 All sectors of postwar Germany were characterized by what Eve Kolinsky has called a 'culture of physical survival.' Shortages of food, heating materials, clothing, and household goods meant that most Germans had to develop pre-industrial methods for meeting daily needs. Poor health and malnutrition were common, and some individuals in fact 'lived close to starvation levels.' See *Women in Contemporary Germany: Life, Work and Politics*, rev. ed. (Providence, RI: Berg, 1993), 26–8.
17 Annemarie Troeger, 'Between Rape and Prostitution: Survival Strategies and Chances of Emancipation for Berlin Women after World War II' in *Women in Culture and Politics: A Century of Change*, ed. Judith Friedlander et al. (Bloomington: Indiana University Press, 1986)
18 The statistics on Mennonites who were repatriated and those who remained in the west and later emigrated can be found in a number of sources, although the means for arriving at the numbers are unclear. See Frank H. Epp, *Mennonite Exodus: The Rescue and Resettlement of the Russian Mennonites since the Communist Revolution* (Altona, MB: D.W. Friesen & Sons, 1962), 363; Epp, 'Mennonite Immigration to Canada,' 114–15.
19 Detailed discussions of the policy and negotiations surrounding the postwar

Mennonite migration can be found in Epp, *Mennonite Exodus*, chaps. 24–6; T.D. Regehr, *Mennonites in Canada, 1939–1970: A People Transformed* (Toronto: University of Toronto Press, 1996), chap. 4. A personal memoir from the perspective of two MCC relief workers is Peter and Elfrieda Dyck, *Up from the Rubble: The Epic Rescue of Thousands of War-Ravaged Mennonite Refugees* (Scottdale, PA: Herald Press, 1991).

20 The term 'grab bag' is applied by Sheila Fitzpatrick to families in which individuals with or without a blood relationship come together to share housing, food, and other resources for the purpose of survival under wartime conditions. See *Stalin's Peasants: Resistance and Survival in the Russian Village after Collectivization* (New York: Oxford University Press, 1994), 221. The phrase 'happy united family' is borrowed from Annalee Golz, 'The Canadian Family and the State in the Postwar Period,' *left history* 1 (Fall 1993): 9–49.

21 For discussion of the way in which personal narratives are shaped to fit the communal or social memory of a group, see James Fentress and Chris Wickham, *Social Memory* (Cambridge, MA: Blackwell, 1992); Raphael Samuel and Paul Thompson, eds., *The Myths We Live By* (London and New York: Routledge, 1990).

22 See, for instance, Barbara J. Todd, 'The Remarrying Widow: A Stereotype Reconsidered' in *Women in English Society, 1500–1800*, ed. Mary Prior (London and New York: Methuen, 1985), 54–92. Also Ida Blom, 'The History of Widowhood: A Bibliographic Overview,' *Journal of Family History* 16, no. 2 (1991): 191–210.

23 Pamela E. Klassen, *Going By the Moon and the Stars: Stories of Two Russian Mennonite Women* (Waterloo: Wilfrid Laurier University Press, 1994), 66–7

Driving towards Death

ARITHA VAN HERK

Florence, the noose is a necklace. Not quite as soft as a velvet ribbon gracing your wedding best neck but a line dividing breath from choke, head from body. The rope, Florence, can form the shape of a question. Or a knot.

Florence Lassandro knew how to drive. Florence drove the rumrunning cars: first Model T Fords, then Buicks, McLaughlin Six Specials, McLaughlin Sevens. Cars capable of ricochet, of a swift plunge into a ditch or over an embankment, of out-racing the Alberta Provincial Police patrols, thick men designated to smell out liquor and confiscate bottles, pour their liquid into the thirsty ground. Women didn't drive, but Florence drove, her hands on the wheel, the canvas canopy above flapping in the wind. Fifty miles an hour. Fifty miles an hour – in the 1920s, when cars veered at a leisurely amble, their horns asquawk. Fifty miles an hour, the McLaughlin's thick tires solid and bouncing, the front bumper a steel pipe filled with concrete for smashing through roadblocks. Driving became a dance, a whirl through air as crystalline as the hoods of snow on the Crowsnest mountains. Florence drove the Red Route, the Rumrunner's Trail, from Fernie, British Columbia, to Pincher Creek, via the Crowsnest. Using Phillips Pass, 1550 metres high, an ant crawl over the continental divide. Florence Lassandro at the wheel. 'You drive,' someone (Pic or Charles) must have said. *'You drive.'*

What was the subtext? The Alberta Provincial Police wouldn't shoot a woman? If a woman drove, the rumrunners could slow down, keep to the speed limit? If a woman drove, the men's hands would be free to count the money? No answers to these questions, but there was Florence at the wheel, and not asleep, oh no, awake, wide awake – before Bonnie and Clyde, before Thelma and Louise, before the idea of a woman at the wheel (permission or not).

Philomena Costanzo. Born 1901, presumably, since she was twenty-two years old when she was hanged, hanged not as Philomena but Florence (her Canadian name), hanged not as Costanzo but Lassandro (her husband's name, although there is some evidence that his real name was Sanfidele). Birth name a different appellation from her hanging name, its newspapered condemnations and implacabilities. Florence Lassandro, born in Calabria, Italy, and immigrated to Canada in 1910, with her father Vincenzo and mother Angela. The same mother, Angela, who would be the last family member to see her (on 28 April 1923) before she was, according to the dour sentence of the court, Judge Walsh presiding, 'taken from your place of confinement ... and ... hanged by the neck until you are dead and may God have mercy on your soul.' The same Florence Lassandro executed at Fort Saskatchewan on 2 May, after having been charged and found guilty (with Emilio Picariello, the Bottle King of the Crowsnest Pass) of the murder of one Stephen Oldacres Lawson, Alberta Provincial Policeman, despite appeals, despite two reprieves, the noose finally settled, and Florence fell. Tripped more like it, tripped into the tight asthma that accompanies hanging.

So what was it, Florence Lassandro? Why did you fall? Who did you fall for? Fast cars and faster company? Or just Emperor Pic, that two-hundred-pound philanthropist cum rumrunner cum ice-cream pedlar cum innkeeper cum town counsellor, family man, father, husband?

What was Emilio Picariello to Florence? Sidekick? Boss? Lover? No way of knowing, only that they were together, both in the car from which the shots that killed Lawson were supposedly fired. Only that they were hanged from the same prison (Fort Saskatchewan) on the same morning, not at the same time but one after the other, possibly even with the same rope, certainly by the same hangman (Wakefield).

So why did you get involved with Picariello, Florence? Was it inevitable, Pic the godfather of the working-class Italians in the Pass? The sacks of flour that he distributed to the poor, after they had camouflaged their forty-ounce incubated bottles, flour a perfect cushion and container? Pic's ice-cream wagon patrolling the streets of Fernie, British Columbia, on hot August afternoons? Or the bear cub on a chain that he kept behind the old Macaroni factory, the wolf cub that he tamed? Or was it simply Pic's actual kindness, the intense bluster of a tender man, feelings hidden inside his 200-pound wall of a body?

Pic's mustache was fierce, bristling with intent and waxed to its pointed ends above his certainly sensuous mouth. Pic was the ice-cream man, hotelier, the Bottle King: 'Emperor Pic, the Bottle King, requests that all persons selling bottles hold them until they see E. Picariello, who

Mrs Florence Lassandro, 1922. An accomplice in the Picariello murder case,
she was convicted and hanged at Fort Saskatchewan.

pays top prices.' A monopoly on empty bottles, selling price, quarts
forty cents, pints twenty-two cents a dozen. Temperance drinks, he
advertised, served out of the Alberta Hotel in Blairmore, with the player
piano discordant in the lounge and a tunnel branching off of the basement, stacked with innocent sacks of flour in front of burlap bags of
'illicit booze.'

*Did you drink, Florence? Did a young lady dare to take a nip or two to fortify
her intentions, or did you wave the passing bottle away, avert your eyes as if it
were immoral, a liquid indelicacy? Had you heard the speeches of the Woman's
Christian Temperance Union, the Temperance and Moral Reform League, the
Dry side outshouting the Wet, prohibition flourishing its intricate set of loopholes and agitations, moral spectatorhood implemented by plebiscite as a measure against the demon drink?*

'July 1, 1916, whereas and wherefore ... all beer and liquor not to be
purchased or sold, with the exception of the medicinal, scientific or
sacred.' Intemperance: the cause of social ills, falling down drunk, public incontinence, the Antichrist, poverty, misery, and crime. Pure thirst.
Temperance pulling itself up hand over hand from the wet days to the
damp days to the dry days, and it wasn't a handkerchief or an umbrella
that was needed but a good solid shot glass filled to the brim and strong
enough to burn the hairs in your nostrils.

Were you, Florence, a temperate woman, careful to starch your lace collars and to perm you hair, smoothing your eyebrows with a wet forefinger? You combed your hair before they took your mug shot, prisoner 483 C, the crown teased into a bouffant, the sides crinkled and springy, and the flower embroidered on your transparent collar leafing palely upward. You look temperate enough, sad even, your eyes dark and enigmatic above an almost aristocratic nose. Stone cold sober, and not a drop in sight. Yet.

But what came first? The Alberta Provincial Police, created to close loopholes in the Prohibition Act. Magistrate Primrose (nomenclature beware) appointed, in February of 1917, to head a Provincial Police Commission, created expressly to suppress liquor and its warming flow. By April, APP officers (new and zealously sworn) had been dispatched to various detachments in Alberta; their uniforms were on order. Amendments to the Liquor Act were such that it was illegal for anyone to have in their possession more than one quart of liquor or two gallons of beer. Not much for a long hot summer. Housewives bought illicit bottles of extract, and patent medicines were moved behind the counter. Prescriptions required. Medicinal purposes, aids to delicate constitutions.

Delicacy, Florence. You looked shyly tough, as if the steel of your actions was postural. Your smile hid itself, secretive, willing to be unwilling. Indelicate questions, these, who you were and where you lived, how many times you had driven the Red Route and whether you enjoyed clothes too much, whether you were Pic's mistress or his housekeeper, his wife's best friend, or his business associate's wife. All the alternatives so tempting in their display, their speculation, a beautiful if darkly foreign young woman in a red tam, her (was it nervous, or merely a statement of fact?) outburst, 'Well, he's dead and I'm not.' So far so good, Florence. And the story was that they would never hang a woman in the West.

Charles Lassandro and Maria Picariello; Charles the husband of Florence and Maria the wife of Emilio Picariello. Picariello was married to Maria; Florence was married to Charles. If those marriages mattered, de facto unions, how were they configured? Florence was living, not with Charles, but in the Picariello household when the shooting occurred; her clothes were in the children's room. It is unclear where Charles Lassandro was living (in the hotel?), but he was not lodged in the Picariello household. Had Florence left him? Were they estranged? Or was it merely a convenient arrangement, a way to save rent money? Another gap in the bootleg, another escape clause in the flight that led directly towards 2 May 1923 and the hemp rope's hairy knot.

Florence, were you capable of speaking for yourself? Was it Italian or English you spoke when you were passionate? Did you pray in English or Italian? Did you speak at all, on those trips over the continental divide, through weather or beauty or scenery or whatever the pass implied, or did you maintain a discreet silence, as you did on the witness stand, your mouth demurely set, your eyes downcast, a lady but caught with your pants down, your hand on a gun.

Various motives for killing Lawson were ascribed to Florence Lassandro. Love for Steve (Pic's son), loyalty to Picariello, a penchant for the bottle herself. Or maybe she just loved driving and she knew that well-intentioned law-abiding citizens were going to make her give up the wheel, the permission of 'you drive' suddenly revoked. Florence back to driving a dishpan, waiting on tables, hacking vegetables for soup.

Whisky gets drunk, and guns go off.

The noose is a rough necklace, a hemp choker.

They wouldn't hang a woman but they did.

Where did the story of Florence Lassandro start? With Emilio Picariello's ambition, his energy, his dark eyes and severe posture, a godfather in the making, children and partners and payoffs to the police (the same police eager to ensure that their own celebrations were enthusiastically well-supplied). Pic saw intoxicating possibility – a business venture, a chance to get rich, money not money but instrument, to gain power, help the poor, the stumbling miners and labourers, WOPs without papers, the thick-fingered workers who came to him for assistance, a bag of flour, a few bottles of oil, philanthropy, money for toys for Christmas. Pic can hardly be blamed for seeing an opportunity and laughing his big man's laugh, erasing borders, speeding prohibitions. They were there, those opportunities, waiting to happen.

And Florence, how could you resist? Could you have turned that shy smile the other way, could you have prohibited your own necklace? Was Pic the temptation? Or Steve, Pic's son, young, engaging, quick to laugh? Was it the speed of the car as it crested the pass, the high cerulean air of running, the complex of signals and cross-signals, subterfuge and sheer high octane excitement? There couldn't have been much for you to do, and Charles Lassandro was no prize. Not much besides the drudgery of ritual – weddings, funerals, christenings. A shoot-out. A court case. A noose.

Florence often drove, but she wasn't on the particular run that knotted her noose. Emperor Pic was bringing in a load of liquor from British Columbia, the McLaughlin Buicks were fired up, full of spark-plug popping energy, their bumpers weighty, their windows polished. The drivers knew the side roads, the potential detours, the ditches and hills.

Police pay-offs should have settled matters, but there were new men on the APP force, adamant, unwilling to turn a blind eye, entranced by their own heroism, machine guns mounted on their motorcycles, with the power to stop every vehicle and search under the seats, in the boot, below the dash. No such thing as an innocent hatbox or picnic basket, no such thing as a car without a few bottles stashed in the boot, not any more. The unwritten rules that legitimate rumrunners (their own equipment, their own vehicle, no theft or violence) were to be treated gently, were eroding.

On 21 September 1922, Pic loaded his liquor in Fernie, British Columbia. McAlpine, Picariello's mechanic, drove one car, another was driven by Steven, Picariello's eighteen-year-old son. Picariello followed in the third car, the decoy; he carried no liquor. They paraded, slowly, funereal, almost taunting, through the Crowsnest Pass, the necklace of towns strung like beads along its shoulder, from Fernie through to Natal, Michel, Coleman. Passing through Coleman, they were spotted by Alberta Provincial Police officers Lawson and Houghton, who made no attempt to stop the cars, but telephoned to the detachment at Frank, Alberta, farther up the road, warning that Picariello was making a run (wet or dry), in broad daylight. APP officers Scott and Dey, wanting to catch Pic booze-handed, drove from their quarters at Frank to Blairmore, with a warrant to search Picariello's hotel, expecting that he would have begun to stash the load.

Picariello must have been nervous. He was parked squarely in the middle of the street, waiting; the three cars had arrived but they hadn't begun to unload. Seeing the APP, he reached into his car and sounded the horn, a brisk warning to Steven, who roared away, back to British Columbia. Picariello jumped into his own car and tried to block the APP from following Steve. But although they manoeuvred around his father, Steve Picariello was too far ahead of the APP, the McLaughlin too powerful to be easily overtaken. As a stop measure, Dey phoned Lawson (still back in Coleman) from the hotel in Green Hill (another bead on that string of towns), informing him that Picariello was doubling back, taking his load back to safety in Fernie.

And where were you while this was going on, Florence? Did you hear the commotion in the street, the roar of engines as Steve spun away, as Pic tried to prevent the APP from following? Were you daydreaming, doing your hair, mending a button? You should have been mending that loose button on your coat, it fingered you later, got you hanged just as sure as the gun or your red tam-o'-shanter.

In Coleman, the APP were unprepared, and officer Houghton was trying to arrange to borrow the most powerful car possible for a pursuit, when Steve Picariello's McLaughlin approached the main street. Lawson acted as roadblock, stepping into the street and holding up his hand to stop the car, but Steve sped towards him, swerving at the last minute, and continued despite the warning shots that Lawson fired. Commandeering the car of one Mr Bell, proprietor of Coleman's Grand Union Hotel, Lawson and APP Officer Houghton followed, trying to gain on the fleeing vehicle. Leaning out of the window, Lawson fired at the car ahead. Unknowing, Stephen Lawson hit Steve Picariello in the hand, injuring him, but still the McLaughlin did not stop, and the commandeered Bell's car developed a flat tire, forcing the APP to abandon the chase.

While they were fixing the tire at the side of the road, Emilio Picariello pulled up. Words were traded. Picariello's are lost, but records state that Lawson approached Picariello's car, and said, 'You had better bring your son back, because if you don't get him I'll go and get him.'

Picariello shrugged and drove away.

That shrug, Florence, is that where the answers lie? Or in the missing words traded between Stephen Lawson and Emilio Picariello, mostly over Steve Picariello, one Steve demanding that the other be brought in – or Picariello demanding that Lawson retrieve his son? Both Stephens of a sort, and even martyrs, Lawson the protomartyr who won you the martyrdom of a pre-dawn death, the fifth woman to be hanged in Canada since Confederation, the first in twenty-four years, but not the last, fast woman needing to be stopped in her tracks, made an example of.

After Bell's tire was changed, the APP met a vehicle driven by Sergeant Scott, who took Lawson back to Coleman, then turned around and continued his own return to Blairmore. Just past Coleman, alone, Scott encountered Picariello's car, stopped beside the road. Picariello signalled Scott to stop, and asked him if the APP had gotten his load. Scott told him that they had not gotten the whisky but that he, Picariello, would be charged with various motor vehicle offences and that both Picariello and his son would be charged for failing to stop when ordered to do so. Picariello told Scott that he did not care, just so long as his load was safe, and then added, 'If Lawson shot Steve, I would kill him.'

Of course, Florence, this is Scott's word for it, and you know how much Scott was to be trusted, eager to do his job, trigger happy, his square brutal face set in its own enforcement expression. The same face that sat across the table from you and watched what you said without writing it down, the same face that swore in the courtroom that you had pulled the trigger.

Here begin the multiple suppositions. Picariello did not know that

Steve had been shot; Lawson did not know he had shot Steve; Steve was injured, but not badly, certainly alive. Picariello returned to his hotel in Blairmore, determined to devise a way to get Steve home and to smuggle the load through later. He sent McAlpine, the mechanic, to find Steve; then received a phone call – in Italian – from a man (unidentified) who told him that Steve had been shot. Here the story begins to contest itself further, begins to unravel. Some versions say that Picariello was told that Steve was alive; some maintain that Picariello believed his son dead; others assert that Picariello knew that Steve's injuries were minor but he was so angry that he could not contain himself, and said, 'I don't like this shooting business, but if they are going to shoot, I can shoot too.' And later, or earlier, 'If he has shot my boy I'll kill every policeman in the Pass, by God.' Somewhere in Picariello's rage or grief or inconvenienced fury, he decided that he had to confront Lawson, had to insist that Lawson go with him to retrieve Steve, assure his son's well-being. And somewhere between his decision and his leaving the house, Florence volunteered to accompany him, saying 'Wait until I get my gun.' Yes, she *asked* to go along.

Your request, Florence, has been microscoped and revisited. All I can imagine is you, Florence, rising to your feet, pulling a red tam over your hair, shrugging into a green coat, that coat with the loose button, saying nothing, whether or not you had your own gun, whether or not you knew you were going on a mission of retrieval or vengeance. Like the first 'You drive,' was this 'I'll come' an admission or a defeat, enforced or volunteer?

But Florence Lassandro was in the car, the gun in her lap, as Picariello slowly nosed through the streets of Blairmore, towards the APP house where Lawson lived with his family; Florence was there when the car pulled up and Lawson came outside, walked towards the car, asked his law-enforcer's question, 'Yes, sir?' Florence heard the whole conversation, between Pic and Stephen Lawson, over the other Steve, Lawson standing at the driver's side, resting his foot on the running board, Picariello demanding that Lawson go with him to get his son, Lawson refusing, Picariello accusing Lawson of shooting his son, Lawson arguing that he was allowed to shoot at the car tires, that Picariello had to pay the price for bootlegging. Did Pic wave a gun? Lawson leaned into the car window, wrestled his arms around Picariello's neck, and it was then the shots were fired. But from where? Picariello's hand? Florence's hand? From behind the alley and not near the car at all?

Those moments in the car, Florence, what went through your head? The gun (in your lap? in your hand?) was heavy, bluntly blue. The air softening into autumn, leaves ready to turn, the light hazy. Did you pull back for a moment and watch those men, their body powerplay, their jockeying for the upper hand, their voices rising into threat? You were there, you knew what happened, heard it, saw it. You might even have squeezed the trigger of the gun. Maybe, when you weren't looking, your hand simply held the weapon and fired.

There were shots – three shots or possibly four. One shattered the windshield, another struck the speedometer and went through the floorboards, another killed Stephen Oldacres Lawson, who the story claims was running away, towards the side of his house. His nine-year-old daughter, Pearlie, saw him fall.

Florence, did you intend to shoot? Did you intend to kill? Did you intend to confess? Were you, as the Morning Albertan *headline declared on 2 December 1922, BOTH GUILTY!*

Pearlie pointed at Florence in the courtroom. 'The woman was wearing a red tammie.'

Unmistakably Florence.

'They would never hang a woman in the West.'

Whisky gets drunk, and guns go off.

The noose is a rough necklace, a hemp choker.

They wouldn't hang a woman but they did.

Pearlie Lawson: nine years old and put on the witness stand. Cute, bathetic. 'Daddy was standing by the car. He put his arm around the man's neck and then they shot, the lady shot and then the man shot and then they shot again, the lady let off the last shot and Daddy fell down.' How to erase this testimony, the nine-year-old child, too old to lisp but too young for dissemblance, or so it would seem, Pearlie innocent of intention, and no red tam-o'-shanter can stand up against that condemnation, the child watching her father fall, standing around the corner of the house, but hearing the shots, their sound carved into the air like a rope falling in dust.

Florence was either an accomplice or an accomplice. Or she might have been accompliced. She confessed that she had shot Lawson in self-defence. But Lawson had no gun, had emptied the shells and left his gun in the house. Lawson was unarmed, a policeman, a veteran, an Englishman, a war hero, a father, a straight-ahead, do-the-right-thing officer who needed nothing more than marching orders. And he had been hit in the back, gunned down by bootleggers, Catholic foreigners with dark eyes, seemingly by the 'lady in red tam' firing the two shots that brought the tussle to a noose.

Florence, you were the woman in the tam-o'-shanter, the red your marker.

You were the woman in the red tam, the woman wearing the hat. Was it getting colder, as it does in the Pass, September turning the poplar leaves yellow, the air beginning to bite the morning? The tam a bright contrast to your dark hair, your Toni curls springing out below its edge, red a happy declaration. Florence, you weren't afraid of being seen, or recognized. That hat (your last hat before an execution) a bright blaze when Maria (Pic's wife) cleaned your clothes out of the house, sent them over to your mother, Angela. There is character in the red tam, its brave signal almost sorrow in the passenger side of the car (why weren't you driving that night, what were you doing in the passenger seat?), a flare of identification.

The car roared away then. They ditched the vehicle; Pic ran into the hills, while Florence stayed with a friend. But the next day, Pic was caught and Florence surrendered. Interrogated by Scott, in the kitchen of the barracks in Coleman, she said that she shot Lawson in self-defence. In self-defence, denying every responsibility except accomplice, the pure possession of the gun, Picariello throwing it into her lap and saying, 'You keep the big gun.'

'You keep the big gun.' Did you thrill to those words, Florence? The same invocation as that earlier directive: 'You drive.' The same power? The same freedom suddenly unfurling its suggestive hands? Or were you a stray bystander, an accidental woman, along for the ride? Were you the victim, a soggy girl caught in the middle of an unexpected thunderstorm, poor Florence, taking the blame, ready to carry the gun, scared, shivering, a misled innocent? Why do I doubt this? Your maundering defenders accuse Picariello of manipulation and distortion, of setting you up to take the fall. 'They would never hang a woman in the West. You take the blame, say it was self-defence. I will go free and hire expensive lawyers to get you off.' Why do I doubt that you were quite so gullible, so sacrificially inclined? Because you liked to drive.

They were, Picariello and Lassandro, both in the car. They were along in the car at the time of the shooting, and all shots presumably came from the car. But Lassandro and Picariello made no effort to conceal themselves; innumerable people saw them as they drove through town, as they drove to Lawson's house. Lawson was shot while fleeing; the autopsy concluded that the bullet entered his back. But Picariello and Lassandro's revenge motive was unsubstantiated. If Picariello knew that Steve was alive, why would he want to harm Lawson? Both Lassandro and Picariello admitted that Lawson was unarmed. A .38 calibre bullet caused Lawson's death, and Picariello owned a .38 calibre gun. The Crown would argue that while only one bullet took effect, both Lassandro and Picariello fired, and all shots came from the car; therefore both were guilty of murder. But the question of intent seemed strangely skewed – Picariello and Lassandro could have waylaid Lawson, instead of confronting him openly, in broad daylight. And why did Lawson grapple with Picariello? No shots were fired before the physical altercation. Did Lawson have a gun? Or did Picariello think he had a gun? Did Lassandro imagine a gun? Or did the shots come from some person in the shadow, standing at the peripheral edge of the story, determined to cement a noose for one or another candidate?

Florence, you must have known that you were in trouble; you must have thought about the possibility of murder, death's shadow, you must have anticipated the enclosure of a jail cell. Or did you merely remember driving, the wheel under your hands, the grind of the engine, cool air against your face?

Florence Lassandro hid at the Gibeau (Gibault?) house. When she was arrested there, without resistance, by Constables Moriarty and Scott, she seemed unconcerned more than resigned, declaring her own indemnification. 'I have nothing to fear. He's dead and I'm alive.' She complained of hunger, and the first thing Scott did after her arrest, back at the barracks in Blairmore, was to make coffee, fry eggs.

What did you think of them Florence, the two men in their multipocketed uniforms and brimmed hats, what did you think of their questions, their hands? They patted you down, found cartridges in your coat pocket, the same coat that had lost the button you should have sewed on more securely, the button they would find when they searched the car later, a green button for your green coat. They put you in their car, they fed you, they leaned across the kitchen table listening to your story. Moriarty and Scott, APP specials, guys trying to invent a gangster's moll. And were the eggs good, could he make coffee, or was it dishwater, too weak to be effective?

Sergeant Scott fried her eggs and then asked her questions. Florence sat at the table in the kitchen, saying, yes, she shot in self-defence, yes, she held the gun, but Scott was too busy listening (too interested in the conversation) to write her words down. He could produce no signed confession, just as he produced no search warrant when he searched Picariello's house. The story and its confession hearsay, Scott reconstructing, and Florence reconstructed, shivering in the necklace of a misintention. At the trial, when defence lawyer McKinley Cameron asked why Scott had not taken down Florence's alleged confession, Scott was the one to shrug and say that he was too busy, and he was too interested in the conversation. Too interested in Florence telling him that two shots were fired *at* the car. 'I did not shoot until I saw a gun pointed at me,' she said. 'When Lawson put his arms around Picariello's neck, I fired.

Picariello didn't fire at all. Lawson had hold of him around the neck, I killed Lawson by accident.'

You were calm, Florence, calm and clear, as if self-defence were a matter of your voice speaking across a wooden kitchen table over a plate smeared with egg yolk, the coffee cup steaming in your hand. Scott listened as if what you said mattered, he leaned across the table towards your voice, your unerring eyes. You were alone together and caught inside a story, an interesting story, between climax and denouement, that hiatus of breath when the adrenalin is still high, when the chase is just subsiding, but the noose has not yet been fitted.

Scott left Florence in the kitchen while he went to get the revolver from Mrs Gibeau's house, mulling over her story, this dark-eyed woman whose brows almost met, whose hands (solid, red-knuckled) seemed capable of motion and strength, whose head tilted slightly at an angle, whose mouth secretly remembered a wide, ear-splitting grin. Scott was the nub of her alleged confession; no need to write down what a woman says. Although he told her, 'You have eaten the last Christmas dinner you will ever eat in this world.' So much for due process.

Florence never denied herself, or her red tam, or her green button, or even the gun. They seemed to belong together, there under the eye of the Crowsnest Pass, southern Alberta and the stern waggings of the attorney general's finger, there to ensure a pass at justice and its mitigations. Attorney General Brownlee was a squinch-eyed man who wore his pince-nez with severe intention: justice would be served. And these were Catholic foreigners, dark-skinned to the tips of their incomprehensible lingo, Pic a shady character for all his success and his election to the town council, and better the whole damned arrogant lawless lot be stopped than that they be shown clemency or even too much courtesy, whether they were women or men. Just as Judge Walsh instructed, 'In a British court of justice we do not consider or recognize sex.'

Florence, could you feel their British scorn, their condescension, the way that you were painted as a moll, a paramour, out for the race, fast cars, excitement, new clothes? The gangster's moll, the Bottle King's mistress or housekeeper or even 'daughter,' as if the connection with Pic was variously detextable, irrevocable. But whether you were Pic's mistress, or Steve's mistress, or Charles's wife, or just a gullible girl, it was all the same to them. You were a woman with her finger on the trigger.

Somewhere in their conversation Scott apparently told Florence that she had eaten the last Christmas dinner that she would ever eat. Just as Scott said to Picariello, when Pic asked about the welfare of his son, Steve, 'He's much better off where he is, probably better off than you.'

Scott the tough, unerring one, the one who carried Florence's story in his head, refusing to write it down, his memory playing over and over again her mouth saying, 'I killed Lawson,' that phrase edited from the others. Which would made defence counsel McKinley Cameron fulminate in his final address to the court, a summation that lasted some four hours, after Judge Walsh had ordered the corridors cleared, the noise of those spectators waiting outside so loudly curious that the court could not hear itself speak or think. Cameron played on Florence's youth and gender, his speeches carefully constructed around the order of his days, his laundered collars and meticulous hotel bills, the fee that Pic was paying him, Florence and Pic on trial together, but separated, without the chance to speak to one another.

'Sergeant Scott is the champion confessions man for the crown. He got this confession alone with this poor girl in his kitchen, while the detachment was filled with police and while the assistant superintendent of the provincial police was only two rooms away, as Scott knew. Were it not for these confessions, where would the case for the crown be? Scott was their heavy artillery and he was marshalled into court at the last minute with his head crammed full of confessions and confessions.

'The reason Scott did not take down notes when this confession was purported to have been made is that he might have been requested to have produced those notes in this court. Scott attended the inquest and still the confession was not put down in writing, and then he comes into this court at the trial for their lives of the lives of these two people and he has nothing but his memory to rely upon for the accuracy of his statements here. He didn't have the time to ensure the protection of this poor little girl.'[1]

Cameron pointed at Florence, 'this poor little girl.'

What did you think then Florence? 'This poor little girl?' Did you want to tell him you were your own woman, the story was yours and nothing Scott or Cameron or Judge Walsh could do in their examinations and accusations and exfoliations could take it away, erase its blunt outcome, your hands were on the wheel, you were driving.

It did not work. The Crown insisted that Florence had 'put on her toilet of death with malice aforethought' by going to get her gun before she left with Picariello to find Lawson. The jury returned a verdict of guilty.

They reported your weeping, the way that you cried while the judge summed up, still sure that they would never hang a woman in the West, too much chivalry, but that's for white women, northern Europeans who speak English without an accent, careful with their petticoats and their hands, afraid of garlic

*and inclined towards starched pillowslips, refusing the bite of anchovies and
olives.*

There were the usual appeals, and two brief reprieves. They were
originally to be hanged on 21 February, but, pending an appeal, the date
was commuted to 21 March. Cameron did his best, his applications for
clemency playing on Florence's gender. 'One of the defendants under
sentence of death is a woman. In fact, the evidence establishes that it
was she (if either of them) who fired the fatal shot, and it is submitted
that it is not in accordance with the trend of modern thought to execute
a woman no matter how great a sinner she may be.'[2] There was considerable prejudice against the accused, Cameron insisted, especially given
that the defendants were 'of foreign origin' as opposed to Lawson's reputation as 'a returned veteran.'

*Sinner, Florence? Did you feel yourself a sinner, a victim, a foreigner? Or
did you, despite the newspaper reports that claimed you were on the verge of
utter collapse, exhausted by long days contemplating your fate, resist repen-
tance? They said you lay for hours on your cot, moaning and rocking restlessly.
What did you contemplate then? Death? Or your life, driving the high winding
roads of the Crowsnest Pass, from Fernie to Blairmore and back again, driving,
driving.*

On 13 March a new reprieve was ordered and the date of execution set
for 2 May 1923. Which is when Picariello and Florence were both executed (hanged, that is) in a grey pre-dawn covered with low clouds. Pic
was first, at 5:10, stepping into space after his final question, 'Why are you
hanging an innocent man?' And Florence followed, at exactly 5:51, the
same bleak pre-dawn of the same day, escorted on her long walk across
the yard from the women's prison by Matron, a priest, the warden, the
sheriff, and three guards. The doctor had injected her with half a gram of
morphine. The hangman fitted the hood over her head. Florence Lassandro took eleven minutes to die, after saying, 'Why do you hang me when
I didn't do anything? Is there anyone here who has any pity?'

*But you did do something, Florence. You laughed, you wore lace collars and
danced, moving your body in time to a fiddle and squeezebox, you loved the
thrill of the chase, the excitement of driving, the wheel jolting and vibrant
under your hands, you lived in Picariello's house, you were part of a moment
that was pitched with pleasure, every sense on edge, whether it was in chase or
simply around a table, but that'll teach you to be a rumrunner, that'll teach you
to run with rumrunners, and as for carrying a gun, be careful, it may go off.*

Her story, the narrative under the narrative under the narrative under
the already expected car chase, shoot-out, manhunt, escape and capture,

trial and appeal, death and demarcation, what is it? The bare bones, the facts? Punishment or pleasure? Or just a woman gone wrong?

Florence, I want to drive with you, over the rumrunners' trail, the wheel under your capable hands. None of the shooting would have happened if you had been driving, you at the wheel instead of Picariello, his temper working between the handbrake and the clutch. The night before your death, a young woman showed up at the First Baptist Church on the South Side of Edmonton, and asked the Reverend O.D. Priddle if she could take Florence's place on the gallows. She was, she said, ready to die, but she was certain that Florence was not. She seemed normal in every way, except that she kept repeating a phrase to the effect that she had been driving. I admit it, Florence, that woman was me. I would have taken your place, stood in for you, worn your necklace, as I now try on the lace collars that fanned your dark dresses.

In the earlier picture, Florence, your grin is a wide bite. Your Cuban-heeled shoes are full of snow, and your dress, as you perch against the ledge of a back-yard fence, is hiked so that an edge of lace shows below the hem, like the lace that scallops the collar. You have your arm around your sister, Rose, and your brother Martin, serious under his toque, stands beside. It can't be very cold, although the snow is thick on the ground, wet in its frost on your shoe. One foot, Florence, is already off the ground, and the other is on the accelerator. You are ready to take off, laughing, full of life, your lace collar a metaphor for your final necklace and its aching clasp around your neck, a final lover, a final adventure, before the run of death.

CHRONOLOGY

1901 Philomena Costanzo is born in Consenza, Calabria, Italy.

1910 Family emigrates to Canada, settling in Fernie, British Columbia.

1915 Philomena marries Carlo Sanfidele (age twenty-three). They move to Pennsylvania, but return to Canada within a year. They change their names to Charles and Florence Lassandro. Charles works for his former employer, Emilio Picariello, at Blairmore, Alberta, in the Crowsnest Pass.

1 July 1916 Prohibition begins.

1 March 1917 A new provincial police force, the Alberta Provincial Police, is formed to control the making and distribution of illicit liquor.

1919   Florence begins rumrunning with Picariello.

1922   Picariello is arrested for unlawfully keeping liquor for sale at Blairmore. Picariello is found guilty and fined $500 and costs.

23 March 1922   Stephen Oldacres Lawson is taken on as a first-class constable and posted to the Crowsnest Pass.

21 September 1922   Picariello attempts to get a carload of liquor through to Blairmore from Fernie, British Columbia. Lawson shoots Steve Picariello in the hand. Emilio Picariello and Florence go to Coleman to confront Lawson. Lawson and Picariello, who is inside the car, exchange words, there is a struggle, shots are fired, and Lawson dies.

23 September 1922   Both Picariello and Florence are arrested. Florence confesses to firing the shots, either by accident or in self-defence.
    An inquest into the death of Stephen Oldacres Lawson determines that he met his death by a bullet fired from a revolver in possession of the occupant of a car parked in front of the Alberta Provincial Police Barracks in Coleman, Alberta. At a special sitting of the Alberta Provincial Police Court on the same day, both Emilio Picariello and Florence Lassandro are charged with the murder of Stephen Lawson. Emilio Picariello is transferred to Lethbridge Jail; Florence is transferred to Calgary.

25 September 1922   Lawson's funeral is held in Fort Macleod, Alberta.

2 October 1922   A preliminary hearing is held in Coleman, Alberta. Emilio Picariello and Florence Lassandro are charged with murder and committed to stand trial. The venue for the trial is changed from Fort Macleod to Calgary. Picariello is retained in Lethbridge; Florence is sent to Fort Saskatchewan.

27 November 1922   A special sitting of the Supreme Court at the Calgary Provincial Courthouse begins.

2 December 1922   Emilio Picariello and Florence Lassandro are found guilty of murder and condemned to death by hanging, 21 February 1923.

16 February 1923   Stay of execution to 21 March 1923.

13 March 1923   Stay of execution to 2 May 1923.

2 May 1923   Emilio Picariello and Florence Lassandro hanged at Fort Saskatchewan Penitentiary.

NOTES

1 McKinley Cameron Papers, Glenbow Archives, Calgary, Alberta
2 Ibid.

CREATING FACTS

Dear Ruth: This Is the Story of Maggie Wilson, Ojibwa Ethnologist

SALLY COLE

What precisely ... is [it] that interests us in the lives of other women?

Barbara Caine, 'Feminist Biography and Feminist History'

In the summer of 1932, two women met at the Manitou Rapids Indian Reserve between Fort Frances and Kenora in northwestern Ontario. One was Maggie Wilson, a world-weary Scots-Cree grandmother in her fifties who walked with a limp and suffered from dropsy and other ailments related to age and poverty, who had lived her entire life on Ojibwa reserves along the Rainy River. The other was twenty-three-year-old Ruth Schlossberg Landes, who had been born and raised in New York City, the daughter of Russian-Jewish immigrants, and who had recently separated from her medical student husband. An urbane, attractive woman, Mrs Landes had rejected marriage and 'domesticity' in order to devote herself to graduate studies in anthropology at Columbia University.[1] This unlikely pair began a collaboration that resulted in three books, *Ojibwa Sociology*, *The Ojibwa Woman*, and *Ojibwa Religion and the Midéwiwin*,[2] and three scholarly articles, including 'The Ojibwa of Canada,' which was solicited for the volume *Cooperation and Conflict among Primitive People*, edited by Margaret Mead.[3]

Manitou Rapids was then a community of under 300 people enduring hard times. The economic depression was having its impact, but more important had been the Canadian government's forced consolidation and relocation in 1915 of seven formerly autonomous Ojibwa bands. This relocation at Manitou marked the end of a process that had begun with the signing of Treaty 3 in 1873. Ojibwa had engaged in the treaty

Ruth Landes, age twenty and married, summer 1929, New York City

expecting protected reserve lands and government assistance to develop their small farms along the Rainy River. But the government's aim to secure access to lands to build the railroad and open the area for Euro-Canadian settlement had exactly the opposite effect. In 1881 federal legislation passed that reduced the ability of Indians to sell their produce to non-Indians.[4] This effectively closed Ojibwa commercial markets with fur traders, logging companies, and settlers who bought their corn and potatoes. The closing of markets, lack of training in farming techniques, use of poor-quality seed and implements, sickness, and demoralization contributed to Ojibwa eventually abandoning agriculture. Later, in 1887, a dam built at the mouth of the Rainy River at Lake

Maggie Wilson, about fifty-four years old, 1933, Emo, Ontario

of the Woods flooded many Ojibwa gardens and rice fields so that even raising food for household subsistence became difficult and, by the 1890s, many were starving. The government meanwhile appropriated arable reserve lands for Euro-Canadian settlers, arguing that the Ojibwa were not cultivating them, and ultimately relocated the people to one reserve.[5] By the 1930s, Ojibwa at Manitou relied on a diverse annual round of subsistence activities, exploiting resources that included deer and other game, fish, wild rice, berries, maple sugar, and garden produce. Fur trapping and seasonal work in local resource industries (logging, timber mills, commercial fisheries, and mining) offered limited and unpredictable wage earnings for some. Chronic destitution was the lot of most.

Into this world came the young anthropology student Ruth Landes to work with Maggie Wilson, who was to teach her about Ojibwa social organization and religion for her PhD dissertation. It was the standard practice of anthropologists of the time to hire Native research assistants, who were referred to in that era as 'key informants' whom they paid to sit and tell them about a culture, a place, and its people. These key informants were usually, but not always, male elders who were knowledgeable about the origins of the tribe, its myths and geneaologies, its social, economic, and religious organization. The data thus collected were transcribed by the anthropologist during painstaking hours of oral dictation. Mrs Wilson's participation in the project was both economic (she was paid $1.00 a day) and cultural: it was Ojibwa practice for older women to teach younger women by telling stories of women's lives, and of women's skills and resourcefulness.

ANTHROPOLOGY AND OJIBWA WOMEN'S STORYTELLING

Through the winter months, older women often tell their life stories and devote a great amount of time and interest to elaborating past affairs with lovers and husbands.

Ruth Landes, *The Ojibwa Woman*

So it was that on 6 July 1932 Ruth Landes arrived in Fort Frances, carrying letters of introduction from the deputy superintendent-general of Indian Affairs in Ottawa to the local Indian agents at Fort Frances and Kenora. In this colonial context, she followed then-standard anthropological practice: she first approached government authorities, not the people themselves, for their endorsement of her research. She arrived in Fort Frances with the name of one Ojibwa person, Mrs Maggie Wilson, whom she immediately set about contacting. Mrs Wilson had first collaborated in ethnological research as early as July 1919 when Minnesota ethnomusicologist Frances Densmore visited Manitou Rapids. She later became known to Father John Cooper, an ethnologist from Catholic University in Washington, when he spent a few days in the Rainy River district in 1928. A. Irving Hallowell, of the University of Pennsylvania, who had begun his extensive research with Algonkians in Manitoba in 1930, had also heard favourably of Mrs Wilson's ethnological skills. These scholars had advised Ruth Benedict, who was supervising Ruth Landes's dissertation research, to send her young student to Manitou Rapids to work with Mrs Wilson.

Ruth Landes's ethnography carries with it the hallmarks of 1930s anthropology. It is often ahistorical in its neglect of the wide-ranging and traumatic changes aboriginal societies were undergoing at the time. And the textual representation may be guided by a psychologizing, often ethnocentric, voice of an absent but omniscient ethnographer. These characteristics of some early anthropological writing have been justly criticized.[6] Landes has also been challenged for her portrait of Ojibwa society as individualistic and conflict-ridden. In particular, her description of some and economic relations as 'atomistic'[7] has been disputed, and subsequent ethnographers often emphasized instead communality and cooperative (not individualistic), egalitarian (not atomistic) relations.[8] For example, anthropologist William Dunning, in his classic *Social and Economic Change among the Northern Ojibwa* (1959) describes marriage as a life-long economic partnership in which women are 'passive' and 'submissive' to their husbands, who are described as 'active and gregarious.'[9] In such accounts marriage choices follow prescribed cultural rules, not individual choice, and there is no mention of love, conflict, domestic violence, desertion, separation, or divorce – the topics that most interested Maggie Wilson and Ruth Landes. Particularly striking in the Landes–Wilson ethnography is the attention given to the hardships and struggles of women. While this attention to women led critics to charge that the work represents 'an idiosyncratic female viewpoint' and is 'less than scientific,'[10] I suggest that this woman's point of view is the key to understanding Landes's portrait of conflict and social tension.

In addition to the oral accounts that Ruth Landes transcribed at Manitou, Maggie Wilson sent over forty letters to Landes after she returned to New York, dictating them to her daughter Janet. The letters were a kind of anthropological piecework: Columbia University paid Mrs Wilson fifteen cents per double-sided page of a stenographer's pad. The typical opening is: 'Dear Ruth, This is the story of ... She was an Ojibwa woman who ...' These story-letters testify to the harsh lives of women in northwestern Ontario in the early years of this century. Her stories construct women as social actors and document their lived experience. They tell of women's boldness and resourcefulness in overcoming hardship. Based on the lives of as many women as Maggie Wilson could recall, the stories are about being lost or abandoned; of running away from an abusive husband, mother, stepmother, or co-wife; of enduring cold, starvation, sickness, and the deaths of children; of hunting and butchering a moose; of building a canoe and paddling long distances; or

of constructing a shelter and surviving alone in the wilderness by fishing, snaring rabbits, and collecting berries. Often they tell of women
who became medical or religious specialists. Mrs Wilson punctuates the
stories with statements like, 'She lived a rough life; she was a real Indian
woman.' The 'real Indian woman' narratively constructed by Maggie
Wilson, although non-existent in conventional Ojibwa ethnography,
resembles the skilled and resourceful Cree and Ojibwa women that historian Sylvia Van Kirk describes in 'Many Tender Ties.'[11] Regarding Mrs
Wilson's story-letters, Landes wrote to Benedict: 'I've read only two
Wilson stories in the batch ... and I find these excellent. One is her old
and thorough line about the woman deserted, mistreated, rewarded,
shamed, combatted over, etc. The theme is damned familiar to us by
now.'[12]

The overall picture in Mrs Wilson's stories is of women living under
duress. It is not the kind of tale that anthropologists seeking to recon-
struct the social life of noble and pristine 'primitive man' were hoping to
tell. Nor are these the kinds of lives that are usually recorded in history
and biography. The actual identities of these women and standard biographical details of their lives (place and dates of birth, marriage(s),
births of children, death, for example) will probably never be known.
Yet the common denominators of women's lives emerge in a pattern
that, as Landes says, becomes 'damned familiar' in the reading of these
letters-stories-lives. The realities of survival in a harsh environment
(both physical and social) are repetitive and oppressive in their ultimate
predictability.

One such story is of 'Hawk-Woman,' whose husband, after years of
beatings and repeated desertions, finally abandoned her one day when
the couple was out moose hunting:

They travelled by canoe up the Lake for two days. The third night they stopped
on the shore. The next day they killed two big moose, and she cleaned them, and
dried the meat. So they (separately) went up into the woods to get some birch to
make a birchbark wigwam, and also birchbark for a canoe. She came down with
her load of birchbark, and saw their gun there, so she took it along and went back
for another load. When she returned, their canoe was gone, also her husband. So
she was left there alone with no canoe. But everything else was there ... her kettles, tea pail, knives, all her clothing and blankets, and she also had the gun. She
walked along the shore thinking that her husband was out paddling, but it got so
dark that she returned to the wigwam and went to bed. The next day she waited,
and still he didn't come. Then she knew that her husband had left her there for

good. She made up her mind to stay until death came to her. She made birch-barks, tanned the moose-hides, and pounded meat, and then she got some cedar and made the frame of a canoe. She stayed there and did all her work, made mats, and all kinds of things. She had her sewing with her. One evening she went around the point of the bay and sat there. She saw a moose in the water. She waited until it came closer, and then she shot and killed it.[13]

Hawk Woman survived by doing the work of a man, in addition to using her woman's skills. Eventually, she met and happily married a younger man.

Mrs Wilson's storytelling was her attempt not only to educate the neophyte anthropologist but also to serve as witness to Ojibwa women's experience. She told stories about women's lives as metaphors, as 'narrative resources,'[14] to elicit understanding of Ojibwa women's lives – and of her own life.[15]

Would Mrs Wilson have told these same stories to another anthropologist, male or female? This is not clear. It is especially important to recognize that she did not tell her stories to Ruth Landes simply because they were both women. But the fact that the communication between them was remarkable when contrasted with the relationship that often prevailed between other women anthropologists and Native women in this period facilitated the process. According to Deborah Gordon, women anthropologists often held an attitude of liberal reformism and 'matronization' towards aboriginal women.[16] Gordon maintains that women anthropologists commonly projected idealized early twentieth-century passive maternal and feminine roles onto Native women, inevitably portraying them as self-sacrificing 'communal mothers.' She refers, as an example, to Gladys Reichard's biography of a Navaho woman, *Dezba: Woman of the Desert*, published in 1939, the year after Landes's *The Ojibwa Woman*.

Why, one wonders, did the relationship between Maggie Wilson and Ruth Landes not follow this same course? The answer in part lies in their mutual recognition – despite their differences in age and cultural background – of a shared experience of social marginality. For, what Deborah Gordon does not note is that the women anthropologists of whom she writes were all raised as members of established old New England families whose liberal reformism was the response of a particular social class to conditions in 1930s American society. Ruth Landes, however, was the daughter of immigrants, a Jew, an outsider in early twentieth-century American academe. An academic future was for her uncertain and, indeed, unlikely.[17] Furthermore, her termination of her brief marriage had strained relations with her family and placed her outside her ethnic immigrant milieu, which prescribed marriage and motherhood. Mrs Wilson, who at Manitou had been ostracized for her visionary powers and her insights into human behaviour, recognized in Landes a keen fellow observer and social critic. Landes, recently separated from her husband, was especially sensitized to hear about other women's experiences of marriage, separation, and divorce; and, many of the stories that Maggie Wilson had to tell were those that spoke of marital stress.

In the preface to *The Ojibwa Woman*, Landes wrote, 'I did not tell her what kinds of stories to report, but she knew from our intensive studies that I wanted the whole life – its warm breath, its traditional forms. She had the storyteller's instinct and a dramatic flair. These biographical accounts are unique as a gifted woman's view of her fellow women, usually under stress. Since the characters come alive despite the crude English, how powerfully they must have emerged in the original Ojibwa!'[18]

In her writing, Landes often makes reference to her youth, inexperience, fears, and revulsion at the conditions of life in northwestern Ontario in the 1930s. She acknowledges that there was probably much in Mrs Wilson's accounts that she missed, since she did not speak Ojibwa. Unlike many anthropologists, who claim intimacy to assert authority for the ethnographic portrait they have constituted, Landes maintains no pretense of intimacy or friendship between herself and Mrs Wilson. She is certain, however, of the exceptional working relationship and mutual respect between them. She credits Maggie Wilson's genius, intellect, and careful attention to detail as largely responsible for the success of their joint endeavour. Landes considered the ethnography 'a product of [Mrs Wilson's] genius and my conscientiousness' and describes their relationship as follows:

I never supposed that she liked me, but she treated me well in every way. The times were desperately poor, so I made a point of paying her one dollar at the close of each day, besides small extras. She respected this punctilio, which happened to coincide with Ojibwa requirements surrounding the relationship of teacher and learner. Her work habits were meticulous and I surmise she respected my own conscientiousness. During the several years I visited her, I never saw her smile. Perhaps it was because I did not truly trust myself to expand, aware always of the language barrier, of the strange Indian presences, of the tom-tom at the gambling games, of the smells and ugliness maintained by chronic destitution.[19]

For Ruth Landes, Maggie Wilson was a teacher, an intellectual, a philosopher, a visionary, and an ethnologist. Near the end of her second summer among the Ojibwa, she wrote to Benedict: 'I consider her a gem and believe that we will have her with us till she gives up the ghost. I think that by now she is as good an ethnologist as any of us. I gave her some instruction this summer, which she snapped up. She gets the real point of what we want.'[20]

MAGGIE WILSON, ETHNOLOGIST

She was highly skilled in Ojibwa women's crafts, and furthermore a celebrated visionary ... [S]he loved to ponder and talk reflectively in the Ojibwa's rather whining, nasal, light tones; she embroidered with porcupine quills for which she used native grassy dyes; she embroidered also with trader's beads; she tanned hides of deer, elk and moose, and cut them up for mocassins and 'firebags' (carrying tinder for tobacco); and she bit designs into new birchbark .... Seeing her shining, shrewd black eyes peer through rimless spectacles (worn only when embroidering), one would not have supposed she was a mystic who had produced mighty 'dreams.' Those eyes, the broad cheekbones, the tight-clamped mouth exposing constant harassment, belonged to her needle-sharp mind, ever at grips with reality. She had a sardonic humor that my young self could record but not truly follow.

Ruth Landes, Preface to the second edition of *The Ojibwa Woman*

Twice Landes's age when they met, Maggie Wilson was born about 1879 at the Little Forks Indian Reserve on the Rainy River west of Fort Frances. She was the first child of Benjamin and Elizabeth Spence. The previous year her parents had begun receiving payments from the Canadian government under Treaty 3 as members of the Little Forks band. Her mother, Elizabeth, was the daughter of a Scottish Hudson's Bay Company trader and a woman whom Maggie Wilson describes as a 'Cree halfbreed woman.' In a letter to Ruth Landes, Maggie told a story of her mother's life: when Elizabeth was about five years old (ca. 1865), her father wanted to return to Scotland and take his Native wife and their three small daughters to live with him there. Elizabeth's mother, however, did not want to go, and he left for Scotland alone; Elizabeth never saw her father again.[21] Soon afterward, her mother married a Cree man, and the new family camped near Fort Alexander on Lake Winnipeg. The stepfather, however, was abusive, and the little girls were soon taken into the care of their mother's sisters, who were also married to Scottish men. At seven, Elizabeth went to live with a cousin who was married to a Hudson's Bay Company man to help care for their young daughter. Elizabeth endured years of abuse with this couple: she was regularly beaten, deprived of food, and locked alone in the company warehouse. When the man was transferred to Fort Frances, Elizabeth accompanied the family. She finally ran away when she was fourteen and found work at the Anglican minister's house. Here she met Ben Spence, who worked as a driver taking the minister by dog team throughout the Rainy River district.

Elizabeth and Ben married the following summer and moved to Little Forks reserve to live with his parents. Ben's father, Peter Spence, was a bilingual (English-speaking) Cree from Fort Alexander who taught at the Church Missionary Society school in Little Forks. Ben took a succession of seasonal jobs, working for land surveyors or on the steamers that plied the Rainy River between Fort Frances and Kenora. Mrs Wilson recalls frequent conflict between Elizabeth and her mother-in-law over rights to the wages, trade goods and purchased items, such as cloth ('print') and food that Ben brought home. When, in 1881, Peter Spence was moved to the Anglican mission at Long Sault reserve, Ben rented a house in Fort Frances and brought Elizabeth and Maggie there to live for the winter. Maggie was then about three years old. In the spring, at Peter Spence's request, they moved down to Long Sault. After building a house there, Ben went to work on the riverboats for the summer and Elizabeth worked breaking the soil for a garden and planting corn and potatoes. Maggie Wilson reports that she and her mother nearly starved that summer until Ben returned, bringing with him blankets, a shawl, cotton yardgoods, tea, flour, and other groceries and 'things that were nice to eat.' For several years, they farmed at Long Sault and Ben worked on the riverboats in the summers. In March 1885, when Maggie was six years old, Ben and Elizabeth's second child, also a daughter, was born. That year the Anglican Church moved Peter Spence and his family back to Little Forks, and Maggie's parents decided to join them and accept treaty provisions to farm there. Ben cleared land, and Mrs Wilson describes four happy years during which her grandparents 'were different people,' doting on their new granddaughter and now being kind to

Maggie and Elizabeth. Elizabeth began her profession as a midwife, receiving payment in food and animals – her first pay was a young calf from a non-Native woman whose baby she had safely delivered at Little Forks. The small farm apparently prospered as the Spences raised cows, pigs, and chickens and grew potatoes and corn.

Then tragedy struck, tragedy from which Maggie's parents and grandparents never fully recovered. One of Ben's brothers became ill. The entire Spence family, including Ben, Elizabeth, and their children, moved into Kenora on the last steamboat before freezeup to be near the hospital. Maggie's uncle died in November. Then in Kenora in March 1889, when Maggie was ten years old, her four-year-old sister contracted measles and died. Her grandparents' world had been destroyed. They both turned to alcohol, Maggie Wilson recollects, 'and from that time my grandfather was out of his mind ... [I]t was a hard time to get him to wash his face or change his clothes. It was only my mother who could get him to change his clothes and he always tore the collars off his shirts.' When the ice was out in the spring, the shattered family returned by steamboat from Kenora to Little Forks and took up farming again. They gardened and raised pigs, cows, and poultry for the next few years. Maggie recalls that her parents often quarrelled and blamed one another for their young daughter's death. One summer, Maggie's father, distraught, simply left them and moved into Kenora. In September, Maggie, then fourteen years of age, went by boat to Kenora to find her father and, once she found him, refused to leave until he returned to Little Forks with her. She reports that when they returned they brought with them her father's seventeen-year-old orphaned cousin, Thomas Spence, who became a member of their household. Ben died five years later. Elizabeth married Thomas Spence and moved to Long Sault where she lived until Spence died sixteen years later. She then married John Bunyan at Manitou Rapids in 1915 or 1916 and died in 1932.

Maggie Wilson married at the age of sixteen, shortly after her father's death. Her husband, however, died within the year, and she then married Tom Wilson of the Hungry Hall band further west on the Rainy River in 1895 or 1896. Their first child, Christina, was not born until 14 September 1902 when Maggie was in her early twenties. A son, Leonard, was born 20 February 1908. Her husband's death is noted on the Hungry Hall annuity paylist of June 1911, and Maggie's second son, Albert, was born on 26 February 1912.[22]

People at Manitou told Landes that, within a remarkably short time after her husband's death, Maggie Wilson had amassed the necessary wealth to ransom her freedom from her in-laws (*giwenige*), who always maintained that a lover must have aided her. 'This was wrong and punishable, for she should have been celibate and sorrowing – sorrowing in guilt, as the survivor.'[23] Landes, however, saw this as evidence of Maggie Wilson's individualism, courage, and pragmatism – for as a widow with three young children she might otherwise have been forced into service for her husband's kin. Maggie apparently was determined to control her own destiny. Under such difficult conditions, it is a considerable feat that she also managed to keep her children with her and that she appears to have remained close to them throughout her life.

Maggie Wilson lived at Hungry Hall until 1914 when she married Chief Namepok's son, John Wilson, at Manitou Rapids. A daughter, Janet, was born in 1915. Her last child, a girl, was born about 1919 when Maggie was forty, but died within her first year. In 1925, she adopted a non-Native baby boy who was seven years old and known simply as 'Shaganash,' meaning 'white boy,' when Landes arrived at Manitou in 1932. Maggie lived with John Wilson at Manitou Rapids until her death sometime between June 1939 and June 1940; John Wilson died in January 1952.

LIFE AT MANITOU RAPIDS

Maggie Wilson's life spans important years of transition during which she witnessed the erosion of the political and economic autonomy of the Ojibwa living along the Rainy River. She was born about five years after the signing of Treaty 3 in 1873 when the seven Rainy River bands were settled on reserves and brought under the administration of the Department of Indian Affairs in Ottawa. By the time of her death in 1940, the seven bands had had all of these lands appropriated, with the exception of the Manitou Rapids reserve, and had been consolidated at Manitou under the administrative authority of the indian agent in Fort Frances.

Prior to their consolidation in 1915, the people had lived in small bands of related families who came together in the spring and summer to garden at villages along the Rainy River. From these villages they would fish and harvest berries along the river and its tributaries. Mrs Wilson remembered travelling with her father and mother up and down both shores of the Rainy River from Little Forks to fish sturgeon, which they smoked for winter food. In fall, Maggie camped with her parents and grandparents near the wild rice beds on Rainy Lake, where they spent several weeks harvesting and preparing the rice for winter storage. In the late fall they gathered at her grandfather's fishing grounds at Whitefish Creek on the American side of the Rainy River, three miles below Fort Frances. People regrouped again briefly at the summer villages before disbanding in family units for winter hunting and trapping grounds; Maggie's father trapped north of Little Forks. As spring approached, families gathered at family-owned sugar bush stands to collect the sap and make maple sugar, which could then be stored and eaten with wild rice, vegetables, and fish. Maggie Wilson recalled that she, her father, her mother and her father's cousin used to work a stand of about 300 trees on the American side of the mouth of the Little Forks River, a stand that had belonged to her father's mother. Larger families worked larger stands of from 400 to 500 trees. After the maple sugar harvest, families returned to the villages to plant their gardens of wheat, barley, oats, potatoes, and corn, and the seasonal round began again.[24]

Political organization was family-based. Each band was under the leadership of an individual who was also the head of the extended family unit. Most decisions, however, were made by consensus. Some individuals, usually men, but on occasion women, held authority that was based on visions or supernatural experiences. Marriage, divorce, inheritance, and adoption practices were all considered family matters.

When the Rainy River bands were consolidated at Manitou Rapids in the fall of 1915, questions of political authority arose. The people had foreseen these problems and had, in February 1915, sent representatives from each band to meet with Canadian government officials in Ottawa to express their concerns. The bands did not want to be under the domination of the Manitou Rapids band and requested that, if moved there, each band would retain its own chief and councillors.

Upon consolidation, Manitou Rapids suddenly had a population of 277. Most of the people had never lived in villages of more than forty to sixty people, and then only seasonally and not year-round. Little Forks, where Maggie was born, was a reserve of forty-nine people. The people faced many new challenges in their efforts to construct a viable community. Economic difficulties were built into the system. As noted above, Ojibwa efforts to develop agriculture had been permanently undermined by federal legislation that deterred them from selling their produce. Given this historical context, a government farm instruction program instituted at Manitou after the relocation, and after the best farmlands had been appropriated for Euro-Canadian settlement, was doomed to failure. Nonetheless, Mrs Wilson describes the efforts people made to farm at Manitou. Her husband John cleared a few acres, built a two-storey frame house, and planted wheat, barley, oats, potatoes, and corn. When Maggie's eldest daughter, Christina, married in 1916 at the age of fourteen, she and her husband cleared bush adjacent to John and Maggie Wilson's farm. When her son Albert planned to marry, Maggie and John gave him land on which to farm and build a house. John was ill and unable to cultivate all his land when Maggie's youngest daughter, Janet, married at the age of thirteen in 1927. He invited his new son-in-law, James, into partnership with him. James contributed a horse and plough, helped his father-in-law farm his lands, and they divided the produce between them. James also cleared additional new land for himself.

Maggie Wilson describes the increased stresses in marriages under the new living conditions as well as the new restrictions on marriage and divorce that the Indian agent sought to enforce. Historically, the choice of marriage partners had been an individual decision, although family members, especially mothers, could become involved. Maggie herself recalled how her mother had forbidden her from marrying her first sweetheart, who was also her fourth cousin. Once married, however, it was an individual woman's choice to remain in or to leave a marriage, and notions of romantic love and sexual fulfilment were, according to Mrs Wilson, important components of a successful marriage. Separations, divorces, and remarriages had been common occurrences. Once settled at Manitou, however, women were less free to leave unhappy marriages or abusive partners because there were no longer other villages to go to. But, more important, the Indian agent took an active hand in keeping marriages intact that would not have survived previously. As an example, Maggie described how a young neighbour was abused by her husband, who experienced continual frustration and disappointments in farming and who took up gambling and often stayed away from home for days. This young woman would often cry herself to sleep at Maggie's house or Maggie would find her at home in bed 'helpless from her husband's kicks.' Maggie Wilson explained to Landes: 'That's why she's so thin and unhappy. But the Agent said they had to live together, otherwise he wouldn't help [her husband] with his wheat. I tried to tell the Agent that they should separate, but he said no.'[25]

The forced co-residence of members of different bands at Manitou required the negotiation of new social relationships as neighbours and as members of one community. According to Mrs Wilson, new rivalries and jealousies abounded; she herself experienced these as a result of a leadership role she had at first reluctantly assumed and later, also reluctantly, relinquished.

MAGGIE'S VISION: THE UNION STAR DANCE

I would wake up singing.

Maggie Wilson, quoted in Landes, *Ojibwa Religion and the Midewiwin*

Maggie was a thirty-five-year-old widow and mother of three when she married John Wilson and moved to Manitou Rapids in 1914, a year before the Rainy River bands were relocated there. On her first night at Manitou, she had a vision that was to recur in a sequence of vision-dreams, each lasting several nights. In the vision, supernatural thunder-birds told Maggie to perform a dance to save the lives of Ojibwa soldiers, including her daughter Christina's husband, who were fighting overseas in the First World War. For a long while Maggie resisted and feared the visions. 'The head Thunderbird [came], saying they were going to take me somewhere – and I did not want to go. I heard them singing. I wakened, got out of bed, thought about the dream, returned to bed, and dreamt again. They repeated that they wanted me to go with them, to a big mountain.' She was afraid, but they assured her that they meant to console and 'amuse' her and the village. When she continued to resist, the thunderbirds threatened, 'something will befall your family and all the people.' So, with the assistance of her husband, who would hear her singing the songs in her sleep, Maggie taught the Manitou people the dance and oversaw its performance for seven or eight years. In vivid and detailed visions in which Maggie was transported to a super-natural mountain, the world of owls and thunderbirds and eagles, the thunderbirds taught her the dance sequences, drum patterns, and eighty songs. Sixty thunderbirds appeared in the visions, and Maggie Wilson reports that she recruited sixty villagers to represent the Thunders in the dance.

People were glad to help and join the dance for I dreamt that the soldiers would come back if their relatives danced ... This would be a new war dance. The head Thunderbird told me to name the dance the Union Star Dance. The sixty birds all came in a flock, flying with a tremendous noise, like a rattling train. They would tell me how to lead the dance and how to fix things. I would dream and waken and return to dream from the place where I had left off. They said, 'Count us – as many as we are, so many will you have in the dance.' I would sit awake for the dream to leave me alone – I couldn't understand it for a long time. But it would come back. I do not know what would have happened if I had not obeyed the dream. Maybe I wouldn't have lived.[26]

After having the vision for several years, Maggie gave the dance for the first time in September of 1918. 'During the seven or eight years that I gave the dance, other people had dreams about it. They would not understand their dreams and talked to me about them. Several people dreamt songs that I put into the dance.' She continued to dream and to learn new songs during the years she sponsored the dance at Manitou: 'I would wake up singing,' Maggie recalls.

Although neither Ruth Landes nor Maggie Wilson suggest this, it is possible that the Union Star Dance came to provide a focal point for the people around which to unify and to try to overcome their differences and develop a sense of community.

All who danced and who came to the dance brought tobacco, food, some print [cloth], which we offered to the Thunderbirds, asking protection ... The dance was given fall and spring because Thunderbird leaves in the fall and returns in the spring. You seldom hear the Bird in winter. But sometimes we gave the dance oftener because the Birds told me to commercialize it. The Indian agent helped. We gave it at a ball ground near Fort Frances and charged twenty-five cents admission. We all shared and did well. Sometimes we gave the dance five times a year: at Christmas, New Year's, spring, summer, fall. The dance had to run two to four nights ... But after seven or eight years, the people became mean and jealous, and the whole thing too expensive. If anyone sickened or died, it was blamed on me. Then my leg became too sore to dance. And about four years ago [circa 1928] we turned Christian. So we gave up the dance. We laid all the furnishings in the bush to rot. But I still dream of Thunders and I do not think they are angry at me for having quit.[27]

Maggie Wilson had experienced tragedy and disappointment during these years. A year after she started the dance, she gave birth to her last child, the daughter who died in infancy. Her son-in-law had died overseas, and Maggie felt this happened because of her initial reluctance to recruit and train personnel to perform the dance. Her husband had become ill and so had Maggie. By the time Landes met her, Mrs Wilson lived a somewhat solitary life, surrounded by her family, but isolated from the social life of the community. She often told Landes that she felt 'hollow' and 'empty' since the community had discredited her and her dance. Although she still dreamed, she missed the beauty of the performance of her Star Dance. The people said she was a proud egoist; she said they were jealous of her visionary powers. Landes said that Maggie Wilson had experienced the traditional disciplining of a woman who exercised power rooted in vision experiences, a domain that, according to Landes, was culturally sanctioned for men, not women. Landes wrote, 'I surmise the burden of the Vision, the exhaustion, the shock when it was denied by the people, the emptiness which she tried to fill through Conversion [to Christianity] ... After she lost her Vision or it was taken away from her by her fellows who withdrew their faith, she had no self.'[28] In 1932, Maggie's songs, the songs she dreamed for the Star Dance, were 'still sung at native dances within an area of about one hundred square miles, often by people who never saw her, always by people who are not interested in her personally although they know that "the songs come from her dance."'[29]

By the 1930s Mrs Wilson confined her imaginative life to designing porcupine quill embroidery, beadwork, and birchbark, crafts at which she excelled. As well, she skilfully tanned deer and moose hides and sewed mocassins and other clothing. She made an income selling her handiwork to whites and, in this way, supported herself and her asthmatic husband. She was also well-known for her knowledge of herbal cures and midwifery, which she had learned from her mother. And, because she was a Christian and English-speaking, she occasionally found work as an interpreter. Maggie Wilson's biculturality was typical of indigenous collaborators with anthropologists in the early decades of this century.[30] Her bilingualism and biculturalism as a woman of Scots-Cree descent who had been raised in an Ojibwa cultural world and had married Ojibwa men gave her 'insider-outsider' status that made her a keen observer of Ojibwa life. But it was probably through her Star dance that Maggie Wilson had begun her career as an ethnologist.[31] Her shamanic powers spoke to her intelligence and knowledge about Ojibwa custom and belief. They also placed her on the margins of Ojibwa social life, for Maggie could not be of the people if she possessed powers and knowledge that they did not. These characteristics that no doubt made her later life a lonely one are also the traits that made her a superb ethnological observer.

METAPHORICAL AUTOBIOGRAPHY: INTERPRETING THE STORIES OF
MAGGIE WILSON

All autobiographical memory is true; it is up to the interpreter to discover in
which sense, where, for which purpose.

Luisa Passerini, 'Women's Personal Narratives'

The stories that Maggie told Ruth are ostensibly the stories of other
women's lives. She constructed the stories from the orally transmitted
details of people's lives that circulate daily in all face-to-face societies.
The events of these women's lives were undoubtedly well-known in the
local context, and Mrs Wilson had known many of the women herself.
Although she did not directly tell Landes the story of her own life, my
rereading of the ethnography is that Mrs Wilson's stories of other
women's lives and her account of Ojibwa society and culture are illus-
trative of her own life and, in this sense, autobiographical. Landes's ethnography should be interpreted not only as the collaborative vision of
Ojibwa culture of Maggie Wilson (narrator) and Ruth Landes (interpreter) but as *about* Maggie Wilson (and Ruth Landes).

Maggie Wilson used the experience of telling stories as a way of symbolically situating herself in history and in Ojibwa culture. She did not
see her self as separate from her context. Ojibwa society for her com-
prised not individuals (or selves) but men and women whose lives took
their meaning from their relationship to a whole embodied in cultural
values and customs. Her notion of self is paralleled in the findings of
anthropologist Julie Cruikshank, who recently recorded the lives of
three Yukon Athapaskan and Tlingit women in the book *Life Lived like a
Story*. Cruikshank found that these women told stories of their lives not
in order to secure their individuality and immortality but in order to
resurrect a sense of shared experience and community: 'Individual
autonomy is only a means to an end for these protagonists; their goal is
reconnection with the community.'[32]

I would argue, then, that Maggie Wilson's stories of other women's
lives may be interpreted as metaphorical autobiography. The recurring
images in her accounts of Ojibwa women's lives – of harshness and of
overcoming struggle – can be read as her perspective on her own life, a
life that she shared with other women of her time, place, and circumstance. She told these stories in the last years of her life because a young
woman came along who was able to hear them. In the context of the

anthropological research, Maggie Wilson's purpose in telling them was in part to inform Landes and in part to testify to Ojibwa women's experience. But in their telling, Maggie Wilson symbolically transformed her life from memory to narrative.[33] While the self that emerges might be a synecdochic self, the life is not an exemplary life.[34] And it is this, no doubt, that lies at the root of critiques of the Wilson-Landes portrait of Ojibwa culture. For Wilson, through Landes, offers a world with the contradictions and tentativeness of experience intact. The narrative voice is not an authoritative one; it is open to criticism – and to reinterpretation. There is no single 'truth' in history, and Maggie Wilson's narratives offer an important, complex, contesting voice. Luisa Passerini offers useful advice to the listener/reader of such narratives: 'The guiding principle could be that all autobiographical memory is true; it is up to the interpreter to discover in which sense, where, for which purpose.'[35]

Two women met at Manitou Rapids in the summer of 1932. The older woman, in the last years of her life, told the younger one stories of the lives of women of that place. The younger woman at the time interpreted these stories as ethnographic narratives. Half a century later, I am interpreting these stories as metaphorical autobiography. While there are many conventional biographical details of Maggie Wilson's life that we will probably never know, rereading her stories beside Ruth Landes's ethnography tells us much about a woman whose life would otherwise go unrecorded. Like the women whose stories she tells, Maggie Wilson lived, struggled, and overcame hardship. The story we can now hear is a 'true' one in which Maggie Wilson emerges as an actor in history, a participant in culture, and the author of her own life.

Dear Ruth: This is the story of Maggie Wilson, Ojibwa ethnologist. She lived a rough life. She was a real Indian woman.

NOTES

Unpublished sources consulted and cited include the Ruth Landes Papers in the National Anthropological Archives at the Smithsonian Institution in Washington, DC, and the Ruth Fulton Benedict Papers at Vassar College. This research was conducted as part of my work on a biography of Ruth Landes supported by the Social Sciences and Humanities Research Council of Canada. I would like to thank A.O.C. Cole, Ellen Jacobs, and the editors of this book for their comments on an earlier version of this chapter.

94 Sally Cole

1 Ruth Landes, 'A Woman Anthropologist in Brazil' in *Women in the Field*, ed. Peggy Golde (Chicago: Aldine, 1970), 122

2 Ruth Landes, *Ojibwa Sociology* (New York: Columbia University Press, 1937), *The Ojibwa Woman* (New York: Columbia University Press, 1938), and *Ojibwa Religion and Midéwiwin* (Madison: University of Wisconsin Press, 1968)

3 Ruth Landes, 'The Ojibwa of Canada' in *Cooperation and Competition among Primitive Peoples*, ed. Margaret Mead (New York: McGraw-Hill, 1937), 87–127

4 Leo G. Waisberg and Tim E. Holzkamm, '"A Tendency to Discourage Them from Cultivating": Ojibwa Agriculture and Indian Affairs Administration in Northwestern Ontario,' *Ethnohistory* 40, no. 2 (1993): 186

5 This is the argument developed by ethnohistorians Waisberg and Holz-kamm, ibid.

6 Jonathan Spencer describes the conventional style of ethnographic writing as 'ethnographic naturalism': 'the creation of a taken-for-granted representation of reality through the use of certain standard devices such as free indirect speech and the absence of any tangible point of view.' Jonathan Spencer, 'Anthropology as a Kind of Writing,' *Man* 24 (1989): 152.

7 Landes, 'Ojibwa in Canada,' 102

8 See R.W. Dunning, *Social and Economic Change among the Northern Ojibwa* (Toronto: University of Toronto Press, 1959); Harold Hickerson, 'Some Implications of the Theory of Particularity, or 'Atomism,' of Northern Algonkians,' *Current Anthropology* 8 (1967): 37–63; Eleanor Leacock, 'Women's Status in Egalitarian Society: Some Implications for Social Evolution,' *Current Anthropology* 19, no. 2 (1978): 247–76.

9 Dunning, *Social and Economic Change*, 131

10 Herbert Alexander, review of *The Ojibwa Woman*, *American Anthropologist* 77 (1975): 110–11

11 Sylvia Van Kirk, *'Many Tender Ties': Women in Fur Trade Society, 1670–1870* (Winnipeg: Watson and Dyer, 1980)

12 Ruth Fulton Benedict Papers (RFBP), 20 March 1935

13 Landes, *The Ojibwa Woman*, 87–8

14 Luisa Passerini, 'Women's Personal Narratives: Myths, Experiences, and Emotions' in *Interpreting Women's Lives: Feminist Theory and Personal Narratives*, ed. The Personal Narratives Group (Bloomington: Indiana University Press, 1989), 191

15 The way that Maggie told other women's stories as a metaphor for her own is similar to the story-telling practices of Yukon Athapaskan women described by Julie Cruikshank, who recalls, 'When I asked women to talk about the past, they used traditional stories – particularly stories having a strong competent woman as the central protagonist – to explain events in

their lives.' Julie Cruikshank, in collaboration with Angela Sidney, Kitty Smith, and Annie Ned, *Life Lived like a Story: Life Stories of Three Yukon Native Elders* (Vancouver: University of British Columbia Press, 1990), 347. The Yukon women repeatedly told Cruikshank that young girls should be learning from the stories. Also similar is the way the Yukon women's stories, like Maggie's, tell of women who have been captured and escaped or who were lost or abandoned and survived through their resourcefulness and practice of a range of skills taught to women at puberty. The stories teach that 'women who rely on learned, shared, "practical" knowledge to achieve their ends eventually succeed.' Ibid., 342–3

16 Deborah Gordon, 'Among Women: Gender and Ethnographic Authority of the Southwest, 1939–1980' in *Hidden Scholars*, ed. Nancy Parezo (Albuquerque: University of New Mexico Press, 1993), 129–45

17 Anti-Semitism at Columbia University in the 1930s has been well documented. See Russell Jacoby, *The Last Intellectuals: American Culture in the Age of Academe* (New York: Farrar Strauss Jiroux, 1987), and Diana Trilling, 'Lionel Trilling: A Jew at Columbia,' *Commentary* 67 (1979): 44. In her diaries, Landes frequently refers to Margaret Mead's snobbishness for things 'Old American,' and there was always tension between them because of Mead's exclusionary practices.

18 Landes, preface to the second edition of *The Ojibwa Woman* (New York: W.W. Norton, 1971), viii

19 Ruth Landes Papers (RLP), Box 36

20 RFBP, 12 Oct. 1933

21 This account is from a letter Maggie Wilson sent to Ruth Landes around 1934, which begins 'Dear Ruth, This is the story of my mother, Mrs. Bunyan.' It is catalogued as Story #119, Box 38, RLP. According to Maggie, her Scottish maternal grandfather was 'named Simpson.' I have, however, found no archival sources to confirm the name. The predicament of Native 'country' wives and children abandoned by fur trade employees who returned to Scotland or married white women has been well documented. See Jennifer Brown, *Strangers in Blood: Fur Trade Company Families in Indian Country* (Vancouver: UBC Press, 1980); Jean Murray Cole, *Exile in the Wilderness* (Seattle: University of Washington Press, 1979); Van Kirk, '*Many Tender Ties.*'

22 The dates of Maggie Wilson's marriages and the births of her children were obtained from copies of the Treaty 3 annuity paylists that are in the Ruth Landes Papers. In the last decade of her life, Landes had been writing notes for a biography of Maggie Wilson and had conducted research in Ottawa at the Public Archives of Canada and the Department of Indian Affairs. These notes are among her papers at the National Anthropological Archives.

23 Ruth Landes, 'Remembering the Ojibwa after Fifty Years' (unpublished paper, n.d.)

24 Landes, *Ojibwa Sociology*, 87–102

25 Ibid., 83

26 Landes, *Ojibwa Religion*, 210

27 Maggie Wilson, quoted in ibid., 212

28 RLP, Box 36

29 Landes, *The Ojibwa Woman* (1938), 130

30 Cf. Mary Black-Rogers, 'Dan Raincloud: "Keeping Our Indian Way" in *Being and Becoming Indian: Biographical Studies of North American Frontiers*, ed. James A. Clifton (Chicago: Dorsey Press, 1989), 226–48; Brown, '"A Place in Your Mind for Them All": Chief William Berens' in *Being and Becoming Indian*, 201–25; Jeanne Cannizzo, 'George Hunt and the Invention of Kwakiutl Culture,' *Canadian Review of Sociology and Anthropology* 20, no. 1 (1983): 44–58

31 Maggie had given the Star Dance for the first time in the fall of 1918. It was probably because of her dance and songs that she became known to ethnomusicologist Frances Densmore, who visited Manitou Rapids the following summer, in July 1919, to record Ojibwa music. See Densmore, *Chippewa Customs* (Washington: Bureau of American Ethnology Bulletin 86, 1929).

32 Cruikshank, *Life Lived like a Story*, 355. According to Arnold Krupat, in Native American autobiography, the self is an 'I-am-we' self defined in relation to and as part of a cultural whole. See Krupat, *Ethnocentrism: Ethnography, History, Literature* (Berkeley: University of California Press, 1992), 219; see also Helen Carr, 'In Other Words: Native American Women's Autobiography' in *Life/Lines: Theorizing Women's Autobiography*, ed. Bella Brodzki and Celeste Schenck (Ithaca: Cornell University Press, 1988). Krupat refers to this self that exists only as part of a whole as a 'synecdochic' self. According to Krupat, a synecdochal notion of self is found among minority groups generally, including women and immigrants.

33 Cf. Cruikshank, *Life Lived like a Story*, 357

34 Cf. Marjorie Mbilinyi, '"I'd Have Been a Man": Politics and the Labour Process in Producing Personal Narratives' in *Interpreting Women's Lives*, 204–27

35 Passerini, 'Women's Personal Narratives,' 197

Casting Light on Women in the Shadow of the Law: Toronto at the Turn of the Century

CAROLYN STRANGE

'The lady vanishes,' the title of Hitchcock's 1938 film announced. The director's legendary misogyny led many of his screen heroines to disappear – off mission towers, behind shower curtains or, more often, into the arms of the hero. Feminists have also been drawn to the metaphor of the disappearing woman. However, our project has been to restore women to history after centuries of benign, and not-so-benign, neglect. That demands to include women in historical debates persistently raise eyebrows attests to the still-radical, semi-magical act of making ladies reappear.

As magicians perhaps realize, it is more difficult to make some ladies reappear than others. Early women's histories documented the heroines of the past – saints, feminists, writers, suffragists, revolutionaries, educators, and politicians. They were women who, by and large, were conscious of their contribution to their own time, if not to history, and records of their exploits in anything from club meeting minutes to hagiographies provide the raw material for the reconstruction of their lives. The feminist biographer's mournful refrain is that so few women leave behind a complete portrait, primarily because their contributions are not taken seriously by unappreciative families or hostile peers.

Understandably, biographers of women are drawn to subjects about whom it is possible to speak with provisional authority. The discovery of diaries, letters, photographs, or paintings attracts us to a subject simply because it is so rare to find such precious information. In spite of our commitment to press feminist historiography beyond its early preoccupation with prominent women, biographers recognize the difficulty of capturing personal material on any women but those of sufficient economic standing, literacy, or talent to make a mark. The vast majority of poor and uneducated women, in contrast, are visible to us only as statistics: so many domestics, so many women on strike, so many women marrying at a certain age.

To make these ladies reappear requires different tricks but the same concern with documentation. A largely untapped reservoir of evidence lies in records generated not by women but by institutions and practices of surveillance and control. The Catholic Church and mental health systems, for instance, allow us to say something of the lives of nuns and of women diagnosed as mad. The criminal justice system is an equally rich source for the documentation of otherwise obscure women's lives. Magistrates', quarter sessions, and assize court records, as well as police and prison records, contain evidence every measure as intimate as the personal reflections jotted into a diary: mug shots take the place of studio portraits; notes intercepted by prison guards parallel the perfumed letters of upper-class women; newspaper accounts of trials expose information that might otherwise have surfaced only in a literate woman's private papers. Of course, the crucial difference is that records produced through the policing and prosecution of crime are always, ultimately, the products of coercion and the unwanted probing of investigative agents, even in cases initiated by women complainants.

Documentation regarding victims of crime, particularly those whose sexuality emerged as a factor in their victimization, is also produced through coercion. Rape shield law, for instance, has only recently restricted inquiry into the sexual past of sexual assault complainants. Women who barely survived bungled abortions were scrutinized with equal avidity. Prior to the legalization of abortion, these victims were often pressed to testify against abortionists or face jail themselves. In the course of investigating crimes against women, then, the state has pried into the most painful and intimate aspects of women's personal lives. Female victims who recounted their stories to the police and the courts may have thought they could retain their authorial voices; as it so often turned out, they soon found themselves snared in legally constructed narratives that veered from their own sense of the truth.

Both as victims and as prosecuted persons, then, women inhabit a shadowland of deviance, defiance, and tragedy. At the same time, however, their encounters with the law expose them to sudden bursts of official and cultural inquiry. This paradoxical combination of shade and light – a kind of empirically constructed chiaroscuro – permits glimpses of the lives of women who would otherwise have vanished from sight and memory.

Domesticity was the antidote prescribed for women in conflict with the law,
as this photo of Mercer reformatory inmates illustrates.

Unlike most of the 'great dames' who appear elsewhere in this book,
the women whose lives I document were exposed to the glare of history
hesitantly or protestingly. Prostitutes, shoplifters, or women who killed
their own infants had good reason to seek out the shadows, but so did
victims of illegal abortions and survivors of sexual assaults. To encounter the law was to suffer the scrutiny of magistrates and lawyers but
also, in many cases, newspaper reporters eager to fill columns with
colourful accounts of 'birds of paradise' who had drifted from the path
of moral rectitude. Those convicted underwent further surveillance by
probation officers, well-meaning ladies, prison matrons, psychiatrists,
and doctors. Official and unofficial observations produced an extensive
paper trail that tells us more about these women than they would have
liked us to know.

An historical account of the unfortunate cannot provide anything that
could be described as an accurate picture of women in the shadow of the
law. Rather, what we have are fleeting glances at women's experiences.
If the human condition amounts to living in a world not of our own
making, then erring and victimized women are further disadvantaged
by the production of stories not of their own telling. This account is,
thus, another phase in that process of mediation and interpretation,

although it attempts to read official and media accounts of women's lives with a questioning gaze. What I see are stories of women who struggled and lost, and those who defiantly proclaimed their disrespect for authority and convention, even if it did them little good to do so.

Who were the women whom the criminal justice system and, in some cases, the popular press came to know as deviants or as victims of crime? Late-nineteenth-century Toronto was home to a city jail and a reformatory for women, so it is possible to profile the lives and crimes of many who ran afoul of the law. Newspaper accounts of trials in which women appeared as defendants or witnesses were filled with sketches of their lives in intimate, if narrow, detail. The metropolitan press thrived on crime reportage and grew to five or six dailies over this period. In this sense, the evidence on women in the shadow of the law is anything but sparse.

This kind of evidence, however, lends itself more to snapshots than to fleshy narratives that flow seamlessly from women's childhood to death. Most contemporary accounts of women in trouble with the law collapsed their life histories into stories of inexorable descent. Whether that descent was tragic depended on the extent to which the woman in question could appear as a victim. The most colourful accounts in turn-of-the-century Toronto came from police court reporter Harry Wodson. To him, the 'petticoated birds of paradise – and prey' who squawked at the court rail were the polar opposites of virtuous 'ladies,' over whom he enthused warmly. Certain misguided ladies, in Wodson's opinion, lacked judgment in attempting to rescue their fallen sisters. They twisted their handkerchiefs over the plight of prostitutes, seeing them as victims, whereas the tough-minded court reporter saw them simply as degraded and a menace.

Conflicting stories of one 'Rose,' a young woman who appeared in court on a vagrancy charge, illustrate the elusiveness of victim status. According to her telling of her tale, Rose had been forced into prostitution because she was poor and friendless. Arrested by policemen and judged by men, her only hope for redemption was the kindly attention of a Salvation Army matron. Wodson's version sprang from a more cynical understanding of prostitution. Rose's face was pale not because of poor nourishment and economic privation, he offered, but rather the 'life she was leading.' Protestations of innocence were mere shams. The *real* Rose was a recidivist, Wodson reported. He also remembered that after a previous conviction, she had flown into 'an ungovernable tantrum, and made the whole [court] loathsome with her vile language.'[1]

Rose's conflicting stories, one a tale of victimization, the other an account of a depraved soul, illustrates wider problems in the retelling of women's lives. Her swearing and protests against confinement were enough to convince Wodson, and doubtless most of his readers and others who came to know Rose, that she could not conceivably be a victim. In the reporter's account, it mattered little what had prompted Rose to take up prostitution: what counted was that she was a 'daily menace to society.' If Wodson's story is unsympathetic, is the competing, sentimental version of Rose and others of her ilk as 'fallen angels' more compelling? The lady visitors of the courts – first in the persons of clubwomen and Salvation Army workers, then as Big Sisters, probation officers, and social workers – were on missions of mercy and rescue. Portraying their charges as obdurate criminals would have rendered their efforts moot. Wodson, in contrast, told stories like Rose's to sell copy, and his gritty style of urban realism was a genre of reporting that set the tone of crime writing by the early twentieth century. If Rose had told her own story, how might it have gone?

Statistics gathered on women in prison arguably provide more reliable, if less colourful, evidence. Prison registers, dry-bones accounts of incarcerated women's backgrounds, seem to offer something like objective knowledge, untainted by the preoccupations of story-tellers. Even still, the light they shed is cast at odd angles, leaving us, inevitably, with knowledge deemed relevant by authorities curious about individuals' social, economic, and bodily characteristics and uninterested in contextual matters. With these caveats in mind, we can read prison registers as documents of marginality.

PROFILES

The single most consistent characteristic of convicted women was poverty. Not surprisingly, we do not find the names of middle-class women or professionals on the books, but we can find a handful of the more typical women workers of the newly industrial age, including office workers, saleswomen, and factory hands. By far the most common occupation of imprisoned women was domestic service. Until the late nineteenth century, working as a maid, laundry worker, or seamstress was virtually the limit of most women's employment options. As the range of paid occupations expanded with the growth of light industry and retailing, domestic service became a badge of desperation. In 1901, for instance, just over 40 per cent of Canadian women workers were employed as domestics, yet at the Andrew Mercer Reformatory for Females in Toronto, fully 60 per cent of women reported having worked as domestics. By 1921, the gap had increased significantly. While almost 60 per cent of Mercer inmates continued to report domestic employment, only 27 per cent of Canadian women workers were in the domestic sector. As a group, then, these women lagged behind their non-criminal cohorts, who jumped at the chance to work in fields that offered better wages and more control over their lives. When a Mercer inmate stepped up to the admitting counter and answered 'domestic' to the guard's enquiry about employment, she might as well have replied, 'poor woman with few prospects.' One out of every four women spelled out her economic marginality even more explicitly when she mumbled: 'No occupation.'

In a period when Toronto was still overwhelmingly an Anglo-Celtic city, women who ended up in prison were not distinguishable, at first sight, from their cohorts. Religion in combination with ethnicity, however, tells another story. The poverty-stricken Irish immigrants who fled famine and crowded into Toronto's cheap lodgings confirmed, in the eyes of staunchly Orange Torontonians, that intemperance, crime, and Catholicism were linked. Longtime police court magistrate Col. Denison had definite views about the moral afflictions of Jews, blacks, and Chinese, but his opinions about Irish Catholics were equally strong. In his recollections, he portrayed them as brutish, drunken, and given to fisticuffs and great verbal assaults.[2] His characterization was not confined to the male population. The overrepresentation of Irish Catholics among incarcerated women suggests that they, like their menfolk, were more vulnerable to arrest than Protestants. The Mercer inmate register shows that in the early twentieth century, when only 12 per cent of Torontonians were Catholics, more than a third of the inmates professed that faith.

The rowdy style of behaviour with which the Irish were popularly associated was precisely the type of morals offence that typically led a woman to be arrested in late-nineteenth-century Toronto. Women of all faiths and ethnicities were arrested for behaving indecorously and thereby violating prevailing standards of public, feminine decorum – after all, over two-thirds of the women in Toronto prisons were Protestants of one variety or another. Drinking, swearing, or yelling on the streets was the shortest route to a 'drunk and disorderly' charge. This was, by far, the most common charge laid against women in the nine-teenth century. Most women served short jail terms, only to face rearrest – as many as thirty or forty times in some cases. For these women, the historical record reveals nothing more than lives trapped in revolving doors that swept them from grog houses to jail houses to the streets and back again. Only when they died under suspicious circumstances can we catch more than a glimpse.

Coroner's records tell the story of Jessie Layton, alias Nellie Pearson, whose addiction to alcohol and inability to share a brothel peaceably with her fellow prostitutes led to an early pauper's grave in 1880. Called to testify at the inquest into Layton's death while in custody at the Toronto Jail, one of her former co-workers described her as 'girl on the street' – the lowest echelon of the commercial sex hierarchy. Locked up in the jail on previous occasions for drunkenness and disorderliness, she died as a result of blows to the head, whether at the hands of a guard or a customer the coroner did not inquire. Layton's sad end was the sober side of the common 'drunk and disorderly' charge: insecure housing, alcoholism, and violence were as much the inspiration as the results of impoverished women's disorderliness.[3]

This theme of victims charged with victimless crimes remained evident into the twentieth century, when vagrancy and prostitution charges began to supersede drunk and disorderly charges. For women, especially young, single women, vagrancy did not mean penury or homelessness but implied sexual immorality. After several waves of repression against organized brothels in Toronto in the 1890s and the 1910s, the industry was dominated by street prostitution and pimp-controlled commercial sex. That did not mean, however, that a police officer required proof that money had been exchanged for sex. The vagueness of the vagrancy charge allowed the police to arrest any woman whose behaviour hinted at promiscuity.

Hortense Flambeau's arrest and incarceration in 1917 show how non-compliant behaviour – in this case leaving her family while a minor – could be interpreted as a crime. Hortense claimed to the constable who retrieved her that she had run away because her father had sexually assaulted her. Striking out on her own, she encountered a generous Mr Thibideau who took her out to movies and loaned her cash to pay her board. Whether her father was guilty of incest, or whether Mr Thibideau was a pimp seemed hardly to matter to the authorities: Hortense was made to serve an indefinite term at the St Mary's Reformatory for Girls because she was guilty of 'delinquency.'[4] Young women who had been raped were sometimes shown the same treatment. When a fourteen-year-old Italian girl was raped by a boarder in her own home, a crime that may have occurred in many households where strange men lived in close quarters with young women, *both* parties ended up in prison – he for violating the law, and she for 'her own good.'[5] Again, the criminalization of victims is the common thread in these women's stories.

CLOSE-UP: LIZZIE LESSARD

Occasionally, a woman who fit the general profile of poverty, unemployment, intemperance, and unlady-like behaviour appears as more than a momentary flash on our historical screens. In Lizzie Lessard's case, her notoriety was assured by her extraordinarily violent behaviour. In the first fifty years (1880–1930) of the Mercer Reformatory's life, there was not a single disturbance that could compare with even the minor riots that broke out periodically in men's prisons. Inmates sometimes rebelled by screaming, breaking their furniture, or sabotaging their work, but only a very few took out their frustrations on others. Lessard was an exception.

Elizabeth 'Lizzie' Lessard was born sometime in the 1870s. As a child she moved with her family from Quebec and settled in Hamilton. Barely into her teens, she and her sister began what became a life spent before courts and behind bars. In 1893 the Hamilton magistrate sent her to Mercer after convicting her on the summary charge of vagrancy. When she stepped through the reception corridor of the imposing building, she was given a quick scrub, issued a plain prison tunic, and marched in front of a guard who took down her particulars. The reformatory register telescoped her life story into the minutiae of official knowledge:

Age: 16
Physical Appearance: brown hair, fair complexion, grey eyes
Weight: 97 1/2 pounds
Height: 5 feet
Civil State: unmarried
Education: read and write
Religion: Baptist
Offence: vagrancy
Occupation: none

The lives of women like Lizzie Lessard were laid out in columns and rows, and, in a final stroke of the bureaucratic pen, they were given numbers. If one looked solely at the register, Lizzie Lessard's story seems typical: young, guilty of a victimless crime, poorly adapted for legitimate employment. Lessard's personality, however, defied anonymization.

Reformatory life failed to steer Lessard away from a life of lawbreaking. After her release from the Mercer in 1895, she lingered in Toronto and was arrested numerous times for vagrancy, theft, and prostitution, and she spent more time in jail than out. With each incarceration, Lessard entered prison more recalcitrant, intolerant of guards who thought they could tame her wild spirit. Lessard did everything in her power to subvert the dehumanization of institutional life, where petty infractions such as chewing gum or speaking sullenly could put a woman on a discipline report. The punishment register at Mercer indicates that Lessard committed more than her fair share of institutional offences. While each inmate in the early twentieth century committed an average of 1.2 infractions per annum, Lessard was often charged with two on a single day.[6] Whether she was idle, using foul language, wilfully destroying her cell furnishings and dishes, or attacking her fellow inmates, she was a prime source of staff frustration and fear.

By the time of Lessard's final committal to Mercer in 1909 on a charge of theft, she was determined to make those around her as miserable as she had become after a life of hard drinking, prostitution, and petty thievery. Syphilis had also begun to ravage her body and, perhaps, her mind. In the month before her ultimate act of rebellion at Mercer, her punishments included restriction to her cell, deprivation of privileges, four days in the dungeon, four days on bread and water, and, lastly, two weeks in 'basement' isolation. Her final punishment had been dispensed after Attendant Mick put Lessard on report for 'calling names, vile language, threatening etc.'[7]

The matrons may have anticipated that Lessard would rebel against this latest punishment, but they were hardly prepared for her murderous attack on Attendant Mick. As the Toronto *World* reported, Lessard took a pair of scissors (a handy weapon in an institution that taught dressmaking skills) 'in a fit of passion' and, 'infecting them with a loathsome malady from which she suffered, she stabbed the attendant in the breast, inoculating her with the disease.'[8] In a desperate, brutal moment, Lessard had performed a deeply symbolic act, puncturing both the prison guard's uniform and her mantle of propriety, exposing Mick to the disease that would soon claim Lessard's life.

Violence of this magnitude called for a stiffer sentence than the one Lessard was then serving. On 29 April 1909, she was convicted on a charge of wounding and was sentenced to serve three years at the Kingston Penitentiary, the federal prison that was authorized to incarcerate women serving sentences of more than two years. The austere regime at Kingston failed to modify her rebelliousness, but she committed no further assaults. Her health was failing, and, although only in her early thirties, hard living and eighteen jail and reformatory committals had begun to catch up with her. In the final stages of syphilis, she died at the Kingston Hospital on 3 April 1911.

The Kingston *British Whig* reported her demise as the 'Death of a Hamilton Lady,' decorously omitting the fact that she was a penitentiary inmate. But the Hamilton *Spectator* remembered her as one of the city's most colourful criminals. Describing her as 'at one time a well known character in this city,' the obituary recalled her wounding offence as 'one of the worst on record,' no doubt on account of her attempt to infect a guard with venereal disease.

In his book on Toronto police court, Harry Wodson remembered her as well. He devoted a section of his chapter on women criminals to the Lessard sisters, 'Liz. and Min.,' who, in his opinion, were 'notoriously evil.' When it came to hard drinking and ferocity, 'these girls had no rivals.' As with Rose, the 'moral menace,' his greatest concern was their influence over other men and women: 'They seemed to enjoy their degradation and never missed an opportunity to lure another into their web of vice.' He went on to describe her scissors assault as the work of a 'she-devil.'[9]

Lessard did her best to sear herself into the memory of those who judged her. Granted, her assault was flamboyant and potentially fatal, but that should not foreclose the possibility that other, less pugnacious, women shared her anger. Mercer Superintendent O'Sullivan contended that all recidivists were 'hardened' and 'vicious.' Indeed, this is the reason that she redoubled her efforts in the wake of Lessard's attack to restrict the inmates of Mercer to young first-time offenders. When it came to moral reform, prison administrators recognized that older, intemperate, and streetwise women like Lessard were lost causes.

CLOSE-UP: SARAH FOX

At the turn of the century, there were undoubtedly more women killers than there are today. However, most of the victims were the women's own offspring, and few mothers were ever convicted of infanticide. In newly industrial cities where a few cents could buy a cheap night's lodging with no questions asked, women (most of them young, poor, and unmarried) tried to conceal their pregnancies and dispose of their infants. The scores of tiny infants 'found dead' in back alleys and vacant lots each year attest to the frequency of the practice among desperate women who felt that they had no other choice but to kill.

It would be morally bankrupt to portray such women as heroic, yet it would be equally obtuse to describe them as callous criminals. Their contemporaries rarely thought them so. Juries were notoriously reluctant to convict women of anything other than the lesser offence of 'concealment of birth,' a crime that overlooked the accused's volition to kill. Judges, too, played their part by doling out minimal sentences and suspending sentences altogether. After all, the victims, had they lived, would have been illegitimate and therefore a burden to respectable society. Moreover, the large proportion of domestic servants among those charged raised suspicions about the paternity of the infants. Whether the father had been a farmer or a financier, the criminal justice system reinforced the culture of denial and dismissal that drove women to infanticide in the first place.

Occasionally, a woman like Sarah Fox, who admitted that she killed her infant, could not be ignored because her act appeared to have been clear-headed. Juries and judges rationalized their merciful inclinations by asserting that women who committed infanticide were *irrational* – that is, that they were labouring under a kind of temporary insanity. Simply put, they did not know what they were doing, since any 'normal' mother would naturally care for her child. Although this chivalrous attitude saved many women from jail or the gallows, it decontextualized their acts, reducing them to murderous, biologically-driven impulses. Sarah Fox's decision to murder her baby could not be reconciled with that scenario of exculpable infanticide.

There was no question in the mind of the Crown attorney that Sarah Fox was guilty of murder. At first, the young unmarried mother's story sounded typical of the experiences suffered by poor, single women. She had given birth to an illegitimate child and, because she was a self-supporting woman, she gave the infant to a 'baby farmer,' a person who took in babies for a fee until adoptions could be arranged. Fox soon ran out of money, so she transferred her infant to another baby farm, leaving the operator a false address. Most baby farmers would have thought little of letting the baby starve (as several trials of notoriously neglectful baby farmers indicate), but this one managed to track down the penniless mother. In response to the baby farmer's demand that she pay up or retrieve her baby, Fox reportedly told her to 'throw it away as she did not want it.' Shocked at her unmotherly response but unwilling to care for the infant without payment, the baby farmer left the infant with Fox. At this point, the story took a more sinister turn. Only moments later, Fox strangled the baby and threw it over a wall.

Over the course of Fox's trial, elements of her life prior to her crime brought a human face to the monstrous mother. In 1890, at the age of twenty, she had come to Toronto, like thousands of other young, rural women, in search of a job. Although she drifted from one menial position to another, she did find a prospective husband – a bricklayer who proposed marriage. Once she told him she was pregnant, he abandoned her and, fearing the wrath of her parents, she decided to stay in the city and conceal her shame. The defence in this case did what it had to do to soften the hearts of the jury: it manipulated this picture of the seduced and abandoned country girl, a victim of the big city and its wickedness, to counteract Fox's cold-hearted decision to throw her child away. The result was a compromise – a conviction on a charge of manslaughter and a recommendation to mercy.[10]

CLOSE-UP: CARRIE DAVIES

If Sarah Fox's culpability could be reduced by constructing her background as a story of fallen womanhood, domestic servant Carrie Davies' biography was fashioned by the press into a tale of noble maidenhood. Like Fox, she had confessed that she had intended to kill the victim – in her case, her wealthy employer. She had shot him point-blank as he walked up the path to his fashionable home on 8 February 1915. Astonishingly, sympathy gushed from the pens of crime reporters as soon as she appeared in police court. In contrast to the other 'carefree' women assembled on the usual charges of drunkenness, vagrancy, and theft, Davies looked more like 'a mild and gentle Sunday School pupil ... very subdued and sorrowful.'[11]

Although the victim's family tried to have Davies declared insane, it soon became evident that they had something to hide. 'Bert' Massey, the man she killed, had allegedly forced sexual attentions upon the unwilling maid; out of her escalating fear that he would rape her, Davies claimed, she shot him. If this was true, she had done Sarah Fox one better by protecting her virginity and, thereby, preserving her character.

As a recent British immigrant, she attracted loyal supporters from 'the Old Country.' In the context of the opening months of the First World War, it was downright patriotic to rally behind the campaign to exonerate Davies. The teenager's life story fit the bill perfectly. When she was arrested, a letter to her mother and an envelope with thirty dollars (almost a month's wages) were found on her person. Apparently, she had left England to secure a job so that she could help support her blind, widowed mother and younger siblings. She had a beau, but not of the welshing suitor variety. Rather, he had been one of the first to volunteer to fight in Europe. A doctor added a final, medical seal of approval on her character by confirming at her trial that her hymen was intact.

By all accounts, Davies was a remarkably solicitous, chaste young woman to whom sexual threats spelled a fate worse than death. But she was also a gun-toting maid who blasted her master for indiscretions that most domestics suffered in silence. How did the gentlemen of the jury and her multitudinous supporters come to see the self-confessed murderer as guiltless?

Carrie Davies' story was easily appropriated into a wartime parable of the just cause. No one dared to question the morality of loyal soldiers of the empire, who claimed German lives to fight the evil 'Hun.' Davies was as noble a guardian of virtue as her soldier sweetheart. Her defence lawyer, Hartley Dewart, left no room for doubt about his client's innocence: 'It is no more murder or malice than it is for our brave troops to defend the honour of the empire they are so splendidly doing at the front.' While the Crown tried feebly to suggest that she might have overreacted and exaggerated the threat, the jury and the judge would have none of it. Davies' acquittal brought a tear to the judge's eye and raised a tumult of approval from the assembled crowds. Uncomfortable with the attention, Davies shrank from the limelight. She later married and conducted the remainder of her life in what she undoubtedly preferred: quiet obscurity.

CLOSE-UP: JENNY IRVING AND GERTRUDE KERR

Ironically, women whom the law, rather than popular justice, defined as victims were rarely treated so compassionately. Faced with a living, breathing male defendant in a rape or abortion trial, jurymen and judges were more interested in the sexual history of the victim than the alleged offence of the accused. Just as establishing Davies' credibility depended upon disclosures about her virginal state, so women who claimed to be victims traded painful, degrading memories for a stab at justice. The catch, as most discovered, was that criminal courtrooms are treacherous places for telling one's story.

On the same day that the *Globe* reported the decision of the coroner's jury in the Davies case, it included (on the same page) an account of a trial in which a seventeen-year-old servant accused her employer of rape. This might easily have been Davies' story. If she had read the papers regularly, she would have known that no master in recent memory had been successfully prosecuted for rape on the complaint of his servant.[12] As coroner's files confirm, some domestics preferred suicide to the burden of living under the shadow of disgrace that sexual assault cast upon them. In 1888, twenty-year-old Jennie Irving, a live-in seamstress, claimed that a male relative of her mistress had pinned her to the sofa. Having heard these allegations, the man's wife, searching for evidence to secure a divorce, forced Irving to sign a statement that she had been having an affair. In vain, Irving protested that the man had forced her to go with him. As one witness recalled, Irving felt the injustice keenly: 'I am disgraced now and I will go and throw myself in the bay.' After her body was discovered, floating in the harbour, aspects of her life came to light through a search of her personal effects. In death, she could offer no alternative to a salacious interpretation of the amorous letters that were found. One letter, addressed to 'darling Jennie,' and another from Irving to a man for whom she could not 'resist the temptation of loving more,' painted her as a manipulator who dangled several suitors. About the alleged sexual attack nothing was mentioned in the coroner's verdict. The official end to the narrative of this young seamstress's life was that she had committed suicide because her spirits were low.[13]

What is remarkable is that any woman decided to proceed with sexual assault charges. Concern about the possibility of wrongful convictions in rape cases (where the defendant could theoretically face the death sentence) might account for the defence's willingness to 'blacken' the woman's character to inspire sympathy for the defendant. Because of this tactic, though, the only things we can 'know' about rape complainants' lives are insinuations that they were sexually promiscuous or, failing that, simply malicious. Prostitutes and madams had the pluck to stride into police stations and lay complaints but desk sergeants rarely gave them the time of day. Furthermore, women who did not work as prostitutes were suspected of being 'good times' girls precisely because they were willing to talk publicly about their sexual encounters.

A young stenographer named Gertrude Kerr anticipated such an ordeal but decided nevertheless to press charges of indecent assault against a man from whom she bought some sheet music in 1918. She claimed that William White had offered her a ride to the Conservatory but had instead driven out of town to a secluded area so that he could have sex with her. Kerr successfully fought off his advances and eventually convinced him to drive her back to the city. Once home, she laid a complaint.

Kerr was a country girl who had come from the town of Collingwood to wartime Toronto in search of a job in the expanding office sector. It had not taken her long to learn what she described as 'city ways.' In answering the defence's inquiry as to why she had retained the sheet music, she stated: 'If I went out in the car [and] if I did not have the songs to show I had done business with Mr. White, they would naturally think I went out for a good time.' As it turns out, this is precisely how the defence interpreted the case. Taunted, and accused of fabricating the whole incident, Kerr battled valiantly to tell her story her own way: 'I did not come here for notoriety but I do not want Mr. White to go about saying to everybody he can do what he likes to me and get away with it.' Here, it seems, are the words of a young woman who, like Carrie Davies, cared deeply about her sexual reputation. The assault was only the first blow; the lasting repercussions would be Mr White's freedom to spread lies about her character. 'I thought he was a perfect gentleman,' Kerr reflected on her earlier innocence. The court's dismissal of the case assuredly left her a little wiser and a lot more cynical.[14]

CLOSE-UP: ANNIE SWEET AND RUTH DEMBNER

Although Toronto's campaign against urban immorality in the early twentieth century aimed for a reformed sexual environment, the policing and prosecution of morals offences was piecemeal. The most visible effect was a well-publicized crackdown on brothels and street prostitution. Consensual sex without pay was also policed more strictly than before, particularly because sex outside of the procreative context of marriage was assumed to lead to venereal disease and 'feeble-mindedness.' At the same time, declining birth rates (from 191 live births per thousand population in Ontario in 1871 down to 79 by 1931) raised fears that 'race suicide' would dilute the concentration of fit, Anglo-Celtic Canadians. In this context, a woman's decision to control her fertility by having an abortion was a serious matter, with implications not only for her own health but, more broadly, for the future of the nation.

Infanticide by the turn of the century was a relatively rare event. Women like Sarah Fox had more options for private adoptions or state institutional care, and even married women who decided not to keep their infants could turn them over to the newly formed Children's Aid Society rather than a baby farmer. Of course, infants were still suffocated, with few questions asked at inquests, but increasingly, contraception and abortion became the preferred means of restricting the number of children. In the eyes of the state, however, these strategies constituted serious offences; moreover, a woman's decision to have an abortion could not as readily be tagged to an unbalanced mind.

Women who had abortions were not prosecuted themselves for 'procuring an abortion,' although this was technically possible and an ever-present threat. Rather, efforts to prosecute abortionists hinged upon testimony from women who had undergone the procedure. Unlike infanticide, characteristically carried out in secret, abortion was a crime that often involved networks of co-conspirators, including women relatives, boyfriends, nurses, druggists, husbands, and doctors. The police claimed that they were powerless to penetrate these closed circles because women who had abortions, understandably, tended not to advertise that a crime had been committed, unless forced to testify at an abortionist's trial.

Women who testified in rape trials, in most cases, made conscious decisions to use the courts in the pursuit of justice. In contrast, women's evidence in abortion trials was presented against their wills, either because they had been coerced by the police or because they were dead by the time their stories were aired in court. As with other women caught up in the criminal justice system, they were robbed of the power to keep their secrets hidden and instead suffered the humilation of public exposure that reduced their complex lives to a single sexual mistake.

Annie Sweet's experience illustrated the tenuous control that working women had, not only over their reproductive capacities but over their means of managing the consequences of inadequate medical care. She was an eighteen-year-old woman who claimed to be a 'general office worker,' a term that, by 1916, suggested that she eked out a living as a clerk or errand girl. Her home life is unknown, but whether she lived with her family, in a boarding house, or a residence for 'working girls,' such as the YWCA, she would have found it awkward to carry out trysts with her lover, one Mr Good. Instead, the couple met at the Globe Theatre, a cheap vaudeville house, and there they managed to have intercourse in the flickering darkness. Soon, she found herself 'in trouble,' particularly as she could ill-afford to pay her rent, let alone an abortionist. In a period when a competent, medically trained abortionist charged between $50 and $200, all that Mr Good could come up with was $20. Unfortunately, at this price, she received inferior service and ended up haemorrhaging. Mr Good seems to have disappeared from the scene at the point when Sweet went to the emergency ward at the Toronto Western Hospital as a charity patient. Stamped on her admission card were the words that would add humiliation to her physical pain: 'N.B. Notify [Morality] Office, City Hall, before this patient is released.' Told to keep silent by the blundering doctor who had performed the operation, and anxious to hide her sexual affair, Sweet resisted morality squad inspectors' demands that she disclose the abortionist's name. Finally, under threat of jail for contempt, she grudgingly agreed to testify against Dr Coulter, who had performed the operation. The doctor, like most, was well defended, and his counsel used the time-worn tack of exposing as many sordid details as possible about the complainant's past. Indeed, it is only through the doctor's trial that we now know about the affair and its nearly fatal results. The criminal justice process placed a blinding light on Sweet's darkest secrets; the doctor was acquitted.[15]

It was rare that a woman other than those who struggled, licitly and illicitly, to survive came to the attention of the criminal justice system. Women like Gertrude Kerr had a solid sense of their own respectability, but women from the so-called respectable classes could exercise options to redress grievances and to release themselves out of tight binds. For instance, when wealthy women stole merchandise from department stores, the price of their purloined goods was discreetly entered on their accounts, or their husbands simply sent in cheques. Poor women who stuffed undershirts and ribbons into their pockets were more likely to find themselves featured in Harry Wodson's police court columns.

There were occasions, nonetheless, when class privilege failed to protect middle-class women from scrutiny in the criminal justice system. One notable trial in 1927 blew the cover off stuffy, respectable Toronto by publicizing the fact that there was a lively abortion trade among the middle class. In order to bring the abortionists to justice, the prosecution exploited the tragedy of Ruth Dembner, a woman whose untimely death allows us to know something of her life. The press and the abortionist's defence lawyers actually handled Dembner's reputation quite gingerly. Death seemed to wash her of the sins that stained Annie Sweet's life, and her genteel background cocooned her from portrayals of sordidness. In contrast to her fiancé, who had helped arrange for the abortion, and the abortionist, Dr Oswald Withrow, who was a leader of the Ontario birth control movement, Dembner emerged as an innocent figure, coerced into committing an act of race suicide.

Dembner seems to have been a daughter of the jazz age. Well-educated, employed as a private secretary in an large insurance firm, and comfortably ensconced at her parents' High Park home, she was free to pursue the enjoyments of her day – motor rides in the country, dining out, dancing until the wee hours. Her parents worried that she was 'burning her candle at both ends' but, even after the family doctor warned her to slow down, she continued her life of gaiety. Weekends away with Bartlett Brooks, her intended husband, provided more discreet opportunities for intimacy than Annie Sweet and Mr Good enjoyed. In January 1927, Dembner discovered she was pregnant, two months before her planned marriage. She sought out Dr Withrow, whose abortion practice was an open secret. She dipped into her savings and paid the doctor $75 to perform the procedure at a private hospital. After the operation, Brooks paid for her accommodation at a Muskoka rest home. The whole affair would have remained a secret had Withrow not nicked her uterus and exposed her to sepsis.

In a way, Dembner did write her life story, or, more precisely, the story of the last moments of her life. When she arrived in Muskoka, feverish and vomiting, the staff alerted the police, who managed to capture the tale of her abortion in her last breaths. Her 'ante-mortem' statement, an official document certified to represent a witness's dying words, recounted her attempt to keep the matter secret from her family. The only people in whom she had confided were her husband-to-be and the doctor. Before Brooks could bid goodbye to his fiancée, she died of peritonitis.

As it turned out, both Dr Withrow *and* Bartlett Brooks were charged with manslaughter. Withrow's guilt seemed clear: hospital workers confirmed that he regularly performed abortions under the guise of dilation and curettage procedures, and that Dembner had applied under a false married name; furthermore, Withrow had released Dembner before ascertaining that she was free of infection. Brooks' culpability was murkier. True, he had conspired with her to keep the operation a secret, but he was only twenty and still technically a minor. In his defence, he claimed that Dembner had planned the whole scheme and that he had merely played a supportive role. The judge and the press branded him as an unmanly coward for suggesting that 'a dainty and well-brought up girl [from] a Christian home' could have considered such a solution to her dilemma on her own. 'I believe that she was a good and innocent girl,' Justice Logie lectured Brooks, 'and that you ruined her and led her to make desperate efforts to avoid the results of indiscretion.'[16]

A naïve girl, cruelly interfered with? A jazz baby who took a fall? A business woman trying to plan her family? Dembner may have rejected each of these renditions of her life. In any event, her death deprived her of the opportunity to offer a counter-narrative. The successful prosecution of Brooks and Withrow depended upon portraying her as a weak-willed creature, easily swayed by unscrupulous men. However much Dembner may have felt victimized, she undoubtedly walked into Withrow's office with her eyes open. Hundreds of women each year made conscious, painful decisions to control reproduction. Using any means at their disposal, they would have known that they risked death. For Dembner and unknown numbers of other 'Mrs X's,' that possibility was evidently more palatable than the stigma of unmarried motherhood or the burden of an unwanted child.

REFRAMING THE PICTURE

It is difficult to picture the women who most often encountered the justice system in turn-of-the-century Toronto beyond the labels conferred upon them. 'Vagrancy' and 'drunkenness' are offences, but they also defined a convicted person's status and personhood. Women who were otherwise neighbours, mothers, or workers were recorded as drunks, prostitutes, or thieves – descriptions that mock the complexity of their lived experience and self-conceptualization. Even when we know more than usual about a person, we still see them through the eyes of court reporters or prison matrons. Women like Rose, the hypocritical 'fallen angel,' or Lizzie Lessard seemed to be rebels without a cause, but their abusive outbursts may have been their only means of articulating their rage over the injustice of poverty that sliced daily through their lives. Or perhaps they simply preferred their freedom to jail.

Although most women in conflict with the law could claim that their troubles began through their economic vulnerability or physical victimization, the criminal justice process only rarely conferred unequivocal victim status on women. Ironically, women like Gertrude Kerr, who claimed that she had been sexually assaulted, were much more readily dismissed than Carrie Davies who admitted to premeditated murder. Women who committed infanticide could attract sympathy in most cases, but those like Annie Sweet who nearly died after an abortion could appear as morally corrupt ingrates. When middle-class women made rare appearances in the limelight of the law, they were granted more credibility. Still, had Ruth Dembner been available for cross-examination, it is possible that such a 'well brought-up girl' might have emerged from the crucible of the court as a conniving temptress who had manipulated her younger fiancé. Irrespective of her courtroom portrayal as a victim or the orchestrator of her own fate, a woman complainant or defendant would have realized by the end of her ordeal-by-law that her story was no longer her own. Indeed, this realization apparently provided the momentum behind Jenny Irving's suicidal plunge into the Toronto bay.

The women in this story – prostitutes, violent offenders, victims of rape or bungled abortions – are too often forgotten, let alone recalled as 'great.' Yet the epic dramas of their lives, dramas that rival any heroic woman's story, were exposed through the criminal justice process. They inhabited a darker world than women poets, doctors, writers, and adventurers but, as this volume confirms, their lives need not remain forgotten in the obscurity of the past. We will never know their 'true' lives, but they may very well have preferred it that way.

NOTES

1 Harry Wodson, *The Whirlpool: Scenes from Toronto Police Court* (Toronto: n.p., 1917), 148
2 George Taylor Denison, *Recollections of a Police Magistrate* (Toronto: Musson Books, 1920)
3 Toronto (York) Coroner's Inquests, 1880, Archives of Ontario (hereafter AO).
4 St Mary's Training School for Girls, Case Files, 1900–1930. AO, R.G. 60, D-12, Reels 1–11. 'Hortense Flambeau' is a pseudonym.
5 Ibid., 'Geminiani,' 1912
6 Carolyn Strange, 'The Velvet Glove: Maternalistic Reform at the Andrew Mercer Ontario Reformatory for Females, 1874–1927,' MA thesis, University of Ottawa, 1983
7 Carolyn Strange, 'Elizabeth Lessard,' *Dictionary of Canadian Biography*, 14 (Toronto: University of Toronto Press, 1992), 386
8 *World* (Toronto), 5 April 1911
9 Wodson, *The Whirlpool*, 149
10 *World* (Toronto), 2 March 1891
11 *Telegram* (Toronto), 9 Feb. 1915
12 Between 1880 and 1930, there were no successful prosecutions of men

accused of raping their servants. See Carolyn Strange, *Toronto's Girl Problem: The Perils and Pleasures of the City, 1880–1930* (Toronto: University of Toronto Press, 1995), for a fuller exploration of sexual assault in this period.

13 Toronto (York) Coroners Inquests, AO, RG 22, 1888
14 Toronto, General Sessions of the Peace, Criminal Assize Indictments, AO, RG 22, 1918
15 Ibid., 1916. Sweet was a charity patient, so it is unclear if paying patients would have been subject to such scrutiny. This method of medico-legal regulation was also used to investigate knife or gun wounds, as well as venereal diseases.
16 *Telegram* (Toronto), 18 May 1927

STRUGGLE TO CREATE

From *Bovarysme* to *Automatisme* (and Beyond): Thérèse Renaud and the *Refus global* Women

PATRICIA SMART

In August 1948, a small group of Quebec artists under the leadership of painter Paul-Émile Borduas published a manifesto that would later be regarded as the first decisive cultural gesture rejecting the values of traditional French Canada and announcing the emergence of a modernity that would become fully visible with the arrival of the Quiet Revolution twelve years later. Entitled *Refus global* – Total Refusal – the manifesto denounced the conservative and church-dominated values that held Quebec in a stranglehold, and passionately affirmed the link between artistic creation and the possibility of social transformation:

The frontiers of our dreams are no longer the same ...

Beyond Christianity, we are touching the burning human brotherhood to which it has become a closed door.

The reign of fear in its many forms is ended ...

We invite those tempted by the adventure to join us.

We dare to imagine a time when man, liberated from his useless chains, will realize the fullness of his individual gifts – in the unpredictable and necessary order of spontaneity, in splendid anarchy.

Until then, without rest or pause, in a community of feeling with all those who thirst for a better life and regardless of the waiting, the encouragement or the persecution we may encounter, we will joyfully pursue our savage need of liberation.[1]

The fifteen young artists who joined Borduas in drafting and signing the manifesto had honed their ideas over six years of discussion and artistic experimentation. They read Marx and Freud, listened to modern music ranging from Stravinsky to jazz, blues, and voodoo rhythms, and experimented with avant-garde theatre and dance productions – always testing their own creative abilities against Borduas's dictum that all authentic art must spring from the deepest and most mysterious realms of the self. If any one influence on their esthetic and social ideas predominates, it is that of Surrealism, with its emphasis on the interdependence of art, the liberation of the individual unconscious, and the transformation of society. But the 'Automatists,' as they called themselves, were strikingly different from the Surrealists in at least one important way: seven of the young artists grouped around Borduas were women.

None of the seven women who signed the manifesto can be said to be typical of the Quebec woman approaching adulthood in the late 1930s and early 1940s; indeed, the differences of class, education, and family background among them give the lie to any attempt to typify the Quebec woman at all. What they have in common is the fact that each of them was rebellious and courageous enough to put her name to an incendiary document – a document on the basis of which their mentor, Paul-Émile Borduas, was fired from his position as an art teacher, abandoned by his Catholic wife and three children, and forced into exile in New York and later Paris, where he died in 1960. Six of them – Marcelle Ferron, Françoise Sullivan, Madeleine Arbour, Françoise Riopelle, Louise and Thérèse Renaud – are still very much alive and, for the most part, still questing and daring to risk exploring new avenues in their lives and artistic production, despite the solid body of work in painting, writing, sculpture, dance, choreography, and design represented by their work. The seventh, Muriel Guilbault, probably the best-known of all the manifesto's signatories at the time of its publication, thanks to her acting on stage and radio in the 1940s, tragically took her own life in January 1952, at the age of twenty-nine. A star at fifteen, best remembered today for her role as the female lead, Marie-Ange, in Gratien Gélinas's *Tit-Coq* (1948), Muriel was a striking physical beauty, surrounded by male admirers throughout her career, and yet plagued by depression and alcoholism. Placed alongside the undoubtedly happier lives of the other women in the group, her tragedy reminds us of the almost insurmountable difficulty that must have been experienced by many women attempting to break out of traditional female roles and develop to a confident sense of self in the stifling climate of 1940s Quebec.[2]

The artistic productions of the *Refus global* women tend to flaunt the

Thérèse Renaud with Bruno Cormier (left) and Fernand Leduc on her
departure from Montreal for Paris, October 1946

traditional borders separating the arts not only from each other but from
life, and while this flexibility and openness to change are undoubtedly a
result of certain gender-based realities in their lives,[3] they also reflect
Borduas's teaching that true artists must free themselves from an obsession with the work as product, and learn to listen without preconcep-
tions or censorship to the promptings of the psyche. Marcelle Ferron is
best-known as a painter, but her stained-glass windows adorn a number
of public buildings in Quebec, providing a dramatic illustration of the
manifesto's aim of transforming society through art. Françoise Sullivan,
the founder of modern dance in Quebec, has in the last fifteen years
returned to her original artistic interest, painting; Françoise Riopelle
also made important contributions to choreography and dance; Madeleine Arbour is known not only for her work as a weaver and interior
decorator, but for a successful career in children's television in the 1950s
and 1960s. Louise Renaud, the group member whose influence, support,
and friendship are most often singled out by the others in their reminis-
cences of their own development in the 1940s, is the only one of the
group to have abandoned her artistic work when she married and
became a mother (a choice that may be related to the fact that she has
lived almost all of her adult life not in Quebec, but in the English-

language environment of New York). Many of these women have made statements about the challenges they faced, particularly in the 1950s, in trying to reconcile their creative work and their responsibilities as wives and mothers; and certainly the difficulty of combining maternity and artistic creation is at the heart of much of the work of Thérèse Renaud, the only writer in the group.

In many important respects it was Borduas's artistic daughters, more than his sons, who carried on the *Refus global* legacy, moving art literally outside the frames, the galleries, and the boundaries of academicism and into the public domain. And yet – perhaps precisely for this reason – none achieved celebrity as quickly or as dramatically as some of their male counterparts (notably painters Jean-Paul Riopelle and Fernand Leduc and playwright Claude Gauvreau), and the numerous books and articles on *Refus global* and the Automatist adventure habitually ignore their existence.

Nonetheless, each of the women who signed the manifesto deserves a biographical portrait, not only for her contribution to contemporary culture, but as a record of the complex negotiation between life and art demanded of women, particularly in an era of dramatic transition for women's roles like that of mid-twentieth-century Quebec. Attempting to find a coherence in their often rich and prolific artistic output, but also in their varied life choices and in the inevitable periods of silence that, for a few of them at least, coincided with marriage and childrearing, the biographer is dramatically confronted by what is perhaps the major dilemma of those who seek to tell women's stories: the resistance of much of what makes up the texture of a woman's life to taking on the shape of narrative.[4] In spite of feminism's important recuperation of the private realm, the fact remains that, in women's lives as well as men's, what is truly memorable – at least as far as biography is concerned – is what exceeds the private: whether art, political activity, scientific endeavour, or other contributions to the public domain. But while the biographical enterprise may well be 'justified' by the woman's achievements outside the private sphere (as is the case in men's biographies), there remain important differences between the projects of writing about men's and about women's lives. The typical biographer of a man, secure in the awareness of the public importance of his subject, can refer back to the private life as a colourful and informative backdrop to the central story. But the biographer of a woman cannot avoid recognizing the greater centrality of the private realm to the story the writer seeks to shape – whether in fact the subject has sought to ignore the constraints imposed on women, escaped them with a greater or lesser degree of success, or been blocked or silenced by them at various stages of her life. Like the subject, the biographer must, according to Carolyn Heilbrun, 'struggle with the inevitable conflict between the destiny of being unambiguously a woman and the woman subject's palpable desire, or fate, to be something else.'[5]

In the case of the *Refus global* women, even a straightforward presentation of their artistic evolution and accomplishments would reveal something of the interface with their lives (as in Françoise Sullivan's use of spaces and objects from everyday life in her sculpture and painting, or the recurrent obsession with blocked doors and windows at a certain period of her evolution, for example). But such a traditional narrative structure could only hint at the spaces between the lines and outside the frames of their works (that is, the spaces of their lives as women). For this reason (and because a single article cannot hope to do justice to the lives of seven women), I have decided to focus on writer Thérèse Renaud, whose often autobiographical works have as their primary *raison d'être* the understanding and revelation of her life as a woman, with its inevitable hesitations and blockages. Renaud's refusal to conform to the repressions and hypocrisies of her society, proudly flaunted when she placed her name on Borduas's document, is also a lifelong *narrative* refusal to conform: a gender-based insistence on telling her own story in her own way, often at the price of lengthy and painful periods of silence. The autobiographical record her writing provides, while not necessarily *typical* of the lives of the *Refus global* women, should be seen, as in some sense *emblematic* of them: a written account of the often ignored private dimension of the movement, and of one of these lives that came briefly together in the 1940s to challenge the status quo.

When Thérèse Renaud put her name to the manifesto that was to create a storm of controversy in her home province, she was twenty-one, living in Paris, and married to painter Fernand Leduc, also a signatory of *Refus global*. For her the manifesto's insistence on refusal – 'refusal to knowingly operate at anything less than our psychic and physical potential; refusal to close our eyes to the vices and falsehoods perpetrated in the name of knowledge'[6] – must have felt absolutely right. It was a public and political statement of what she had long felt to be the deepest and most authentic parts of her own self: refusal to conform and hatred of hypocrisy. Her meeting with the Automatist group in the summer of 1944, when she was seventeen years old, had helped to give shape to a rebellion that went back as far as her earliest memories – against the rules and constraints of her comfortable bourgeois family, a convent-school education that stifled her creativity and intelligence, and the larger society of Duplessis's Quebec, with its rigid expectations regarding women's role. 'We were raised in the purest *bovarysme* it is possible to imagine,' she later wrote.[7] All of Therese's writing – poetry, autobiography, and fiction – is a rebellion against this upbringing and an attempt to undo its negative effects. For if it took courage to put her name to an incendiary manifesto, it would take more than that – indeed a whole lifetime of struggle – to extract herself from the effects of an unbringing that had prepared her for no function in the world other than the passivity and sense of uselessness that have plagued many women's lives in patriarchal society, and which Flaubert captured so accurately in the character of Emma Bovary.

Thérèse was born in the working-class area of Saint-Henri in Montreal on 3 July 1927, the third child of parents who were both members of French Canada's cultural elite. Her father, a dentist and later a professor of dentistry at the University of Montreal, was the grandson of one of the first members of the Canadian Senate, Louis Renaud, who had begun his career as a cart driver, made and lost a fortune in the grain business, and sat in the Quebec Legislature before being named a senator by Royal Proclamation in 1867. Her mother, Blandine Lesage, was the descendant of a family whose roots in Canada went back as far as New France, to Urbain Tessier *dit* Lavigne, who was a friend and advisor of Maisonneuve and after whom Montreal's Saint-Urbain Street is named. In the nineteenth century the family produced a number of notable sculptors and musicians, including Thérèse's great-uncle Ernest Lavigne, the charismatic conductor who almost single-handedly brought classical music to the Montreal public by founding Parc Sohmer, where internationally known musicians played daily in the summer months, and where Maestro Lavigne himself conducted his orchestra on Sundays for many years after the park's opening in 1889. Thérèse's cousins on her mother's side were Guy Mauffette, who would become one of Radio-Canada's best-known announcers and directors, and his sister Estelle, an actress who became famous in the 1940s playing the saintly and much-abused Donalda, wife of the miser Séraphin Poudrier, in the hugely popular radio drama *Les Belles Histoires des pays d'en haut*, based on Claude-Henri Grignon's novel *Un Homme et son péché*. In her early adolescence, Thérèse's imagination was kindled by evenings when the entire family would gather at the Mauffette's house to recite poetry, stage a ballet scene, or make music – a quartet, quintet, or septet, depending on the availability of musicians.

And yet Thérèse's earliest memories, as evoked in her first autobiographical work, *Une Mémoire déchirée*, contain almost nothing of this stimulating milieu. Not until she was in her forties and seeking to understand her own daughter's various rebellions would she begin to explore the reasons for the cloud that seemed to hang over her early years, and the unresolved relationship with her mother that was to mark her own life and work, reflected in a constant and unfulfilled quest for reconciliation.[8] At the time of Thérèse's birth, her mother, Blandine Renaud, had just turned forty, and in the preceding two years had seen not only both her parents die within days of each other, but also her only brother commit suicide (ostensibly from grief) a few months later. Much later Thérèse's father would tell her of the anguish of those years and of the desperate desire shared with his wife that by having another child Blandine might find new reasons to live. Instead she seems to have been overwhelmed by the birth of two new daughters within the space of a year and a half and by her own deteriorating health. By the time Thérèse was six her mother would be dead of cancer, and the little girl would be left with a lifelong sense of having being rejected by a mother she barely knew. In the atmosphere of worry and foreboding that permeated the household during those early years, the naturally daring and spontaneous little girl would soon come to see herself as a rebel and outsider, someone whose curiosity and desire for adventure were always getting her in trouble and who, no matter how hard she tried, was unable to conform to the strict rules of family and milieu.

By the time Thérèse was four or five her family had moved to a large house on Dunlop Street in Outremont, next door to the Lalonde family, whose daughter Mimi (who later married actor Jean Gascon) would become a lifelong friend of the three Renaud sisters. Mimi remembers Thérèse as the most vulnerable of the three, and sees the mixture of acute sensitivity, artistic talent, and rebelliousness that characterized her as typical of the Quebec of her era. 'She was too self-willed for the adults to deal with,' she says, 'and at the same time extremely unsure of herself.'[9]

Thérèse's own account of her childhood confirms and gives depth to her friend's observation, but roots her drama more specifically in gender-related realities. One of her earliest memories is the desire to 'grow up, so I could be free,' a desire that merged with the awareness that being a girl was more limiting than being a boy: 'Boys were much more at ease in their actions and allowed to express themselves freely, to be independent and order us around, and it goes without saying that I'd have liked to be one of them. But I was stuck with the bad luck of being a girl' (*Mémoire*, 8). Her insatiable curiosity seemed always to come up against the fact that the knowledge she craved belonged to a forbidden realm – whether the mystery-enshrouded space of her father's dental consultation room on the main floor of the house, from which inexplicable cries emerged, or the 'black, inert and seemingly inoffensive hole' of an electrical outlet into which she couldn't resist putting her fingers, 'to find out what it was hiding' (*Mémoire*, 9) resulting not only in her own burned hands, but a short circuit that upset the entire household.

The ultimate taboo in the culture of Thérèse's childhood was the body and sexuality, and her fascination with them trapped her from early on in the image of a 'bad' little girl. At four, she remembers seeing the gardener urinate and asking him to reveal the details of his anatomy, all the while both thrilled and frightened by the knowledge that her mother would be horrified by what she was doing. At six, she accepted a dare to take off her clothes and run naked down the street, only to collide with her dismayed father and find herself banished to the porch for a week. Unable to deal with her unruly daughter, Blandine (whom Mimi Lalonde remembers as extremely ill, with a stomach bloated by excessive radium treatments) would punish Thérèse by shutting her in a closet or subjecting her to cold showers, ordeals that Thérèse remembered later as unsuccessful efforts to 'contain' her: 'She had difficulty in keeping my impetuous urges and my insatiable curiosity under control. I knew of no law more imperious than my own' (*Mémoire*, 13). Somewhat more patient, but distant and distracted by his many worries, Thérèse's father tried to explain to her the need to respect the rules of society, an effort that seems only to have convinced her at a very young age that she would 'never be capable of fitting into this oppressive society. I felt it was hopeless' (*Mémoire*, 15).

For the little girl, the worsening illness of her mother was experienced as the arrival of darkness in a 'house full of light.' Mysterious things were whispered about by the adults, while the children, excluded, took refuge in looking through the books in their father's well-stocked library. Thérèse's first experience of books is associated with this sense of worry and foreboding, exacerbated by the heavy Victorian furniture and dark maroon colours of the room, and the enforced silence imposed on the children by their mother's condition: 'We looked nostalgically through the illustrated books, and the silence that weighed on everything took us further and further away from the gaiety of our childhood' (*Mémoire*, 19). As she sat on the front steps of the house one afternoon, Thérèse was suddenly overwhelmed by the certainty that her mother was dead, a presentiment that would be confirmed later that day when her father arrived home from the hospital.

This experience of being the vehicle or vessel of a larger consciousness was to be a formative one, which would later find an esthetic shape in the Surrealist-inspired experiments of the *Refus global* group: 'I was learning to descend into myself and to listen to the voice of intuition that goes beyond all logic, for in spite of my mother's long illness there had never been any mention that she might die' (*Mémoire*, 21). This first, devastating experience of death would also be her first experience of religious doubt and rebellion: 'They tell us that our mother is in heaven and that she's happy. I can't believe it. How can she be happy without us? How can she know happiness, knowing we are unhappy? Already I'm starting to have questions about this heaven that seems to me a pale and disagreeable place' (*Mémoire*, 22). A few months later, the aunt for whom Thérèse was named and who had cared for the children during their mother's illness also died, leading the terrified little girl to wonder if all the adults in her life were going to be taken away from her.

Their mother's death precipitated the Renaud girls into an even worse, indeed a nightmarish, period of over a year, during which they were cared for by Mademoiselle Rose, a sadistic and vindictive woman hired by their father on the priest's recommendation. The original readers of Renaud's autobiography must have been reminded on reading this segment of her work of the famous 1920s play, which later became the first French-Canadian film hit, *La petite Aurore l'enfant martyre* – the story of a little girl brutalized by an evil stepmother whose piety tricks her husband, the neighbours, and the village priest into believing her tales about the child's wickedness. In fact one cannot help wondering whether the mythical pull exerted on the collective unconscious of Quebec by little Aurore's story[10] may have shaped Thérèse's own narrative in some way. In any case, the reality of their persecution at the hands of Mademoiselle Rose is confirmed by all three Renaud sisters as well as by Mimi Lalonde, and in it modern readers will recognize the now familiar mechanisms of child abuse.

Under Mademoiselle Rose's control, the children were subjected to a regime of forced labour, discipline, and punishment meant to instil in them a sense of their unworthiness.[11] Every evening they were obliged to recite the rosary with arms extended in the form of a cross, while Mademoiselle Rose watched over them, ready to tap them with a ruler if their arms weakened. Thérèse, with her independent spirit, became the chosen victim, the one who had to be 'broken' by extra mortifications. She was forced to go to Mass every morning, and Mademoiselle Rose would awaken her at 5 AM by pulling her hair. Most humiliating was the walk home afterwards, when she feared her friends would see and laugh at her as she walked behind the limping Mademoiselle Rose, reciting the rosary. At lunch the children were often deprived of food, and Thérèse would sometimes be required to kneel throughout the meal, while Mademoiselle Rose gave her kicks under the table. During her first year at school, she would often return home to find her younger sister Jeanne scrubbing and vacuuming, 'dead with fear and exhaustion' (*Mémoire*, 26), but the two little girls were forbidden to speak to each other.

While Thérèse's response to this treatment was outwardly that of defiance and rebelliousness, she long retained the anguish of an inner split: the knowledge that, in spite of her best efforts to be a model Catholic girl, she was inhabited by impurity and evil. On the day of her First Communion, overwhelmed by guilt at the memory of her experience with the gardener two years earlier and by the consequent fear that she was committing a sacrilege, she fainted, spitting out the host – making the adults more convinced than ever of her evil nature. Deliverance from Mademoiselle Rose eventually came, thanks to the intervention of a neighbour, but the pattern of persecution and defiance had been set and continued throughout Thérèse's years at convent school, where a dreary succession of hypocritical nuns and mindless teachings seemed expressly conceived to stamp out all traces of her spontaneity and individualism. Punished for her refusal to conform to the prescribed mediocrity, she became more rebellious than ever, and more desperate than ever for understanding and approval. Her intuitive approach to learning particularly enraged her mathematics teacher, who on one occasion, when Thérèse had arrived at the right answer to a problem without following the rules, strode to the blackboard and inscribed a huge red zero on her work, then grasped her by the ear and threw her against the blackboard, while the other pupils docilely chanted the correct formula. Marched to the principal's office, Thérèse remained defiant, replying, when the nun threatened to call her father, 'Do what you like; I can only do what I must.' Later, although devastated when her father called her 'the black sheep of the family,' her sense of the injustice of the situation made her refuse to apologize: 'Father, you're asking for the impossible. I will never utter a word of apology for something I'm not guilty of' (*Mémoire*, 39–45).

Thérèse seems to have survived the trauma of these early years by clinging to a number of truths that would remain as constants in her life and writing: a belief in the power of her own intuition against the rigidity of dogma and social convention, a passion for justice, and a sense that her own destiny lay in the exploration of the forbidden, the mysterious, and the marginal realms of existence – 'The place where mystery resides is the place I belong' (*Mémoire*, 49). When she was eight, the economic difficulties of the Depression years forced her father to sell the Outremont house and move the family to a poorer neighbourhood, where Thérèse's desire for justice and intuition of a beauty and truth outside the confines of her bourgeois world began to take the shape of social consciousness. In the streets and back lanes of her new neighbourhood, she learned with astonishment of the existence of hunger and poverty: friends who had gone without lunch and dinner because there was no food in the house, a family evicted from their home when their father lost his job. Equally troubling was the indifference of her family and school friends, their assumption that the poor themselves were to blame for their situation. On the whole, though, these were exhilarating years, for in the streets and with her new friends Thérèse had a taste for the first time of the freedom she had always craved: 'Did it come from the fact that I was breaking the rules? From the need for personal affirmation? Certainly the discovery of another milieu, of a moral code that was less conventional and closer to the heart, of a more spontaneous language and a simplicity in human relationships awakened in me a great desire to change life' (*Mémoire*, 52).

By early adolescence, although still a rebel, Thérèse had begun to show the effects of the long years of socialization and training in conformity. Her desire for mystery and for a mystical fusion with a larger entity was now equally shared between God and sex, and she recalls reading the lives of the saints and waiting anxiously for God to speak to her, all the while tormented by 'evil thoughts' exacerbated by fiery sermons about the sinfulness of such things as 'the kiss on the mouth.' Although as a younger child she had had an instinctive sense of the hypocrisy of religion, she had become a typical Catholic girl – dreaming of sacrificing herself for Christ, tormented by the suffering caused him by humans, and aspiring to help those in misery. And yet her friends' recollections of her at the time are of her irrepressible *joie de vivre*, her freshness and teenage beauty: 'She always had the ability to make herself glamorous with a bit of ribbon put into her hair in just the right way, or an inexpensive scarf,' recalls Mimi Lalonde.[12] This sort of 'vanity' (really an aesthetic sense) enraged the nuns, whose teachings aimed rather at instilling in their charges a disgust and fear of the body. Once, after curling her hair with particular care in preparation for an academic awards ceremony, Thérèse had the curls violently ripped out by a nun brandishing a hairbrush and a lecture: 'God gave you a body not so you can make it beautiful but to better serve Him' (*Mémoire*, 61). Her reaction was rage, but also self-hatred that would take a lifetime to root out.

Thérèse's account of the mentality of these years is an important contribution to Quebec cultural history, one whose honesty about the process of internalizing a hate-filled and even racist ideology is reminiscent at times of Christa Wolf's famous account of her childhood in Nazi Germany.[13] As a child Thérèse had been attracted by the mystery of the 'other,' whether the neighbourhood ragpicker in Outremont or her working-class street friends, but as a young adolescent she and her convent school companions fantasized about the abominations of all who were different from themselves: Communists, Jews, Freemasons, and even the students of a neighbouring co-educational English school, whose short skirts and comfortable way of relating between the sexes inspired the uniformed French-Canadian convent girls with erotic fantasies worthy of Sade, always ending with the trampling of a crucifix. In the anti-Communist films shown in school, the anti-Semitic propaganda so distressing to the mature Thérèse that she cannot bring herself to put it in writing, and the lurid stories of the secret society of Freemasons bent on destroying all Catholics, the message drummed into the young girls' minds was consistently one of fear. The violent and sadistic imagery in which it was communicated touched the deepest layers of the adolescent psyche: 'We were literally surrounded by evil forces aimed not only at our moral destruction but our physical mutilation. I imagined myself submitting to torture up to the point of death rather than giving in to their injunctions and denying Christ, who had given his life on the cross to save humanity' (*Mémoire*, 60).

But during those same years there was also the formative influence of weekly sessions with her cousin Estelle Mauffette to study theatrical and poetic recitation, and of long talks with her older sister Louise, by then a student at the École des Beaux-Arts, who was herself discovering Marx, Engels, and avant-garde poetry with a group of friends who would a few years later form the nucleus of the Automatist group. By the age of fourteen, Thérèse had stopped going to Mass on Sundays and had abandoned the lives of the saints in favour of the art books in her father's library, one of which contained a question that went to the heart of her dilemma: 'HOW CAN ONE REACH THE BEAUTY IN ONESELF AND EXPRESS IT?' (*Mémoire*, 67). At a performance of *The Nutcracker* by the Ballets Russes, she burst into tears and confided to Louise, 'I never knew such beauty could exist.' Most decisive was her discovery of the poetry of Rimbaud (a surprising choice for a fourteen-year-old, and one that scandalized her cousin Estelle when she brought it to one of their weekly recitation sessions). Years later, Thérèse would remember her first reading of his famous 'Lettre du voyant,' with its stirring description of the pain and risk inherent in the quest for poetic vision and its prophetic lines about the as yet unspoken potential of women's vision, as overwhelming, 'a terrible blow.'[14] The desire for mystery that went back as far as her earliest memories was reawakened as well by a book lent to her by a nun who was 'doubtless unaware of its contents' – Alexandra David Neel's *Voyage d'une parisienne à Lhassa* (*Mémoire*, 71). With trembling and anxiety, feeling very much alone, she was becoming aware once again of the possibility of an unknown beauty that could be reached through the intuitive faculties.

By the time she was fifteen, at a standoff with the nuns, who would no longer read her work, claiming it was 'too personal,' Thérèse had convinced her father that school was stifling what was most precious in her. The compromise solution reached was that she and Jeanne would instead have private tutoring with the nuns for the next two years. Thérèse is still bitter about the waste of those two years, after which both girls failed their baccalaureate examinations, and which left her confused, untrained in any area, and still torn between rebellion and the need for approval. But they were the years in which, to fill her inner void and counter her growing desperation, she began writing the poems that would later – under the title *Les Sables du rêve*[15] – become the first Automatist publication.

Unlike anything then existing in Quebec literature, these poems, with their witty and yet disturbing combinations of words and images flowing from the unconscious, are an eruption of desire and the need for laughter in a grey and stifling landscape of sameness. The young girl who speaks in them is depicted as hungry for sensation, 'biting into' flowers that are given her to smell, wanting to dance and fly off on the wings of 'negro music,' but blocked by her 'long feet' and by 'storm clouds,' or – in another poem – waiting naked for a 'sad lover' who after making love with her yawns, steps out in the street, takes his revolver, and fires two shots into his temple. Often there is a fairytale atmosphere: the young girl sets off into the night at the beckoning of an 'interior eye' with its 'inviting smile,' but is tempted to stop on her route by a 'gay and welcoming' old woman who invites her into her house ('But what is it that disturbs me about this house made for tranquillity? I'm bored I'm forced to abandon the little old woman. What is waiting for me in the night? ... I have to unfold the road that I had rolled up in my pocket, and continue, without ever growing pale with shame'). Everywhere present beneath the playful surface imagery of this thin volume and the whimsical accompanying illustrations by Jean-Paul Mousseau is the underlying current of sexual desire and, more generally, of the desire to grasp the beauty of life, chafing against constraints that block and stifle it.

> At dawn on an inebriating morning I am at the window. A note carried by the wind comes to caress my cheek – I am the note that you haven't been able to grasp, the forgotten musical note.
> I lean forward to listen to it but a gust of wind carries it away among the dead leaves.

Less gentle, and more expressive of the erotic energy that would animate the *Refus global* group and their anger against a stultifying society, is the poem that would later inspire one of the choreographies of Françoise Sullivan and Jeanne Renaud:

> What disgrace of a race can it be that reigns over the crystals and blocks the water's reflection! ...
> I hear a soundless voice that calls me from the mysterious shadows of the craters ...
> In a burst of laughter: ...
> I am of the red and thick race that borders on volcanic eruptions and craters in movement.

During the years when Thérèse was writing these poems alone in her room at night, Louise and her friends at the Beaux-Arts had come into contact with Borduas and begun to meet regularly in his studio on Napoleon Street in the Plateau Mont Royal area of town. For Thérèse, the golden years of her association with the group began in the summer of her seventeenth year, when to be closer to Borduas's home some members of the group (all three of the Renaud sisters, Françoise Sullivan, Mimi Lalonde, Fernand Leduc, Pierre Gauvreau, Bruno Cormier) rented a rundown old house in Saint-Hilaire, forty miles south of Montreal. For all of them it was the first experience of a bohemian lifestyle very different from the way they had been brought up – shocking to the local farmers and especially to the curé, who railed against the ungodly ways of the young artists in his Sunday sermons, but (as they all now recall with amusement) totally innocent and even puritanical. 'The girls slept upstairs and the boys on the main floor, we didn't drink alcohol or smoke marijuana, and we would gather in the evening around a wood fire to question everything: our relationship with society, with art, with mankind,' wrote Thérèse later.[16] When Françoise's parents announced they were coming for a visit, the men were sent off to amuse themselves elsewhere for the afternoon, and all traces of them removed from the house. Unfortunately, Borduas also chose that afternoon to drop in for a visit, and the young women frantically tried to send him signals so he wouldn't betray his perplexity at the absence of his young disciples (*Mémoire*, 103–4). All of the members of the household were painting or writing furiously, devouring the Surrealist works Louise had brought with her from New York, trying out avant-garde theatre productions, which would invariably end in laughter. For Thérèse it was a glorious summer, a taste of freedom at last (writing of it later, she tells of a trip they took around the Eastern Townships that probably qualifies them as the first hitchhikers in Quebec), although a bittersweet freedom at times because of the attitudes they encountered in the tightly conformist society around them. One evening they dressed up in their best clothes and decided to treat themselves to a restaurant dinner, but were frustrated and furious at being relegated to the kitchen because of their bohemian appearance. And the girls soon gave up their attendance at Saturday night dances in the village because of the vulgarity of the village men, who assumed they were easy conquests.

This was also the summer when Thérèse fell in love with Fernand Leduc, the articulate and somewhat intimidating painter eleven years older than herself, who had abandoned his training to be a Brother shortly after enrolling in the École des Beaux-Arts in 1939, and whom she would later marry. Back in Montreal that fall, Leduc rented a studio on Jeanne-Mance Street, and it was there that members of the group would congregate almost every evening over the next few years to share ideas about Surrealism, Freud, the evils of religion and capitalism, and the possibility of transforming society through art. In October 1946 Thérèse left for Paris on a cargo steamer, having raised the money for her ticket with help from her friends (Borduas's contribution was a painting that was raffled off), and on her arrival she was picked up at the Arc de Triomphe by future prime minister Pierre Trudeau on his motorcycle. Fernand Leduc arrived the following May, and he and Thérèse celebrated his arrival by getting married. In August 1948 *Refus global* appeared in Montreal, carrying both their signatures.

Often women's writings about their lives cover the period of their childhood and adolescence, but stop at the moment of marriage: one thinks of the autobiographies of Gabrielle Roy, Maya Angelou, Christa Wolf, and Mary McCarthy, to name only a few. It is as if the intimacy of the couple operates as a veil of secrecy pulled over the woman's life, or – more disturbingly – as if the very individuality of that life has come to an end. Thérèse Renaud's autobiographical writings are an exception to this rule, for in both *Une Mémoire déchirée* (1978) and *Le Choc d'un murmure* (1988) she speaks with unusual honesty of some of the difficult moments of marriage and motherhood, and of her often desperately felt need to find an expression for her own creative voice. Unlike her account of her childhood and adolescence, the portrait of her adult life is not linear, but fragmentary and at times repetitive, like the lives of so many women; a circling around the defining truths that recur throughout a life, which increases in depth and understanding even as the outer reality (marriage, motherhood, the passion for truth, freedom, and creativity) remains more or less the same. 'It is very difficult, to be honest, to recount an interior journey. It takes shape in small successive layers, and through an imperceptible movement' (*Mémoire*, 134). The shape of Thérèse's writing – often interrogative, hesitant, or awkward, yet propelled forward by the imperious need to record the self's journey, interrupted at times by imaginary dialogues with herself, her husband, or her daughter, at other times veiled by transparent fictional devices – is the mirror of a reality that resists shaping, a constant falling back into disorder and yet a transforming of the failure and frustration into a life direction: 'What matters most to me is to find the words for that inner journey [which corresponds to] the discovery of one's deepest truth through the many wanderings of life' (*Mémoire*, 143).

During the early years in Paris, Thérèse's attempts to make a place for herself in the theatrical world led nowhere, whether because of her French-Canadian accent, her inability to tolerate snobbishness and hypocrisy, or her tendency to efface herself before the greater importance of her husband's work – most likely a combination of all of these. By 1949, she and Fernand were the proud but desperately poor parents of a daughter, Isabelle, and had moved to the suburbs of Paris, where living was cheaper, but where Thérèse's isolation from people and events related to her own artistic aspirations was complete. *Une Mémoire déchirée* contains a moving account of the hardships of those years, openly discussing such painful aspects of her life as depression, overindulgence in alcohol, and marital difficulties – experiences shared by many women, but rarely acknowledged in written accounts of their lives.

On the surface at least, the serious depression that Thérèse faced when she was twenty-six was a not surprising reaction to the situation in which she found herself. Life in the Paris suburbs with a four-year-old daughter, who seemed to have a constant cold, and a husband who felt no need for social life and had little patience with his young wife's tears, was a far cry from the dreams that had brought her to Paris six years earlier – and from the bourgeois comforts in which she had grown up. In fact, when she had set sail in 1946 with her father's admonitions about the dangers Paris held for a virtuous young girl ringing in her ears, Thérèse had had no intention of finding herself married within seven months, much less a mother within two years. But for her generation of Quebec women, raised in 'the purest *bovarysme* it is possible to imagine,' it was obviously easier to sign one's name to a revolutionary and anti-Catholic manifesto than to break with the expectations that had been drummed into one about marriage.

In fact, the contrast between the reality described by Thérèse and the rhetoric of the *Refus global* manifesto, with its proud affirmation of an erotic liberation of creativity that would burst the shackles of a repressive society, is a revealing comment on the distance between private lives and public discourse, perhaps especially in an age of cultural transition. For example, even though she and Fernand had ceased going to church years earlier and were married at the *mairie* in Paris, they were totally ignorant about the possibilities for birth control. And after the rebellious eroticism of *Les Sables du rêve* (and of Thérèse's letters to Fernand while she languished alone in Paris awaiting his arrival), the reality of sex was a rude shock: 'Something in the deepest part of me was blocked [about sex] and a kind of modesty kept me from even thinking about the problem ... During adolescence we were always made to understand in devious ways that women don't enjoy the physical aspects of love, and that men don't want them to! You were supposed to hide your pleasure if you wanted to keep your husband' (*Mémoire*, 129).

Thérèse's descriptions of the confusion and depression of her years as a young mother in the 1950s are equally frank. Over and over again in her writings she returns to the loss of identity experienced by the women of her generation, who had been brought up to believe their fulfilment lay in marriage and motherhood. 'I wanted to get involved in something, direct some of my excess energy outside of myself, into theatre or singing, but I had absolutely no self-confidence. I needed to be encouraged; like many young women of the 50s I was marked by the fear of not being good enough, and filled with enormous doubts and inhibitions.'[17] And, while desperate for a career of her own, she also came to a conscious decision that in a marriage of artists, one of the partners must take on responsibility for the practical realities of life and accept the fact that priority is placed on the career of the other: 'One day I realized that we couldn't both be artists, that one of us had to be realistic – so I got up all my courage and capitulated.'[18]

The 'capitulation' was never complete, however, for it was resisted by the part in Thérèse that demanded expression – that 'inner demon' whose voice, after more than twenty years of marriage and literary silence, would finally push her to write *Une Mémoire déchirée*.[19] Before that, though, there were other attempts at finding a creative expression, notably in singing, for which Thérèse had always had a talent. On the advice of a doctor concerned about her depression and isolation in Paris, the couple returned to Montreal from 1953 to 1959, and there, in spite of her nervousness and the demands of her maternal role,[20] Thérèse began to put together the beginnings of a moderately successful career as a singer, specializing in the type of poetic song then popular in Paris but still relatively unknown in Quebec. After the years of feeling trapped in domesticity, she felt she was beginning to find herself: '[Singing] was the part of me that reflected the pleasure of being alive. It was me ... a me that was able to love and also be free.'[21] Recordings of her weekly appearances on the Radio-Canada morning program 'Radio Bigoudis,' hosted by her cousin Guy Mauffette, are evidence of her rich alto voice and engaging musical style; but although she had a certain following, the conditions were not yet ripe for the flowering of the *chansonniers* and the *boîtes aux chansons* that would begin after 1960, with the arrival of the Quiet Revolution. And by then Thérèse and Fernand had returned to France.

Always torn between Quebec and France, and frustrated by Isabelle's convent school education, which seemed a repetition of Thérèse's experiences twenty years earlier, the couple decided in 1959 to return to

Paris for good. There, Thérèse made what turned out to be a disastrous mistake, enrolling in singing lessons with a teacher who over the next few years would destroy her voice by making her sing above her alto range. The realization of what had happened was not to come until 1963, when Thérèse, once again determined to explore her career possibilities, returned to Montreal in the spring for an audition with Radio-Canada. It was while listening to the tape of that audition with some close friends that she became aware of the disaster – her tonal range had been destroyed, and with it all her dreams of a musical career. Her almost daily letters to Fernand during those weeks reveal the tenacity of her struggle to adapt to this loss, even as she devotes almost all her time and energy to promoting her husband's work and shoring up *his* artistic ego. On May 11 she tells him of the devastating discovery: 'I have never felt such a sense of loss! Yesterday I went with Jeanne, Jean-Paul Filion and Gilles Potvin to listen to the audition tape ... What a terrible singer I am! What a horribly shrill voice I have now! Truly, Fernand, I trembled when I heard myself. And if you could have seen the faces of Jean-Paul and Jeanne ... I know I'm going to have to start over again from ZERO ... But I must find some kind of expression, or I will die of boredom.'[22] A week later she has bounced back enough to tell her husband of the admiration people were expressing for the paintings she has brought with her ('Guy Viau came to see your work and he was literally carried away by it. "You see," he said to me, "they justify his new *plasticien* manner – the forms and colours are in perfect unity."'). Already she is starting to plan for other possible work for herself, determined not to fall back into depression. But despite her efforts to hide it, the pain of her situation is apparent:

How am I going to tell Mme D. that I'm not singing any more? I'm afraid to write to her ... I have other projects, I'd like to get into interviewing, and I've met some people who might be able to help me ... I don't really know what direction to take. You know that I have to get involved in something right away, otherwise I may fall into something painful and destructive. I have to *do* something with my life, I can't sit around doing nothing, I'll die of boredom and despair. Last night at the B.'s place, they put on a record of Kathleen Ferrier, and I started to cry like a little kid – it was as if I was being shown my arm that had just been amputated. So I absolutely must find some work, immediately.[23]

The creative direction that Thérèse would eventually find was, not surprisingly, writing; what *is* surprising, and yet typical of the pattern of many women's lives, is that in spite of having been a published writer at the age of nineteen, it would require half a life before she could find the time, the discipline, and the confidence to go back to that art. In November 1968, with Isabelle waiting to start university during the exhilarating and unprecedented student and worker strikes that were rocking Paris, Thérèse wrote to her friend Margot Lespérance:

Forgive me for not replying to your letter before this ... but can you believe I've been possessed by the demon of writing, and writing a letter is quite different ... What should I tell you? So little and yet so much is happening ... I never seem able to put the essential things into a letter, because I'm always caught between what's happening inside and the events taking place outside (you see? even the word 'outside' is hard for me to write). When I got back from London I said to myself 'Ma petite, you have to do something with yourself or you'll die of langour ... And now every morning, like a studious schoolgirl, I sit down in front of my notebook and write. I've gotten caught up in it and it's still going on and taking shape and causing me all sorts of problems ... and nothing else matters![24]

This letter marks an important moment in Thérèse's life, not only because it signalled her choice at the age of forty-one to commit herself once again to writing, but also because in it she recognized the centrality to her artistic vision of the inner dimension of reality. From then on, whether in autobiography (Une Mémoire déchirée and Le Choc d'un murmure), poetry (Plaisirs immobiles[25] and Jardin d'éclats[26]), or fiction (Subterfuge et sortilège[27]) her writing would focus on the personal and the private, often revealing uncomfortable truths and hitherto unspoken aspects of women's lives. Just as Thérèse as a child had been blessed (or cursed) with an honesty that often scandalized, the writing of her mature years has often met with resistance and even hostility on the part of publishers and critics. Une Mémoire déchirée, written in the early 1970s, finally found a publisher in 1978, but before that there were numerous rejections, including one that stated, 'Your past is of interest to no-one.'[28] Writing to her friend Jacques Allard (who eventually would be instrumental in finding her a publisher) in 1974, Thérèse tells him of her frustration with these responses and her refusal to give in to the demands that she place more emphasis on the public dimension of the events she recounts: 'I want to justify this supposed "discretion" that they all seem to be reproaching me for. In fact, I think my little piece is actually quite indiscreet, for my aim was to reveal the evolution of my soul and not to describe the places and people that more or less shaped it or contributed to its rebellion. It seems to me that if things have changed in Quebec, it's because some people of my generation felt [that rebellion] in the deepest part of their being. Of course each person's circumstances are particular ... but I don't believe my talent lies in historical evocation.'[29]

Resistance to revelations about the private realm can also be a resistance to the recognition of women's voices and perspectives, for as feminists have realized, the invulnerability of patriarchal institutions – particularly the family – was long guaranteed by women's silence about their experience within those institutions. In this regard, Thérèse's most 'indiscreet' book is her reflection on mothering, *Le Choc d'un murmure*, an autobiography thinly veiled by the use of fictional names, in which she attempts to come to terms with her daughter's various rebellions and with her own stormy relationship with her mother by exploring the closeness of the mother-daughter link, and the brutal rupture that must sometimes take place in order for daughters to accede to autonomy. Writing to Denise Boucher (the author of the controversial feminist play *Les Fées ont soif*) in 1985, she reveals her awareness of the risks she is taking in the book: 'I'm working on "The daughter's struggle" [her provisional title] – and what a struggle it is to write it! I'm so afraid of not succeeding with this book in which I reveal myself completely, warts and all. It's not all beautiful to look at.'[30] Her worst fears were realized on publication, when the book received an extremely cruel review in *Le Devoir* by the powerful and ultra-conservative critic Jean Ethier-Blais. Significantly, Ethier-Blais is put off by what he sees as the confidence of Thérèse's tone ('The "murmur" we hear is a very strong voice, sure of its right to speak, exceedingly affirmative'), and even more by her lack of *pudeur*, her frankness in revealing things that in his view should have remained private: 'A mother is, by the very definition of maternal love, the depository of ... the secrets of her children.' Besides, he goes on, attacking her as well for her earlier volume of memoirs dealing with convent school life, there was nothing wrong with the education given to girls: 'I recall my sisters and their friends coming home after school, laughing and joking, completely free in their relationships with their teachers, and, in August, their joy about returning to the convent.' Thérèse Renaud, he concludes, is 'a spoiled, over-protected and vindictive child.'[31]

More open-minded readers would be struck, on the contrary, by the searching tone of Thérèse's two books of memoirs, their honest admission of doubts, hesitations, and mistakes that by the 1980s Thérèse had come to understand from a feminist perspective: 'I wonder whether the weight of generations of silenced women hasn't affected our freedom to think. So much energy unused or deflected from its goals, so many unexpressed conflicts, so much aggression turned in on itself, aren't these things imprinted in each one of us? ... Amid all this women's silence, or excessive talkativeness, how is it possible to find a voice, a language that corresponds to what one wants to say?'[32]

Her own writings are a breaking of that silence, not only about women's lives, but about the cultural past of the country that formed her and that, despite her long years of residence in France, is still perhaps the primary object of her love and her anger.[33] And while for future generations these writings will undoubtedly be regarded as Thérèse Renaud's primary creative expression, they are only partial traces of the much more complex creativity of the life behind them – that of the daughter, sister, wife, mother, and friend who, by her own avowal, never succeeded completely in giving her writing priority over the other demands of her woman's life:

I don't consider myself so much as a writer as a searcher, someone with a quest ... For me life remains a very mysterious thing ... Do we really choose our direction or are we driven by forces outside ourselves? I can't answer that question ... I'd like to get to a point where I could elucidate the mystery of it all ... Because there are a lot of things I'd have liked to have done and that I certainly could have done, but that I didn't do because of love, because of the people around me, through a sort of *why me rather than someone else?* One thing is certain [and she laughs]: I still haven't reached the point of serenity![34]

NOTES

1 Paul-Émile Borduas, *Refus global et Projections libérantes* (Montreal: Parti pris, 1977), 29–30, 39–40 (translation mine, here and in all subsequent citations from French-language texts and interviews)
2 For more detail on Muriel Guilbault, see my 'Unearthing the Subject behind the Woman-Object: The Representation of Muriel Guilbault in Claude Gauvreau's *Beauté baroque*,' *University of Toronto Quarterly* 63, no. 4 (Summer 1994): 528–37.
3 For example, Françoise Sullivan's decision to turn to sculpture, rather than the art of painting in which she had been trained, after the birth of her four children in the 1950s made it impossible for her to continue her dancing

career. Sullivan recalls that she felt her husband, who was also a painter, would feel threatened if she began painting again.

4 See Carolyn G. Heilbrun, *Writing a Woman's Life* (New York: Norton, 1988), for a critical study, and Carol Shields' *The Stone Diaries* (Toronto: Random House, 1993) for a novelistic rendering of this incompatibility between women's lives and the shaping quality of narrative.

5 Heilbrun, *Writing a Woman's Life*, 21

6 Borduas, *Refus global*, 35

7 *Une Mémoire déchirée* (Montreal: L'Arbre HMH, 1978), 143

8 See Renaud's second autobiographical work, *Le Choc d'un murmure* (Montreal: Éditions Québec/Amérique, 1988).

9 Mimi Lalonde, interview with the author, 30 Sept. 1994

10 *La petite Aurore* played continuously in Quebec from its inception in 1920 until the arrival of the film version in 1952. The film still appears fairly regularly on Quebec television, making the story one of the most formative myths of the Québécois consciousness. See Heinz Weinmann, *Cinéma de l'imaginaire québécois: de la petite Aurore à Jésus de Montréal* (Montreal: L'Hexagone, 1990).

11 Lalonde remembers the Renaud sisters as exceptionally creative and full of life, and Mademoiselle Rose as determined to block that creativity in every way possible. She recalls how they were made to wear shabby clothing to teach them 'humility,' and how Jeanne, the youngest and 'most feminine' of the three sisters, would try to hide the frayed cuffs of her blouse in front of her classmates in their bourgeois convent school.

12 Lalonde, interview

13 Christa Wolf, *Patterns of Childhood*, trans. U. Molinaro and H. Rappolt (New York: Farrar Strauss & Giroux, 1984)

14 Philippe Haeck, *Naissances: De l'écriture québécoise* (Montreal: VLB 1979), 125

15 Montreal: Les Cahiers de la file indienne, 1946 (unpaginated); reprinted in *Les Herbes rouges* 29 (août 1975)

16 Thérèse Renaud, 'Au temps du Refus global,' *Perspectives*, 4 Dec. 1971, 22–8

17 Renaud, *Le Choc*, 136

18 Thérèse Renaud, interview with the author, 25 Oct. 1993

19 The memoir opens with the following lines, which Renaud says unlocked a flood of inspiration and memory after twenty-five years of literary silence: 'The only real preoccupation of my life has been to be attentive to my inner demon. I know how to recognize the urgency of its voice, to navigate through the maze of the various situations it gives rise to, and choose the appropriate direction.'

20 'I wanted to be everything at once: mother, wife, lover, and free in my comings and goings ... not easy for a young woman imbued with the slogan

"There is no salvation outside the home"! ... And I was horribly timid, and
on the defensive. I hated having to beg an audition from these pretentious
and arrogant men.' Thérèse Renaud, 'Ah! vous avez dit chanter ...,' unpublished typescript, 1993, 4.

21 Ibid., 1
22 Letter to Fernand Leduc, 11 May 1963
23 Letter to Fernand Leduc, 20 May 1963
24 Letter to Margot Lespérance, 12 Nov. 1968
25 Saint-Lambert: Éditions du Noroît, 1981
26 Trois-Rivières: Écrits des Forges, 1990
27 Montreal: Éditions Triptyque, 1988
28 Renaud, interview
29 Letter to Jacques Allard, 10 June 1974
30 Letter to Denise Boucher, 8 March 1985
31 Jean Ethier-Blais, 'Quand l'immodestie frise le tragique,' *Le Devoir*, 12 nov.
    1988, D-18
32 *Le Choc*, 26–7
33 'It seems obvious to me that, as I had lost my mother at a very young age, my
    country took her place in a sort of identification and revolt that is difficult to
    explain, but that every young woman goes through at some point in relation
    to her mother.' *Le Choc*, 130
34 Renaud, interview

The Wrong Time and the Wrong Place: Gwethalyn Graham, 1913–1965

ELSPETH CAMERON

I used to tease her that everything she wrote was about herself. It was all about Gwen.

Isabel Lebourdais, Gwethalyn Graham's sister, 1994

I see novelist Gwethalyn Graham, age nineteen, standing on the end of a dock at Go Home Bay in Northern Ontario. She seems caught forever – as if in a photograph – on that windswept Muskoka Island that inspired her father's friend, painter A.Y. Jackson. This late-blooming woman, who had just won a scholarship for a second year at Smith College in Massachussetts, was about to meet her fate.[1] For driving towards her in a sleek, powerful boat with his father that summery day in 1932 was Jack McNaught, thirteen years her senior. A man recently returned from abroad, whose reputation as 'playboy of the western world'[2] preceded him. 'Jack saw her on the dock, and that was that,' a family member would later recall.[3]

When she had reached the island, Petra repeated to herself in a low voice the first line of 'Western Wind': 'Western wind when wilt thou blow,' and heard a masculine voice repeat the second: 'That the small rain down can rain.'[4] The voice was Richard Grey's ...

The understanding between them was almost instant and complete. Wading in the water and sitting on the sun-soaked granite of the island, each permitted the other to see into the inner core of their individual existence ... Richard was the first man she had ever known whose mind roamed the same by-paths, and who knew what she was talking about.

'West Wind,' c. 1940[5]

But I also see twenty-five-year-old political activist Gwethalyn Graham returning to Montreal from six months abroad in 1938, shaken by the suffering of refugees from Hitler's voracious imperialism. As if she were the subject of a compelling documentary film, she whirled into purposeful action: amassing statistics on the refugees pouring into Canada; identifying the insidious and pervasive anti-Semitism of the time; writing articles to make Canadians see the terrible truth she had witnessed; pitching her impassioned plea to dispel hypocrisy wherever and whenever she could; opening her home to the 'displaced persons' who arrived destitute in Montreal during the early years of the war.

The Nazis jeer at us [Canadians], say we make a great show of equality of race and creed, and criticize them for not wanting their Jews, while in actual fact we don't want them either. There is just enough truth in these accusations to make any honest Canadian uncomfortable.

'Refugees: The Human Aspect,' *Saturday Night*, 1938[6]

Gwethalyn Graham: a name now forgotten. Gwethalyn Graham: naive romantic and astute socio-political analyst. Gwethalyn Graham: passive victim and raging activist. Gwethalyn Graham: tragic failure and brilliant success.

What sense can I make of her? In the absence of the massive archival holdings and other documents typical of her male literary contemporaries – such as Hugh MacLennan or Morley Callaghan – what sense can I make of a career that encompassed one novel so saccharine that the movie rights were snapped up by Sam Goldwyn, and another so politically volatile that it was blacklisted by the Nazis? And both books deemed so excellent they won Governor General's Awards? Since no one bothered to save her personal letters (unlike the mothers of male writers whose hoardings in anticipation of the fame of their young sons are now carefully filed in various library collections), how am I to understand a woman so elastic that the tension between nineteenth-century notions of femininity and late-twentieth-century feminism finally tore her apart?

I must rely on the few documents that do exist and glean what I can from the few, often wary, interviews available. The paucity of such information is discouraging. But to give up, to let the inviting array of materials on male writers dictate who will be canonized by biographers is to confirm a skewed, male-centred literary tradition and further silence the women who were their equals, if not their superiors. As a biographer who has succumbed to the lure of the library in writing of

Gwethalyn Graham, with Earle Birney (left) and E.J. Pratt (facing Graham)

three male writers, I am challenged to redress the imbalance I have helped create. To do so in Graham's case is to fly in the face of the injunction almost universally agreed to by literary critics: fiction is not truth, it is *untrue*. I am convinced, on the contrary, after twenty years studying the connections between the lives of writers and their art, that all creations are autobiographical. Some, like the writings of Elizabeth Smart, are virtually indistinguishable from diaries or journals. Indeed, Smart's 'fiction' strikes me as more autobiographical than, say, the 'journals' of Susanna Moodie.

As Gwethalyn Graham's older sister's blunt remark that I have used as my epigraph indicates, those close to Graham testify that her experience fed her writing. The choice for me is between an academically self-righteous silence, which imprisons writers like Graham in unfair anonymity, or a no doubt flawed attempt to interpret the incomplete assemblage of documents, interviews, fiction, and non-fiction in order to release at least the echo of her voice. I believe her fiction is the site where the personal and political issues that gripped her can most authentically be heard.

'What do you do on the Post?' Marc Reiser asked.

'I'm the Woman's Editor – you know, social stuff, fashions, women's interests, meetings, charities, and now all the rules, regulations and hand-outs from the Wartime Prices and Trade Board that have to do with clothes, house furnishings, food, conservation of materials – that sort of thing.'

'How many pages?'

'Three or four, usually. Depends on which edition it is ...'

'Do you like your job?'

Erica paused, and said finally, 'Yes, I like working on a newspaper because I like people, particularly newspaper people, but I'm not a career woman, if that's what you mean.'

Earth and High Heaven, 1944[7]

'I'm always willing to play my part,' said Elsa, 'provided it's recognized that my part is anatomical drawing and not breeding children like guinea pigs.'

Christina looked a little worried. 'I wish you wouldn't be so ... so direct,' she said mildly.

'Scientific language,' said Elsa.

'Well, after all we're the ones who have children ... I mean men don't ...'

'They help,' said Elsa.

'Elsa!' said Christina reproachfully.

'All right, lambie.'

'And no woman wants to be married to a man who keeps house while she goes out to work,' said Truda, continuing in spite of them.

'I don't want to get married, though,' said Elsa. 'I don't mean that I've any objection to marriage ... I dare say it's all right, but I'm certainly not going to give up the work I've wanted to do all my life for the sake of it, any more than I'd expect my husband, if he were a doctor or a lawyer, for example, to give up practising medicine or law in order to marry me.'

'Well, it's not up to you to get in the way, either,' said Truda. Elsa raised her eyebrows but said nothing. 'And since it's a choice between you getting a job and some man who is either supporting a family now or will in the future, getting it, then you should stay home.'

'Why can't both Elsa and the man work?' asked Christina unexpectedly.

Swiss Sonata, 1938[8]

The naive romantic in Gwethalyn Graham was rooted in dreams that dodged distress. At Rosedale Public School, where the children of Toronto's wealthy elite were groomed – boys to seize power, girls to be decorative – Gwethalyn Graham Erichsen-Brown, born 18 January 1913, was huge and awkward. 'I remember,' her older sister Isabel says, 'the picture of the kindergarten class and all the other youngsters were the same size and there was one standing out like the classroom dunce – she [Gwen] said that later – even though she was the youngest.'[9] By age eleven, Gwethalyn was 5'8" and almost two hundred pounds. Her nose was too broad and her teeth protruded a bit.[10] By age twelve, enrolled in the prestigious girls' school, Havergal College, it was worse. 'Now we shall see the elephant perform,' her gym teacher announced.[11] It did not help that Gwen had an exceptionally pretty sister four years younger.

Gwen had fled into the dreams spun by such writers as Stendahl (her favourite), Willa Cather, John Steinbeck, Ernest Hemingway, Ford Madox Ford, Somerset Maugham, Thomas Wolfe, and Bessie Breuer to escape a vague but persistent sense of loss.

Someone had taken her downtown to stand on a street corner before a bluish-green fence and watch the soldiers going off to the Front [where her father had gone]. The band was playing 'The Girl I Left Behind Me' as they went by, and all about her were men and women crying in the street.

'West Wind,' c. 1940

Graham also escaped the ordeals of school at the movies – stealing money and playing hookey to do so.

School was hell. But summers were heaven. Immune from the Great Depression at Treasure Island in Go Home Bay, she mastered wind and wave by sail and canoe, lazed in the hammock reading, swam through delicious cool water, and put her strong body to good use chopping wood. One friend remembers the transformation this summer life wrought: 'She looked absolutely beautiful in a canoe.'[12] And it was at Treasure Island that she began writing – a career she had decided on at age six. 'She didn't go to family picnics, she was always typing away,' her sister recalls.[13] She wrote – then tore up – two novels before she was nineteen.[14]

Meeting Jack McNaught that summer of 1932 fired a relationship of such passion it consumed her. 'Jack was a spoiled playboy who had served in the navy, and who exuded culture in word and accent,' Graham's older brother John recalls. 'He had a wife who divorced him and three children who lived at Aurora [Ontario] who[m] C[harles] B[loyd] McNaught [Jack's father] was supporting. He was reputed to have slept around with more than one woman. He was the despair of his parents. The glaring example of a rich man's [only] son spoiled to the point that he had nothing to commend him ... It must have been apparent to him that this latest infatuation [with Gwen] also offered a prospect of rehabilitating himself in the eyes of his parents.'[15]

Jack's whirlwind courtship – like the west wind that bent Muskoka's trees one way and inspired the title for Graham's autobiographical novel – twisted her life to his will. Like Catherine in Emily Brontë's *Wuthering Heights* (a novel whose Yorkshire setting of wind-bent trees also inspired its title), Graham merged with the object of her love. Just as Catherine exclaims, 'I *am* Heathcliff,' Petra in 'West Wind' extols the merging of her soul with Richard's.

Graham lasted less than a month at Smith that fall. Jack followed her there, and – because a request for marriage had provoked her father's anger instead of his blessing – he persuaded Gwen to elope with him. All they had between them when they married 24 September 1932 was 'five dollars and a small volume of John Donne's poetry.'[16] 'It would not be true to say that if not McNaught it would have been someone else,' Isabel recalls, 'for he was a very unusual man, like a "matinee idol" from the London stage. I found him fascinating myself, though I never would have fallen in love with him ... But Gwen at nineteen had no defences. He beguiled her with every skill in the book.'[17]

Graham's father, Frank Erichsen-Brown, who as solicitor for Charles McNaught's insurance brokerage firm of Reed, Shaw and McNaught was privy to the financial chaos Jack's divorce had caused, was 'livid' about the elopement. He was soon convinced that Jack 'had deliberately got his daughter pregnant so as to cement his control over her, his parents, and their money.'[18]

Anthony Graham McNaught was born 1 July 1933.

Initially, Gwen was ecstatically happy with Jack. But others were sceptical. 'I didn't think he gave a damn about her,' recalls Isabel, who was a witness at their marriage in New York State. 'I remember thinking he was much more bossy than I thought he would be as Gwen's husband.'[19]

'I'd much rather take the very low spots [with Richard] in order to get the high than run along on the average level halfway between ... I'll take three days of hell to get twenty-seven days of heaven each month, and call it a bargain.'

Petra in 'West Wind,' c. 1940

Within a year, Gwen discovered that Jack was not just 'bossy,' but also physically violent. He could not control either his drinking or his temper. Worst of all, he had a mistress. Even more distressing than his physical and psychological abuse was the realization that their romance had been an illusion from the start. He had rekindled an earlier affair directly after their elopement. Graham began divorce proceedings before Tony was a year old. Her settlement was an allowance for Tony and herself of $50 a week from Jack's mother, Violet.

Given that for the Erichsen-Browns, who loved the theatre and entertained drama people, Sarah Bernhardt was off-limits because she had led an immoral life,[20] Gwen's short-lived romance and failed marriage incurred shame and – eventually – anger. In a fierce gesture of independence and a determination to begin life anew in Montreal, she had her surname and that of her son legally changed to 'Graham.'

The political activist in Gwethalyn Graham was rooted in reality. Her father's family were well-to-do English and Scots people. Her great-grandfather Brown (known as 'Gentleman Brown') was an ear, nose, and throat specialist who not only wrote an important textbook but also three historical novels set in southwestern Ontario where he retired to a farm. Her grandfather and father were lawyers.

But it was with her mother's side of the family – a much less conventional and decidedly more outspoken group of Maritime Scots – that Graham identified. She adored her maternal grandfather, James Frederick McCurdy, who lived with them in Toronto. The youngest gold medalist ever to graduate from Edinburgh, he was an outstanding and widely published scholar of Hebrew and Sanskrit. After being made unwelcome at Princeton for his radical views, he headed the Department of Oriental Languages at University College in the University of Toronto from 1906 until his death in 1935. 'He was an individualist in the finest sense of the word,' she is reported to have said of her 'strongest influence,' 'and I remember that he would not tolerate the use of any of the defamatory slang words which label national or religious groups on this continent – such words as 'Wop,' 'Mick,' 'Hun,' or 'Chink.''[21] Even McCurdy's father – her great-grandfather – had been noted for eccentricity. A Presbyterian minister in New Brunswick, he insisted – despite the disapproval of his elders – on having an organ in his church for the sheer pleasure of singing to an accompaniment and he encouraged his wife to wear colourful dresses instead of the conventional black to celebrate the happiness of religion.[22]

Graham's mother, Isabel Russell, carried forward and even exceeded her family penchant for unconventional behaviour. Marrying shortly after completing her BA in classics in 1904, she threw herself into a public life of politics, culture, and travel at the same time as she raised her four children in an extensive household that included her parents, her maternal aunt, and her husband's father, Dr John Price Brown – 'the ancestors' as they were jokingly called – and four servants. For a time her sister Hattie also lived with them after returning from a lengthy stint as a missionary for the Central Presbyterian Church in New York in Hwai Yuen, Anhwei Province, China.[23] A writer *manqué*, the matriarchal Isabel (who had once translated part of *Alice in Wonderland* into Greek for fun) took up writing satiric verse in her forties, and was given to sitting in the upstairs hall, reading loudly from one of the family's library of 6,000 books, while the rest of the family were in their rooms with doors ajar.

Isabel Erichsen-Brown was a woman of prodigious energy and commitment to the betterment of this world. She toured Germany in 1911 between the births of Isabel in 1909 and Gwethalyn in 1913; assisted as secretary for the Equal Franchise League in Ontario until 1917 when women secured the vote; served on numerous patriotic committees during the Great War, including the Serbian Relief Committee of Toronto (she received the Order of St Soba from the Serbian government); acted as secretary for the League of Women Voters, a group dedicated to educating women on public issues; campaigned for pasteurized milk and isolation hospitals; visited Italy, France, Palestine, and Egypt in 1929–30 while Gwethalyn was at Havergal College (her own alma mater); helped administer the Women's Musical Club, the Women's Canadian Club (she convened the annual literary contest), the Toronto Ladies' Club, the University Women's Club, and the Women's Art Association.[24] In all these activities she was encouraged by her husband, Frank. On one notable occasion he jumped onstage to quiet a crowd of men who were heckling a suffragist advocating the vote for women.[25]

The Erichsen-Browns' spacious, three-storey, flower-filled home resounded with family debates on every possible subject. Sunday at-homes were memorable, as Isabel gathered a motley assembly of artists such as A.Y. Jackson, actors such as Maurice Colborne and Barry Jones from London, political refugees or activists such as the British suffragette leader Sylvia Pankhurst, musicians such as the Adaskins, and entertainment personalities such as Walter Huston of Broadway and Hollywood fame.[26] Gwethalyn was in her element in this milieu. At eight, she had named her goldfish after several of her family's guests and had composed a newspaper called 'Life in a Goldfish Bowl.'[27] As her sister Isabel (who would later publish the controversial bestseller

The Trial of Steven Truscott)[28] recalls, 'I was very shy in talking to adults, who I figured were much wiser than I was. Gwen was never. Not a bit. I can remember Gwen when she would be about thirteen, carrying on an animated discussion over one of Shaw's plays with, oh, I think somebody who was an editor or something; and he was just flabbergasted that this youngster expressed herself so well and was so intensely interested in telling him what she was thinking.'[29]

Gwethalyn Graham's privileged life, the models set by her parents – especially her mother – and the family ideology of individualism, political crusading, cultural sophistication, and internationalism, were being confirmed and enlarged at Smith College. Her marriage to Jack McNaught and the birth of Tony abruptly terminated any further education – a situation that limited the degree to which she could later become a socio-political commentator.

In 1929, Graham had been taken from Havergal College and placed in a school she hated even more – the Pennsionnat des Allières in Switzerland. This international girls' school later formed the basis for Pensionnat Les Ormes in *Swiss Sonata*, the autobiographical novel she drafted between November 1933 and July 1934 immediately after leaving Jack McNaught, then rewrote in 1935, and again in 1937.[30] At the Pennsionnat des Allières she was horribly homesick, feeling such distress that she considered jumping from a window to certain death.

The nun still walked back and forth, back and forth ... Hail, Mary, full of grace, gratia plena ... then before Rosalie's terrified eyes she stopped, holding the railing with both hands, looking downward. She stood there a very long time, then, so quickly that Rosalie could hardly see her, she put one foot over and was gone, her skirts flying out as she fell.
Swiss Sonata, 1938[31]

But as the school year progressed – especially after a Christmas Mediterranean cruise with her mother and sister Isabel during which she had her seventeenth birthday in Nice – she began to enjoy it. 'I don't know how the Swiss schools can take students of fifteen or twenty nationalities with nothing in common except their ignorance of French,' she would later comment in grudging tribute, 'and provide them in a matter of months with a knowledge of the language that remains with them for the rest of their lives; but Swiss teachers are trained to do just that.'[32] At the Pennsionnat des Allières, Graham befriended a number of girls; in particular, an Armenian, an Italian, a Pole, and an American Jew. There, too, she met Joyce Tedmen from Toronto to whom she dedicated *Swiss*

Sonata (originally called 'Vicky' after the Torontonian main character), a stunningly incisive political allegory in which twenty-seven female characters – staff and students at the pensionnat – represent in microcosm the fierce international currrents swirling through Europe in the three days that preceded the Saar plebescite on 1 March 1935 that returned the Saar to Hitler's Germany. The school symbolized the League of Nations as Mlle Tourain, the headmistress, attempts 'to weld together the various nationalities.'

If the atmosphere of this school continues to be as strained, as unpleasant, as it is at this moment, we shall lose our pupils ... and our means of livelihood. It's hard enough combining an American Jewess of Theodora Cohen's temperament with a hysterical fourteenth-century Fascist like Truda Meyer, without throwing in a peace-loving and devout Bavarian Catholic like Anna von Landenburg, a half-Jewish girl from the Saar who doesn't yet know what nationality she is, and adding a Swiss and English staff who are too detached to consider these girls as anything but so many troublesome children learning lessons in the schoolroom of a mountain village.

Swiss Sonata, 1938[33]

It is not surprising that *Swiss Sonata* was blacklisted by the Nazis. Graham includes details about the political and economic situation in Germany that were not widely known (or, if known, not acknowledged), even in Germany, until much later. Anna von Landenburg, the Catholic half-Jewish girl from Nürnberg, fears for her father, who is a counter-revolutionary.

She had heard of torturing and violence. The summer before, she and her aunt had been walking in the town; her aunt had suddenly caught her arm and pulled her into an alley, in time to prevent her from seeing some Communists being driven through the streets of Königsberg to a concentration camp ... but not in time to prevent her from hearing the whistling of whips in the air; the screams and wails of women.

Someone had told her ... was it Ida? ... of a small village where one of the men had flown a red flag. The Nazi Storm Troopers came and beat up the men in full sight of their wives, mothers, sisters and children, then loaded them into lorries and took them away.

Swiss Sonata, 1938[34]

Graham's six-month trip to England, France, and Switzerland, right after the publication of *Swiss Sonata* in early 1938, confirmed her grasp of these sinister events. From the stories of refugees in the streets, she obtained first-hand information about Hitler's *Anschluss,* in March 1938, and the Sudetenland crisis, which erupted in April of the same year.

Graham concluded that democracy is vulnerable and precious. But she saw, too, that democracy was only partially realized in the western world. Much work was needed to dispel smugness, dismantle prejudice, and free the individual to become the basis of an economic system based on consumption rather than profit. 'Both in national and international fields,' she, like her grandfather, was to observe, '[the individual] must be freed from the prison of judgements based on so-called "group religious or racial" characteristics.'[35] It was an idea that found expression in her journalism at the time and one that led directly into her next novel, originally titled 'The Case for the Defence' but published as *Earth and High Heaven.*

In *Earth and High Heaven,* the romantic and analytic sides of Gwethalyn Graham's nature coalesced. Her move to Montreal – the city she especially loved – in 1934 had given her a new start. She had long since emerged from awkward adolescence to become a glamorous blue-eyed brunette of remarkable poise and presence. As one journalist put it, she was by 1938 'a tall, dark, striking-looking girl ... and a brilliant, persuasive conversationalist.'[36] Jack McNaught had reinvented himself as James Bannerman and disappeared from her life. She had set in place her career as a journalist. Now the success of *Swiss Sonata,* which won the Governor General's Award for fiction, paved her way into the cultural community of Montreal. Writing by day, she entertained in her elegant Dorchester Street apartment, all whites and pale furniture, by night. A goddess-like presence remembered especially for her dramatic red velvet hostess gown, she attracted a stellar salon: fellow writers such as Gabrielle Roy or Hugh MacLennan and Dorothy Duncan (later also a painter); political activists such as F.R. Scott and painter Marian Scott; professionals such as Trotskyist lawyer Maurice Spector, and a host of newly arrived refugees from Czechoslovakia, Austria, and Germany whom she met through her work with Montreal's Committee on Refugees. Among these were many who were later to contribute to Canada's intellectual, cultural, or business life: Frederick and Gertude Katz, for instance, and Victor Block, Eric Koch, Henry Kreisel, John Newmark, Franz Kramer, Henry Finkel, Walter and Greta Schmolka, and Helmut Blume.[37]

It was in Toronto, though, where she and Tony – now seven – spent much of 1940, that she met a Canadian Jewish lawyer and once again fell in love. Despite the fact that her father had supported her mother's social activism, which because of the war had taken the form of opening their home to refugees – Jewish and non-Jewish – he refused even to meet Gwethalyn's suitor. According to Isabel, there were actually four or five Jewish lawyers pursuing her sister at about this time, and their father disapproved of them all.[38] The 'titanic struggle' (as John, their brother, had described the earlier conflict involving Gwethalyn, Frank, and Jack),[39] between the infatuated daughter with an unsuitable lover and the father who was certain marriage spelled disaster, was taken up again. This time Frank Erichsen-Brown won.

Out of this situation, Graham devised the plot for *Earth and High Heaven*. Twenty-eight-year-old journalist Erica Drake falls in love with an Austrian Jewish lawyer, Marc Reiser, and their courtship is blocked by her father, Charles, an importer of rum and molasses and resident of Westmount, Montreal's Anglo-elite bastion. Charles, like Frank, suspects Reiser of wanting to use Erica to 'rise' professionally and socially – just as Jack McNaught had done. Graham suggests Charles's motive is Oedipal.

> 'I suppose you realize that there's never going to be anyone Charles will let you marry,' [her sister Miriam said.]
>
> 'Why not?'
>
> 'You're too important to him. Sometimes I think he could get along without Mother better than he could get along without you, at least in some ways ... He's going to hang onto you as long as he possibly can, and I'm willing to bet you anything you like that no matter whom you pick, [Father] will try to stop you from marrying him.'
>
> 'There's no way he can stop me,' said Erica. 'This is 1942, not 1867.'
>
> Earth and High Heaven, 1944[40]

Half Harlequin romance in which true love conquers all, half socio-political exposé of the prejudices and politics of church and state in war-time Montreal, *Earth and High Heaven*, which was published simultaneously by Jonathan Cape in England and Lippincott in the United States, was a success beyond anything Graham or anyone else could have anticipated. *Collier's Magazine* paid $7,500 to serialize an abridged version before its October publication and soon bought back every available Canadian copy to meet American demand when the magazine series sold out. The novel was the October selection for the Literary Guild of America, earning $42,000. The book eventually sold, in all editions, including a special American armed forces edition of 350,000 copies, a million and a half copies. For the first time ever, a Canadian novel topped the American bestseller list for a year in 1945. Sam Goldwyn bought the movie rights for $100,000. *Earth and High Heaven* garnered Graham's second Governor General's Award for fiction and tied for the *Saturday Review of Literature* Anisfield Wolf Award for the best work on race relations. Eventually, it would be translated into Braille and eighteen languages.[41]

Ironically, the stunning success of *Earth and High Heaven* was a coup from which Gwethalyn Graham never recovered. Suddenly she was famous, and rich. Her earnings from journalism and *Swiss Sonata* over the previous decade had been a meagre $1,100 – an income she had had to supplement by working during the winters in New York as an occasional agent for Jonathan Cape, her English publisher. Now the relatively huge income from her second novel plunged her into tax problems that occupied most of her time and energy for the next two years. Eventually, by spearheading a committee of the Canadian Authors Association with her father's legal advice and the help of Hugh MacLennan (whose early publications *Barometer Rising* [1941] and especially *Two Solitudes* [1945] were also taxed as if major novels could be produced annually), she convinced the federal government to amend the tax law to allow authors to prorate their income over up to three years, the usual time span for writing a novel. This amendment was finalized on 27 June 1946, too late for her to benefit from it for the windfall of *Earth and High Heaven*. Her taxes for 1944 were $65,000 – the equivalent of the cost of one wartime destroyer, as she liked to say.[42]

No film of *Earth and High Heaven* was ever made, despite the fact that six writers produced screenplays between 1945 and 1947, and Sam Goldwyn sent photographers to shoot Montreal in preparation for designing a set. Graham and Goldwyn had agreed that Katharine Hepburn and Gregory Peck should be cast as Erica Drake and Marc Reiser.[43] Goldwyn was interested almost solely in the novel's romantic plot. As screenwriter Garson Kanin would recall in his memoir *Hollywood*, he thought it 'the most beautiful love story [he'd] ever read.' But the script writers focused instead on the novel's timely exposé of racial prejudice: 'They were all infected with the idea that in their adaptations they should preach against anti-Semitism,' Graham said in a 1960 interview, '[and] Mr Goldwyn did not want that kind of treatment.'[44]

The events that followed the publication of Laura Z. Hobson's *Gentleman's Agreement* in 1947 – a romance involving anti-Semitism – dashed all hope of transferring Graham's novel to the screen. Twentieth Century-Fox quickly made an Academy Award–winning film of

Hobson's novel, starring Gregory Peck. Sam Goldwyn announced that he did not intend to make another film on the same subject.[45]

The turbulence of fame and fortune so affected Graham that she could not complete another novel, though she did continue to produce articles on such subjects as immigration, Quebec politics, publishing problems, and – when she married David Yalden-Thomson, an Englishman who taught philosophy at McGill – the experience of renovating and moving into a house, for such magazines as *Maclean's*, *Chatelaine*, and *Saturday Night*. Reasons for her creative paralysis were widely offered. Monica McCall, her friend and New York literary agent, recalls, 'She was flabbergasted by the big success of her novel ... It overwhelmed her and she panicked that she could never repeat it.'[46] Her son recalled much later, 'She felt a compulsion to become an achiever, to vindicate herself, to acquire value. When she acquired it, she realized that it was hollow. She was not spiritually or philosophically prepared for success in any way and she didn't realize that it's empty. And so when she became successful ... the things that she thought she wanted ... were not what she wanted really. And it left her in a complete vacuum, completely demoralized.'[47]

Graham's choice of subject for the novel she began after *Earth and High Heaven* was ill-fated. She intended to deal 'principally with English-French relations and the effects of monopoly capitalism working jointly with the church to maintain the status quo.'[48] It was a subject she was well able to tackle: she had already dealt deftly with it in the sub-plot of *Earth and High Heaven* through the character of René Sevigny, a Quebec Catholic and politician; and she had written articles such as 'We Are a Self-Satisfied Nation ... Feeding on Racial and Religious Prejudices,' which thoughtfully analysed what was about to become *the* Canadian subject. In fact, Graham was in most ways better-suited to deal with the subject she had chosen than the novelist whose name became indelibly associated with it before she could complete her book: her friend, Hugh MacLennan. His *Two Solitudes*, which appeared a year after *Earth and High Heaven*, presented somewhat woodenly through social and political stereotypes what she was capable of presenting in more fluid emotional and political complexity. It is tempting to speculate that in conversations these two novelists probably had, the ideas for both books originated. If so, it may well be that MacLennan's success was at Graham's expense.

Angered by unfair tax laws, her energy drained in mothering Tony (who would go on to medical school at Cambridge, England) while trying to establish a career, overwhelmed by a success she found hollow, frustrated by the long dance with Sam Goldwyn to make her novel a film, thwarted by her father in her desire to marry, unlucky in the publication of both *Gentleman's Agreement* and *Two Solitudes,* and finally devastated by the infidelity of her second husband after following him to his new post in Virginia in 1958, Graham crashed into serious depression. She began drinking far too much, and sought help from a series of psychiatrists.[49] Her Montreal friends helped her financially, since she was capable only of piecing together part-time jobs such as marking high school final examinations. 'Her illness was not mental,' her son would later observe, 'it was spiritual ... Her self-image always stunk.'[50]

By 1960, she had begun to recover her equilibrium, writing scripts for television,[51] a new medium for which her talents were eminently suited. And, in November 1962, she met and befriended Solange Chaput-Rolland (a Liberal later elected to the Quebec National Assembly), whom she met on the 'Peace Train' when they both took part in a large delegation of women who presented briefs in Ottawa protesting nuclear arms. During that trip, the two women conceived *Dear Enemies* (originally titled 'A Curtain of Prejudice'[52]), the book they co-published in 1963 as the Quiet Revolution swept Quebec, an affectionate exchange of wise and politically incisive letters discussing English-French difficulties and proposing constructive solutions.

The two women had just obtained grants of $5,000 each from the Canadian Centennial Commission to prepare a joint diary ('The Picnic Papers') of their travels across Canada, and Graham had three other projects well in hand (a CBC-TV script, 'Death of a Stag,' on Quebec terrorism; and translations of Raymond Tanghe's *Laurier, artisan de l'uniti canadienne, 1841–1919* and Réal Benoît's *Quelqu'un pour m'écouter*)[53] when she sank into alcoholism and depression for the last time. She began to doze off mid-sentence, or fall suddenly in the street or down stairs.[54] 'First she was placed by her son and by others into a hospital for alcoholics in North Toronto,' recalls Isabel.

I had a call from the doctor there. He told me she was not an alcoholic, that she didn't fit any of the patterns. So she was released. Next Tony took her from the cottage to the psychiatric hospital in Penetang. She was drinking an awful lot at the time ... When I saw her she told me she was about to die. I didn't believe her. They took some X-rays, and the doctor said, 'You should get her to the best neurological hospital in North America.' So she went to the Montreal Neurological

Hospital. When I visited her there she told me she should go to a psychiatric hospital. So we put her in the Allan Memorial Institute in Montreal. When I went to see her there, she was very confused. She thought I had come from across the river for some reason. She pointed to a flower in her room and told me it was from our mother. Well, Mother had been dead for years. Soon after that visit, the doctors called to tell me they thought they saw some kind of a thing in the front of her head. They operated [back at the Montreal Neurological Hospital], and I saw her a few hours later. She looked as if someone had badly socked her and given her two black eyes. They had removed a cancer the size of your fist. She never recovered.'[55]

On 25 November 1965, Gwethalyn Graham died. Her son scattered her ashes into the west wind over the waters of Georgian Bay.

Very few Canadians remember Gwethalyn Graham. Certainly her reputation was eclipsed by that of Hugh MacLennan, though his literary sales were lower, his awards later, translations of his work fewer and his attempts to sell a screenplay futile. Even the reprinting of *Earth and High Heaven* in McClelland and Stewart's New Canadian Library series in 1960 stirred hardly a ripple in the currents of Canadian literature. For Gwethalyn Graham was in the wrong place at the wrong time. Born into an elite family that believed in women's rights and encouraged her to contribute to society, that same family could not grant her sexual equality with men. Had she, like her mother, engaged in her 'causes' within a respectable marriage, she would have been regarded as an interesting eccentric. But to conduct her life without reference to such upper-middle-class codes was intolerable. Her susceptibility to the romantic view of woman, love, and marriage was retrograde. It rendered her tragically vulnerable in her life – especially to the early marriage that cut her off from the education that would have augmented her career as a political journalist. And it made her prone to banality in her art. The melodramatic amours of Stendahl – the writer she most wanted to emulate – bore little resemblance to the tough 1940s glamour and pragmatic sexual relationships of wartime North America, which were quickly supplanting the codes her family espoused. On the other hand, her political activism, much more than her mother's, was far ahead of its time, and would be, with rare exceptions, the exclusive territory of male writers until the feminist revolution that began in the mid-1960s. Her hopes for individualism and ethnic equality would not be realized – even in principle – until the ethos of multiculturalism took hold in the late 1960s, after the public action as a result of John Porter's *The Vertical*

Mosaic (1965). Her interest in internationalism was out of step with the anxious nationalism that swept the wartime Canadian literary scene. She frankly discussed many feminist issues – abortion, illegitimate children, anorexia, domestic abuse, employment equity, sexual freedom for women, and the organization of women as a group against patriarchal social structures – that would not become common concerns for years. Her distaste for male hierarchies and entrenched elites, and her corresponding enthusiasm for interconnected individuals admired for intrinsic rather than inherited merits, anticipates feminist writings like those of Carol Gilligan, who compares male paradigms to ladders and female paradigms to webs in *In a Different Voice* (1982). And her exposés of anti-Semitism in Canada anticipate such studies as Irving Abella and Harold M. Troper's *None Is Too Many* (1982).[56]

Graham's major works won awards at a time when competitors were few. I am convinced that they could have won awards of the same calibre had they appeared when contenders were many. *Swiss Sonata*, with its all-female cast and brilliant three-part sonata structure, was a literary experiment too exceptional to be appreciated in its time. Nor could it receive its full due in a country with no publishing infrastructure and a minuscule literary community. *Earth and High Heaven* was a success for all the wrong reasons: it played to a sentimental audience, many of whom – like members of the Allied forces – were experiencing or knew of wartime romances like Erica and Marc's. This banal romance – so much less interesting than the subtle intrigues among the girls at Les Ormes – attracted droves of unsophisticated readers and obscured the remarkable literary skills and complex profile of social, political, ethnic, and feminist issues that the novel displayed. Canada was not ready to appreciate Gwethalyn Graham's extraordinary talents.

Even Graham's efforts to persuade the government to amend the tax laws regarding authors benefited others, but not herself. There is something poignant in *Dear Enemies*, her last work. In Solange Chaput-Rolland she found a soulmate – a woman who called forth her enduring interest in the French, her mother's political idealism and crusading spirit, a Liberal whose politics of individual rights so happily corresponded with her own philosophy of individualism, a federalist who loved Canada, a woman with whom she could communicate and co-operate as an equal on a mission, like her mother's, to make Canada a better place. Had Graham lived longer than fifty-two years, she would have seen many of the issues that consumed her interest come to the fore, and some of them, at least, realized.

The word for Gwethalyn Graham was committed ... *It does not mean going overboard for causes. It does mean the holding of some steadfast convictions and the willingness to translate them into action. Miss Graham in her all too short life had beliefs which burned like a steady flame. She did something about them.*

Obituary, *Montreal Star*, 1965[57]

What one word would capture her in my mind? Passionate. *She was always passionate about everything. She never did things by halves. She really was a plunger. She'd plunge in and out of anything, and while she was in it, it was very much a complete preoccupation with her. I think that's the one word I'd apply to her. It made her a sort of genius.*

Anthony Graham, 1979[58]

NOTES

1 Anthony Graham (Gwethalyn Graham's son), letter to Barbara Opala, 30 March 1980, as cited in Barbara Opala, 'Gwethalyn Graham: A Critical Biography' (PhD thesis, Université de Montréal, 1980), 22. I am on many occasions in this essay indebted to Dr Opala's research and to her personal cooperation in the preparation of this article.
2 Isabel Lebourdais, interview with the author, 22 Dec. 1994, Toronto
3 Leslie Sirluck, interview with the author, 7 Jan. 1994, Toronto. Leslie Sirluck (née McNaught) recalls her family's accounts of the meeting of her cousin Jack and Gwethalyn Graham as reported here.
4 'O Western wind, when wilt thou blow,
   That the small rain down can rain?
   Christ, that my love were in my arms
   And I in my bed again!'
     O Western Wind (c. 1530)
5 Gwethalyn Graham, 'West Wind' (unpublished novel, c. 1940, property of Catherine Graham [wife of the late Dr Anthony Graham] and of Isabel Lebourdais)
6 Gwethalyn Graham, 'Refugees: The Human Aspect,' *Saturday Night*, 19 Nov. 1938, 8
7 Gwethalyn Graham, *Earth and High Heaven*, New Canadian Library Series, ed. Eli Mandel (Toronto: McClelland and Stewart, 1969), 32. The original edition was published in London by Jonathan Cape, 1944.
8 Gwethalyn Graham, *Swiss Sonata* (London: Jonathan Cape, 1938), 112
9 Isabel Lebourdais, interview with Barbara Opala, 2 Oct. 1979, Toronto
10 Ibid.

11 Monica McCall (Graham's New York literary agent and friend) told Barbara Opala of this anecdote of Graham's in an interview 21 Sept. 1980, New York.
12 Ibid.
13 Lebourdais, interview with author
14 Main Johnson, 'Toronto Girl Writes Book, Tears Up Three of Four,' *Toronto Daily Star*, 19 Nov. 1938, 14
15 John Price Erichsen-Brown, letter to Barbara Opala, 30 March 1980
16 George Grishkalt told Barbara Opala of this anecdote of Graham's in an interview 23 May 1980, Rosemere, Quebec.
17 Isabel Lebourdais, letter to Barbara Opala, 30 March 1980
18 Erichsen-Brown, letter to Opala
19 Lebourdais, interview with author
20 Gwethalyn Graham and Solange Chaput-Rolland, *Dear Enemies* (Toronto: Macmillan, 1963), 49–50
21 'Gwethalyn Graham,' *Current Biography* (Jan. 1945), 6:16–18; Alexandrine Gibb, 'Blood, Sweat, Tears Writer,' *Toronto Daily Star*, 26 Nov. 1965, 14; Johnson, 'Toronto Girl Writes Book,' 14
22 Lebourdais, interview with Opala
23 Beth Paterson, 'Gwethalyn Graham,' *Liberty*, 1 June 1946, 14–15
24 'Mrs. Frank Erichsen-Brown,' *National Reference Book on Canadian Men and Women*, ed. H. Harrison, 6th ed. (Montreal: n.p., 1940), 107–9
25 Lebourdais, interview with author
26 Paterson, 'Gwethalyn Graham'
27 Margaret Aitken, 'Gwethalyn Graham: A Canadian Author with a Crusading Spirit,' *Saturday Night*, 28 Oct. 1944, 36
28 Isabel Lebourdais, *The Trial of Steven Truscott* (Toronto: McClelland and Stewart, 1966)
29 Lebourdais, interview with Opala
30 See Opala, 'Gwethalyn Graham,' 110, 30
31 Graham, *Swiss Sonata*, 314
32 Graham and Chaput-Rolland, *Dear Enemies*, 37
33 Graham, *Swiss Sonata*, 31, 33
34 Ibid., 103–4
35 Gwethalyn Graham, as quoted in *Current Biography*, 17–18
36 Johnson, 'Toronto Girl Writes Book,' 14
37 See Opala, 'Gwethalyn Graham,' 232–3
38 Lebourdais, interview with author
39 Erichsen-Brown, letter to Opala
40 Graham, *Earth and High Heaven*, 86–7
41 See Opala, 'Gwethalyn Graham,' 154–5. See also 'Gwethalyn Graham,'

Current Biography, 247. The novel tied with Gunnar Myrdal's *An American Dilemma: The Negro Problem and Modern Democracy* (New York and London: Harper and Brothers, 1944), an academic analysis of the problems of Blacks in the United States.

42 Lebourdais, interview with Opala, 2 Oct. 1979, and Anthony Graham, interview with Barbara Opala, 12 Nov. 1979
43 Paterson, 'Gwethalyn Graham,' 14–15; Gwethalyn Graham, letter to Edith Stanley, from Oaxaca, Mexico, 21 Jan. 1945; Mrs F. Damant, interview with Barbara Opala, 1 April 1980, Montreal; and Bernard Dubé, 'Shoestring to Do Script by Gwethalyn Graham,' *Gazette* (Montreal), 11 March 1960, 7
44 Dubé, 'Shoestring to Do Script,' 7
45 See the details of this situation as in Opala, 'Gwethalyn Graham,' 232–3
46 Monica McCall, interview with Barbara Opala, 21 Sept. 1979, New York
47 Anthony Graham, interview
48 *Current Biography*, 247
49 See Barbara Opala, 'Gwethalyn Graham,' 236–8; Lebourdais, interview with author
50 Anthony Graham, interview
51 Graham adapted two literary works for television: W.W. Jacob's 'The Weaker Vessel' and Dorothy Parker's 'Wonderful Old Gentleman.' See Opala, 'Gwethalyn Graham,' 240 for further details.
52 Thomas Sloan, 'Fluttering the Curtain of Prejudice,' review of *Dear Enemies*, *Globe and Mail*, 23 Nov. 1963, 24
53 See 'Award-Winning Novelist, Gwethalyn Graham, Dies in Montreal Hospital,' *Montreal Star*, 25 Nov. 1965, 1, 5.
54 See Opala, 'Gwethalyn Graham,' 246.
55 Lebourdais, interview with author
56 John Porter, *The Vertical Mosaic: An Analysis of Social Class and Power in Canada* (Toronto: University of Toronto Press, 1965); Carol Gilligan, *In a Different Voice: Psychological Theory and Women's Development* (Cambridge: Harvard University Press, 1982); Irving Abella and Harold M. Troper, *None Is Too Many: Canada and the Jews of Europe, 1933–1948* (Toronto: Lester & Orpen Dennys, 1982)
57 *Montreal Star*, 26 Nov. 1965
58 Anthony Graham, interview

'TRADITIONAL' LIVES

Settling the Score with Myths of Settlement: Two Women Who Roughed It and Wrote It

HELEN M. BUSS

One has to claim, with authority, the very grounds of identity that patriarchal ideology has denied women: a self worth its history, a life worth remembering, a story worth writing and publishing.

Leigh Gilmore, *Autobiographics*

Learning to read Canadian women settlers' memoirs in archival collections has been, for me, an education in unlearning myths of 'settlement.' One myth is the heroic one of men who explored, ranched, farmed, and harnessed the natural resources of the vast territory of Canada's western provinces in the name of progress. Another is the heroic one of women, which presents the Canadian West as a place where they could escape gender binds and share equally in the adventure, work, and benefits of the settlement experience. However, when I read the unpublished archival accounts of women settlers, I find that, although the writers may try to conform obediently to these heroic stereotypes, they are in fact writing accounts that also contradict these myths of settlement. After reading many accounts, I have become aware that no matter how upbeat the surface narratives of women's settlement memoirs may be, there is an undercurrent of forbidden discourse, a discourse of rebellious accusation and multiple breakings of the code of silence that families require of their female members regarding the deeds and misdeeds of men.

This forbidden discourse gives me a different definition of 'settlement': one that involves a different reality than the heroic myths. This reality reveals the unfairness of having to settle for a woman's place while performing men's work, of contributing without getting credit, of discovering that the keenness of men wears thin quickly, and of finding in the end that a woman may have to settle for a very different result than the adventure promised.

At the same time, these women's writings settle some important scores concerning the treatment of women at the hands of men. For those of us who read and publicize these writings, the score that most needs to be settled is the setting straight of the history of settlement. The achievement of these women is of a different mythic quality, one figured not by actions, but by the subversive use of words that serve to interrupt and rewrite patriarchal myth in ways that the writers may not have been entirely aware of. Thus, the 'greatness' of such women lies not in their deeds (although their struggles often stagger the imagination), but in their self-represented written lives as *read* by women in search of a female culture.

My emphasis on 'read' acknowledges my contribution as reader in the relationship between writer, text, and reader. As Philippe Lejeune has pointed out, the reader tends to merge the identity of author/narrator/protagonist when reading an autobiographical document and to 'overestimate the problem of the "reading act."'[1] We 'overestimate' only in the sense that in traditional literary criticism, the acts of reading are 'underestimated' in the text of the critic, theorized into impersonality, or hidden in carefully constructed, objective argument. The adoption of a critical method in which the reading act is foregrounded is particularly necessary in the case of settler women's memoirs for two reasons. Firstly, the writers are usually concerned with obeying codes, and a resistant reader, such as myself, is seeking the small breaks in the codes, not obvious on the surface.[2] Secondly, as Lejeune has pointed out, reading in archives involves the critic in an ethical dimension for, unlike reading published texts in established genre contracts, we are reading documents that may have been written and collected for reasons far different from the uses they are put to by present readers.[3] I propose that one of the ways in which we can solve the ethical dilemma of reading autobiographical documents in archives is to self-consciously examine our reading acts as we make them.[4]

Both the memoirs I will work with are chosen for their difference within a similar historical and cultural framework. Both women settled in the West during the first and second decades of the twentieth century, in areas not previously farmed by white people. Nellie Boon, a young mother of two children, left a comparatively settled area near Kamloops shortly before World War I to settle with her husband at

Pioneer woman washing

North Bonaparte in the Cariboo region of northern British Columbia. In 1903 Hermina Maria Nagel, a little girl of five years, left Austria with her family to settle near Grenfell, Saskatchewan. Later in life she wrote of growing up as part of a settler family.[5]

Nellie Boon certainly has the most positive attitude of the two writers. This may be because she did not have to move from one country to another to settle in a new place. If the venture failed, going back to Kamloops was much simpler than returning to a homeland across the ocean. As well, the interior of northern British Columbia has a less harsh climate than Saskatchewan prairie. Boon characterizes her husband, Bob, and herself as mutually enthusiastic in favour of the move north to the Cariboo. They are both, 'keen with anticipation over our new venture,' despite the fact that her 'relatives tried to persuade me not to take the trip. They said I was not cut out for roughing it.'[6] In fact, despite the difficulties of the trip and the trying conditions they meet living in a one-room cabin infested with pack rats and working an acreage seemingly haunted by the wailing spirit of a woman the Indians call 'stone woman,' Boon makes a very deliberate effort to participate positively in all aspects of the venture: 'As I wanted to do my share towards carving out our future home, I cooked enough to last two meals every evening when it grew dark. Then after the breakfast dishes were washed I went with my husband and children down to the lake. At times I helped Bob cutting the pines with the crosscut saw, and when I found the work too tedious, I chopped down slender cottonwoods with an axe while the children piled the branches to be burnt' (23).

This tendency in such women's memoirs to record daily life in detail allows alternative readings such as my own. Thus I note that although Boon does not analyse her situation, her devotion to detail allows me to see that the price of a woman's full participation in the pioneering venture involves doing double duty: she must do her woman's work as extra labour.

Despite her keenness for the possibilities for the new roles that the homestead adventure brought, it is when Boon is left alone with her children for the first time that she confronts the full impact of the 'adventure.' The retelling of that confrontation changes the writing in a subtle but real way. Her husband goes to Kamloops to bring back a herd of cattle, and she experiences an encounter with a particularly vicious bull (in new territory farmers were allowed to let stock range free), which chases her and her children into their cabin and keeps them prisoner for a whole day 'like a sentry on guard' (31). Ever confident, Boon tries frightening the bull with an umbrella, since she has heard that opening an umbrella in front of a bull is somehow terrifying to the beast. It proves not to be, and the enraged animal takes after her. Always a fast thinker, Boon remembers that running in a zigzag fashion is supposed to confuse a bull. This seems to work. On other days when the bull returns she learns to set the dog on him.

The incident would seem a small, even comic one, but it proves to be a turning point. It is as if being left alone gives her permission to write of her adventures *alone*. Early pages of the account are filled with the pronoun 'we': 'we were now thoroughly discouraged' (9), 'unharnessing the horses, we tied them to a tree' (9), 'we made a roaring fire in our stove' (10), and 'we went on a tour of inspection' (22). Certainly, the Boons begin as a team, since a basic subsistence level of life must be established together if they and their children are to survive. However, for Bob Boon at least, settlement quickly becomes gendered. More of his activities are necessarily undertaken in the company of male friends among the neighbours. Raising beef cattle and harvesting requires cooperative effort. As well, there are always reasons for going to town. The result is that Nellie Boon, who dreamed of a shared adventure, is more and more on her own. The pronoun 'we,' almost by circumstantial necessity becomes a rather tentative 'I.' At first it is an 'I' that can only claim its fear of bulls as its own: 'I was terrified' (32). But very soon Nellie Boon's 'I' has a slightly interruptive, if apologetic, quality. As she narrates the very important male activity of climbing on top of sod roofs to see if a forest fire is coming, she observes tangentially: 'I must not forget to mention that up in this lofty position we had a little garden where lettuce, radishes and spinach grew. All this *I* watered by hand and we had enough greens to last us a greater part of the summer. But *I* must not interrupt my story' (34, emphasis added). Here Boon's 'I' would seem almost incidental, especially since she dismisses it as an interruption. However, this casual 'I' becomes an 'interruption' in the sense that it interrupts the generic contract of the female settler memoir. A memoir, by definition, is one's record of the 'I' as part of a community, not the self-actualizing 'I' of autobiography. The construction of an 'I' that undergoes an individual or self-development is not typical of the memoir genre, a form that, as Marcus Billson has noted, concentrates on 'being-in-the-world,' whereas autobiography emphasizes 'becoming-in-the-world.'[7]

Soon Boon's 'I' seems a little braver as she describes a day when her children are lost and, searching for them, desperate with panic, tiredness overcomes her and she collapses in the forest. Lying there, telling herself not to give in to this strange lassitude, she suddenly undergoes a uniquely personal growth experience: 'To this day I don't know what happened. Something came to life – broke loose in me – something potent. I was now imbued with a new strength and will power. Not the same woman that had lain there a moment before – a poor helpless creature' (51).

Even the diction of the passage – 'potent,' 'imbued' – indicates a great change, a concern with self-development that is a rebellion against, a subversion of, the female place in the male-dominated settlement story. I am not arguing that the actual activity of seeking lost children is a rebellion; certainly it can be argued that in itself it is the very opposite of an emphasis on the 'I.' But the way Boon chooses to write of it is a rebellious gesture, a subversion of the contract that women take on (genuinely or as disguising rhetoric) when they take on the traditional form of a memoir recounting settlement. I note that Boon's record lacks the usual disclaimers that the memoir is being written at someone else's urging and is not a personal story, but which is retold to honour others and is written for posterity.

The pages that follow this incident in Boon's memoir show that she is, in terms of her written record, 'not the same woman.' She is willing to confess much more of her personal investment in the activities of homesteading. She informs us openly that when the men begin haying she has 'all the chores at home without assistance' (52), brags that she learns to calm a cow who will not be milked by the simple act of singing to her (54), and actually highlights her new physical strength developed hauling logs. While describing the communal nature of the cutting and hauling of trees as part of the Boons' mutual effort to build a home, she observes: 'We were happy working together this way, and the children loved to help ... Quite often I rolled my sleeves back and scrutinized closely the upper part of my arm to see how much muscle I was developing. Some people would think this was childish of me. But it had always been my desire to be the hardy Spartan type of woman, and not a so-called weakling' (55). Her husband teases: 'that's just flab, that's not muscle' (56), but later recants after she has cleared an astonishing amount of brush while he was away: 'You bet you've got muscle. I can feel it now' (56). Thus, while taking pride in her new strength, she carefully frames it in a discourse of community. She seems truly 'happy working together,' finding her 'Spartan type' of self in actualizing a shared dream with husband and children.

It takes two or three readings of this woman's memoir to realize that it is Bob Boon's loss of that shared dream that allows for the greatest rebellious gesture of Nellie Boon's 'I.' Gradually one becomes aware that although Bob is represented as keen on the adventure at the start, his enthusiasm flags easily. The first hint comes two-thirds of the way through the account, when the otherwise cheerful, oft-quoted Bob, who seems to be an authority on everything from birds to Indians, is portrayed in a less than positive light: 'At times he was moody, and I had to be tactful on these occasions. So I kept a silent tongue' (57). What worries Bob has troubled the venture from the beginning: the raising of cattle for profit. Unlike the milk cows brought with them and kept for family use, beef cattle are herded from Kamloops and then let loose to range freely in the bush where they are prey to rustlers or can feed on poisonous plants that eventually kill them. Bob Boon is frustrated by the loss of cattle, worried about the price of beef and the distance from market. Ignoring his wife's advice that 'the best thing we can do is not to put our eggs in one basket' (58), he finds that the Cariboo is a poor place to run the kind of specialized operation he is used to. As well, he thinks the early frosts will be a danger to wheat, and there will be no market for poultry. Nellie Boon, on the other hand, seems to be adjusting to the subsistence lifestyle of mixed farming dedicated primarily to the family's needs. Despite the dangers of bears, the bother of leaking roofs, plagues of flies, and constant work, she recounts the variety of activities necessary for survival, from berry picking to brush clearing, with obvious pleasure, a pleasure that is greater because of the company of her husband and children.

However, an extended period alone while her husband is in Kamloops harvesting her brother's crop (the brother has enlisted in the army at the outbreak of the World War I) undermines Nellie Boon's desire, no longer a mutual one, to make a success of the homestead. Once again, it is not in the events themselves, but in the retelling that the rebellion against a failure she feels was not hers takes place. She makes no secret of the fact that the arrangements made for her and the children while her husband is away are insufficient. The bull is still a problem; the wood supply runs out; and she is reduced to killing her laying hens, who are dying anyway because they have insufficient feed. At no point does Nellie Boon portray herself as heroic. She cannot even watch her ax fall as she beheads the unfortunate hens. Her nonheroic retelling is, ironically, part of the rebellion of this text, eliciting the reader's sympathy for the woman left alone. Indeed Boon cleverly crafts her reunion with her husband (after two cries for help by way of letters finally bring him home) into a dramatic retort: 'Shortly he arrived, and I will never forget the first words he said to me, as he drew up. "Have you got any meat? I've not tasted meat for three days." "Meat!" I repeated in an astonished tone. "I've never tasted meat for months"' (76). The retort may not be quite true (she did have the occasional scrawny chicken for the soup pot); however, it works quite well in terms of 'settling' a score in the retelling, a score she obviously felt to be important, considering the way the account now progresses. Her husband asks her why she didn't 'take a walk in the woods and pop off some game, like other women of these wilds do' (81). After suggesting that hunting 'with two little tots trailing behind me' might be difficult, she quickly invents a successful scheme to trade old clothing with the Indians for wild meat (which entails Bob having to look after the 'tots').

Reading many women's settler memoirs, by so-called 'naive' writers, has taught me to pay particular attention to moments when narrative is interrupted by the reconstruction of spoken exchanges, which the reader is implicitly asked to accept as a verbatim recounting of words spoken many years previously. It is possible that they are exact. Some occasions are so traumatic that we can recall exchanges in detail. The more likely case, however, is that when a writer reconstructs her exchanges with others in this testimonial fashion, an important scenic device is being used to good purpose. Dramatic reconstruction lends emphasis, authority, and verisimilitude to an account; it sets things straight for the writer and allows her to draw the reader into her version of history. Boon's account ends with their return to the more settled areas of Kamloops despite Nellie's attempt to cheer Bob up by suggesting that 'if we are patient we'll find the pot of gold at the end of the rainbow' (92). She represents her husband as responding with 'sarcasm' by telling her she is 'always building castles' (92). Boon portrays herself as a woman who has done her best and lost her dream; she has to settle for going back to Kamloops where she will also have to settle for the gender roles of a farm life that she briefly escaped, but she does not do so without settling a few scores and making at least a symbolic bid for equal status with her husband.

When Bob finally decides to 'pack up' after the loss of more cattle, she informs the reader that she 'was expecting this outburst' and responds to her husband by asking him what he will do 'with all the land' (93). When he announces 'bitterly' that he is 'through with it all ... It can go back to the government,' she 'eagerly' suggests, 'how would it do if you gave all this land to me to do as I like with?' (93). It is agreed between them that she will own the land, which she intends to sell, although her husband thinks she will 'have a job on your hands' to do so (94). She does sell the land, thereby becoming one of the rare women to own and sell homestead land (since women could not own land under the conditions of the Homestead Act[8]).

The modest Nellie Boon does not make this last point explicit in her account; however, the dramatization of her conversation with her husband in the concluding paragraphs of the memoir makes the point quite well nevertheless. Her ending is, on the surface, conciliatory, as is typical of a rebellion that must remain covert. She observes: 'I really think that all we went through gave us a different perspective on life' (94). The 'I' that has been constructed in this memoir carefully subsumes its subjectivity in the 'we' and the 'us' of the helpmate stereotype of women settlers' accounts. However, given my subversive reading of her rebellious writing, I cannot help but see the seemingly impersonal and factual final sentence of the memoir as yet one more retort to the husband who gave up too soon. Boon ends her account by observing of the Cariboo: 'There has been a big change there however. As the country became more settled, good, hard roads took the place of blazed trails, besides many other improvements' (94).

For a woman like Nellie Boon, merely choosing to end her memoirs with an account of her successful land dealings is enough of a rebellion. For some women, the scores that must be settled – especially the harshness of the gender position they have had to settle for after the settlement experience has proved they can do anything a man can do – are more complex. Temporary or symbolic acts of rebellion are not enough. History must be set straight. The act I have characterized as 'setting history straight' is what Marcus Billson says happens as a personal story inserts itself into long-accepted public history in the form of memoir: It 'defamiliarizes the common experience of the past, transforms it and makes it new.'[9]

Such is the case with Hermina Maria Nagel's memoir, called, significantly, 'Saskatchewan Prairie Girl.'[10] While Boon generalizes and communalizes her account by calling it 'Pioneering Days in the Wilderness,' Nagel's title speaks more directly to her own identity, forged from a childhood settlement experience. The fact that she settled in the Canadian West at the age of five and experienced the demands such a life involves for a child, a teenager, and a young woman, gives her a special viewpoint that women who experienced settlement as adults cannot have. In addition, at first she and her family did not speak or write English, thereby lengthening the period of isolation from their community and increasing the hardships that community-making tends to lessen. Like most settlement stories written by the children of pioneering families, this is primarily the story of the parents' struggles, which backgrounds the shaping of the personal self of the writer. The development of the self of the narrator is primarily available through the reading act by adopting the strategy that the parents are the (often opposing) models that shape the growth of the child's psyche. Therefore, when we see the focus of the memoir returning again and again to these figures we may read this focus in terms of the writer's self-development. As well, since memoirs thrive on an abundance of detail, detail can also be read metonymically, to discover the typical patterns of a growing child's psyche within her family.

In studying Nagel's memoir I have wondered why the book-length (340 pages) manuscript has never been published. It is one of the most vigorously written and gripping tales of the West that I have read. It fulfils what Billson has named as an important requirement of memoir, that it present a cogent 'moral vision.' The memoir writer 'thinks it is his duty to fix in form and imbue with significance the random, haphazard, and accidental that once existed but would be forgotten without his narrative.'[11] This desire to give personal meaning to historical events, meaning that can explain the self, is particularly a drive for women in the twentieth century. As Lee Quinby had pointed out, various forms of memoir can act as a 'material practice' through which marginalized persons can refuse 'the totalizing individuality of the modern era' and map out 'new forms of subjectivity.'[12]

Nagel's text certainly offers both a moral vision of the world and an experiment in alternate self-construction. However, when I think of the kind of stories written by settlers' children that do get published (and I have read a number), I realize that Nagel's memoir breaks a basic rule of settlement myths: it portrays a typical settler father who is a hard-working, goal-oriented, talented, ambitious man capable of enormous work – as men had to have been to undertake the monumental tasks of settlement successfully – but also reveals a narrow-thinking, demanding, impatient, dictatorial, and abusive man.[13] As soon as I write these words, I must assure my reader that this is not a one-sided, whining memoir that puts down Dad as bad and validates everyone else as innocent victims. Part of the exceptional nature of this account is its fairness. Nagel often interrupts her narrative to be fair to both mother and father, explaining their motivations, delighting in their talents and abilities, giving accounts of good times as well as bad. She also gives much more attention to the lives and motivations of siblings than is typical of such memoirs. Most importantly, her account suggests that families pay a terrible price for the father's dream of settlement in the new world.

Nagel takes two opening chapters to establish the groundwork of her complex portrait of her family. She dramatizes the division between the father who is gradually convinced by the rhetoric of the land agents and the mother who resists the move. Anton Stradecki is at first sceptical: 'Why should I! I have my job and security here! It is my home, my life!' However, he quickly thinks of good reasons to undertake the adventure: 'But what is the future for my boys? As soon as they become eighteen they have to serve in the army for several years and will they be able to get a good job?' (4). The mother worries about his search for information about Canada: 'Will he be able to distinguish between what is true or what is not true?' (4–5). Nagel portrays her mother as actually hostile to her husband: 'A feeling of dislike welled up in her chest towards her husband' (5).

It is important to distinguish between the intentions of Nagel and a writer such as Boon. In Boon's account the rebellious content may well be unconscious, or at least veiled. I find Nagel's writing acts to be a deliberate rhetoric directed towards an alternate version of the settler experience. Nagel was under the age of five when she immigrated and could not possibly have remembered the detail of parental decision making that she constructs in chapters 1 and 2. Although other details – such as the beauty of their small acreage in the lush Austrian countryside, and her grandmother's extreme grief at their departure (she had to be pulled bodily from her daughter) – might quite conceivably be part of a small child's factual memory, the detailed dramatization of parental disagreement is an act of creativity, no matter how closely the creation may resemble the stories retold in the household later. It is these writing acts, acts that work from a factual base while using the imaginative devices of fiction, that make Nagel's account an exceptional memoir in its ability to set history straight through construction of a different version of the truth than is typical in the settlement myth.

Her detailed dramatization of the decision to leave what is portrayed as a good life in Austria is part of the construction of the 'moral vision' of this text, one in which Nagel highlights the viewpoint of her mother, Sophie, on the man who is the 'hero' and instigator of the family's settling enterprise. She does this through an imaginative recreation of her mother's thoughts after accepting that her husband is 'boss' and they must go with him:

I suppose once we get to Canada and are somewhat settled there, I will like it. What's more I have my husband and my children with me. I know Anton is much too strict with me and our children. Also if he would at least try to check his wild ferocious temper. Still I appreciate him. He never drinks much. Doesn't gamble. He lives a decent life. He is as honest as the day is long. He hardly ever smokes more than six cigarettes, which I roll for him everyday. He doesn't mind working hard for us, though he makes sure that our children do their share too, according to their ages, at least by helping me to work our land and look after the cows, which is only right! We are richly blessed. He is a good provider! We always had a roof over our heads. We never had to go hungry. I am sure he would give his life for us! More he could not do! Again thoughts came to her mind, 'Does he want to go to Canada to satisfy his own venturesome nature? Or is he doing it to give our family a better chance in life?' (7–8)

I offer this lengthy quotation from the early pages of Nagel's memoir to show how she portrays the typical patriarchal family working successfully, both economically and socially, but also suggests the possibility of how individualism ('his own venturesome nature') may be the cause of later problems. It takes over three hundred pages to historicize the settlement experience in the daily detail necessary to allow the reader to understand just how enormous the pressures on the family became.

The dichotomy I have found in all settlers' stories is that it takes a man who privileges his 'own venturesome spirit' to embark on such an enterprise as settlement in a foreign country where his skills and energy will be severely tested. Ironically, in successfully meeting the demands of the adventure, he may sacrifice the one thing that he believes justifies the undertaking: the welfare of his family. This is Anton's story as told by his daughter. Even before they leave Europe, the baby of the family dies of pneumonia during the train journey to Hamburg, and the family cannot attend her funeral without missing the boat. When Anton and Sophie and their seven remaining children reach western Canada, the father arranges to leave the two eldest girls, aged fourteen and twelve, in Grenfell to work as maids in the homes of townspeople. Except for the father, who must make biannual or sometimes annual trips to town, the rest of the family does not see the sisters for years (he takes the mother on one trip). It quickly becomes obvious that the eldest brother will need to supplement the family's cash income by working summers on the railroad. Each of these divisions, engineered by the father and agreed to (if reluctantly) by the mother, is seen as a sensible decision, good for the whole family: fewer mouths to feed, more cash for the homesteading endeavour (machinery, a big item not available in Austria, is now tantalizingly within Anton's reach, even if he can only afford second-hand items).

What makes Nagel's narration of these harsher elements of the settler story so believable is the detail with which she balances negative with positive experiences. She describes her mother's delight at her first glimpse of Canada and her pleasure at finding a Catholic Church and some German spoken in Grenfell. She describes, in full detail, the father's excitement when discovering Canadian farm machinery and fully credits the canny talents that allow him to make good bargains and make old machinery work efficiently. Typical of her strategy of giving both sides is this observation about their homemade furniture: 'In no time, Father had made furniture, which just a few days ago were proud trees standing grouped together. They had formed what we called a bush, that had given shelter to the countless varieties of birds, also wild animals ... Only the straightest logs were split evenly then smoothed with the hobel (plane) cut to the needed lengths and nailed together. We called that furniture, of which we were proud!' (58).

During my first reading of this passage I wrote in my notes, 'Is this conscious?' because I could not quite decide if this 'naive' writer was aware that she had both praised the father's ingenuity and described how the settlement activity adversely affected the natural world. But once this conjunction of a discourse of settlement and a discourse of ecology occurred a number of times, I began to accept it as a deliberate rewriting of the settlement myth, which normally is negligent of, if not actually hostile to, the original flora and fauna.

One of the most disturbing realities acknowledged by Nagel's memoir is the possibility that the enterprise of homesteading can not only stress families, but make them dysfunctional. With the absence of the eldest son and two elder daughters, activities that would seem very difficult for small children become the necessary duties of Nagel and her elder brothers Karl, ten, and Fergi, eight. The boys eventually graduate from cattle herders to full helpmates to their father, and responsibility for the cattle falls to Nagel: 'I was now 8 years old and so I was given more responsibilities, besides helping poor Mother who was already doing work for three men. We now had four milk cows, a young bull, five calves of different ages' (115). Nagel describes her work as herder, the dangers of wild packs of coyotes, which sometimes attacked calves in unsettled country, her own fear that she is small enough to be attacked, the problems of keeping mosquitoes from driving the cattle wild, the pain of her shoeless condition and the bleeding feet and legs that are her continual problem as nettles and stones cannot be avoided. As well, she must contend with the debilitating loneliness and fear experienced by an eight-year-old child spending her days entirely alone for the first time: 'For the first month or more, when I was out with the cattle, I was crying my eyes till they got blood red. I felt so lost and so utterly lonely!' (117). By age eleven, as brothers graduate to paid work and her father's energies are diminished by poor health, Nagel becomes a full field hand. This follows on an offer to her of a place as a domestic servant, which her father turns down since he needs her too much on the farm. (Nagel's formal education lasted three months, curtailed because her work was essential on the farm.)

I am not trying to argue that the dysfunction of this family lies in its overworking the children, since hard work was everyone's lot, and Nagel is the first to acknowledge that the whole family worked hard. I am arguing that the fact that Nagel had to take up boys' and later men's roles early in life and had to develop the physical strength and independence of body and mind that come with those roles, and yet found her family unchanged in their gender expectations of their daughter, causes a severe dysfunction between them. Besides being beaten by her father anytime she cannot quite manage the demanding tasks he sets her, she is whipped for any behaviour that indicates she might be a rebellious girl. The parents, perhaps in overcompensation for having to exploit their older children, give special attention to the youngest child, Liz, who never wears boys' hand-me-downs as does Nagel, and who is not introduced as early in life to farm work. Nagel becomes very jealous of her little sister and often fights with her. At the same time, her older brother Fergi excludes her from his companionships with neighbourhood boys, actually allowing another boy to drag her into the stable in a quasi-sexual attack, one that she cannot tell her parents about, because by now she has become known to both father and mother by her mother's term for her, 'der teibl' (that devil) (231). Nagel observes: 'I had a fear of my parents, more so of my Father, even though I had considerable love for both of them. Many times I wished that they would show a little more love and kindness toward me. They kept me a great distance apart from them' (230). It seems obvious, from a present day psychological perspective, that Nagel had become the family scapegoat: a girl never good enough to fulfil all the physical tasks required of an adult male farm hand exactly the way her demanding father wants her to and yet never quite appropriately gendered as a female to please her parents. She becomes the odd child, an embarrassment to her siblings, who often take advantage of her scapegoat role in the family.

Ironically, her inappropriate gendering results in the only concerted rebellion she makes against her parents: the refusal to marry young. The family arranges marriages in the traditional way (in fact, Anna the second eldest daughter, is forced to give up the boy she loves to marry inside her own religion and ethnic group). These marriages take place early in life, and the pressure begins for girls around age fifteen. Nagel resists, for several years, the combined efforts of father and mother (and, after her father's death, the equally intent efforts of mother and sister Anna) to marry her off.[14] Finally convinced that she will be that most dreaded of entities, a spinster, and finding herself without the actual freedom or even the knowledge to imagine another possible destiny, even one to which her love of reading (largely self-taught) might guide her, she accepts the offer of marriage of George Nagel. She does not represent the acceptance as an experience of falling in love, observing instead: 'Was it romance? or was it just because we were both ready to get married and I had no prospects? The matchmakers hit the Nagel (nail) on the head at the right time! And so it happened very suddenly' (324). The narrative that follows this observation indicates that Nagel feels hit on the head in more than one sense.

The last chapter of the manuscript, entitled 'Getting Ready for the Wedding and the Life Thereafter,' is a detailed account of how a daughter is prepared to be a 'bride.' It does not romanticize the process, but emphasizes the lack of opportunity for the young couple to get to know each other, the family politics involved in the arrangements, and the fear felt by a young woman entering a new family. Nagel offers us no details of the actual ceremony, except this observation, one charged with symbolism for a reader such as myself: 'As George and I stood before the priest, repeating our vows, I hardly realized that a very great miracle was taking place. From Mary Hermina Stradecki, I became Mina Nagel. My husband liked the name Hermina better than Mary, but he cut off the first part and from now on I will be Mina!' (330–1). It would seem that the 'Life Thereafter' of the chapter's title requires a truncated and imposed identity, being renamed by another to begin in a new role.

Nagel does not say whether this renaming was to be one more imposition of others' needs on her identity, or a freeing of the self from past impositions, since the manuscript ends with the marriage and move to the husband's district. However, it is interesting to note that the woman who is designated as 'H.M. Nagel' on the archival file does succeed – if not in the acts of her life, then in the act of her writing – in constructing a memoir that subverts some of the most dearly held tenets of the settlement myth and that, carefully read, can help us to a fuller understanding of this period in our history.

Memoir writers such as Nellie Boon and H.M. Nagel give the concept of 'settling' a new meaning. Reading their memoirs reveals the full unfairness of the gender inequalities of the settlement experience. Yet there is a positive side to the experience of having to be amazingly adaptable and learn new skills outside the domestic realm, even if it does not lead to gender equality in personal life. I think their hardships gave these women the courage and desire to write in opposition (however muted) to the ideology of their time and place. In doing so, they offer feminist researchers in the present the opportunity to revise our cultural myths and settle the score for women involved in the history of the settlement of the West. In doing so, we 'claim, with authority, the very grounds of identity that patriarchal ideology has denied women: a self worth its history, a life worth remembering, a story worth writing and publishing.'[15]

NOTES

1 Philippe Lejeune, *On Autobiography*, ed. Paul John Eakin, trans. Katherine Leary (Minneapolis: University of Minnesota Press, 1989), 157. Lejeune quotes the work of Elizabeth Bruss, *Autobiographical Acts: The Changing Situation of a Literary Genre* (Baltimore: Johns Hopkins University Press, 1976), who transfers the work of speech act theorists into a theory of autobiography.
2 I do not mean to suggest a traditional deconstructive reading, where the critic reveals an ideology the writer is completely unconscious of; rather I seek signals of complicity between myself and the writer, verifying them by their repetition, through unusual acts of dramatic reconstruction, unusual diction, and other emphasis added. For explication of this reading method, see my *Mapping Our Selves: Canadian Women's Autobiography in English* (Montreal and Kingston: McGill-Queen's University Press, 1993), 21–7. For an analysis of 'emphasis added' and other reading techniques used in decoding women's autobiography, see Nancy Miller, *Subject to Change: Reading Feminist Writing* (New York: Columbia University Press, 1988).
3 Lejeune, *On Autobiography*, 210–13
4 See my articles 'Constructing Female Subjects in the Archive: A Reading of Three Versions of One Woman's Subjectivity' in *Working Women's Archives*, ed. Helen Buss and Marlene Kadar (North York: Robarts Centre for Canadian Studies Monograph Series, 1995), and 'Decoding L.M. Montgomery's

Journals / Encoding a Critical Practice for Women's Private Literature,' *Essays in Canadian Writing: The Gender Issue* 54 (Winter 1994): 80–100.

5 Spelled 'Grenfel' in Nagel's account

6 Nellie Boon, 'Pioneering Days in the Wilderness,' British Columbia Archives and Records, File E/D B643, p. 2

7 Marcus Billson, 'The Memoir: New Perspectives on a Forgotten Genre,' *Genre* 10, no. 2 (Summer 1977): 261

8 The Homestead Act gave free land to any man who could 'prove up,' that is, clear a set acreage and build a dwelling in a designated time period. Although women's labour was often essential to this effort, women were not eligible to undertake the effort under their own names.

9 Billson, 'The Memoir,' 262

10 H.M. Nagel, 'Saskatchewan Prairie Girl,' National Archives of Canada, File 30 C 237

11 Billson, 'The Memoir,' 269

12 Lee Quinby, 'The Subject of Memoirs: The Woman Warrior's Technology of Ideographic Selfhood' in *De/Colonizing the Subject: The Politics of Gender in Women's Autobiography*, ed. Sidonie Smith and Julia Watson (Minneapolis: University of Minnesota Press, 1992), 297–8

13 Published accounts by children of settlers, such as Mary Hiemstra's *Gully Farm* (Toronto: McClelland and Stewart, 1970) and Nellie McClung's *Clearing in the West* (Toronto: Thomas Allen, 1935), tend to idealize the male settler figure and show the mother as eventually accepting his ways as right. It is only in recently published accounts, which have been rescued from archives by (primarily feminist) scholars, accounts such as Susan Allison, *A Pioneer Gentlewoman in British Columbia: The Recollections of Susan Allison*, ed. Margaret A. Ormsby (Vancouver: University of British Columbia Press, 1976), that we can begin to hear the other side of the settlement story.

14 Nagel's father died of complications brought on by an unnamed allergic reaction that went untreated for some time. The symptoms listed sound remarkably like hay fever.

15 Leigh Gilmore, *Autobiographics: A Feminist Theory of Women's Self-Representation* (Ithaca: Cornell University Press, 1994), 51

Anna of Intola:
A Finnish-Canadian Woman with *Sisu*

BEVERLY RASPORICH

I never met Anna Koivu, but as I listen to a tape of her voice, recorded when she was in her eighties, I am struck by its animation. She is on stage, performing, as she recounts her life, with the perfect timing of an expert storyteller. I am mesmerized by her. I am comforted, too, by a familiar Finnish-English accent, which, in its recognizable rhythms and intonations, recalls for me the voices of my grandparents. My grandmother first inspired my admiration for Finnish women like Anna. The daughter of a judge in Finland, my grandmother was an immigrant woman who bought her own real estate with money earned by scrubbing floors, a woman who said that had she been born a man, she could have become a millionaire. To her, making money in this new country seemed such an easy thing to do if you were the right gender. Although she doted on her sons, she seemed to me, from a child's point of view, to be somewhat disconnected from the world of the men around her. A number of Finnish women that I came in contact with in the community of Thunder Bay where I grew up had that same quality or attitude. It puzzled me then and, to some extent, still does. Why were they more independent in their thinking, more confident in their self-determined goals, than the mature women I knew in the Anglo-Canadian cultural mainstream?

The answer lies partly in immigration history. From 1900 on, many Finnish women emigrated as single women; they found economic freedom in the new world because they were in such high demand as housemaids;[1] as well, independence was the cultural heritage of Finnish women.[2] When, and if, they did marry, many probably retained emancipated mindsets. This explains the odd phenomenon, at least from my youthful perspective, of the stylish, middle-aged, married Hannah who

Anna Koivu and her children, 1915

lived three doors down from my grandmother. In the early 1950s, while Anglo-Canadian women were dutiful housebound homemakers, she came and went at her own discretion, making good wages as a bush-camp cook during the winter, and flaunting an elegant and enviable wardrobe.

My grandmother and Anna Koivu were turn-of-the-century immigrants who married yet attempted to achieve some personal ambitions within marriage. I have no record or knowledge of their knowing one another, and I expect that they travelled in different circles, my grandmother being a townsperson and Anna a country woman. Nonetheless, I see their lives as being connected, in that Anna's life can be read, on one level at least, as being symbolic of many Finnish-Canadian women. In her independence, her industry, her self-reliance, her firm belief in the rights of women, and her defiance, Anna is representative of the self-determined women who came from Finland in the first part of the twentieth century.

As wife, mother, and, later, grandmother, Anna played conventional female roles, but she was also Anna the politician, a Finnish-Canadian farmwoman who, through her own efforts, sat at the dinner table with prime ministers. And she was Anna the writer, the vocal and feeling *mokin muori* (log-cabin granny) who wrote about Canadian affairs in her Finnish-Canadian newspaper column to a devoted immigrant audience. In the beginning and throughout much of her long life, she was a typical pioneer 'stump farmer' (*kantofarmari*), settling the land in northwestern Ontario.[3] In this capacity, she was Anna of Intola, a pioneer Everywoman and a mythic first ancestor in the landscape of settler culture. She was one of many ordinary women who led brave, tough, untold lives, and built the country. Hers is the true story of a vigorous and indomitable female spirit that is much neglected in Canada's national mythology.

Anna came to Ely, Minnesota, in August 1903 with her mother and her two younger sisters from Helsinki, Finland. Her father, who had worked as a horse taxi driver in the old country, had emigrated earlier to take up work in the mines. He left Finland because Russia insisted that drivers wear the Russian insignia on their uniforms. At the turn of the century, Tsar Nicholas II of Russia, the 'Finland-eater,' disbanded the Finnish army and declared the right to legislate Finnish affairs. Having endured Swedish domination for over six hundred years, prior to their approximately eighty years of independence in the nineteenth century, the Finns, often remaining fierce nationalists, emigrated for political freedom as well as economic opportunity.[4] From 1897 to 1914, 30,060 Finns emigrated to Canada from overseas and from the United States.[5] Anna was one of these.

Although she attended the Girls' Academy in Finland, Anna had to be reschooled in Ely, where she did eight grades in four years. Her father had further ambitions for her, but she stubbornly resisted his plans. 'I told him that I'd rather go working, that I'd rather work, that I'd had enough schooling, that thirteen years was enough for me.'[6] She took a job at the local hospital.

An athletic young woman, barely five feet tall, Anna was exceptionally headstrong, a scrapper, and was defiant of male authority for her entire life. Neither did she have any regard for women who did not appreciate the independent paths that other women might take. Minnie, her best friend in Ely and a woman ten years older than Anna, became a school teacher and a University of Michigan graduate and then went on to Finland to take a diploma in Finnish. When the young women in Ely criticized this relationship, saying to Anna 'What do you learn from that old maid?' her reply was, 'Maybe I learn more from her than I learn from you.'

Anna soon challenged her father's wishes again and aroused his anger when she fell passionately in love and left home to marry Esa Smedberg, a tall, handsome young man who had come from Eveleth, Minnesota, to Ely as part of a volunteer fire brigade at a fireman's picnic. Anna recognized him as a familiar face from Helsinki. In Finland, he had lived in the same house where Anna's family had resided, in a cooperative of fifty owners.

A miners' strike in Minnesota led Smedberg in 1907 to seek his fortune by skiing over one hundred miles through thick bush to Port Arthur (now Thunder Bay). He arrived on New Year's Day, 1908, and Anna joined him, travelling by train, in October of that year. Anna, aged twenty, and Smedberg, twenty-one, rented a single room in a boarding house and both became store clerks. Smedberg, the son of a lay preacher, spoke four languages: English, Finnish, Swedish, and Danish. Anna was proud that he became the first Finnish clerk in McNulty's, a clothing store that only recently closed its doors in Thunder Bay and that over the years served the city's elite. Anna clerked at a small store called Alexander's.

At this time, Finnish immigration into the city was intensive. Lured by the offer of 160 acres of free homestead land and spurred by the folk myth that Canada offered gold that could be cut with a wooden knife, Finns arrived daily at the land office above the store where Smedberg worked. John Oliver, the land office agent, regularly called upon Smedberg to interpret for the incoming Finns. Anna was inspired by the homesteading possibility and assured Smedberg that she had farming experience from spending the summer on her aunt's farm in Finland. Overcoming Smedberg's objections that both of them were Helsinki-born and city-bred, she convinced him to file a homestead ten miles out-side of town in McIntyre Township.

Anna was eager to demonstrate that she was in charge of her land. When the man who first showed them their property laughed at her for walking barefoot, suggesting that it looked like she was born in the country, she retorted, 'No, I was born in the city, but I get electricity from the land when I walk barefooted ... It gives me some energy.' As both men waited for her to cross a cedar log spanning a creek, Anna took a decisive action that symbolized her commitment to what lay before her: 'They were watching [to see] if I [would fall] in the creek – I was the last one – my petticoat got caught, there was some lace on it and it got caught in the brush ... I just took hold of it and pulled it so that – the whole thing came off, and I threw it in the bush ... the old man said, "... she's going to be a farm woman!"'

Anna's pioneer life in the bush of northwestern Ontario had begun. Both she and Smedberg continued with their store jobs, using off hours to walk long miles out to the land, which was not unlike the wooded countryside of the Finland that they had left. They turned their hands to the back-breaking labour of cutting and clearing, building themselves at first a small shack and then a log cabin in 1910. That same year, Anna undertook another pioneer venture. Smedberg, offered a clerk's job at a railroad construction camp for the Grand Trunk Railway, did not want to leave without his young bride. He appealed to his boss for her to come with him, arguing roguishly that she might die of coffee drinking if left on her own.

Anna went as a cookee in the company of two other Finnish women. All three, she was proud to say, were among the first women to work in the construction and lumber camps of the North. The camp, made out of logs, held a dining room sixty feet long, and a thirty-five-foot kitchen. She recalled travelling to the camp, by streetcar, then a little railway line, and finally by sleigh, on 'the coldest day in Canada – New Year's Day, 1910.' They arrived late in the evening, the men having made fires in the stoves for their arrival. In her recollection of having immediately to prepare dinner for seventy-two men, she tells a lumberjack tale of the northwestern Ontario bush. Innumerable pancakes are made, mixed in a washtub with water obtained from a hole in the ice on the lake, and cooked in a pan the size of a kitchen stove top. The salt pork the men ate with the pancakes was 'so tough it was just as if you were chewing your mouth,' and the tables were so cold with frost that the plates slid off them and had to be dipped in hot water to stay put.

Anna, even while pregnant and often nauseous as a cookee, remembered this year as one of the happiest of her life. She gloried in her pioneer presence as a woman in the men's camps, although she had come close to being driven out. The boss of the camp decided to replace the women, worrying that there had never been women on the line and that their presence would drive the men out of control. Smedberg rallied the men to the women's side, and ultimately the boss decided that 'I guess we can control our own camp.' Women like Anna would become regular and important figures in the construction and lumber camps of the North. The Finns insisted on their sauna (bathhouse) and would not tolerate unhygienic conditions or poor cooking, and these women were necessary to maintain the standards of cleanliness and domestic order that the men demanded. In return, the Finnish cooks, cookees, and laundresses who peer out of early photographs, dressed in their long white aprons or freshly starched white uniforms, and who often stand supportively together in a large clump of men, were paid quite well and treated with respect.[7] For the young Anna, the hard physical work and lack of luxury in the bush was offset by the fun of community and being with Smedberg. The railway built a little office for Smedberg, and Anna was allowed to stay there with him.

Anna's first baby, a son, was born in town with the assistance of a doctor. She was alone prior to the birth, having returned to occupy the homestead in April 1910 so that she and her husband could get ownership in three years. The night before the birth, Anna walked by herself the ten miles into town to stay with Smedberg's brother and his wife. The baby was born in their home, and not long after Anna hiked back to the cabin. Anna's daughter Aili has written a literary reconstruction of her mother's life, focused on this early period and based on stories passed from mother to daughter. In the following excerpt from Aili's narrative, *Mother of the Cabin*, Anna, having recently given birth, returns to fend for both herself and her newborn baby.

A delivery horse and buggy had brought her to the trail and from there she had come by foot. Halfway along the trail she stopped to rest and feed the baby, talking to him even if he didn't understand ... He would be company for her until [her husband] came home.

When Olaf had eaten his fill she continued her journey ...

Anna lay the sleeping child on the bed and let the straps of her pack slide off her shoulders. She felt shaky but knew that a meal would be the cure for it. She gathered dry sticks of fire wood and lit a fire in the stove, then she ran to fetch water from the river and she put a pot of potatoes to boil while she sliced salt pork into the frying pan. When she had eaten her meal of potatoes and salt pork gravy she felt much better and sat down on the doorstep to admire her little clearing they had managed to clear. She saw a rabbit run out of the bush and fetching her rifle, she got it at first shot. Skinning it carefully so the fur would not be damaged, she placed the pieces of meat into the stew pot to cook for supper. At the edge of the clearing she found some wild strawberries.[8]

A month after the birth of his son, Smedberg returned home with a male companion, Alex Koivu, a man who knew the Finnish art of building log cabins. With his help, the cabin that Anna was to occupy for sixty-five years was constructed, and at Christmas of 1910 they moved into it. Alex found himself a homestead next to Anna and Esa's. He was to become a next-door neighbour, a working companion on the road construction gangs where he and Smedberg found employment, and Smedberg's loyal friend. But Koivu had a secret – according to Anna's daughter Aili, he was later to reveal that he had fallen in love with Anna the moment that he saw her.[9]

The community was growing quickly and was dominated by Finns. In 1910 a meeting was held to discuss the naming of the settlement. The Finns chose the name of Intola (place of eagerness and enthusiasm) over the name of Jarkela (place of reason, sense, intelligence), having decided that Jarkela would be an immodest choice.[10] In 1960 Anna herself wrote of the naming and of the positive growth of the community, remembering that they had first come together because they had wanted their own post office. '"They all agreed to call it Intola. They all had lots of eagerness in them. They cleared fields, cut trees in the bush and built their homes out of logs ... The days were filled with hard work turning tree stumps and clearing rocks from the fields." Anna delighted in Intola's progress: in the mail that arrived from around the world, the new school, hall and a violin orchestra, as well as the villagers themselves such as "Ville Airola [who] entertained the villagers with his presentation of comic songs."'[11]

When her child was a year old, Anna took a trip to see her parents, travelling by boat to Duluth, Minnesota, and by train to Ely. Here she met only disappointment. Her father remained angry about his daughter's choice for a life. Although he refused to speak to his daughter, Anna was undaunted, and she and Smedberg continued to work their homestead. According to Anna's daughter Aili, 'As the clearing around the log house grew wider, a barn and stable were built; with credit they bought a team of horses and for show a buggy ... and Anna had to learn to milk the cow.'[12]

While Anna loved the horses, having grown up with them at the livery stable where her father worked, she hated tending the cow that provided so much: milk, butter, and the clabbered cream that the Finns love. Wild game was abundant, too, and was shared by the community. A communal steambath was available in the village. Most importantly for the women, the 'women's bible,' Eaton's catalogue, came in the mail twice a year. As recounted in *Mother of the Cabin*, Anna buys a pair of stylish shoes, only to discover that she prefers the comfort of her home-made shoe packs.[13] In 1912, Anna did buy a treasure from the catalogue: a black and silver cookstove, purchased for $12.00, seemed beautiful to her; it would be a long-time companion.[14]

As part of their homesteading life, Anna and Smedberg, both youthful sports-minded people, skated and skied for pleasure and purpose in the winter months. Anna was a natural gymnast and was involved in the first gymnastic club of the kind that would later mean much to Finnish life in Canada. The Finns were wildly keen about sports, and men and women participated equally. In retrospect, Anna described her feelings: 'There was enthusiasm, we did gymnastics and competed and received prizes. Song opens hearts but a beautiful sports team makes the heart quiver.'[15] As an 'old gymnast' she viewed a young people's gymnastic performance as beautiful and virtuous, emphasizing that 'A healthy soul lives in a healthy body.'[16]

These were golden years for Anna, who apparently revelled in a vigorous physical life. She recalled fondly, with a characteristic Finnish humour of self-deprecation, her skiing 'first.' She remembered herself as the first woman to come down the hill where the local city high school was built. Skiing beautifully down the steep slope, she met at its base a farmer turning the corner. His horse dropped a number of 'horse buns' at the moment of their encounter: 'My ski got stuck and gee, I tell you, I went two times like this, and there was [an] English gentleman on the sidewalk and he doubled [over] laughing ... I lost my other ski ... We had to hunt two hours for my ski.'

Despite such entertainment, the trials of pioneer life for Anna, as for many women like her, had only just begun. Even though Finnish standards of cleanliness were beyond the ordinary and the common practice of birthing in the sauna made infant mortality rates relatively low, babies were still lost at birth. Anna gave birth to a second son, only to see him die two weeks later. She buried him in a sunlit spot behind the house.

Worse was to follow. The kind of work that immigrant men were engaged in made them prone to accidents, and Smedberg was no exception. Aili's imaginative recounting of the tragic turn of events pictures Anna preparing the steambath for the men, who would be home for two days during Easter. When they arrive, she is told that Smedberg is not with them, that he is finishing chores and will return home the next day. In the night she hears Alex Koivu sobbing, but she does not register alarm. The next day Koivu tells her that Smedberg is dead, and leads her to the hayloft to see his cold body.[17] Esa Smedberg was killed instantly when a gravel pit caved in, in the spring of 1914, leaving a shocked Anna with two children, a baby girl having been born ten weeks previously, and a homestead with many debts. She buried Smedberg beside their son near an evergreen tree and mourned him, romantically, her entire life as her lost, young husband-lover.[18]

Anna's father was not long in arriving to take her back to Ely, and at the same time Alex Koivu began to make his long-standing love for her known. She refused her father's request out of hand, once again angering him with her self-determined view of herself as belonging to the place she had created. 'My roots are in Canada,' she purportedly told him, and he left in a huff.[19] In the family photographs of the time, a portrait of Anna and her two small children shows a little woman demurely dressed in black, slightly bent forward to the camera, with dark brown hair parted in the middle, not entirely tidy, in the smoothed winged style of the day. Her eyes are intense, passionate, in a small, attractive face. In a picture of Esa and Alex Koivu standing together before Esa's death, Esa Smedberg holds the reins of one of a team of three large, healthy, white-faced horses and faces the camera boldly. In contrast, Koivu stands to the right, on lower ground, he, too, holding one of the horse's reins, but clearly the less dominant figure, a supporting, smaller player in the photograph. He became that, as well, in Anna's life.

Anna had no insurance and was deeply in debt. Koivu had brought a Finnish woman home to live with her to provide company while the men were away; this woman was to live with Alex once his house was completed. Although the union of Alex and H—— was practical rather than romantic, Anna was reluctant to become a third party to their affair; they were having a child together, and she mourned Smedberg.[20]

After Smedberg's death, Anna seems to have become more self-possessed, although not above invoking sympathy for her widowed position if need be. In one instance, she drove her own horses home when an unreliable teamster from the city stable forgot his driving obligations and got drunk. As a tiny person perched on the high seat of the buggy, she was ridiculed by an 'English' man she met on Four Mile Hill. He called from afar, 'Is your husband so drunk you have to drive the team home?' Anna pleased herself with her meek reply, 'No, I am sorry, I am a widow.' She further enjoyed his embarrassment and apology, as 'he stood there and said, Madame, please forgive me.' She was later to demonstrate her temper and active outrage at the same undisciplined teamster; she took a whip to him for abusing her horses, Frankie and Danny. She gleefully recalls that he fled yelling, 'Help me, help me, that woman is going to kill me!'

Later, in a similarly fearless style, she negotiated with an Anglo-Canadian timber boss for the just payment of Koivu and his friend as cordwood cutters, driving as hard a bargain as she could in a male world where immigrant men had little real economic, social, or political power. When she said, 'They want what is coming to them,' and the timber boss insisted they sign his agreement or lose their cordwood, she replied, '"Let it stand there until the Judgement Day." And I pushed the guys out and we came home.'

Clearly, Anna became an even more determined and authoritative woman after the death of her first husband. She had what the Finns call *sisu*. A cultural code that is not translatable into English, *sisu* insists on 'having guts' or absolute courage in going forward.

Anna did not consent to marry Alex Koivu until 1917. They were married in a triple ceremony that was orchestrated largely so that the men would not be drafted into the army, as many single men were during World War I. At least, this is how Anna's daughter reconstructs the wedding, in part from her own memory as one of the noisy children, in *Mother of the Cabin*:

'I think we will have to be married legally by the pastor,' said Kusti [one of the bridegrooms].

'Well, it wouldn't be fatal even if we did. [L]et us see what the women folk think,' answered Taavi [Koivu].

Both women were willing and as the news spread, a third couple joined them. The pastor performed the ceremony at Anna's house, marrying all three couples at the same time. Anna decided afterwards that she had not made the obedience vow for at that part of the ceremony she had been disciplining the children who got too noisy in the bedroom.[21]

If Anna seems to have entered this marriage casually, it is probably because she would not have felt much community pressure to marry at all. As Varpu Lindström points out, 'there was no great social stigma attached to being single in the Finnish community.' Moreover, Finnish socialism of the day was 'extremely anti-religious,' with 'free unions' of men and women encouraged by the left-wing Finns. These were marriages cemented in socialist halls, and with simple announcements in the newspapers.[22]

Although Anna never demonstrated any obvious support of radical, left-wing politics, Intola was a socialist community that in the 1920s saw the typical split in the Finnish community between the syndicalists and the communists.[23] Anna herself did not take sides as the political schisms deepened and grimly intensified in the 1930s, both among the Finns and between them and the larger Canadian society. She refused, in fact, to work for the Finnish Communist Women's Movement when aggressively approached, preferring later to focus on mainstream Canadian politics. Eventually, she would rejoin the Lutheran Church, but here, too, her independent thinking and her defiance of authority came to the fore. She fell out with the minister because he would not support the Finnish ladies of Kaleva lodge, a cultural society that takes its name from the Kalevala, the national folk epic of Finland. As her daughter put it, 'Mother had a way of making an issue of things.'[24] Anna could not be coerced by groups or individuals. She kept her own counsel.

Anna had four children with Alex, a man who treated all her children, including Smedberg's, with kindness, affection, and love. Significantly, Koivu, who became the blacksmith of the community, took over the considerable debts of Anna's place, which were to be with them for many years. Although Koivu was a likeable man of great humour, one who rarely got angry and who loved delightful excursions with his children, Anna, romantically and probably unfairly, retained the memory of Smedberg as her ideal. Ironically, her daughter Aili reports that it was only after Koivu's death that Anna felt her second husband's real worth.

Life continued to be hard for Anna and the other Finnish women in Intola. The *sisu* that characterized Anna as a pioneer woman was also characteristic of many others who endured physical hardships, endless work, and sickness with little medical assistance. The Spanish flu epidemic, which raged at the end of the First World War, took Anna's favourite sister; the news, delivered in a letter edged in black, was a hard blow to her. Soon the epidemic attacked Intola, striking Anna and her children in the winter while she was alone and Koivu was in the bush earning extra money. Caring for children while one is ill oneself is a grim feat. Even more extraordinary is childbirth in the context of mass illness where there is little practical assistance. In *Mother of the Cabin*, Anna recollects an incident during the community's epidemic: 'The whole family had been ill when the mother had to give birth and old Susanna [the community midwife] had crawled from her sick bed to tie the cord. In the morning the mother had to get up to do the chores which included water carried from under a steep hill. Many other families experienced the same but the little girl grew and thrived.'[25]

Thriving depended not only on *sisu*, but on female community and cooperative enterprise. Aili Lehto, a second-generation Finnish Canadian who made soap before washing machines and commercial soap came into use, describes a venture in women's soap making as a community project:

When the butchering was done and waste fat collected, the women got together ... [W]here there was a big iron pot with the fire-box beneath [they built] the fire while the others carried soft spring water into the big pot. The fat and lye were added, in earlier days even the lye was home-made from birch wood ashes, but it was easier to buy the lye by the can. While working the women also talked for this was one of the occasions when they were all together ... [T]he coffee pot was kept hot on the hostess' stove and by turns they stirred the boiling soap and kept the fire going until the contents of the pot turned white and creamy. It was then ladled into low wooden containers to cool and harden. This would take days before it was firm enough to cut and each one take their share.[26]

For Anna and Intola the 1920s was a period of pioneer growth. The school was well established, as was a local cooperative store. Anna gained some new material comforts and leisure of sorts. Alex purchased a model-T Ford and filed a homestead on a lakeshore, which they visited regularly through complicated treks by car, boat, and foot. Anna also had time for civic affairs. She appears to have had a short stint as a member of the McIntyre Community Hall Board, and records show that in 1930 she was elected as a trustee to the Intola Board of Education. Later, in *Canadan Uutiset*, she would remark on the importance of women in these offices: 'It's pleasing that we got a woman on the executive [of the Intola school district] for the second time in Intola's history. This "cabin granny" was the first and now Mrs A ... J ... Women should be more enthusiastic about following school affairs.'[27] Anna's election to public office is a marker of the next remarkable phase of her life.

Anna's daughter Aili identifies her mother as an early feminist in

Canada. In Finland Anna had come of age when, along with socialism, the Finnish woman's movement had flowered and certain rights for women had been attained. She could not have been unaffected by the spirit of women in Finland, who by 1907 had already achieved the right to equal education and the vote. In effect, Finnish immigrant women would carry this spirit forward in demonstrating and agitating for suffrage in North America.[28]

Anna had a strong social conscience, which was focused on the domestic issues and concerns of women. Aili recalls her mother's strong commitment to community during the Depression. Working for the Relief Board at a time when families were receiving five dollars a month in relief payments, Anna always went to check to see whether families and mothers had received their money. Sometimes she would ski long distances, arriving home late in the evening after spending considerable time in extended conversations.[29] It is easy to imagine her as a tiny, solitary skier, braving the fierce and numbing cold, racing blizzards in the vast northern moonlit landscape of snow and black trees. Anna was fearless and competitive in pitting herself against nature – while being interviewed in old age, her conversation turned to a recent failed attempt to outwalk a rainstorm.

During the Depression, Anna was also propelled into politics. In her own 'Memories of Election Time' she asks, 'How did I, a Finnish pioneer's wife, become a speaker at election time? That is what I often think about.' She goes on to explain that Charlie Cox, a candidate in the Ontario provincial election of 1933, came to speak at the Big Hall at Intola, which was filled with both farm and city folk. When Cox asked if there were any questions, one woman 'stood up and asked to speak. She turned to me and said, "You Anni, go to the platform and interpret our complaints and demands." I said: "I'll interpret but I won't go to the platform." Anyhow, Mr. Cox called me to the platform and I introduced myself and interpreted. That was the time of the big depression in Canada.'[30]

Anna became a political conduit between the Finnish-Canadian community and mainstream Anglo-Canadian politicians. In choosing to get involved in mainstream politics rather than the internal political world of the Finnish-Canadian community, she was demonstrating that she knew where the real power in Canadian society resided. After hearing a speaker at the Charles Street Women's Institute Hall in Port Arthur, Anna, who had formerly voted Conservative, became a lifelong member of the Liberal Party. Although the CCF would seem to have been a more likely choice for her, given her early socialism, it might not have seemed open to her as an immigrant woman. One anecdote has her telling of meeting a woman on the street, a prominent townsperson and member of the CCF, who greeted her in a patronizing way, with 'Hello Mrs. Koivu, and how are the Finns today?' Anna, forever quick in her responses, replied, 'The Finns are fine ..., and how are the English today?' After her initial meeting with Charlie Cox, she worked for the Liberal Party for twenty-three years, promoting the interests of women and her community.

Cox convinced Anna to come to other meetings to speak on his behalf. This was shrewd, given the large concentration of Finns in northwestern Ontario. It would seem that she was equally shrewd in that she wanted certain improvements for her community, such as rails for street cars and milking machines for Finnish women, who would be freed from the barn work they did while the men did other jobs or were away. Anna herself could only afford to be away on speaking jaunts because she had trained her daughters to do the chores and keep house. In her initial speeches for Cox, she recalled, 'I spoke in Finnish and some words in English, asking the people to study the programs of all the parties; especially I urged the women on election day to use their right to vote.' In fact, above all, Anna seemed concerned in this election with the rights of women in the political process. The Election Act had been revised so that a woman could get citizenship after her husband got his. Anna accompanied many 'Finnish women to the lawyer's office where they filled the applications and swore the oath of loyalty so that they could get their papers before election day. Here in the country there were many women that I helped. And how glad they were to be eligible to vote. Mr. Cox won many elections.'[31] From the day she met Cox, Anna became enamoured of politics. One of her daughters is credited with saying, 'We had municipal politics for breakfast, provincial politics for lunch and federal politics for supper.'[32]

In 1934, Anna, as a rural representative, attended a nomination meeting for the Liberal candidate for the 1935 federal election. C.D. Howe won this nomination and went on to become Prime Minister Mackenzie King's right-hand man in government and an extremely influential politician. Although Anna worried about Howe's slow delivery in speaking, she thought him a quiet, nice man and supported his candidacy. Howe, like Cox, asked Anna to speak on his behalf in Finnish in Port Arthur, Nipigon, and other rural areas. Her daughter Aili recalls that she would be away for days at a time, and they would not know where she was. Her strong political presence is documented in the election of 1935.

Anna spoke to a crowd of 300 to 350 in Nipigon, at a number of meetings in outlying rural areas, and at homes within the city. A most sensational speech is recorded in the *Port Arthur News-Chronicle* on 10 October 1935. The column's headline reads 'Asks House Cleaning at Dominion House,' while the subhead reads 'Finnish Farmwife Speaks for Liberals at Rally in Labor Temple.' Anna's speech is reported as follows:

Monday is the proverbial wash day and probably has been since people began wearing clothes. Mrs. A. Koivu, Finnish farmwife, advised at a Liberal rally in the Labor Temple last night. 'But, ladies,' Koivu urged, 'forget about your household washing next Monday, October 14. Do a bigger and more important washing and wash the Conservative Party out of control of our government. With more than fifty per cent of the voting power, we can do so even without any assistance from the men.' Mrs. Koivu suggested that 'Blue Monday' and every other blue day be wiped right out of the week. 'Why not do a real old-fashioned Fall housecleaning at the Federal House,' she asked.[33]

Within the limits of her ethnicity, her class, and her gender, Anna was a political force. She spent all of C.D. Howe's elections with him, urging the Finns to cast their votes for him and the Liberal Party. She also informed Howe of local concerns, explaining to him, for example, before the 1934 election that many of the Finns did not want relief money; rather, they needed better roads so that they could haul their wood out and fulfil their pulp wood contracts. Anna became a local presence in the party. C.D. Howe visited her log homestead on the hill sloping into its cleared meadow while she in turn sat at the dinner table at a number of Liberal dinners and receptions with Prime Ministers W.L. Mackenzie King, Louis St Laurent, and Lester Pearson. In the 1940 election, she sat at the same table as Mackenzie King at Howe's nomination dinner and, as representative of the Liberal women, seconded Howe's nomination.

However, it was not these male leaders whom Anna credited with giving her the understanding of the Liberal Party and its principles, but rather Mrs E.J.B. Dobie, a city woman of the Canadian cultural mainstream, who was prominent in the Liberal Women's Association. A tiny woman, not unlike Anna herself, she became Anna's good friend. Anna's involvement in the party was an unusual one. As a Finnish-Canadian farmwoman, she was excluded from the role open to the wives and daughters of prominent politicians and their supporters. For example, she was conspicuously absent from society page photographs of the 1950s, such as the one that shows Mrs Howe in gown and tiara, with Liberal women pouring tea for her.[34] At the same time, she was credited in national Liberal Party documents as a leader in her district.[35]

The development of Anna's rhetorical skills was encouraged by her community. Because women were equal and active participants in the various immigrant institutions and organizations, they had opportunities for public performance and leadership. The phenomenon of the woman speaker developed in Finnish communities across North America, and many women were in demand throughout their regions to speak in Finnish societies.[36] It is not surprising then that, in some ways, Anna was equal to Howe as a politician. She certainly was not merely his translator. In an interview she explained, 'I didn't translate C.D. Howe's speech. I made up my own you know, about conditions around this country side and what we need.'

It seemed to be easy for Anna to support Howe. Perhaps, given his bland speaking skills, she felt her own power in her relationship with him. She may also have felt that the American-born Howe was like herself, an immigrant. When Howe asked her to come with him to the Finlandia Hall to speak the last time he intended to run in 1957, Anna was happy to be back on the platform again with him after their many times together. When Howe was heckled from the audience as a 'Yank,' he turned to Anna as his ally, asking her when she had come and pointing out their comparable and equal status. Anna recalled, 'So he said, "I have a family growing up and they are Canadian born and I think Mrs. Koivu has – how many have you?" I said, "I have six." So the people shut their mouth. Then when I got to speak I told in English that we are naturalized Canadians, we are not Americans – neither Mr. Howe [n]or I. And I said, "We have given the best part of our lives to Canada."'

That meeting was rowdy, but the meeting in Intola was far worse, with violence being narrowly averted through Anna's intervention. Two communists in the audience began to question Howe and cause trouble, and a person on the platform beside Anna became so incensed that she had to prevent him from leaping up and throwing his chair at the questioner. C.D. Howe lost the election. While Anna's own political analysis of Howe's defeat was based on economic reasons, and the lack of year-round organization of the Liberal Party, she was nonetheless, as she put it, 'ashamed of her people.' In a kind of eulogy for Howe, she thoughtfully expressed her feelings of regret for what she considered to be a lack of recognition of his contributions to Northern Ontario, an area that did, in fact, prosper through him. 'What makes me sad is that C.D. Howe did so much for his riding, but he never received the proper credit for it ... But has anyone ever received the thanks due to them?'[37] Almost twenty years later, Anna herself would receive a plaque from the Liberal Party of Canada in recognition of her many years of service.

Anna also served her community well, not only as a politician but as a writer through her columns for the Finnish ethnic press. Finnish Canadians have the reputation of being avid readers. Even in the remote lumber camps, where hard work ate up time, the Finns were inclined to reading.[38] Newspapers devoted to women and feminist issues were also created, usually in conjunction with the labour movement. One such influential paper was the *Toveritar* (Female Comrade) founded in Duluth, Minnesota, in 1909 and to which Anna contributed some writing. Anna wrote mostly for *Canadan Uutiset*, however, a newspaper that was considered to be conservative in character, although Varpu Lindström makes the point that even this, the most conservative of Finnish voices, in 1915 supported women's suffrage 'with all its might.'[39]

Anna wrote a regular column for *Canadian Uutiset* under the pen name of Mokin Muori, which very roughly translates as 'log-cabin granny.' Aili Lehto explains: 'Mokki means a plain dwelling; Muori is a title given to plain elderly women. It is very difficult to translate into English to get the same meaning.'[40] To some extent, the column was the voice of women: Finnish women across the country, often lonely with their husbands away, looked forward to hearing from a comfortable friend in the newspaper. The voice of the log-cabin granny was clear, intimate, womanly, and encouraging. During the war, for example, she wrote: 'on Christmas Day, I was listening to the radio as a soldier's wife from Toronto sent a greeting to her husband in England. A tear burned my eye as I thought how this woman too bravely hid her heart's longing and sense of loss and tried cheerfully to comfort her husband ... Canadian women can be as courageous as men.'[41]

Anna wrote with a compelling voice and a persuasive style that she turned to both national and local subjects and audiences. In one column, for example, appealing to the Finns' loyalty and generosity and to their sense of gratitude for their good fortune in Canada, she urged them to buy Victory Bonds for the national good. Her disappointment in the poor sales in the village is strongly felt, and her hope for increased sales is infectious. Her message is delivered with rhetorical expertise: 'Aren't all the country's sorrows our sorrows?' she asks. 'Are we not dedicated to helping the country? The government is not asking for free loans ... Who are we depending on if not on the government?'[42]

Closer to home, she provided information to the village about the larger Anglo-Canadian community surrounding it, urging Finns to become involved in organizations like the Kiwanis Club because of its good works. Above all, she stressed political participation, advising her readers on how to vote if their names were not on the voting lists and urging them to 'remember to use your right to vote. It's your business whom you vote for, as long as you do it.'[43] At the same time, she reported on the village news and its people, offering kudos for individual achievement and good works at every opportunity. Always she was concerned for the women and children of the community as she commented on such issues as inadequate school-busing policies or the social isolation of farm women. Despite her base in Intola, the voice of *Mokin Muori* carried far beyond the village to Finnish communities across Canada. Doubtless, a part of her appeal was her projection of self to the reader as a living personality: 'This granny has gotten along as best as I can with gramps working for a lumber contractor as a smith this winter. I haven't had time to write for the paper as it's been enough to tread the path between the cabin, the barn and the woodshed. Sometimes all that is showing above the snow is the tip of my hat.'[44]

As log-cabin granny, Anna performed the function of a village elder who was social conscience, moral authority, doting grandmother, generous friend, and community advocate. When Anna retired after decades of being the vocal *mokin muori*, her daughter Aili took over the column, as readers demanded a continuing presence.

For a married woman with children to have both a political and literary life is, in any circumstances, a marvel. This is even more true of Anna, who had the responsibilities of domestic and farm work, and of caring for a large family without modern conveniences. Moreover, Anna's Finnish culture demanded rigorous rules of housekeeping. Aili remembers her mother as a 'cleanaholic' and a perfectionist, washing and drying the floors with elaborate ritual, only to see them very shortly dirty again. At the same time, she treasures the 'most sacred' memories of Saturday evenings, for 'I remember the smell of fresh scrubbed floors mingling with bread just out of the oven.'[45] This was also the traditional night for the steambath.

In 1957, Anna again felt the anguish of a child's death when one of her sons was tragically killed in an automobile accident. This was the same year as Howe's defeat, and she shifted her attentions to her young orphaned grandson. She raised him to manhood in her original cabin, the logs covered over and the house much improved, the sauna within short walking distance. Even after the death of Alex Koivu, she continued to parent this last child. In 1975 she is pictured in *Weekend Magazine*, chopping wood at the age of eighty-seven, still a tiny, slim, attractive, now silver-haired woman, exuding 'strength and independence.'[46] To the end, she remained physically active. During her last few years in a senior citizens' home, she continued to believe that she had jobs to do, preferring to wash dishes and fold laundry than to idly socialize with the other residents.

Anna of Intola was an uncommon common person who made the most of her life as an immigrant woman. She had *sisu*. Like many other Finnish-Canadian woman of her generation she was schooled in the rights of women, and she acted on this belief in the new world. Although she was, in her own words, just a 'scrap' of a woman, her Finnish culture gave her belief in her physical equality. Finnish society in Canada gave her the authority to be a community builder, and she took this opportunity as well. Faced with a mainstream political culture that defined both immigrants and women as second-class citizens, she seized what chance there was for political power and for making her voice heard. Intelligent, with clear ideas and a talent for writing and speech making, she vigorously applied these talents in the new world.

While Anna's ego was strong and I think the pleasure of personal contest always a motivator, her objectives never seemed to be primarily self-serving. Hers was a communal sensibility, conditioned no doubt by the early influence of socialism. She believed in all her efforts to advance women and her Finnish community. She believed, too, in the making of Canada, and each citizen's responsibility to her new country. The romantic echo of Finnish cultural nationalism is perhaps heard in the patriotism Anna felt for Canada. Aili tells the story of the maple leaf dish. Anna explained that when she was a young bride, a storekeeper, realizing that she had not much money, gave her the dish as a wedding gift. She saw it as a beautiful object. Because she had known the poverty of Finland, where flour for bread was thickened with wood chips – in contrast to Canada, which had the biggest bread basket in the world – Anna always kept the maple leaf dish on her table for bread for all, including widows and orphans. A measure of Anna's commitment to Canada was that she never returned, and never wished to return, to the Finland of her birth. When asked when she might go back to see her first country, her reply was, 'When the North Sea grows hay.'[47]

That is not to say that her dreams were completely realized in Canada. She found neither gold nor enduring romance; hers was an ordinary woman's life of poor times, illness, and family tragedy. She did, however, find frontier adventure and spaces where she made a difference in people's lives, and where she helped to advance women and assimilate the Finnish people in Canada. Her political activities were admirable, and her life a physical triumph. Today, the original homestead in Intola is a suburban community of contemporary homes occupied by some of her descendants. Anna of Intola passed away 29 April 1979 at the age of ninety, an original settler, a steadfast Canadian, and a woman of *sisu*.

NOTES

I am indebted to a number of people for assistance in the preparation of this article. My husband Anthony shared with me his interview material and other historical artifacts about Anna Koivu. My daughter Leslie did the microfilm research. Mrs Aili Lehto was extraordinarily helpful, and I am grateful to her for allowing me to use her unpublished manuscript and for her interview time and permission to quote. Helmi Kirki helped me to locate materials at Five Mile School. Jari Leinonen translated Anna's newpaper columns. Financial assistance for translation was provided by the Multiculturalism Programs of the Department of Canadian Heritage.

1 K. Marianne Wargelin-Brown, 'A Closer Look at Finnish-American Immigrant Women's Issues, 1890–1910' in *Finnish Diaspora II: United States*, ed. Michael Karni (Toronto: Multicultural History Society of Ontario, 1981), 214
2 Varpu Lindström, *Defiant Sisters: A Social History of Finnish Immigrant Women in Canada* (Toronto: Multicultural History Society of Ontario, 1992), 67
3 Varpu Lindström-Best, 'Finns in Canada,' *Polyphony: Finns in Ontario* 3, no. 2 (1981): 8
4 Liz Primeau, 'The Nature of Finns,' *Weekend Magazine*, 16 Aug. 1975, 5–7
5 Marc Metsaranta, 'Finnish Immigration to the Thunder Bay Area, 1876–1914' in *Project Bay Street: Activities of Finnish-Canadians in Thunder Bay before 1915*, ed. Marc Metsaranta (Thunder Bay: Finnish-Canadian Historical Society, 1989), 16
6 Anna Koivu, interview with Anthony Rasporich, Jan. 1971. Unless otherwise noted, all quotes and personal information are drawn from this interview.
7 Ian Radforth, 'Finnish Lumber Workers in Ontario, 1919–46,' *Polyphony: Finns in Ontario* 3, no. 2 (1981): 26
8 Aili Lehto, 'Mother of the Cabin' (unpublished manuscript, Thunder Bay, Five Mile School Archives), 4–6. The original Finnish version of this manuscript, *Mokin Muorin Tarina*, was published in *Canadan Uutiset*.

9 Aili Lehto, interview with the author, July 1994
10 *A Chronicle of Finnish Settlements in Rural Thunder Bay*, Bay Street Project No. 2 (Thunder Bay: Canadian Uutiset), 74
11 Anna Koivu, 'Intola, Ontario,' *Canadian Finnish Calendar*, trans. T. Waino (n.p., 1960), 45–6
12 Aili Lehto, letter to the author, 13 April 1994
13 Lehto, 'Mother of the Cabin,' 18
14 'Anna Marie Koivu Remembers Joys and Sorrows,' *Thunder Bay News Chronicle*, 30 March 1974
15 Anna Koivu, *Canadan Uutiset*, 9 April 1952, trans. J. Leinonen
16 Ibid., 28 Sept. 1949
17 Lehto, 'Mother of the Cabin,' 21–2
18 Lehto, interview
19 Lehto, letter, 13 April 1994
20 This is how the relationships are interpreted by Aili Lehto. Lehto, interview
21 Lehto, 'Mother of the Cabin,' 31–2
22 Lindström, *Defiant Sisters*, 67, 72–3
23 In 1914, of the sixty Finns living in Intola, thirty-seven belonged to the socialist organization. The second public bulding to be constructed was a socialist hall. The ideological dispute after the First World War between the syndicalist socialists, who wanted to take over factories and to strike, and the communists, who insisted on a directly political program was felt in Intola. See *Chronicle of Finnish Settlements*, 74–5.
24 Lehto, interview
25 Lehto, 'Mother of the Cabin,' 36
26 Ibid., 42–3
27 Koivu, *Canadan Uutiset*, 22 Jan. 1941, trans. J. Leinonen
28 Joan Sangster, 'Finnish Women in Ontario, 1890–1930,' *Polyphony: Finns in Ontario* 3, no. 2 (1981): 50
29 Lehto, interview
30 Anna Koivu, 'Memories from Election Times, Personal Reminiscence,' trans. Mrs A. Haapasalo (2 April 1971)
31 Ibid., 2
32 Lehto, interview
33 *Port Arthur News-Chronicle*, 10 Oct. 1935, 3
34 'Mrs. Howe in Coronation Gown,' *Port Arthur News-Chronicle*, 15 July 1952
35 Anna's importance as a cultural broker is documented in the National Liberal Federation Papers. Douglas Owen wrote to Mr H.E. Kidd on 15 November 1951 about the Port Arthur riding: 'We also have two points which might be considered a suburb of Port Arthur, namely Intola and

Kaministiquia. These are not separate organizations, but we do have two very strong supporters there who act as leaders in their representative districts. These are Mrs. A. Koiuv and Mrs. A.H.T.'

36 Wargelin-Brown, 'Finnish-American Immigrant Women's Issues,' 215–16
37 Koivu, 'Memories,' 4
38 Radforth, 'Finnish Lumber Workers,' 26
39 Lindström, *Defiant Sisters*, 148
40 Aili Lehto, letter to the author, 1 Sept. 1994
41 Koivu, *Canadan Uutiset*, 22 Jan. 1941, trans. J. Leinonen
42 Ibid., trans. A. Lehto, Lehto, interview, July 1994
43 Ibid., 22 June 1949, trans. J. Leinonen
44 Ibid., 14 May 1943
45 'Anna Marie Koivu Remembers'
46 Primeau, 'Nature of Finns,' 5
47 Lehto, interview

Soaring to New Heights:
Changes in the Life Course of
Mabel McIntosh

MARIANNE GOSZTONYI AINLEY

The hawks circled overhead on outstretched wings, flapping occasionally, then soaring higher and higher before gliding towards the south over the Lake of Two Mountains. Forty-one-year-old Mabel McIntosh stood on Oka beach, watching a kettle of migrating broad-winged hawks. She was fascinated. Although she was to see more spectacular hawk flights in North and Central America, none would equal this, her first experience with hawk migration.

As a member of the Province of Quebec Society for the Protection of Birds (PQSPB), Mabel McIntosh was on a Saturday field trip on that September day in 1963 with a small group of bird watchers. She had been a more or less solitary naturalist until the early 1960s. Sharing her growing interest with others – women and men of all ages and backgrounds – was still a novelty. Having the companionship of like-minded people was comforting at a time when her relationship with her husband, Alex, was deteriorating.

Mabel McIntosh's life was undergoing drastic change. In the space of a few months, her father had died, menopause had begun, and her marriage had broken apart. Furthermore, she painfully realized that, as a dependent wife for nearly twenty years, she had no savings, no income of her own, and only limited skills for the expanding job market of the 1960s. Her situation was typical. In Canada during this period, women could not leave their husbands easily, and in Quebec, with its Napoleonic laws, divorce was not even recognized. Until the 1968 Divorce Act came into effect, the residents of Quebec had to petition a federal court for divorce, a costly and time-consuming process.

In Canada, as in most other nations, law protected men more than women. As well, the average Canadian woman who gave up paid work

Mabel McIntosh observing migrating hawks near Valleyfield, Quebec, May 1990

when she married had no money, no access to bank loans, and, since she had been out of the work force for a number of years, was unlikely to obtain a lucrative job.[1] Mabel McIntosh had been a relaxed and easy-going person all her life, but the crises in her personal life left her confused and insecure. Like most women, she was not prepared to give up her children and her home, and until Alex was ready to leave there was little she could do to force a legal separation. In spite of a worsening situation, Mabel remained financially dependent. Though he spent little time at home, Alex continued the traditional role of the provider. They shared the house, but no longer lived as husband and wife.

There were few people in whom Mabel McIntosh could confide. Her closest woman friend had become her husband's friend and lover, her parents were dead, and her three children were too young to be burdened with the details of her life. Not surprisingly, her health began to deteriorate. She suffered from stomach pains, slept badly, and became depressed.

It was these sudden changes at home that prompted Mabel to seek solace in the outdoors. Her love of nature assumed new importance as she took longer walks and ventured further afield. She spent more and more time in the woods and meadows around her home in Pointe Claire and began to observe nature as a serious naturalist. Mabel McIntosh had been interested in birds and nature since early childhood. Now, in mid-life, her interest became a passion. Pursuing bird-study as an avocation, becoming a link in the web of bird watchers across North America,[2] gave her a new focus, new friends, and an acceptable way to express her scientific and artistic interests. Higher education had been unavailable to her as a young woman but now she avidly acquired scientific knowledge by hard work and independent study. In addition, field trips provided an opportunity to learn from those more knowledgeable and experienced than herself. The PQSPB's membership, like that of many other nature or conservation associations, consisted of women and men who joined because of their own interests. Mabel – lively, attractive, and increasingly knowledgeable – was a welcome addition to the organization.

Mabel Aston McIntosh was born on 11 January 1922 in St Louis, Missouri, of English parents. Her mother, Agnes Hardy Aston (1888–1953), was brought up in Yorkshire. Her father, William Aston (1882–1960), was born in Northumberland and spent part of his childhood in Scotland before the family moved to Canada in 1889. When his mother and his sister Mabel returned to England, Bill remained in Canada. In Pocklington, Yorkshire, Mabel Aston and Agnes Hardy became close friends.

At the outbreak of the First World War, William Aston enlisted in the Canadian Army, was captured by the Germans, and spent two and a half years working as a prisoner of war on a farm in Westphalia. Agnes Hardy, looking after her parents at home and resigned to becoming an old maid after a broken engagement, began corresponding with her best friend's older brother. The two finally met after the war, and within a few months they married and moved to Canada.

The Canadian Veteran's Land Act enabled the Astons to settle on a farm near Abbotsford, British Columbia, but they did not like farming. After a brief visit to Agnes's sister, Ethel Hardy Whalen, in St Louis, Missouri, during which time Mabel (named after her paternal aunt) was born, the family settled in Lancaster, Ontario. In 1925 they moved to

Montreal, where William Aston found employment as an accountant and bookkeeper with the Imperial Tobacco Company. The family lived in the poorer part of the affluent Westmount section of Montreal. As an only child, Mabel spent much time with her parents. Her mother was interested in nature and particularly knowledgeable about flowers. She often took her daughter on long walks to Westmount Mountain and Mount Royal – low hills covered with oak, maple, and birch trees – where they saw wildflowers, squirrels, and a variety of birds.

Mabel was privileged to experience nature in the city. She also learned about astronomy, literature, and music, especially opera, her father's chief interests. Mabel enjoyed it all but became most interested in birds. The Astons' apartment overlooked large, mature trees, and from her window Mabel watched colourful migrant birds in the spring. In her seventies, she could still recall that when she was twelve years old Mr Maxwell, a local policeman, showed her a saw-whet owl in Westmount Park. The tiny tuftless owl was hardly visible, hiding among the vines covering a wall; in fact, many people passed it without knowing it was there. Mabel was proud that she could see it and observed it for a long time. She was even more delighted when she discovered another small owl in a tree cavity in the same park. This owl had tiny ear tufts, and its colour resembled the tree bark. It sat motionless, practically filling the hole with its grey-feathered body. It was the first eastern screech-owl that she had ever seen, a discovery she shared excitedly with her friends.

Mabel attended public school in Westmount. She liked geography, biology, and art but, in spite of her father's interest in math, she had a 'mental block about figures.' In high school she suffered through math classes and was delighted when, in her third year, a program change allowed students to take physical geography and biology instead of math, and there was an option for additional classes in literature and art. Dropping math meant that Mabel's school average improved, and in grades 10 and 11 she obtained a scholarship that covered her fees. The fee-waiver was welcome news. Although William Aston retained his job during the Depression, money was in short supply. Mabel knew that she could not even consider a university education. Like it or not, at the end of high school she had to find paid employment.

In spite of her parents' pride in her accomplishments and Mabel's own desire to become an artist, she was unable to accept the graduation scholarship, one year's study at Montreal's École des Beaux-Arts with the famous painter Arthur Lismer. Instead, she took the less prestigious but more practical second prize, which allowed her to attend night school for one year with a commercial artist. At the same time, with the help of her art teacher, Ethel Edgerton, Mabel found a position as a draughting trainee with the Bell Telephone Company in Montreal. A six-month training period enabled her to draw charts and graphs for the monthly financial booklets published by the company's statistical department.

Drawing graphs and charts was similar to the work done by many eighteenth- to twentieth-century women in western culture who either helped the scientific pursuits of their male relatives as unpaid assistants or, increasingly, worked in universities, research institutes, governments, and industries as salaried but 'invisible' technicians and research assistants.[3] It was because she was a woman that Mabel's individual talents were not realized.

Ironically, while her work was still in the tradition of women's invisible work, many women were already performing different, technical jobs for the company. In 'Hello, Central?' Michèle Martin argues that the position of telephone operator, though a poorly paid technical job, was a high status one within the Bell system. While this may have been true between 1890 and 1920, by the end of the Depression the situation had changed.[4] According to Mabel's own recollection, draughtsmen and other office workers never even saw the 'girls,' who worked in a different building, and she was unaware of any status or pay differences between the operators and the draughtsmen.[5]

Mabel Aston met her future husband, Alex McIntosh, in 1941. She was a nineteen-year-old, attractive, brown-haired, lively woman with a variety of interests. He was a seventeen-year-old office boy, hoping to have a career with the company. Alex McIntosh was born in Montreal in 1924 of Scottish parents who emigrated to Canada after the First World War and settled in the Verdun district of Montreal. Alex's father, William McIntosh, worked as a mechanic for Bell Telephone. It seemed natural that, with his mechanical aptitude, Alex should also work there after graduating from West Hill High School. Tall, fair, and handsome, Alex was ambitious. Although he started as an office boy, he soon moved on to become a foreman and later a district manager.

Mabel and Alex married in March 1944 and, because of the wartime housing shortage, lived temporarily with her parents in Westmount. Alex was in the Royal Canadian Air Force (though he never saw action) and Mabel continued to work until he was discharged in 1945. Then, like other married women of the period, Mabel gave up her job. She soon became pregnant. Brien was born in 1946 and Marjorie in 1947. In 1948 the family moved to a rented flat in west-end Verdun, where their youngest child, John, was born in 1950.

Mabel enjoyed herself. Their flat was near the St Lawrence River, and she often took the children to watch the ducks and herons near the Lachine Rapids. She had a copy of P.A. Taverner's *Birds of Canada* (1938), which Alex had given her as a present in 1945, as well as her father-in-law's old-fashioned telescope, but had neither binoculars nor an up-to-date Roger Tory Peterson *Field Guide to the Birds* (1947) to aid her observations. Despite the fact that she had had to give up the opportunity to study with a famous art teacher, Mabel continued doing water colours, took up oil painting when her children were young, and, until 1966, painted landscapes.

Following a miscarriage in 1951, Mabel was depressed for about a year. Her mother was diagnosed with breast cancer and died in 1953. William Aston stayed on his own for a few months, but when the McIntosh family bought a house in the expanding suburb of Pointe Claire near Lake St Louis and Terra Cotta Woods, he moved in with them. In her new environment, Mabel's depression lifted. She liked the district with its woods, fields, and lakeshore. The location was ideal for walks alone or with her family. The varied scenery also provided inspiration for her painting.

The move from Verdun to Pointe Claire was a result of the McIntosh family's improved financial situation, and they lived a more or less typical suburban life.[6] On weekday mornings, Alex left for work on the commuter train while Mabel looked after the home. The children attended school and were involved in after-school activities. They went on walks and cross-country ski trips *en famille*, though there was neither time nor money for longer trips. Alex coached little-league baseball, hockey, and football and was a member of the Lion's Club.

Although phoning from Pointe Claire to some areas of Montreal remained long distance into the 1970s, Mabel kept in touch with a few of her school friends. She also developed new friendships and played bridge with women in her neighbourhood. Like other suburban wives and mothers, she became involved in a variety of community activities. She taught Sunday school at the local Presbyterian church, and there were several 'Bell families' living in Pointe Claire with whom the McIntoshes socialized.

In 1959 the McIntosh family bought a car, which enabled them to travel and take camping trips to Ontario. They bought land in Ontario as a joint venture with friends. Soon thereafter, Mabel became aware of the growing attraction between her husband and her best friend. As she later recalled, she had always been easygoing and casual, lenient with her children, and 'not a very good housekeeper.' Alex was exacting and strict, something that he had in common with Mabel's best friend.

When around the same time Mabel lost her father, the fabric of her life seemed to unravel. Her doctor declared her to be menopausal and put her on hormone replacement therapy. Mabel knew that her mood swings were not entirely due to menopause, but she accepted the prescribed treatment. In the early 1960s, menopause was not yet openly discussed. Most women were unaware of alternative treatments, while gynaecologists considered personal problems simply a part of menopause and prescribed estrogen as a panacea for middle-aged women's afflictions and concerns.

In January 1961 Mabel went to a public lecture that changed her life. When she saw the newspaper ad for the Province of Quebec Society for the Protection of Birds event to be held at McGill University's Redpath Museum, Mabel remembered that a member of the 'bird society' (as the PQSPB was commonly known) had come several times to her elementary school, King's School in Westmount, to talk about birds and bird protection. It was at the McGill lecture that she once again met Gladys Hibbard who, thirty years before, had visited her class. Miss Hibbard was handing out membership forms, and Mabel made up her mind to join the PQSPB and attend the society's monthly meetings at the Mechanics' Institute (now the Atwater Library).

The PQSPB, founded in 1917 by the conservation committee of the Women's Club of Montreal, was in its forty-fifth year. From the very beginning, women were active in the association. They participated in the regular Saturday field trips in spring and fall, worked for public education and conservation, and served on the executive. Mabel attended her first outing in the spring of 1961. More than thirty years later, she recalled that 'a whole new world opened up to me.'[7] Bird watchers who lived near Pointe Claire gave lifts to her and to Terry Thormin, a young neighbour and scout leader who joined at about the same time. In a 1993 interview Mabel recalled that 'one of the first people who impressed me was Lewis Terrill' the first president of the PQSPB. Terrill was 'most interesting, very informative and patient with us novice birders.'[8] She was intrigued with his knack for finding birds' nests. After their initial encounter, at the Philipsburg Sanctuary in southwestern Quebec, she was eager to go bird watching again with the knowledgeable old man. In fact, in one of her first subconscious bids for independence, Mabel, who 'was supposed to go away with the family to Ontario' chose to go instead on another trip with Terrill and a few other members of the PQSPB.[9]

At a time when her marriage to Alex was finished in all but name, Mabel gradually created her own life. She acquired new friends who respected her and new interests that engaged her. Hungry for the education she had missed, she improved her scientific knowledge and observational skills by reading books, practising in the field, and learning from more experienced field observers. Though she had for years relied on the identification of her interests with those of her husband and family for a sense of purpose, her confinement to the home opened into a spacious new world of exciting geographical and social environments.[10] To finance her field excursions and longer trips to Ontario, New York, and New Jersey and to secure some degree of financial independence, Mabel – like many other suburban housewives – took on an Avon cosmetics route in 1968. Alex McIntosh eventually moved out in 1971, by which time their children had left home. They did not divorce until 1977. Meanwhile, a legal separation gave Mabel alimony and ownership of their home and freed her from much stress, though some of her health problems persisted after the divorce was final.

Mabel's involvement in bird study, which started as a personal aesthetic and scientific interest, quickly became the main focus of her life as she realized that the lack of a formal science education did not prevent her from participating in a number of science-related activities. Excited as she always had been by the variety of bird life around Montreal, she soon wanted to understand more thoroughly the distribution, migration, and breeding biology of birds. From other members of the PQSPB she learned that 'amateur' ornithologists had many and varied opportunities to contribute to science. They could do this individually, studying, for example, the life histories of birds, or as part of organized efforts sponsored by various North American organizations, such as the National Audubon Society, the U.S. Fish and Wildlife Service, and the Canadian Wildlife Service.[11]

Mabel began contributing scientific data as early as 1961, as a participant in the National Audubon Society's Christmas Bird Census, organized for the Montreal area by Dr Ian McLaren. In spite of the inclement weather and the scarcity of birds, she enjoyed the experience and still participates in this annual event. Data collected from this continent-wide study provide information on roost locations, species distribution, and changes of centres of bird populations and have implications for conservation.

Later, Mabel became involved in other scientific activities, such as the Breeding Bird Survey. This annual collection of valuable scientific data was initiated by the U.S. Fish and Wildlife Service. Launched in 1965 on local bases, it expanded rapidly, and by 1968 included all of Canada and the United States. From 1966 to 1992, Mabel took part every June. Starting in the early morning hours, while it was still dark, she and one or two other birders drove to specific sites around Montreal, arriving at the study area in time to count birds from half an hour before dawn until 9 AM. Stopping every half mile along the twenty-five-mile route, they noted all the birds seen and heard and recorded the information on specifically designed data sheets. The data culled from the survey are included in a statistical analysis program in which each physiogeographic region in each state and province is analysed separately. The data are made available to anyone interested in analysing bird populations and for preparing environmental statements.

Encouraged by Dr Henri Ouellet, later of the National Museum of Natural Sciences in Ottawa, Mabel also became an active participant in the Quebec Nesting Card Program, part of the larger North American Nest Record Card Program started by the Cornell Laboratory of Ornithology in 1965. In one of her first summers in the field, she found, studied, and provided detailed reports on seventy-eight bird nests. In the late 1960s, she obtained a federal bird-banding permit to band migrating passerine birds. Setting up long nylon Japanese mist-nets in Terra Cotta Woods had its share of problems, one being marauding cats that killed birds caught in the fine netting before Mabel could band them.

Throughout the 1960s, the Breeding Bird Survey expanded into several good bird-nesting habitats in the Laurentians and along the St Lawrence and Ottawa Rivers. Mabel got to know the Montreal area and the sights, sounds, and smells of the countryside, which was being destroyed in the process of building new roads, airport extensions, factories, and housing developments. Although she was appalled by the destruction of natural habitats, and took an interest in the PQSPB's conservation and education programs, she never developed a missionary zeal about conservation and did not join other environmental organizations until, in 1992, she became a director of the local Terra Cotta Conservation Committee.

By the late 1960s, the PQSPB organized longer field trips. Some lasted several days, like the ones to Point Pelee National Park in Ontario, one of the most famous places for experiencing bird migration in North America. However, most were overnight trips to Derby Hill on the eastern shore of Lake Ontario, where one could watch great number of migrating hawks in late April. When the weather was not favourable for large kettles of hawks, the group proceeded to visit Montezuma National Wildlife Refuge near Syracuse, New York. On a day trip to Derby Hill in the late 1960s, they saw about 2,000 broad-winged hawks in 'little groups of 100,' but left early to return to Montreal and did not see the flight of 23,000 hawks in the late afternoon. More than twenty-five years later Mabel still feels frustrated at having missed such a spectacular event.[12] On later long-distance trips she was to see large-scale hawk migration in Texas and Panama, but never in Canada.

Bird study became Mabel's year-round obsession. She consulted ornithological journals and handbooks about birds at McGill University's Blacker-Wood Library of Zoology or at the PQSPB's own small library. She pored over the pictures and descriptions in bird-identification guides. She spent practically all her waking hours observing birds or reading and talking about them. During spring and fall, Mabel visited Terra Cotta Woods, abandoned orchards, Mount Royal Park, or Westmount Summit, looking for migrating hawks and songbirds. During the winter, she walked or snowshoed through the fields and small woodlots that still dotted Montreal Island, to search for owls and winter finches.

Mabel's quick eye, friendly manner, infectious enthusiasm, and impressive knowledge of bird life made her a sought-after companion. People would go out of their way to talk to her or offer her lifts to field excursions. Driving along snow-covered, icy roads sometimes led to mishaps, such as cars sliding into each other or refusing to start, far from the nearest telephone or gas station, and often in the early morning hours or at other inconvenient times. On a field trip in March 1966, four cars ran into each other in a sudden blizzard. The police asked all the drivers and their passengers 'to go to the police station in Brossard. At the time – I was a lot younger than I am now – and in front of the whole group, I had to give my name and age.' She was in her forty-fifth year. 'Not long after I thought ... I don't care who knows how old I am.'[13]

In addition to fieldwork, Mabel became involved in the organizational work of the PQSPB and in 1966 was elected to the twenty-five-person board of directors of the society. She also served as editor of the PQSPB's *Newsletter*. This publication began as 'a notice to inform people of the monthly meetings.' In the early 1960s, Dr David Sergeant, a marine biologist and keen field ornithologist, enlarged the newsletter with information on bird migration and distribution.[14] Under Mabel's editorship it grew into a monthly publication of five to six pages, and, in addition to notices of forthcoming meetings and lists of field trips, it contained a section on Montreal-area bird observations. As editor of the newsletter, Mabel fielded phone calls from the general public with questions or information about birds, as well as from bird watchers, conservationists, and professional biologists. By the early 1970s she was at the centre of a large informal network of communications about birds.

Apart from her scientific pursuit of birding, Mabel competed in a friendly way with other members of the PQSPB, especially with Terry Thormin – twenty years her junior – to see who could observe more bird species in Quebec. This led to a lot of spontaneous trips to see rarities: birds that do not usually migrate through, breed in, or winter in Quebec. The 'chase' – with binoculars, field guides, telescope, and camera – was always exciting and sometimes frustrating. It could involve spending many hours in the freezing cold waiting for an unusual gull to emerge out of a cold steam along the St Lawrence River, snowshoeing or hiking through rough terrain, or waiting patiently in people's backyards to confirm a rare sighting. It could mean a drive to Philipsburg on icy roads to see one bird, such as the first summer tanager in Quebec, or a trip to Chibougamou in midwinter by plane to observe large numbers of willow ptarmigan. It could start with getting up in the middle of a cold night to reach a distant wood by daybreak, or standing still among blackflies or mosquitoes waiting to see a tiny warbler.

Birding was a kind of madness that Mabel shared with others similarly afflicted. Her daughter, Marjorie McIntosh Legault, accompanied her on one long-distance trip and declared it an experience she did not care to repeat. 'They stood there staring at a tree for hours.'[15] It was tiring and boring for the casual, but never for the passionate, observer. For Mabel, birding had everything to recommend it. It appealed to her scientific, artistic, and social interests. Moreover, travelling with others was enjoyable and relatively safe for a middle-aged woman.

Birding also provided her with enormous personal challenges. A breakthrough came in May 1969, when she could no longer stand the increasingly tense situation while she and Alex were trying to work out a separation. A cross-continent trip seemed easy by comparison. She had heard about the bird life of the West from Terry Thormin, Marion and Jack Steeves, and other friends. The only way she could afford to go was by bus, taking a tent. Since her friends were not free to go with her, she decided to do it alone. Nothing could have been further from the

Avon routes she had travelled to finance this trip. Crossing North America by bus exposed her to a variety of habitats with their different plant and animal life, different geographic regions and weather patterns, and people from all walks of life. The challenge of setting out by bus on her own and camping alone in a small tent developed her independence beyond anything she could have imagined. Her childhood, youth, and early married life had been relatively sheltered. Even during the war years, when many women worked in difficult and dangerous conditions in munition factories or on board ships taking children from England to Canada, Mabel had remained in the security of her office at Bell Telephone.

The trip was a daring enterprise, a testing ground for her own resources, as she was forced to be responsible for her own arrangements, to make contact with other people, and to rely on her own intuition. Fending off the amorous advances of male travellers was easy compared to dealing with hungry bears. It was in British Columbia's Manning Park that Mabel discovered being on her own could be dangerous and potentially life threatening. Campers were told to lock their food in their cars, but she had no car. She left tins of food outside her tent and was awakened one night by the sound of a bear moving and sniffing around her small canvas tent. Fortunately, the bear did not harm her – it was too busy trying to pry open the food cans. But the following morning she was chilled to find the scattered tins pierced by bear claws.

After a visit to Vancouver Island, where a solicitous bus driver actively discouraged her, as a woman on her own, from camping at Tofino, Mabel made 'the spur of the moment decision' to go to Los Angeles.' Travelling by bus in the United States was not as flexible as in Canada, and the ticket from Vancouver to Los Angeles did not allow her to interrupt her journey. She was further disappointed when bird watchers in Los Angeles had no time to drive her around: everyone was glued to their television sets watching the landing of the first man on the moon. Eventually, she met Jim Laine, a well-known field ornithologist and author of the Laine 'site-guides,' who took her into the field and introduced her to the avifauna of southern California.

The 1970s confirmed and deepened Mabel's new interest. As a middle-aged woman separated from her husband, she had more freedom than ever before. She owned her own home, earned a small income, and could spend more time in the field. In this freer life, Mabel was joined by two women who were to become close friends: Margaret Hendrick and Jo

(Elizabeth) Wright. Marg and her husband Tim joined the PQSPB in the late 1960s. They lived in Dollard-des-Ormeaux, a suburb with many open spaces. Jo Wright had been active in the association since the mid-1950s and had organized field trips and Christmas bird censuses in her area. A trained mineralogist and enthusiastic gardener and naturalist, she and her husband Wally lived in Hudson, off Montreal Island. The Hendricks and the Wrights each had four children, but by the early 1970s the children were independent enough that their mothers could spend time in the field with Mabel. The three women became practically inseparable.

Mabel continued to follow her birds further and further afield. In 1971 she was off to South America for her first encounter with tropical birds, on a trip organized by a Carleton University professor. She had a 'great time' with her birding companions, part of a larger group of naturalists that included Canadian nature painter Robert Bateman. In Montreal, younger members of the PQSPB began regarding her as a birding guru and were happy to take her 'anywhere, any time.'[16]

Mabel was fun to be with. She was a good field ornithologist, liked people, and was delighted to share her knowledge. She had a new circle of friends and, by the mid-1970s, became increasingly involved in the study of raptors – birds of prey, such as eagles, hawks, and falcons (all of which hunt during the day) and owls (which hunt at night). So it was that she returned to the small owls and migrating hawks that had fascinated her as a child and young woman. From the mid-1960s she had often gone on hawk-watching trips with Marion and Jack Steeves and a few other members of the PQSPB. Ten years later, when she was in her early 50s, she finally had the opportunity to participate in the organized study of raptors.

Since the mid-1930s, there had been local efforts in the United States to study hawk migration in relation to weather conditions. After the Second World War, North American ornithologists began investigating the reasons for the decline of various bird species. There was a worldwide concern among scientists, conservationists, and the general public about animals at the top of the food chain, such as the American bald eagle, the osprey, and the peregrine falcon. These bird populations had become endangered because the DDT accumulation in their bodies produced fragile egg shells and prevented nesting success.

In 1974, the National Audubon Society and the Hawk Mountain Sanctuary Association sponsored the first North American Hawk Migration Conference in Syracuse, New York, which Mabel attended as the PQSPB's delegate. At the end of the conference, the approximately 300 delegates organized the Hawk Migration Association of North America, which was to publish a newsletter and hold meetings to discuss the implications of ecological changes on North American hawk populations.[17]

Following the initial meeting, Mabel contributed her observations to the new association's newsletter and spent more time on hawk observation. She learned that wind direction and velocity influenced hawk migration, and she began to explore several areas around Montreal to find which location would produce the best hawk flight under certain weather conditions. On a week day she would ride her bicycle or take local buses to the western tip of Montreal Island. On weekends she went with friends who drove her to the more distant observation sites.

At about the same time, Mabel took part in a study organized by David Bird, then a graduate student at McGill University, on the migration of saw-whet owls and the impact of habitat destruction on their numbers. These tiny birds, like most owls, hunt after dusk. During the day they roost in coniferous trees, tangles, or dense bushes where their cryptic colouration makes them practically invisible to most observers. The project was time consuming because it required spending many exhausting hours in the field from September to April. The investigators carried equipment while walking or snowshoeing over large areas in Ville St Laurent, which was then in the process of 'development.' They wore falconers' heavy leather gauntlets to prevent the owls' needle-sharp claws from hurting them, and tetanus shots ensured they would not get lockjaw should the owls manage to pierce through to their skin. Once they located an owl, they used a long fishing pole with a snare attached to the top to lift it off its roost; the snare pinned the bird's wings to its body and apparently did no harm to the owl. They weighed the owl on a hand-held scale, recorded its length and wing span, collected parasites off its feathers, placed a numbered aluminum band on one leg, and attached a colourful soft plastic tag to one wing.

Mabel and her friend Marg did the fieldwork for David Bird as volunteer investigators. Other PQSPB members helped to observe the location of the owls' diurnal roosts. Looking for leg bands was difficult, but the wing tags showed up well in the shade of a cedar or spruce tree. Colour tagging provided data on the number of individual owls that migrated through or wintered in certain habitats. Prior to the study, observers thought that few owls migrated through the area. The data proved that numerous owl passed through the observation area in migration.

In the late 1970s, when Marion and Jack Steeves moved from Montreal to Calgary, Mabel acquired a new hawk-watching companion and driver: Bob Barnhurst, a member of the PQSPB, who came to Montreal from England in 1974 to work in the Department of Mining and Metallurgy at McGill University. By 1980, when the owl-tagging project was finished, Mabel devoted herself to the study of hawk migration and travelled in North America with her friends. In 1982, she visited relatives in England; on her return she was devastated to find that Jo Wright had died during a trip to the Himalayas. Moreover, Marg Hendrick had moved to Ontario, so she suffered the loss of two close friends with whom she had shared many enjoyable hours in the field.

Just as the depression that resulted from her crises in mid-life prompted her to forge a new life for herself, the loss of these two friends eventually led to another phase of Mabel's life. Deprived of drivers at age sixty-one, she bought a scooter to get from Pointe Claire to Valleyfield during the spring hawk migration. Some days she made the trip, which took two to three hours each way, in vain. At other times she saw hundreds or even thousands of hawks. In 1990, Mabel estimated that she spent about 250 hours watching hawks in the spring (from late March to mid-May) and about 350 hours during the fall (from late August to mid-November).[18] In retrospect, she thinks that the times spent were closer to 300 and 450 hours, respectively.

Mabel's increased dedication to hawk watching had an unwelcome result: lifting her binoculars every twenty seconds for several hours a day led to carpal tunnel syndrome, a repetitive strain injury. Despite the pain, she insisted that corrective surgery be postponed.

In spite of her remarkable involvement in hawk-migration study during the last twenty years, Mabel has maintained her interest in other aspects of ornithology. She has taken several trips to Central and South America and, in 1990, went to Africa. She continues to be part of a telephone network in the Montreal area that receives and distributes messages about unusual bird sightings. She serves as a resource person for Peter Whelan's bird column in the Saturday *Globe and Mail* and also occasionally provides information about migratory movements, nesting successes and failures, and the appearance of unusual birds in Quebec to television and radio programs.

For her seventieth birthday in 1992, Mabel's friends bought her a telephone answering machine so that she could receive messages about rare birds. She still enjoys the occasional trip to observe a new or rare species, and sometimes regrets that her dedication to hawk-migration study precludes visits to other habitats.

Mabel shows few signs of slowing down, continues her work as a director for the PQSPB, and has been elected its first honorary vice-president. She visits her married sons in Ontario and participates in the activities of her daughter's family in Pointe Claire. She mentors other naturalists, some of whom join her in the field during hawk migration.

Mabel McIntosh's life demonstrates that women can make life course changes and choose alternative lifestyles, even when staggering obstacles must be overcome; that women, who have been socialized to become subordinate to the demands of family, can find other meaningful activities. Mabel's involvement with a community of naturalists enabled her to recover and develop a childhood love of science. Her participation in field ornithology led to independence and a life of her own. She became known and respected across North America as an outstanding field observer and has been the subject of several articles in newspapers and journals.[19] Although she has not published extensively (a common measure of scientific success), she has contributed data to a number of different scientific studies and has published articles on hawk migration.[20]

More importantly, her example indicates that in spite of the pervasive ideology of the media and advertising industry, youth, money, and social position are not the only requirements for having a meaningful life. In a society where middle-aged women are often invisible, Mabel's infectious enthusiasm, energy, and knowledge, her capacity for friendship with all ages, her trips by bus and scooter, and her visibility in the media communicate an engaging, inspiring alternative.

NOTES

I thank Mabel McIntosh for her friendship of more than twenty years, and David Ainley, Betsy Barber, Tina Crossfield, Sarah Jane Hills, Marjorie McIntosh Legault, and Susan Sullivan for their help with various aspects of the project. Unless otherwise stated, information on Mabel McIntosh's life was accumulated during numerous conversations between her and the author from 1972 to 1995.

1 Susan A. McDaniel, 'The Changing Canadian Family: Women's Roles and the Impact of Feminism' in *Changing Patterns: Women in Canada*, ed. Sandra Burt, Lorraine Code, and Lindsay Dorney, 2nd ed. (Toronto: McClelland and Stewart, 1993), 432
2 Bird watchers with serious scientific interests, also referred to as 'avocational ornithologists' or 'field ornithologists,' have contributed considerably to the

science of ornithology. See Marianne Gosztonyi Ainley, 'The Contribution of the Amateur to North American Ornithology: A Historical Perspective,' *The Living Bird* 18 (1979–80): 161–77.

3 On invisible women in science, see Margaret W. Rossiter, *Women Scientists in America: Struggles and Strategies to 1940* (Baltimore: Johns Hopkins University Press, 1982); Phina Abir-Am and Dorinda Outram, eds., *Uneasy Careers and Intimate Lives: Women in Science, 1789–1979* (New Brunswick, NJ: Rutgers University Press, 1987); Marianne Gosztonyi Ainley, ed., *Despite the Odds: Essays on Canadian Women and Science* (Montreal: Véhicule, 1990).

4 Michèle Martin, 'Hello, Central?' *Gender, Technology, and Culture in the Formation of the Telephone Systems* (Montreal: McGill-Queen's University Press, 1991), 57

5 As she recalls it, Mabel's starting salary was $10 a week in 1939, and after six years she earned $16.50 a week. By contrast, Lois Martin ('Women at Work: "Hello" Girls Are Young, Work Fairly Easy Hours under Fine Conditions,' *St Catharines Standard*, 25 Aug. 1943, 16) wrote that 'a new girl' would receive $18.50 per week, and after five years the 'maximum basic rate' would be $29.50 per week.

6 Veronica Strong-Boag, 'Home Dreams: Women and the Suburban Experiment in Canada,' *Canadian Historical Review* 72 (Dec. 1991): 471–504

7 Mabel McIntosh, interview with Sarah Jane Hills, 7 March 1993 (in the author's files)

8 Ibid. On Terrill see Marianne Gosztonyi Ainley, 'Lewis McIver Terrill: Promoter of Bird Study and Conservation in Quebec,' *Tchébec* 12 (1982): 72–85.

9 McIntosh, interview with Hills

10 On women's life course see, Mary Catherine Bateson, *Composing a Life* (New York: Penguin, 1990); Cindi Katz and Janice Monk, *Full Circles: Geographies of Women over the Life Course* (New York: Routledge, 1993).

11 On 'amateur' involvement in the various projects see Ainley, 'Contribution of the Amateur'

12 McIntosh, interview with Hills

13 Ibid.

14 Ibid.

15 Marjorie McIntosh Legault, conversation with the author, 18 Sept. 1994

16 Robert Carswell, conversation with the author, May 1974

17 See *Proceedings of the North American Hawk Migration Conference* (Washington Depot, CT: North American Hawk Migration Association, 1975)

18 Jean Paquin, 'Mabel McIntosh: animée par la passion des oiseaux,' *Québec Oiseaux* 2, no. 1 (1990): 8

19 Ibid., 8–9; Susan Purcell, 'It's Not Pie in the Sky: It's Birdwatching,' *Montreal*

Star, 18 Sept. 1968, 83; Pierre Gingras, 'Mabel McIntosh, à 66 ans, n'a qu'une passion: les oiseaux,' *La Presse*, 22 March 1988; James Quig, 'In Search of the Sharp-Shinned Hawk,' *Gazette* (Montreal), 6 May 1990, A1, A4

20 Mabel began contributing bird observation data to the PQSPB's *Annual Report* in 1962. Later, she co-authored articles with Bob Barnhurst. See Bob Barnhurst and Mabel McIntosh, 'Hawk-watching in Montreal,' *Tchébec* 6 (1976): 67–75; M. McIntosh and R.J. Barnhurst, 'Fall Hawk Migration at the Morgan Arboretum, Ste. Anne de Bellevue, Québec,' *Tchébec* 10 (1980): 97–102; R.J. Barnhurst and M.W. McIntosh, 'The 1981 Fall Hawk Migration at the Arboretum, Ste. Anne de Bellevue, Québec,' *Tchébec* 11 (1981): 100–3. In addition the two authors were regional editors from 1982 to 1993 of the North American Hawk Migration Association's journal, *Migration Studies*.

BREAKING INTO 'MEN'S PROFESSIONS'

Marion Hilliard:
'Raring to Go All the Time'

WENDY MITCHINSON

Marion Hilliard was one of the most famous woman doctors of her time. Chief of Obstetrics and Gynaecology at Women's College Hospital, Toronto, from 1947 to 1957, she was the most sought-after obstetrician in Toronto. What made her a household name in Canada and elsewhere, however, was a series of articles she wrote in *Chatelaine* in the early 1950s and which she turned into the bestselling book, *A Woman Doctor Looks at Love and Life*. At the time of her death in 1958, she was working on another book, *Women and Fatigue*.[1] The popularity of both books is found in the advice that she gave women and the straightforward, no nonsense way in which she gave it. Much of that was influenced by her own life.

Several themes emerging from Hilliard's childhood and continuing throughout her adult years shaped the guidance she gave women. She had a very strong sense of security and confidence that came from family, friends, and the central role that religion played in her life. Out of that sense of belonging came the belief in social responsibility, of giving back to the community some of what it had given her. This combination of private and public reflected a life of balance. Hilliard was good at what she did and she was ambitious, but she did not define herself solely by her work. Other aspects of her life remained significant – family, friends, religion, and social activism, as well as sports and other recreational activities. She firmly believed all were necessary to be a whole person. Balancing different aspects of life and experience necessitated a certain pragmatism. She was a person who worked hard for what she wanted, but if it proved unattainable she shifted focus to something that was. She did not worry about what she could not have or what could not be.

As a physician, Hilliard was very much influenced by the medical world she inhabited. She was trained to have a specific view of the body, in particular the female body. As was her wont, she did not challenge that view directly but worked within the limits provided by that perspective in a way that spoke to her patients. She was sympathetic, she empathized, she was honest, but she was a physician who shared a professional ethic that tended to medicalize events.[2] One of the advantages she had in working with women patients was the fact that she was a woman herself. She knew the female body in a way that no male physician could. She had gone through many of the physiological processes (a major exception being pregnancy) that most women experience and believed she knew the pressures of doing so in the Canada of the mid-twentieth century. When she spoke to her patients directly, or to audiences, or when she wrote in popular women's magazines, women could identify with her advice. Her own upbringing, her personal experience and that of her patients became a generalized experience on which she based this advice. But her experience and that of many of her patients was founded on a very white, middle-class, Anglo-Protestant existence.

Hilliard was born on 17 June 1902 in the small Ontario town of Morrisburg. She remembered her childhood as an idyllic time. It provided her with physical and emotional security and gave her a very strong sense of her own identity. Her memories of childhood were dominated by family events involving both her immediate family and her large extended family, nurturing her feeling of rootedness and her sense of belonging.[3] Marion's parents were very supportive of all their children. There was no doubt that the girls in the family would be educated, although it was a bit of a shock when Marion decided that she wanted to be a physician rather than the teacher her father wanted her to be. While her father did not approve of her ambition, he agreed that she could register at Victoria College at the University of Toronto and take courses in the natural and physical sciences. In her second year, she registered as a biology and medical sciences student. Her father was still not happy with her choice, but he did not place any obstacles in her way and he continued to support her studies. Once Marion finished her undergraduate years at the university, she was still determined to be a doctor. As before, her father did not approve, but he agreed to support her throughout her medical training.[4] No matter what she did, Marion would be loved and supported. The security this provided cannot be overemphasized.

Marion had a rich personal life that provided her with warmth and security. She made friends easily and kept them. One of her closest

Dr Marion Hilliard, Chief of Obstetrics and Gynaecology,
Women's College Hospital, 1947–56

friends was a young woman named Maryon Moody (later Maryon Pear-son), whom she met during her first year at university.[5] Both joined a women's sorority, which Marion saw as an opportunity to share with others; the bonding that occurred in such a group was important to her, for she needed people, and this remained true throughout her life. One of her closest friends (and life partner) was made when, exhausted, she was forced to take a vacation during the Second World War. While away from Toronto she met a social worker, Opal Boynton, who intro-duced her to trout fishing, of which Marion became enamoured. After the war, Opal moved from the United States, and they shared a home in Toronto until Marion's death.[6]

Marion's friends played more than an emotional role in her life. They often helped her professionally. A Morrisburg friend had been one of the earliest to encourage her to be a physician. Another financed a year in England for Marion at the end of her studies in 1927. On arrival in England, she presented a letter of introduction from another friend to

Miss Gertrude Dearnley, a gynaecological surgeon who was just beginning a successful career of her own. Despite the difference in experience, Miss Dearnley took Marion under her wing and encouraged her to sit the exams for the Royal College of Physicians and the Royal College of Surgeons. She and Dearnley became good friends and remained so for the rest of Marion's life.[7]

On her return to Canada, Marion began work at Women's College Hospital (WCH), where she had interned.[8] She remained there for the rest of her career. The women who worked at WCH were a dedicated group who appreciated what the hospital offered – the chance to practise medicine in an environment that was supportive of women. Marion inhabited a woman's world at WCH, consisting of a network of women who were willing to help and support one another. For example, Dr Sproule Manson, herself from WCH, offered to share her office when Marion was setting up private practice in the Depression.[9] Manson became one of Marion's mentors, a function Marion would perform for other women in her turn. This support was also reflected in Marion's treatment of her women patients and in their high regard for her.

The security and confidence provided by family and friends were reinforced by her religious upbringing and beliefs. Both of Marion's parents, Anna and Irwin Hilliard, came from strong religious backgrounds. Anna's father was a Methodist minister of the old school who disapproved of women wearing any kind of jewellery, even wedding bands. In deference to her father, Anna did not wear her ring until after his death in 1912. Anna, herself, seemed to be a mover and shaker within the local Methodist community, especially in the foreign mission field. Irwin, too, was involved in the church – teaching Sunday school and later as superintendent of the school, and it was his habit to lead his family in prayer every morning.[10] They were earnest people whose religious faith directed them to community involvement.[11] From her parents' activities, Marion drew her image of what an ideal marital relationship was. There was no doubt that Irwin was the head of the household, but he was supportive of Anna's work outside the home and made sure that domestic help was available to ensure that she could develop her own interests. Of course, the comfort of the home and the ability to have domestic help was preconditioned by the middle-class status that the family was able to maintain.

Through her parents' relationship and activities, Marion learned to give back to society something of what it had given to her. During World War I, when so many young men were overseas, she and other young women pitched in and helped local farmers plant and harvest their crops. In her late teens, she set up one of the earliest locals of the Canadian Girls in Training. She taught the younger girls on Sunday, and one evening during the week they would get together for games and projects relating to the Sunday lesson.[12]

This sense of social responsibility backed by a very firm religious faith never left Marion. At university she may have been away from home and enjoying the freedom that absence provided her, but she was her parents' daughter. During her years in Toronto, she became involved in the United Student Christian Movement of Canada, which was founded the year she began university. Disillusioned by war, this group of young people wanted to address social problems from a Christian, but nondenominational, perspective. Marion was leaving the narrow limitations of her Methodist upbringing behind, but her faith was real and deep and the SCM was an organization through which she could express her desire to help society in a way that made sense to her. It provided her with a wider vision of belief at a time when she was ready to embrace it.[13] The SCM, too, was another network for Marion, as were her childhood friends and her sorority sisters.[14] After her student years, Marion became involved with the YWCA and thus continued her social activism within a Christian context.[15] Faith always remained central. In her later years she formed a group of women who met during Lent to discuss religious issues, and in 1950 she and her friend Poppy (Opal) formally joined the Anglican Church.[16]

When Marion entered medicine, she took her sense of commitment with her. She later reflected, 'How a woman can undertake such an arduous, time-consuming course without a definite sense of mission and the beginning of a career, I do not know.'[17] Medicine was not a job, it was a mission for her. Indeed, originally she had hoped to become a medical missionary. She certainly gave back to the profession. She was a president of the Federation of Canadian Medical Women and a vice-president and president of the Medical Women's International Association.[18]

Marion's religious beliefs and social commitment, however, did not make her an ideologue. If anything, they reinforced her pragmatism. She wanted to see things get done, and if that meant compromise and shifting perspective, that was fine.[19] This flexibility was exhibited very early. As a teenager, she did chafe under the constraints placed on her and her activities by her parents, but she loved them, respected them, and understood that the prohibitions on dancing, card playing, and activities on the Sabbath were a result of their deep-seated religious beliefs. She would not disobey directly but, as one biographer put it, 'she was not above abetting others in such pursuits.'[20] An example was her willingness to play hymns at three-quarter time so that her older sister could dance with boyfriends while Anna and Irwin were at prayer meetings. While at university, she began to engage in activities of which her parents would have disapproved – going to plays, playing bridge, dancing. Marion took the attitude that what they didn't know wouldn't hurt them and was very careful not to tell them. In her philosophy, some principles could also be set aside for a greater good. When in 1947 she heard that the United Church had rejected money from the O'Keefe Brewing Company, she arranged to get the money for WCH. Part of that money enabled Marion and others at the hospital to inaugurate a Cancer Detection Clinic for women in 1948, the first in Canada.[21]

If Marion could balance principles with outcome, it perhaps reflected the personal balance in her own life. She may have been one of Canada's most famous physicians, she may have been an ambitious one, but she was by no means driven or one-dimensional. Indeed she had a thirst for life and could no more limit herself to a single activity than stop breathing. As a child, she loved sports, and both parents encouraged her athletic endeavours. Her father saw the effort as character building and her mother as 'distraction from sin.' Marion swam (she was one of the strongest swimmers, male or female, in Morrisburg), played tennis, and participated in other activities that the time deemed suitable for girls. She also revelled in playing hockey. At first, the boys did not want her to play, but she insisted, so they put her in goal and began aiming the puck at her. Undeterred, she would not leave the game.[22]

Marion's years at university were a whirlwind of activity. Her courses were incredibly demanding, but Marion was no narrowly focused individual. She worked hard and played hard – tennis, volleyball, basketball, and above all her beloved hockey. For six years she was the star player on the women's team. The great Canadian athlete Bobbie Rosenfeld remembered Marion as the 'centre who scored the only goal on the Varsity girls' team of '28, a girl who could shoot like a boy and skate like a whippet, a real going concern on skates.'[23] Marion simply abounded with energy and refused to give up outside activities to devote herself totally to her studies. She needed the one in order to be good at the other. This sense of balance would be one of the attributes that made her a good physician and was reflected in her attitudes to how women should live their lives. She conveyed these attitudes through both her influence and advice.

An example of her influence occurred midway through her second year in medical school when she applied for a junior internship at Women's College Hospital. Marion was appalled at the lives the nurses led – twelve-hour days after which they still had to attend lectures and study. This was not a healthy regime. She couldn't imagine how they could survive. Where was the fun in their lives? Where was the physical activity that would sustain them in their incredibly pressured existence? She shocked the staff by appearing in the nurses' living room in basket-ball bloomers and sweater, strumming her ukulele, and encouraging the nurses to join her in song. She prodded them to raise money for tennis and badminton equipment and arranged for them to swim at the local YWCA pool. The nursing supervisor noticed an increased alertness among her nurses and an increase in their energy level.[24] Dr Elizabeth Stewart, chair of the medical staff, caught the essence of Hilliard's work at WCH and her personality when she described her as 'Raring to go all the time. Needs to be held down.'[25]

The first place to begin an examination of Hilliard's advice to women is in her perception of the female body. More than anyone, she should have had a sense of how strong that body was. Yet she was also a prod-uct of her time and, as did most physicians and Canadians, Hilliard believed that women were very much dominated by their bodies. She would probably have made the same statement about men – under-standably, physicians did see people as essentially physiological beings. But in comparing the two sexes, physicians agreed that women, more than men, were biologically determined. As Hilliard herself explained it, 'at certain important periods of a woman's life the activity of their [sic] nervous and glandular systems undergoes a great change, often producing somewhat erratic types of behaviour.'[26]

Hilliard felt that she understood women and their needs because she was a woman but also because she lived her life among women. In addi-tion, Hilliard was convinced of the differences between men and women. She felt that 'women are born with more sensitivity and intuition than men, for very practical reasons. These extra senses must be cultivated and nourished in order to enrich love-making; without them the act of love can be a barren experience for a woman.'[27] In this respect, her attitudes did not differ all that much from those of the nineteenth century.[28]

Hilliard maintained that the sex drive was strong in both sexes but expressed differently.

I ... used to believe that if women had no fear of pregnancy they would enjoy a sex life to the same extent and in more or less the same way as men. I was wrong. A woman's reaction to sex has few points of resemblance with a man's. For one thing, her climax varies from one so slight that it is a sigh to one so profound and deep that it results in an agonizing cry. A man's emotion varies, but his physical climaxes are identical. Millions of women feel nothing, nothing at all; others are so moved that there is a small death within them and they weep. The same woman can experience the whole galaxy of climaxes, from the top to the bottom, depending on her mood. The male enjoyment of sex requires no mood except the basic desire.[29]

It is clear that she believed women to be more complex beings than men. If at times she essentialized women, her men too became very one-dimensional, cardboard figures. They were very much creatures whose libido is mechanistic. The consequences of this for marriage could be disastrous. For women, atmosphere was everything, for men, it was negligible in ensuring sexual satisfaction. She recognized the strength of the sex drive in many women but warned them that they had to differentiate between love and passion, that the two did not necessarily go together, and not to confuse one with the other. She believed that women had basic needs but that passion was not one of them.[30]

Her advice to women about sexuality was given in a very forthright and pragmatic manner. She depicted a world where there was no such thing as a platonic relationship between a man and a woman. At any time passion could erupt. It was a dangerous world because urges could not be contained. Believing this, she recognized that passion did not restrict itself to the marital relationship, although it was socially preferable if it did. She, more than others writing at the time, was willing to entertain – if not advocate – the idea of an active sex life for unmarried women. She was unmarried herself and knew that sexuality was not placed on hold. But neither should it be engaged in. 'Sleeping around,' she argued, was destructive for a woman. She not only had to face the possibility of pregnancy but also 'her physiological pattern is shocked and mortified by the callous emptiness of promiscuity.' Emotions influenced the body as if the body could tell legitimate from illegitimate sex. Instead of succumbing to her sexual urges, a career woman should 'plunge into a professional challenge that is almost too big to handle.'[31] What is apparent in Hilliard's description of the single career woman is how close to home it seems. She herself was one. She was not married, although at the time of writing she had a life partner in Poppy. Her apparent solution was the advice she recommended to others.

Hilliard's perspective on marriage and the family was very much influenced by her own parents' relationship. The husband was definitely the head of the household. His needs seemed to come before anyone else's, and it was the woman's obligation to create a happy marriage. The reason Hilliard gave for this was that 'a man's life is much more difficult than a woman's, full of the groaning strain of responsibility and the lonely and often fruitless search for pride in himself.'[32] This concern about the husband's view of himself and his feelings carried over into the sexual life of the marriage. Many wives lost interest in love-making, but Hilliard believed it was vital for the well-being of the marriage to continue sexual relations and to make husbands believe their wives still found them desirable. In doing so the pretence would become reality.

A man can feel kinship with the gods if his woman can make him believe he can cause flowering within her. If she doesn't feel it, she must bend every effort to pretence. A husband may be offended by this. He does not want a service rendered. He wants love freely given. I am making a fundamental distinction between loving and making love. A wife loves, therefore she woos a tired mate when she knows he needs her. The pretence is only in her physical reaction to the act itself. There is no greater gift and it should be treasured. It's the worthiest duplicity on the face of the earth; I heartily recommend it to discontented wives. It gives a man his manhood, a quality of glorious robustness that cannot fail to reward the giver. Thousands of women who have begun this sort of benign sham have discovered that their pretended delight rapidly became real.[33]

Such a view reinforced her perception of the centrality of sex in men's lives and the centrality of emotion in women's. She separated the two. While we might be appalled at the dishonesty involved in the above scenario, she and many others would have seen this as a consideration for others with little harm to oneself. It was a practical view. It also extended the mothering role of women to their husbands.

It might appear that Hilliard saw the marital relationship as problematic, and at times she probably did. But she considered it the most important relationship in a woman's life. She urged women to delay childbearing so that they could adjust to living with their husbands. Her advice was part of a new trend in marriage counselling that stressed the relationship between the husband and wife as primary, even more significant than that between mother and child.[34] For decades, advice literature had seemed to suggest that marriage was important because it enabled family formation. Women married in order to have children. This did not mean that women did not marry for love but rather that the bond between mother and child was so strong that it superseded all else. But as Hilliard pointed out to women, they usually stayed married to and lived with the same person for fifty years. The time children spent at home was limited. Because of this, wives had to put the needs of their husbands before those of their children.[35] Hilliard had a very idealized view of marriage and family, stemming from her own childhood. She felt that the home should be a refuge from the outside world where its members could gain sustenance to face the pressures of modern society. While the marital relationship might not have been an equal one, the mutuality of love rendered any inequalities manageable.[36]

On the surface, Hilliard appeared to support very traditional notions of gender separation and the subservience of the wife's needs within the marital relationship. Such a view is simplistic. Although she gave due recognition to the pressures on husbands in their quest to support their families and win some semblance of identity for themselves, she did not negate the yearning for identity in women. Indeed, she thought it was essential. Just as she tried for balance in her own life and encouraged the nurses in WCH to engage in physical activity to give them additional energy for their work, she wanted to see young women develop their own lives. It wasn't enough to be married; a young woman should learn about herself and other people.[37] She should be adventuresome. Hilliard made it clear that women had basic needs and among these was the need for status and achievement;[38] but, this need was going to be difficult to fulfil within marriage. Hilliard, herself, had ambivalent feelings about wives and their work at home. While she had tremendous admiration for women and the work they did within the home, her praise was for the never-ending aspect of such work. She did not have a very high estimation of the skill it involved.[39] After all, her mother had run a large home and also engaged in outside activities. So did Marion; but both she and her mother had domestic help.

Hilliard was ahead of her time in her belief that work was necessary for women's happiness and that married women had a right to work. She probably could not imagine her own life without work, and her mother's example of community involvement was a strong one. She felt her mother to be an ideal woman, and she had the example of her father, who recognized the individuality of his wife and encouraged her to engage in activities outside the home. Women should do more than take care of the family, even though that should be their main priority. During the Second World War, the government had encouraged the entry of married women into the paid labour force as a wartime measure, but after the cessation of hostilities it tried to force them back into their homes. At one level it was successful, but at another level the government failed. After the war, the participation of married women in the workforce increased to a considerable degree. In 1941, 12.7 per cent of the female labour force was married; by 1951, that figure had become 30 per cent, and by 1961 it had increased to 47 per cent.[40] Hilliard recognized this. She argued that women needed education because they would have to work for a living, not just before marriage but after – until they began their families and after their families had grown. She was not a predictor but an observer and, significantly, a booster of what was going on. She encouraged women and did not make them feel guilty.[41] What placed her in the vanguard was her ability to see women's employment as more than a temporary phenomenon. She worried that women themselves did not recognize the number of years they would be working outside the home. Women had to plan for this; they had to become better educated; they had to realize that death, separation, or divorce might end a marriage and place the responsibility for providing for a family on them.[42]

Hilliard's ideas on work for women may have seemed ahead of their time, but this does not mean that she had a full understanding of why women worked. Women worked because they had to. Without a wife's income, only 14 per cent of families in the mid-1950s had annual incomes over $4,000; when the wife's income was taken into account, 51 per cent of families had incomes of $4,000 or more.[43] Hilliard refused to recognize this. She criticized the wife who, perhaps frazzled by her family responsibilities and work demands, tired herself and neglected her family, all for 'the $42.97 she gets every week, after deductions.'[44] The money was not worth it from her point of view. But for many working-class families, such money could mean the difference between nutritious food or little food on the table. It could mean clothes on the backs of the children and the possibility of an education for them. In the world Hilliard inhabited, married career women worked because they loved what they did. She dismissed women who worked for money as if this were something shameful.[45] She seemed to feel that women really should not be interested in money.

Hilliard's definition of work was a broad one. Within it she included any activity that fulfilled a woman's need to do something worthwhile.[46] Work was necessary for living, to have a sense of value. Charity work, working for a community organization, working part-time in a dress shop, working full-time, all were approved as long as the homelife of the family was not neglected. In approving of this range of work, Hilliard again indicates how ahead of her time she was. She was willing to lessen the distinction between paid and unpaid work and to acknowledge that the unpaid activities of women were work. Although Hilliard supported the right of women to work, it was clear that she believed the primary responsibility of women was to their families. She recognized that most women wanted to marry and have children. Indeed, some of the most moving parts of her writing are when she describes women who don't marry or who marry and can't have children. She hints at her own pain at not having her early expectations of marriage and family fulfilled. She knew intimately the pressures faced by the unmarried, and she wrote sensitively about the 'shredding sense of failure' that unmarried women felt; there was nothing so painful for a woman as when she had to admit to herself that she was going to spend her life alone. She advised such women that they had to get on with their lives. For her this meant cutting ties with married friends. An unmarried woman could continue to do women's activities with the wife but could not socialize with the husband and wife as a couple. Their lives were simply too different, and it could only cause the unmarried woman pain, akin to 'flattening her nose against the candy-store window.'[47]

Hilliard was an obstetrician, and much of her patient roster would have required her to see a woman through her prenatal months, the birth of the child, and the immediate care of mother and child afterwards. Not surprisingly, given her view of the female body, she believed that pregnant women were very much dominated by their physiology and that the changing hormonal balance could lead to pregnant women being 'out of ... control' and thus not responsible for what they did. Their emotions were volatile and their energy levels uneven. This was why she warned newly married couples to delay having a child. Marriage in its early stages was difficult enough 'without introducing the extra hazard of pregnancy's split personality effects.'[48]

No one would deny the influence of pregnancy on women, the extra stresses that it places on the body, and the emotional nature of what happens to the woman. But Hilliard's words conjure up an almost Jekyll and Hyde personality. Such a view played into the stereotypical notions of the emotionality of women, which had been part of western society's perspective for centuries. It ignored the reality of most women's lives – lives that didn't give them the luxury of being 'out of control.' They had too many responsibilities to meet and, whether pregnant or not, most women met them.

If women were out of control, it was necessary for them to have someone who was in control to help them. This was the responsibility of the physician. Concerned about the tendency of women to talk to one another and to give each other advice, Hilliard warned her patients and readers, 'Don't trust yourself or anyone else ... Ask me instead. I'm taking over while you go through this. When the time comes, I'll give yourself back to you.'[49] Here her role as physician, her own personal sense of confidence, and her desire to take care or to mother came into play. From the perspective of the present day, this is an extraordinary statement and one that few physicians would make. It does, however, give real insight into the nature of patient–physician relationships in the past. The physician, not the patient, was in control. This was not always imposed on the patient; many patients wanted the doctor in control. The patient was vulnerable to what was happening to her and perhaps needed someone else to take responsibility. Certainly women in the '30s, '40s, and '50s were living in a world of experts and were accustomed to looking to someone else for advice.[50] Hilliard was the expert and knew herself to be one and acted accordingly. Where Hilliard had an advantage was in being a woman herself. It meant that her experience was her patients' experience, even though she had never had a child. That didn't matter so much as the fact that she was a woman and seemed to understand other women. She was part of the group, not outside it, as a male physician would have been. She could talk to women and be understood.

Hilliard never diminished the importance of childbirth. Her descriptions of it, in fact, were often poetic. The experience could 'light up a woman's life'; it was a dramatic act, 'the torment wrapped with exultation beyond self,' which 'grants a woman a piercing, dazzling pride in herself that may become dim but never dingy.'[51] She could even wax eloquent about birth in a hospital, an environment that recent observers have criticized as cold and impersonal. 'The scene in a delivery room is especially moving when a baby is being born in the middle of the night. Outside in the darkness people are sleeping but the delivery room is brilliant under the arc lights and filled with the concentration of a well-trained team focused on a single moment, the instant of birth. It holds a heightened sense of friendliness and tenderness rarely found elsewhere.'[52] Whether the woman undergoing the birth would have described it in similar terms is unknown. What is known is that most of her patients found Hilliard wonderful. It was not necessarily the actual technical aspects of her care; they were quite in keeping with the rest of the profession. It was her way of empathizing with them that they appreciated. She had an intimate relationship with her patients, perhaps very much influenced by the world of women in which she lived.

If Hilliard was best-known as an obstetrician, her making menopause a public issue, something to be discussed and not hidden, is perhaps the area where she was most innovative. She was one of the few to write about menopause in a way that laypeople could understand. While some of her ideas appear dated, the fact that she brought the topic out into the open was comforting to many. She recognized that not enough had been written on menopause, with the result that women had some peculiar notions about it – that it would 'whiten [their] hair, make [them] pregnant, and bring on insanity.'[53] She was concerned about this and the lack of sympathy shown to menopausal women.

Hilliard and other physicians depicted menopausal women as 'gloomy,' and compared them to adolescents, people not quite adult. They had all the symptoms of adolescence – they were oversensitive and emotional, and they experienced erratic energy levels. At best, menopause was 'a peculiar and disorganized feminine transition.'[54] What Hilliard was trying to do with such descriptions was to explain to women what they could expect from themselves and to husbands what they could expect from their wives during this time. She was trying to create sympathy for the menopausal woman, to get her to be willing to indulge herself and not hold herself up to a standard that she could no longer meet.

According to Hilliard, menopause was caused by the 'unresponsiveness' of the ovaries, which in turn caused the sex organs to 'deteriorate.' 'Hormones and certain glands behave eccentrically,' with 'emotional upheaval' the consequence.[55] Hilliard's description is full of negativity. The image is of a body that is failing. Yet the body is not failing; it is doing what all women's bodies do. Thus what is normal for a female body is considered eccentric. This view was not unique to Hilliard but was conventional medical wisdom in western society.[56] The normative model for a woman was one who was young enough to be still menstruating and able to bear children. Young women entering puberty were judged by how well their bodies were approaching this ideal, and older women were judged by how much their bodies had deviated from this ideal.

Although she was not painting a particularly attractive picture for women facing the menopause, Hilliard did assure them that whatever upsets they were going through would pass and they would enter a period of their lives where they would regain their energy and then some. Their bodies would once again be dependable. A 'sense of rebirth and exhilaration beyond description' would occur, and they would renew their sexual life, no longer constrained by the worry of pregnancy. For the career woman unencumbered by husband or children, Hilliard predicted 'a marvellous life.' 'The fifty-year-old single women could run the world if the world would give them a chance.' She saw the postmenopausal years as liberating; women would speak out and say what they wanted, without the worry of pleasing others. Her reassurance was believable because her readers and her patients knew that Hilliard herself had gone through the menopause and had reached the plateau about which she enthused.[57] So few people in the 1940s and 1950s saw aging in a positive way that Hilliard's views were quite refreshing and ahead of her time. Thirty-five years later, feminists such as Germaine Greer would rediscover what Hilliard already knew and begin to bring the postmenopausal woman into her own.[58]

Hilliard was very much loved by her patients. Because she was so popular she had a large patient roster and so was unable to spend much individual time with each woman. But what is important is that her patients clearly did not feel part of an assembly line. One patient recalled, 'Although my treatment took only five minutes, when I came out I felt five months better, for the treatment was not purely physical. In those few minutes the mind had been touched and the spirit challenged by something in the manner, in the tone of voice, in the assurance of the movements of this woman.'[59] The person who was Marion was just as important as the physician who was Marion. The person who was Marion, the influences that shaped her life, made her the physician she was.

Marion kept her sense of curiosity and adventure till the end. She died early, barely fifty-six years old, of a brain tumor, on 15 July 1958. According to a long-time colleague at WCH, the institution she had given so much to and where she chose to spend her final illness, her dying words were 'Well, whaddaya know!'[60]

NOTES

1 Marion Hilliard, *A Woman Doctor Looks at Love and Life* (Garden City, NY: Doubleday, 1957), and Marion Hilliard, *Women and Fatigue: A Woman Doctor's Answer* (Garden City, NY: Doubleday, 1960)

2 An early example of work on professional ethics in medicine is Barbara Ehrenreich and Deirdre English, *For Her Own Good: 150 Years of the Experts' Advice to Women* (Garden City, NY: Anchor Press, 1978). For a more recent perspective, see Susan Sherwin, *No Longer Patient: Feminist Ethics and Health Care* (Philadelphia: Temple University Press, 1992).

3 The childhood Hilliard describes is very close to that which experts were advising parents to give to their children. See Katherine Arnup, *Education for Motherhood: Advice for Mothers in Twentieth-Century Canada* (Toronto: University of Toronto Press, 1994).

4 Marion Robinson, *Give My Heart: The Dr. Marion Hilliard Story* (Garden City, NY: Doubleday, 1964), 81

5 Ibid., 62–3

6 Robinson, *Give My Heart*, 152, 209; Hilliard, *A Woman Doctor*, 12; Dorothy Sangster, 'The Spinster Who Lectures Wives on Love and Childbirth,' *Maclean's Magazine* 70 (Nov. 1957): 88; Carol Wilson, *Marion Hilliard* (Don Mills, ON: Fitzhenry and Whiteside, 1977), 46

7 Robinson, *Give My Heart*, 96, 105–6

8 Women's College Hospital opened in 1911 in part as a place for women physicians to practise medicine and for women medical students to intern. Although women had been granted entry into medical school, it was still difficult for them to find internships.

9 Wilson, *Marion Hilliard*, 36; Sangster, 'The Spinster,' 89; Dorothy Henderson, *For the Greater Glory: Biographical Sketches of Six Humanitarians Whose Lives Have Been for the Greater Glory* (Toronto: Ryerson Press, 1958), 33–4

10 Henderson, *For the Greater Glory*, 21; Robinson, *Give My Heart*, 19, 8–9

11 Robinson, *Give My Heart*, 27

12 Henderson, *For the Greater Glory*, 27, 47, 49

13 The SCM was partially a reflection of the movement to lessen denominational division as reflected in the creation of the United Church of Canada. See Margaret Beattie, *SCM: A Short History of the Student Christian Movement in Canada* (Toronto: Student Christian Movement, 1975); Paul Axelrod, *Making a Middle Class: Student Life in English Canada during the Thirties* (Montreal and Kingston: McGill-Queen's University Press, 1990), chap. 6.

14 Robinson, *Give My Heart*, 69, 72

15 Sangster, 'The Spinster,' 18, 86

16 Robinson, *Give My Heart*, 270

17 Ibid., 92, 94

18 Sangster, 'The Spinster,' 18. The idea of combining medicine and missionary work was one shared by many early women physicians. See Veronica Strong-Boag, 'Canada's Women Doctors: Feminism Constrained' in *A Not*

Unreasonable Claim: Women and Reform in Canada, 1880s–1920s, ed. Linda
Kealey (Toronto: Women's Press, 1979), 109–29
19 Henderson, *For the Greater Glory,* 23; Robinson, *Give My Heart,* 53–4
20 Robinson, *Give My Heart,* 46
21 Sangster, 'The Spinster,' 84; Henderson, *For the Greater Glory,* 40
22 Robinson, *Give My Heart,* 10, 51
23 Sangster, 'The Spinster,' 86
24 Robinson, *Give My Heart,* 91–3
25 Ibid., 92
26 Hilliard, *Women and Fatigue,* 14
27 Hilliard, *A Woman Doctor,* 59–60
28 See Wendy Mitchinson, *The Nature of Their Bodies: Women and Their Doctors in
Victorian Canada* (Toronto: University of Toronto Press, 1991), chap. 4. The
twentieth century acknowledged sexuality in women more openly but still
saw a difference between male and female sexuality.
29 Hilliard, *A Woman Doctor,* 64
30 Hilliard, *Women and Fatigue,* 70, 119, 131; Hilliard, *A Woman Doctor,* 88
31 Hilliard, *A Woman Doctor,* 96
32 Ibid., 73, 40, 68
33 Ibid., 65
34 There was some ambivalence about this view. Hilliard certainly made this
point but when she discusses the mother–child relationship it would be difficult to assume that it was not the primary relationship.
35 Hilliard, *A Woman Doctor,* 29
36 Hilliard, *Women and Fatigue,* 102
37 Ibid., 74
38 Ibid., 70, 119, 131; Hilliard, *A Woman Doctor,* 88
39 Hilliard, *Women and Fatigue,* 116
40 Ceta Ramkhalawansingh, 'Women during the Great War' in *Women at Work:
Ontario, 1850–1930,* ed. Janice Acton, Penny Goldsmith, and Bonnie Shepard
(Toronto: Canadian Women's Educational Press, 1974), 294
41 Hilliard, *Women and Fatigue,* 66
42 Ibid., 152–3; Hilliard, *A Woman Doctor,* 107
43 Patricia Connelly, *Last Hired, First Fired: Women and the Canadian Work Force*
(Toronto: Women's Press, 1978), 69
44 Hilliard, *A Woman Doctor,* 109–10
45 Hilliard, *Women and Fatigue,* 72; Hilliard, *A Woman Doctor,* 113, 104
46 Hilliard, *A Woman Doctor,* 104–5
47 Ibid., 94, 13, 92; Sangster, 'The Spinster,' 84
48 Hilliard, *A Woman Doctor,* 23–4

49 Hilliard, *Women and Fatigue*, 52
50 See Arnup, *Education for Motherhood*; Andrée Levesque, *Making and Breaking the Rules: Women in Quebec, 1919–1939* (Toronto: McClelland and Stewart, 1994); Katherine Arnup, Andrée Levesque, and Ruth Roach Pierson, eds., *Delivering Motherhood: Maternal Ideologies and Practices in the 19th and 20th Centuries* (London and NY: Routledge, 1990); Cynthia R. Commachio, *Nations Are Built of Babies: Saving Ontario's Mothers and Children* (Montreal and Kingston: McGill-Queen's University Press, 1993); Veronica Strong-Boag, *The New Day Recalled: Lives of Girls and Women in English Canada, 1919–1939* (Toronto: Copp Clark Pitman, 1988).
51 Hilliard, *A Woman Doctor*, 31
52 Ibid., 17
53 Ibid., 148–9
54 Ibid., 58, 149, 12, 45
55 Ibid., 152
56 See Margaret Lock, *Encounters with Aging: Mythologies of Menopause in Japan and North America* (Berkeley: University of California Press, 1993), for a description of the cultural specificity and construction of menopause.
57 Hilliard, *A Woman Doctor*, 148, 161–2, 78, 144–5
58 Germaine Greer, *The Change: Women, Aging, and the Menopause* (New York: Knopf, 1992)
59 Henderson, *For the Greater Glory*, 19
60 Fanny Cracknell, interview with Janice Dickin, 13 Dec. 1993

'By Title and by Virtue':
Lady Frederick and
Dr Henrietta Ball Banting

JANICE DICKIN

As I sit down to write up my research for this piece, I find myself confronted by my very first memo to file: 'Henrietta Ball Banting, 1912–76, graduated from TO 1945, meets Banting in 1937. She's 25 and he's 46. Treat him as interim in her life.'

I remember precisely what sparked my interest in this woman. I first became conscious of her as an individual in Carlotta Hacker's *The Indomitable Lady Doctors*, while doing general research on women doctors for another project. Here was a woman with a distinguished professional life whose biographical entry nonetheless opened with the sentence: 'Lady Banting, the wife of Sir Frederick Banting, entered the University of Toronto as a medical student a few months after her husband was killed on active service.'[1] I noted with interest that she was referred to by a title gained through marriage, not work; that she was, after decades of widowhood, still being referred to as 'wife'; and that her entry into medical school was linked to the 'heroic' death of her husband. I also noted with interest that I had run into this lady before, had come into contact with this information before, but clearly had thought little of it.

The source of my earlier contact was Michael Bliss's biography of Frederick Banting, the co-discoverer of insulin, *Banting: A Biography*. Writing from the perspective of his own subject, Bliss was interested in Henrietta only as an interval in the elder Banting's life. Despite the high level of education she achieved in an environment hostile to women and the fact that she was in Banting's lab as a graduate student, the place she fills in the book is as a player in Fred's ongoing search for what Bliss terms 'a woman who could cater to his unusual needs.' Bliss's research turned up a story about her fleeing after dropping a jar of live tubercle bacilli and the general impression of the 'men in the lab' that she was 'another sweet kid, an attractive little girl.' She was not, according to Bliss, 'a brilliant researcher.'[2]

When I decided that I wanted to 'do' Henrietta, I contacted Professor Bliss to confirm that I would not be infringing on his territory. He generously spoke to me at length, offered to help me as much as he could, stated no further designs on 'Henrie,' but warned me that there was little material on her in the Banting papers and that he was not sure that she was 'doable' as a topic. This statement alone challenged me to proceed, and when I spoke to him again later, I told him that if 'undoability' were taken too seriously by historians of women, very little would ever be written. We have to take what we can get our hands on, interpret as best we can, and gird ourselves to fend off accusations that we are not 'brilliant researchers.'[3]

Mine was a pompous little speech, backed up by convictions I already held about the meaning of Henrietta's life. Virtually without research, knowing little more than that she never married again, feeling a strong desire to show her life as a continuum lived on her own terms (and personally put off by Fred Banting's personality), I 'expected' to find a strong-minded, independent feminist involved in her professional life. In short, I filled the void of research with my own prejudices.

What I found instead was a woman at once more complex and more simple. What I found was a transitional figure who combined the roles of professional doctor and professional widow. I found a woman who clearly had early career aspirations, and who picked them up almost without a skip after a mere twenty-one months of marriage, but whose personal interests remained domestic and whose views of women's place in the world leaned doggedly backwards. I also found a woman who embarked on another relationship – this one much longer term – with a personality, according to frequent descriptions by those interviewed, equal to Fred's in terms of difficulty and neediness. In addition, Henrietta Elizabeth Ball Banting was not a woman given either to self-examination or to self-revelation. At an age when many people are drawn to autobiography as a means of establishing the meaning of their lives, Henrietta proposed instead to produce a biography of Fred, a project that might fundamentally have shifted her view of her own life.

Henrietta Elizabeth Ball was born 14 March 1912 at Stanstead, Quebec, the first of three daughters of Henry Tenny Ball, after whom she was surely named, and Mary Florence Crocker.[4] Mr Ball worked for Canada Customs.[5] Mrs Ball was a music teacher at Stanstead College

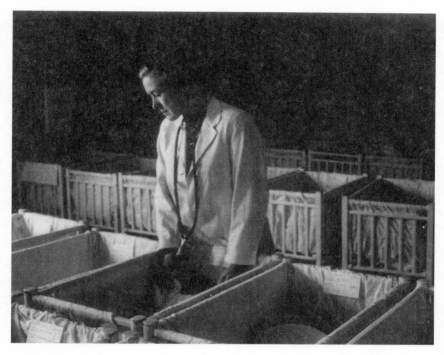

Henrietta Ball Banting, in the nursery at Women's College Hospital, 1955

before her marriage. Perhaps it was the misfortune of her husband's early death that led her to move herself, Henrietta, and younger daughters Eleanor and Lucy Lee from the old family home, Lee Farm, to Newcastle, New Brunswick. Henrietta was educated at Newcastle schools, took her first year of university at McGill, and transferred to Mount Allison in Sackville, New Brunswick, where she received her BA in biology in 1932. Her yearbook entry refers to her as 'Hank,' praises her 'original ideas,' 'noted good taste' and 'steadiness,' and mentions her participation as a character in the senior play.[6]

After graduation, Henrietta worked for three years as a laboratory technician at the General Hospital in Saint John, New Brunswick, before enrolling at the University of Toronto in the MA program, the research segment of her studies to be carried out at the Banting Institute. Clearly her decision to pursue a higher degree demonstrates considerable drive on the part of a young woman, especially in the depths of the Depression. Her acceptance by the University of Toronto and her assignment to the Banting Institute would also seem to demonstrate considerable ability. But, while a young male researcher such as Charles H. Best (with whom Banting shared his Nobel Prize money) or E.F.F. Copp (whose association with Banting gave him a leg up to a distinguished research career in the United States) received help from his mentor in terms of professional advancement, the attentions Henrietta received were more in the nature of what now would be prohibited by university sexual harassment guidelines.

But this is now, that was then. We know little about how Henrietta regarded the courtship and the marriage. We do know that she completed her MA in 1938 and that she went on to further research in London. According to a short notice in the *Globe and Mail*, she was planning a Mediterranean cruise with her Canadian roommates at about the time Banting showed up on her doorstep. The perfectly believable reason given for the cancellation of her trip was 'the international crisis.'

Michael Bliss portrays Banting as very much the pursuer, and not a particularly attractive one at that. Clearly impatient with what he saw as unnecessary hesitation and untrustworthiness, Banting wrote a memo to himself in the summer before he tracked Henrietta to London. 'For eleven months I have, by planning, been able to see this young and beautiful creature at will ... We had had our fights. At times I have been bitterly disappointed in her conduct. She had not been one whom one could rely upon. She has had very much time to herself for I have been very busy and had to go out a great deal. I always told her before so she could know what nights she would be free in advance. And she has often taken advantage of this fact.'[7]

We know that Fred wore down Henrie's defences at this time from a caddish scene he noted in his diary on an official visit to London a year later. He booked into the same hotel he had taken Henrie to on this earlier trip. 'When I registered the clerk said – You were here ago [sic] wern't [sic] you Sir? with your wife. I laughted [sic] & said that the lady was not then but is now.'[8]

Henrietta returned home in December 1938 and stayed with her mother in Newcastle until a few weeks before the wedding. Mrs Ball accompanied her daughter to Toronto and to the very small private ceremony wherein she became Lady Banting on 2 June 1939. The bride was twenty-seven, the groom forty-eight. She seems to have felt some financial obligation to her mother and sisters. He had custody of a ten-year-old son from his first marriage, which had been contracted equally secretively on almost exactly the same date fifteen years previously.[9] After a short honeymoon at his fishing cabin on Georgian Bay, Fred went off to a conference in Washington, and Henrie set up housekeeping in his comfortable home at 205 Rosedale Heights Drive.

Less than two years later, it would all be over. I made a point of asking people who knew her in later life if she often mentioned her marriage. The answer was no, but their impressions ranged from a view of it as a romantic idyll to statements like, 'I can't think it was anything but a happy marriage.' When in one interview I specifically broached the possibility that Fred had a tendency to violence, the answer was 'I can't imagine she'd put up with it.' My questions regarding reasons she might not have remarried brought ventures ranging from 'she never forgot Sir Frederick' to 'People she met after that didn't interest her.' Michael Bliss, however, agreed to be quoted as speculating that Fred was so dreadful she never wanted another man,[10] and my own feelings on the matter are clear from that first memo to file: if this was a fairy tale, it was one in which the princess escaped from the tower and got on with her life as fast as she could.

Henrietta could not have long ignored the fact that Sir Frederick Banting made miserable husband material. We know very little about their courtship and marriage and almost all we do have is solely from Fred's perspective. Even this source has severe limitations, given the decision of Henrietta's executor to comply with a note left by her, dated 1947, to destroy all Banting's love letters.[11] However, Banting did leave among his papers a wartime diary, which barely mentions his young wife except in terms of dissatisfaction. When she is not home to greet him on his arrival, he declares: 'She may be changing toward me. I best go away and let her enjoy herself.' He worries that the problem is that she has not had a child, but he comes home too late and too tired himself to perform the necessaries. He drinks too much even by his own standards and enjoys doing so both alone and with 'the boys.'

Meanwhile, Banting's social time with Henrie seems to be reserved for his much older friends; he was not even willing to wait in a line-up after inviting her to choose a show. Instead, they drop in on some relatives of his, the same couple who show up in his diaries almost as often as Henrie does, even accompanying the Bantings into Fred's 'bedroom on the train' during their last minutes together before he leaves his bride of a few months to spend what he expects may be a perilous crossing and will be a protracted period in England.[12]

While it is true that she could not have familiarized herself with this document before plighting troth, she must have been aware of his drinking, of his scandalous 1932 divorce, which featured accusations of physical abuse within the marriage (and evidence of viciousness in Fred's ending of it) and of his womanizing, particularly of a long-term affair with a faithful assistant in the same lab. Perhaps with a little sniffing around, Henrietta could also have caught wind of Fred's public statements that what he needed as a wife was the equivalent of an Airedale, 'utterly loyal and unquestioning.'[13] But then again, maybe she felt herself capable of being such an animal and was willing as well. Banting-as-husband must also be considered according to her own subjective judgment.

In common Cinderella, marriage-partner terms, Fred Banting fit the stereotype: he was famous, financially secure, and titled. Furthermore, he had excelled in the area of Henrietta's own intellectual interest. He was also a good deal older, which for Henrietta might have been a positive rather than a negative factor, her own father having died when she was young. Banting seems also to have resembled her mother, given the opinion voiced by several of those interviewed that Mrs Ball was a 'difficult' woman. And, for all Banting's coarseness and traditionalism in the area of gender relations, he was genuinely attracted to well-brought-up women who pursued careers, having been seriously involved, in turn, with a minister's daughter become teacher (a failed long-term engagement), a doctor's daughter become X-ray technician (his failed first marriage), and a civil servant's daughter become scientific researcher. His desire to marry Henrietta no doubt felt real to her. Perhaps she was also attracted to his view of her as 'a female with a splendid body that would have strong babies'[14] and his stated desire for a conventional home life.

Fred was also a needy father. Although he invented stories for his young son and invited him to the lab to decapitate mice as a ritual initiation to manhood,[15] Banting complained frequently in his diaries of the boy's shortcomings, referring to him as 'useless, selfish and totally inconsiderate.'[16] Most difficult to take is the painfully abusive scene in which Banting, with revolver and Sam Browne belt, calls his son to his study and informs him he is about to fly the Atlantic in winter in a bomber, telling 'him of the danger but that it was one's duty.' The boy is awkward and stunned; Banting judges him undemonstrative and unsentimental.[17] Less than a week later, eleven-year-old Bill Banting was fatherless. Late in the evening of Thursday, 20 February 1941, the small plane carrying Frederick G. Banting, Canadian medical hero and Knight of the British Empire, crashed on the coast of Newfoundland.

Bill and Henrietta would sit together as chief mourners at the public funeral in Convocation Hall at the University of Toronto. They would hear the tributes, the carillon, the pipes, the gun salute. They would be on display in the foot cortège up to Bloor Street, the motor cortège up to the burial plot at Mount Pleasant Cemetery. Although Henrietta had been an active stepmother to Bill,[18] and would continue to participate in his upbringing, the two can hardly have known one another very well. Surely of more comfort to the boy would have been the presence of his own disgraced mother. Perhaps of some comfort to Henrietta might have been the chance somehow to observe the grief of Sadie Gairns, long-time assistant in Fred's lab, keeper of his scrapbooks, efficient helper, caring adviser, loving friend, a woman on whose support Banting privately recognized a dependence never acknowledged publicly.[19] While the newspaper reports describe approvingly Lady Banting's 'single spray of deep red roses' and her momentary break-down at the private ceremony held the night before, there is no place for the woman in Banting's life who, Michael Bliss notes, came as close to Banting's description of wife-as-Airedale as did any woman in his life.[20]

Fred's death fastened a new persona on Henrietta, one that would identify her even after her own death. She became a professional widow, not simply a woman who does not marry after her husband's death but one who takes up his torch, keeping alight his flame. It is a role that royal and sometimes political wives have been allowed to play, or had thrust upon them, and it has social implications far beyond personal grief. Ever after, Henrie's public life would be defined in terms of this short marriage; her private life would not escape its effects either. She was captured not just by the Banting myth but by the Penelope myth, managing the estate of her absent husband's heroic reputation, refusing to remarry, keeping his vitality alive by participating in an ongoing celebration of a single triumph – a grand coup – the virility of which ensured his victory even in death over younger contenders for glory. His presence had only to be kept apparent; he did not actually have to return as had Ulysses.

The fact that the life Henrietta was weaving would evermore be seen as not simply about her, but also about 'him,' is made clear by both public and private reactions to her decision to enrol in medical school. 'Following in the footsteps of her illustrious husband,' according to the caption accompanying a photo of her posed under Fred's portrait at the time of her graduation almost four years to the day after his death, Lady Banting's enrolment in second year at the Faculty of Medicine at the

University of Toronto in October 1941 was presented – not the least by herself – as motivated by a desire to do 'things that were actually worthwhile.' The clear implication was that the widow was carrying on the hero's work. This impression is heightened by the fact that, before graduation, she joined the army and served almost two years past the end of the war. This mirrors Fred's experience in the Great War, but it mirrors the experience of her contemporaries as well: the majority of the graduating med class of 1945 was in uniform.

There can be no doubt that Henrietta took to the role of professional widow willingly. The only question is, what was in it for her? In 1954, after more than a decade as a widow and almost a decade as a doctor, asked to speak by the Women's Canadian Club of Saint John about the research laboratory named for her famous late husband, Dr Henrietta Ball Banting referred to the Banting Institute only in her introduction and conclusion. In between, the speech is made up of three quite separate parts that do not tie together but that provide insight into how this very private woman saw her life, her work, and her marriage.

The speech starts out with a quick introduction to the 'big things' (a phrase that Banting favoured, along with 'big thoughts,' 'big conception,' 'big ideas' and 'big urge'[21]) accomplished by scientific research. Pasteur, Lister, and Einstein are all portrayed as self-sacrificing men working for the good of mankind. The last section is a straight lift from Banting's own writings, an account of his relationship with one of his laboratory dogs. As the bitch lies dying as a result of his experiments, he wraps her in his old lab coat and takes her in his arms. She looks at him, wags her tail, and departs this vale of tears.

In between these two sections are five handwritten pages about Marie Curie. Henrietta clearly admired Marie Curie and, given the impact of Curie's discovery of radium on Henrietta's later field of cancer detection, this makes professional sense. But Marie had in addition accomplished two things Henrietta had also set out to do – have a successful scientific career and a happy marriage. Marie won the Nobel Prize twice, the first one shared with her husband, Pierre, the second after his accidental death.

There are some fundamental elements here of Henrietta's own life and marriage – Nobel Prize, researchers in same lab, accidental death, woman carrying on alone – but they are all jumbled and not clearly thought through. The fact is that Henrietta was not on the scene for the 'big things' in Fred Banting's life. The experiments that produced insulin took place in 1921–23; Banting received the Nobel Prize in 1923; he was knighted in 1934. By 1935 when Henrietta came to work in the institute, Banting had suffered years of frustration trying to do another 'big thing.' He would never, unlike Marie Curie, manage another Nobel Prize, or even come close.

That Henrietta knew intellectually that she had lost out on the real excitement is underlined by her words in another public speech seventeen years later at a conference hosted by the Eli Lilly Company to commemmorate the fiftieth anniversary of Fred Banting's lucrative (for Eli Lilly) discovery. Her notes for that speech read:

Thank – opportunity – appreciation invitation – celebration.

Sentimental journey – reasons purely sentimental since I am not an investigator in this field and it is true though unfortunate that I did not share – frustration – disappointment – excitement. My experience latecomer – tragically short association. Nevertheless the story thrills – and I can sense an undercurrent of admiration for the two young men whose perseverance honoured here this week ...

Being present has given me the greatest pleasure, indebted to officers of E L Co. for including me.[22]

Henrietta's presentation of the Curie scientific and marital collaboration in the earlier speech is highly romantic. After giving details of Marie's life that identify in her all the ambition and self-absorption necessary to do 'big things,' Henrietta describes the personal relationship as follows: 'In her laboratory work she came in contact with a young teacher at the school of Physics who was attracted by her brilliance and industry and also by personal qualities which shone through the defensive layers of reserve with which she treated all personal relations ... She recognized in him a kindred spirit. They were married and together they formed a team which was indomitable.' In modern terms, Marie 'has it all,' a highly satisfying and successful career and a husband who – literally – supports her in her work. Is this what Henrietta thought she had missed with Fred? What did she expect from marriage? What did she think she'd been deprived of because of Banting's early death?

While it is possible to put forward reasons for Henrietta's continued support of Fred that have to do with outside factors, I find myself increasingly convinced that she was simply enthralled by the story of her life as tragedy. It is true that to support Banting was also to support her profession and her nation, both systems Henrietta passionately believed in, but I don't think this goes far enough to explain why Henrietta stayed 'married' to Fred. Neither do I think she maintained the con-

nection merely for reasons of self-gain. Although doors opened to her as
Lady Banting, and she used her title to raise money for things she
believed in, much of the work she undertook as Fred's widow was
almost purely ceremonial: she reads a proposed Banting script for the
National Film Board; she blesses the use of an excerpt from Fred's thesis; she deals with archives who want his papers; she fields requests
from writers wanting to use his papers for research on other subjects;
she goes down to London, Ontario, to attend a tiny ceremony to unveil a
plaque on the house where Banting claimed to have gotten the idea for
insulin and sends out letters to gain approval for a second edition of
Frances Loring's famous bust of him; she takes an interest in the mapping of the Banting crater on earth's moon and passes on her thanks for
a piece of terrible but sincere poetry deifying Banting as a 'Second Sav-
ior.' And, of course, she dabbled with the planned biography, a project
only just started at the time of her death.

Is the caption under the med school graduation photo correct, then?
Was Henrietta just following in her husband's footsteps? Was her own
medical career more about her husband and her widowhood than about
her own life? There was a myth about Lady Banting that she chose medicine over titled leisure. According to a poem in the Women's College
Hospital files, 'She could have lived her nights and days / In silks ... in
glossy ... fur' rather than choose 'A sterile coat ... a stethoscope.'[23] This
misrepresents the real range of opportunity open to her at the time of
Banting's death. Lady or no, she had not the money for society life.
While her rarity as a Canadian with a title might have allowed her to
live off others for a while, she was too young to be able to bank on a lifetime comfortably spent in such a manner. Remarriage would have rendered her support but also almost certainly meant loss of her title. There
was plenty of war work around for women, but being Lady Banting no
doubt limited her range of options: it is difficult to imagine Henrietta
being hired back at some Toronto lab as an assistant. Ladies volunteer;
they don't usually draw a wage.

At the same time, Henrietta had always demonstrated ambition and
was presented by Fred's death with real opportunity. She was not quite
twenty-nine and had been off the career track for only about two years.
He had left her a property in which she could house her family. She had
no children of her own to look after but had the opportunity for moth-
erly participation in the care of Bill (who would be orphaned with his
mother's death in 1946) and, until 1944, a young 'war guest,' David
Haworth, who had been sent over by his well-placed Birmingham med-

ical family to ride out the war with Banting and whose care Henrietta assumed as part of her widow's lot.

Banting also left a will supposedly 'providing for Lady Banting for life' from his $72,300, estate, which included the Rosedale Heights home, life insurance worth $46,000, the lodge on Georgian Bay, stocks, bonds, and personal effects. This was to be shared with Bill and the Banting Institute. So there was also money, although clearly not enough to allow her complete independence, something she clearly prized: a letter in her student file indicates that her med school fees were waived, probably out of deference to her husband's memory, and that she was not comfortable with this. As soon as she qualified to enter the army and was eligible to receive pay intended to cover the cost of tuition and textbooks, she notified the bursar of the University of Toronto that she would no longer be taking advantage of the exemption.

There is no reason to believe that she received much else in the way of concessions from her husband's former colleagues in her pursuit of a degree. The majority of students entered the program directly from high school. Her admission straight into second year, then, is more than adequately explained by the fact that she already had an MA and had worked in labs for a number of years. A fellow classmate, Dr Isobel Moon, remembers Henrietta on her first day.[24] About 5' 4", slim, a 'tailored person' in a beige tweed suit and oxfords, it was a number of days before students realized who Henrietta was. She stuck out from the first by the simple fact that she entered a group of people who had already been together for a year, but there was the added fact that she was about ten years older than her fellow students, knew all the professors and wives personally, and generally was 'conspicuous' by nature of the simple fact of her husband's identity.

Dr Moon ventures that Henrietta 'had a miserable time in medical school.' She was good at her studies, but there could be no denying that medical education was still waged as a war of nerves against students, particularly against women. On the first day of first year, the dean spoke to the assembled class, telling them that, no matter how well they did, only the top two-thirds would be allowed to go on to second year. Furthermore, only eight of the seventeen women enrolled would be allowed to continue. It is not surprising that such a system and attitude would lend itself to abuse and that the most vulnerable would suffer.

While Moon is under the impression that Henrietta was called on less by professors in class, she was not spared the general reign of male vulgarity, which made it impossible for female students to enter classrooms except en masse and, deferentially, after the professor. Once there, they could not necessarily expect the harassment to stop and indeed could find it reinforced by the professor himself. In this way, male students ensured for themselves the best seats and priority treatment, and male professors ensured continuation of the profession as they knew it. Women seeking entry were to make themselves unobtrusive. Although Moon feels Henrietta persevered partly because 'she didn't want to give up,' she attributes to her a real vocation for medicine, noting that it is not unusual for people who have gone into science to opt later for the more humanistic practice of medicine. In this, Henrietta would reverse rather than follow the course of a husband who started out a doctor but chose instead the lab.

Henrietta's years in medical school were made more onerous by the fact that they coincided with the most public period of her widowhood. In early 1943, she served on a committee organizing a showing of Fred's art work at Hart House on the university campus. Later the same year a special visa was issued by the American government, allowing her to travel to Baltimore to christen the 10,000 ton *Sir Frederick Banting*, the first Liberty ship named after a non-American. On the brisk and windy morning of 20 December, Lady Banting swung the bottle of champagne with such vigour that foam had to be wiped from her army greatcoat before she could be presented with a 'gold floral spray glamour pin set with blue stones.' This gift represented a departure from the usual gift, a gold wristwatch.

Perhaps Private Banting already owned a timepiece – a good, big, sturdy one engineered for the taking of pulses and the keeping of army time. Perhaps she consulted it to get herself back to Toronto in time for an ordeal such as a 'bell-ringer exam' in which students had to sit two or three hours in the pathology lab waiting their turn before spending an hour running from cadaver to cadaver, identifying the labelled parts and answering questions, an exercise that was known to reduce grown men to tears.[25] But before her return to student life, Lady Banting presided at a luncheon in her honour at Baltimore's Hotel Belvedere at which she 'affirmed the fitness of the monument, likening her husband to a great and steady ship.'

If her special widowhood interfered with her education, it would compensate by giving her a leg up once she entered the profession. Upon her graduation, a special position was made available for her to intern at the Toronto General Hospital,[26] and she was invited to Birmingham Hospital by Banting's old friend, David Haworth's father, to pursue her desired specialization in obstetrics. Again, though, such advantages would have a downside: there is evidence that Henrietta had problems accepting her very real successes as her own. When she became the first Canadian woman to pass the necessary exams to be awarded membership in Britain's Royal College of Obstetricians and Gynaecologists in 1948, she speculated that 'it was just a fluke,' and when she was offered a teaching post in Hong Kong by a professor she met at international meetings in Dublin in her own field of specialty, she declared it 'purely a matter of chance.'[27] Upon return from Hong Kong, Henrietta went into practice with Dr Marion Hilliard, an influential obstetrician in Toronto. Being Lady Banting must certainly have helped her build her patient roster.

In 1957, Henrietta became the first recipient of the fellowship established in Hilliard's name at Women's College Hospital. Henrietta made a successful career for herself at the hospital. Given her fellowship in the Royal College and her two years of teaching in Hong Kong, she was a valuable addition to the staff. Within a year, she became head of the ten-year-old Cancer Detection Clinic, which screened well women for signs of breast and uterine cancer. Evidently, she made some attempts at research as part of the clinic work but clearly the focus was on patient care, something at which Henrietta excelled. She wrote personal letters to follow up on patients she was concerned about, was the doctor of choice of many of them, and ran a happy, relaxed clinic. The service was so popular that by 1963 the waiting list extended almost a year into the future.[28]

In addition, Henrietta took an interest in both her profession and in the field of education. For eight years, she served as vice-president of the Medical Women's International Association and she also served on the board of governors of both Stanstead College and Mount Allison University. She retired in 1972 but kept up an active interest in her hospital and in the Faculty of Medicine at the University of Toronto, commuting from the old family home she renovated in Stanstead and staying, at least part of that time, at a suite kept for her at Massey College. After her death (ironically, of cancer of the brain) on 26 July 1976, the hospital memorialized her by naming the retooled clinic the Henrietta Banting Breast Centre.

There is always something sad in photos of Henrietta Ball Banting. While this is easy to explain at the time of Fred's funeral – all widows are under terrible strain, no matter what their marriages were like – this melancholy is not so easy to explain in photos taken years before and years after. She seems to have been a woman who lacked confidence in herself, self-deprecating, even self-effacing. For this reason, some of the things made easy for her may actually have been a disadvantage: those who are valued according to the needs of others often fail to learn their own worth.

She may also have mourned her failure either to manage a research career or a successful marriage, both ambitions of her youth. She may even, in the case of Fred, have had guilt. The abrupt ending of this relationship must surely have left her with unfinished business. This would have included, among other things, the processing of Fred's accusations three weeks before his death that she had been unfaithful to him. Fred had his own method of processing his almost certainly unfounded suspicions – by adding them to the other accusations against her already in his diary: 'I went cold. She wept & kept on weeping throughout the day. I'm licked. I go overseas. I'll not come back. Life to me is not so finite or glorious that I want to take second place to a reject.'[29] Whether he threatened her with a hero's death at the time or whether she read this later in the diaries, these words could not have worked to convince her that she had been a success at this marriage or would be a success at another. Unfounded accusations are the most difficult to defend against. It is possible to interpret her widowhood as an ongoing attempt to convince Fred that she was loyal.

It is also possible that Henrietta did not sufficiently value herself by simple reason of being a woman. Surely success in a research career would have been mightily helped by a change of hormones. For one thing, it would have certainly altered Fred's method of dealing with her. She may also have been coping with residual parental disappointment that their first-born was not a boy. Named for her father, she did opt for an ambitiously 'male' life for that era. Certainly her attitude to women's role in the world was ambivalent. Her obituary would state that 'She was a life-long advocate of the rights of women in medicine and urged young women to consider careers as doctors rather than nurses,' an ambivalent statement in its own right. She was quoted publicly in 1963 in favour of the growing number of women doctors in the Philippines, Japan, and the USSR. In a later interview, she stated that women are better suited for public health and social medicine than are men.[30] She supported women in matters such as rest after childbirth and, later, access to birth control.[31]

But a speech she gave while accepting an honorary LLD from her alma mater in 1954 makes clear a prejudice that higher education for women is, above all, most important in terms of their preparation to be better wives and mothers. 'If the marriage rate among university women were lower than that among the general female population that fact in itself would condemn the system ... There is, however, no need that the years spent in rearing a family should exhaust a woman's physical or spiritual potentialities. A woman in her forties, if her mind has been cultivated in the twenties, should be able to return to community and public life – a mature, useful citizen, having fulfilled her maternal destiny and gracefully accepted the fact that her family no longer needs her exclusively.'[32] It is possible to see such statements as simply postwar woman-speak, a hiding of the ambition that dare not speak its name. It is much the same sort of self-sacrifice recommended to childbearing women by other non-childbearing female doctors during this century, including Marion Hilliard. While there is a celebration of women's contributions, there is neither acceptance that women can combine both home and career nor demand that men take on their fair share of family responsibility.

There has been a tendency in recent years to dismiss women who espoused this approach as merely 'maternal feminists' who somehow sold women short. But perhaps it is time to reconsider them in terms of a real appreciation of women's physical and emotional limits. Certainly later 'superwoman feminists' settled for a compromise that left little time for self, mistook decreased service *to* partners as increased service *by* partners, and condemned women either unable or unwilling to keep up with the pace as unenlightened enemies of progress. Looked at in this manner, Henrietta becomes an interesting transitional figure in feminism: unfettered by husband and children, she could point to the fact that this was only by tragedy, not by choice; having had a hero husband, it was understandable that she was unlikely to settle for less; relieved of the overwork 'having it all' necessitates, she once again made a home of her birthplace, restoring Lee Farm and filling it with antiques and the products of her own loom.

Henrietta combined her career and her widowhood in such a way that she could uphold the importance of homemaking by practising homemaking but with herself as the centrepiece. This has much to recommend it, but it manifests a selfishness she would be unlikely to have supported on the part of women as a whole. In other words, while she could clearly see the attraction of true independence for women, she could not reach so far as to envision the social revolution necessary to bring it about for all. She would settle instead for being an 'exception female,' one who believes the opportunities should be there for certain individuals but that in general the social fabric should keep weaving itself as before. In this way, Fred Banting was not at all the interval in her life I originally thought him to be. He was, one might say, the very woof.

While Henrietta did not remarry, she did not deny herself a serious long-term relationship. For years she lived in partnership with Cecilia E. Long, one of Toronto's first successful advertising women, president of the Women's College Hospital board of directors from 1966 to 1970, eventually a member of the Order of Canada. By all accounts, Cece Long was a flamboyant woman. She dressed all in green, even down to her nailpolish. She also seems to have been a difficult personality, in the model of both Henrietta's mother and Fred: loud, domineering, vainglorious, vulgar, emotionally needy. Cece lived with Henrie in a pleasant, upscale apartment on Avenue Road. She also spent time at Henrietta's farm. They travelled together and clearly were more than just roommates. There can be no doubt that Cece's devotion to Henrie was deep. And not just the fact that Henrie left Cece Fred's amateur art work leads me to believe that this devotion was returned as much as the cool, reserved Henrie could manage.

More than one person I interviewed raised the question of whether these women were lovers. By the time I started my interviews, I already had my own suspicions, not least of all because this scenario fit in with my conviction that Henrietta could not possibly have been serious about her long-term devotion to a man I could not bring myself to like. I concocted a theory that she used Fred as a 'cover' for the true nature of her relationship with Cece. People who raised the issue did so, more often than not, only to discount it, sometimes adamantly. I am left unsure not only about the sexual facts of this relationship but also about any importance they might have. No matter how these women conducted themselves when they were alone, they were a committed couple – living, travelling, entertaining, making plans together – and, in Cece's case, also laying her partner's remains to their final rest.

On a tip of land in Mount Pleasant cemetery stands the monument to Frederick Grant Banting, KBE, 1891–1941 and to Henrietta E. Ball Banting, MA, MD, FRCOG, LLD, 1912–1976. The winged, snaked medical insignia entwines their two names. Below lie quite separately the bones of a man and a woman who spent less than two years entwined in life. My response on coming upon the tombstone was to ask 'Where's Cece?' I found her behind, in the shadow of the much larger monument: Cecilia E. Long, 1912–1988. It was Cece who carried out the arrangements to bury Henrie beside Fred. She undoubtedly also arranged her own tangential, eternal association with them. By several reports, she shared with Henrietta enthralment to the tragedy of the early widowed Lady Banting and her hero husband. It was she who referred to Henrietta at her death as 'a lady, by title and by virtue.' In some curious way, Sir Frederick Banting served Cece for mate as well.

What was the meaning of Henrietta Ball Banting's life? I am convinced that the key is her address at Mount Allison in 1954, exhorting young women to follow a career path she did not follow herself. It is true that she did marry and, given Fred's stated desire for children, at least expressed willingness to have them herself. But the truth is that the values she expressed and the way she actually conducted her life do not fit. No matter how romantic and ingrained her views of marriage might have been, she did not choose to repeat it. Instead she chose to have things both ways – to live an independent life while publicly carrying a torch for a husband who was not in her life long enough to really have much effect on her. In this, she was fortunate but it is unlikely she had any grasp of the advantages. She probably thought her life as easily segregated as her name: Dr Banting professionally, Lady Banting only rarely and for her own purposes. I doubt she saw how the two personas shaped one another. She could manage both roles because of the anomalies of her situation: to wit, her husband was less demanding in death than the run-of-the-mill husband was in life. The importance of her life comes in bringing us some understanding of the ability of the romance of marriage to long outlive its practical advantages.

NOTES

I have sought and received permission to quote from all those I interviewed for this piece. I have not quoted everyone I interviewed. I have withheld certain observations as requested.

1 Carlotta Hacker, *The Indomitable Lady Doctors* (Toronto: Clarke, Irwin, 1974), 233
2 Michael Bliss, *Banting: A Biography* (Toronto: McClelland and Stewart, 1985), 11, 248
3 I spoke to Michael Bliss by telephone from Calgary on 13 October 1993 and in person in Toronto on 13 December 1993. All references herein are to these interviews.
4 Except where otherwise noted, the following biographical material comes

from various records and clippings held under a file in her name in the University of Toronto Archives or from Box 62 of the Banting Papers (hereafter BP) held at the Thomas Fisher Rare Book Room, University of Toronto.

5 'A Rare Humility,' unsourced, undated (probably 1962–63) magazine article, Women's College Hospital Archives

6 Mount Allison Yearbook, Mount Allison University, 1932, 51, Mount Allison Archives

7 Bliss, *Banting*, 249

8 BP, Box 76, 25 Nov. 1939

9 Banting's previous marriage to Marion Robertson took place on 4 June 1924. His divorce from her was final in December 1932. Banting was not knighted until June 1934, hence the first Mrs Banting was never a 'Lady.'

10 Bliss interview, 13 Dec. 1993

11 Katharine Martyn, Assistant Director, Thomas Fisher Rare Book Library, letter to Janice Dickin, 11 Jan. 1994

12 BP, Box 32. See entries for Thanksgiving night, Oct. 1940; 14 Oct. 1940; 17 Dec. 1940; 14 Oct. and 13 May 1940 (he actually uses the term 'the boys'); 23 Nov. 1940; 16 Nov. 1939.

13 Bliss, *Banting*, 161

14 F. Banting, quoted in ibid., 249

15 Ibid., 248

16 Wartime diaries, BP, Box 32, 25 May 1940

17 Ibid., BP, Box 32, 15 Feb. 1941

18 For example, Banting mentions Henrietta going up to collect Bill from a visit to Banting's home town of Alliston. Ibid., 2 Aug. 1940

19 Ibid., 2 Oct. 1940. While the diaries contain no description of his last parting from Henrietta, he notes that 'Miss Gairns' good bye was deep and yet I think she was proud. She did her best to hold in.' Ibid., 15 Feb. 1941

20 Bliss, *Banting*, 240

21 Wartime diary, BP, Box 32, 8 Jan. 1940

22 19 Oct. 1971, Indianapolis

23 Mona Gould, 'Requiem for a Lovely Lady ("Henrie"),' July 1976, Women's College Hospital Archives

24 Dr Isobel Moon, interview with Janice Dickin, Toronto, 7 March 1995

25 Moon, interview

26 According to Isobel Moon, the TGH was considered the plum interning assignment, admitting only two Jews and two women per year. The two top women in the class could in ordinary years count on going to TGH if that is what they wanted. In 1945, however, there was speculation that one of the positions might be automatically given to Lady Banting. Instead, TGH took

three women that year, bending a tradition that would not be entirely eradi-
cated for some time to come.

27 'A Rare Humility'
28 Documents pertaining to a survey of eighty-three women fitted with intra-
    uterine devices can be found in BP, Box 62. Letters to patients are also found
    there. Fanny Cracknell (interview with Janice Dickin, Toronto, 13 Dec. 1993)
    and the Archives of the Women's College Hospital, operated by Margaret
    Robins, are the sources for the daily working of the clinic.
29 Quoted in Bliss, *Banting*, 297
30 'A Rare Humility'
31 Ibid.
32 Henrietta Ball Banting, 'Free and Christian,' *Mount Allison Record* (Fall 1954),
    99, 103

Elizabeth Allin: Physicist

ALISON PRENTICE

As a newly married faculty wife in the early 1960s, I entered the world
of physics at the University of Toronto. The spouses of new physics
instructors were inducted into university life in those days through two
sorts of events: meetings of the Faculty Wives' Association and social
gatherings of the physics department. It must have been at one of the
latter that I first met Professor Elizabeth Allin.

The meetings were not particularly auspicious. Elizabeth Allin was a
senior physics professor, nearing retirement; I was a young high school
teacher and faculty wife oriented, I thought, towards full-time homemaking. To me, Miss Allin – as she was almost universally known –
seemed to belong not only to another generation but to another world. I
was ambivalent about both her single and her professorial status,
despite two facts of my own life that ought to have produced more clarity. One was my acquaintance with some wonderful single women
scholars at the American college for women I had attended between
1951 and 1955. A second was my own deep interest in academic work,
both as an undergraduate and when doing a master's degree in history
at the University of Toronto in 1957–8.

Other facts, however, undoubtedly led to my inability to connect on
more than a superficial level with Miss Allin. Although fascinated by
scientific subjects at the age of fourteen, I had been turned off reading in
the area by the time I was twenty. Certainly no one had encouraged my
interest in science. Nor had I found female mentors, for that matter,
among historians. My favourite professors at Smith College had been
literary scholars, not historians, and no women graced the graduate faculty of the history department at Toronto when I was in attendance in
1957–8.[1] Coming of age in the 1950s may also have had something to

Elizabeth Allin, the first and, to date, only woman to be appointed full
professor in the University of Toronto's physics department

do with my major interests when I first met Professor Allin. Apart from
teaching high school history, these were largely domestic.[2]

It is hard, but not impossible, to account for the sea change that
occurred in my life between those days and my next meeting with Elizabeth Allin, early in the 1990s. An expanding university had swept me
into its teaching ranks; eventually I had also acquired the union ticket
for teaching at the university level, a PhD in history. Secondly, a desire
to understand generally how we came to have the educational systems
that dominate so much of our lives merged with a growing interest in
women's varied and sometimes troubling experience of education. At a
certain point, my research and writing focused on universities and on
trying to understand what was so increasingly apparent: the gendered

character of all of our educational institutions and, particularly, our institutions of higher learning.

Around the same time, events in my husband's department at Toronto could not fail to attract my attention to the question of women in physics. The department that, in the past, had employed Elizabeth Allin and, I now knew from my research into the university's history, other women as well,[3] was experiencing great difficulty hiring a woman in the late 1980s. In fact, there had been no woman in the ranks of the physics professoriate since Professor Allin's retirement in 1972.[4] I found myself wanting to know more about Elizabeth Allin – both about the woman who had made a career in physics at Toronto and the world that had made her career possible.

I sought out Elizabeth Allin in the spring of 1991 and soon found myself an occasional guest in the home of a delightful woman who seemed a far cry from the remote figure of my earlier impressions. My discussions with Professor Allin about her life and work[5] eventually led to a number of taped interviews, conducted by Karen Fejer for the University of Toronto Archives.[6] During her meetings with Karen Fejer, Professor Allin referred to papers that she had left in the physics department at the time of her retirement. Although some of these were subsequently destroyed,[7] eventually a fascinating cache of notebooks and documents, and the appointment diaries of another woman teacher of physics, Kathleen Crossley, made their way to the University Archives. It is from these sources, as well as from Allin's own slim volume on the history of physics at Toronto, published by the department in 1982,[8] that the following account of Professor Elizabeth Allin and her world has been drawn.

I

Elizabeth Allin was born in the township of Brock, Ontario County, 8 July 1905. Her mother, Elizabeth Metcalfe Thompson, had Irish roots; the Irish part of the family had come to Canada from Tipperary. The ancestors of her father, Joseph Allin, had originated in Devonshire, migrating first to the New England states and, after the American Revolution, to eastern Ontario. While Elizabeth was growing up, her father kept a store and was the local postmaster in Blackwater Junction, Ontario.[9]

Enthusiasm for education ran in the family, especially on the side of Elizabeth's father. Joseph Allin had been well schooled, missing out on a university education, according to his daughter, only because he was a younger son; for some years before taking on the store and post office, Allin had been a very successful and popular schoolmaster, as had his father before him. Elizabeth Allin's paternal grandmother had also trained to be a schoolmistress, but had not taught long, owing to her temper, which was 'too quick.'[10] Finally, three aunts on her father's side had been educated beyond the average for the period. One had attended the Ontario Ladies' College in Whitby; another had been an elementary schoolmistress; a third had not only attended university but had pursued a career in secondary teaching before her marriage.

Elizabeth Allin's mother had attended high school in Lindsay for one year prior to her marriage, but ill health had prevented her from completing her secondary studies. Nor did Elizabeth Allin's sisters pursue advanced schooling. The eldest, Sarah, when given the choice between attending high school or staying home to help out in the store and post office, chose the latter. Helen, who was seven years younger than Elizabeth attended high school briefly but, like her mother before her, chose marriage and family rather than further education and a career. Belief in the necessity of such a choice was typical of the era. Certainly few women born at the turn of the century believed that marriage and family could be combined with professional employment.[11]

The woman who would become a physicist seems to have been keen on her educational pursuits from the beginning. Allin described as 'very good'[12] her early schooling, in a one-room school that she attended from about the age of four. Her first teacher, Mr Harvey, was evidently happy to have her, despite her youth. 'If she wants to come, let her come,' was the response that Professor Allin remembered to the idea of her attending school with her older sister.[13] Among her other memories from public school days were the occasions when a particular young woman teacher, who 'only had the Normal,'[14] could not cope with arithmetic problems. Elizabeth took them home for her father to solve. Certainly, neither the weak mathematics background of this teacher, nor the poverty of the local school population, which Professor Allin described as composed of 'poor English, plus Dr Barnardo children,'[15] interfered with the young Elizabeth's desire to learn. Nor was there a debate about sending this second daughter on to high school. Her widowed maternal grandmother sold her house in Toronto and moved to Port Perry, in order to keep house for Elizabeth. Port Perry had a good high school and it was at this school that Elizabeth embarked on the next stage of her education.

Did the high school provide an especially dynamic training in science? Evidently not. The principal taught them chemistry, Dr Allin recalled. His method was to recommend a text that no one could get – and then sit at the front of the room, reading it to the students. Very little lab work was done. In physics, the situation was no better. There was electricity on the main street of Port Perry, Professor Allin remembered, but not in the school. Indeed, when a Toronto friend later checked out Port Perry High School in the Ontario Department of Education 'blue books' for the fun of it, he found that it had less science equipment than any secondary school in the province.[16] Maybe the best thing about Port Perry High School was its case full of books, which included a set of volumes on history and geography, and another set containing stories of children in other lands. These books were 'perhaps not great literature but useful to us ... I read most of the books in the Port Perry Library too – some of them not so useful.'[17] Elizabeth Allin, who was very tall, also enjoyed school sports, especially basketball.

What Port Perry seems to have provided for Elizabeth Allin was the opportunity to grow and to learn as the spirit moved her. When asked if her interest in physics started in high school, Dr Allin replied that she 'was always interested in everything, when it came to that.'[18] She also appreciated the pedagogy of a teacher who 'didn't do much teaching really – he left you to find out things for yourself,' which was, Dr Allin thought, probably a very good idea.[19]

Elizabeth Allin needed little incentive to continue her studies, but her teachers did encourage her to go to university, as did her family, especially her father and her Aunt Lizzie. The latter had not only graduated from Toronto in 1898, but had served as one of Ontario's first woman school principals.[20] When it came to the choice of a university, Allin chose to follow her aunt to Toronto. It was closer to home and therefore cheap to get to; several friends from Port Perry High School were already there, and another would accompany her; and her Aunt Lizzie and Uncle Ted were graduates. Allin picked Toronto's University College partly because of Aunt Lizzie's connection with UC, but also because it was non-denominational – and she regarded herself as a 'very non-denominational person.' Indeed, she 'never thought of going anywhere else.'[21] She chose Honours Maths and Physics because she had done well in these subjects in high school and thought she would like to teach mathematics. In the end, however, it was physics that attracted Elizabeth Allin. She found math too abstract; physics was more practical.

II

Elizabeth Allin entered the University of Toronto in the fall of 1922. This was, in many ways, a good time for a young woman to embark on higher education in Canada. The trauma experienced by the first generation of women to attend university[22] had passed; in theory, at least, the presence of women was now accepted at most Canadian institutions of higher learning. The departure of male students during the Great War had rendered women more visible on campus, as had the founding of new professional programs designed with women in mind, such as household science, social work, and physiotherapy.[23] There is no denying that hostility to women students and faculty continued or that the channelling of women into separate professional training had proven a mixed blessing.[24] Nor can we discount the frivolous and in many ways damaging 1920s image of the flapper: the flamboyant young woman whose interest in clothes, men, and high living supposedly precluded a genuine interest in her studies. University of Toronto women of Elizabeth Allin's generation escaped neither the image nor the frustrations of their continued second-class status on campus.[25] But this decade in Canada also produced the seriousness of organizations like the Student Christian Movement and the University Women's Club and saw women striving for better treatment in universities. Finally, the 1920s were witness to a growing demand among women graduates for the right to meaningful employment, which they increasingly sought in all fields that were open to men. One of these fields was university teaching and research.[26]

Elizabeth Allin recalled much that was fascinating about her life as a student at Toronto. She lived in a University College residence known as Queen's Hall, which consisted of three houses on Queen's Park Crescent. Her house (No. 9) was occupied by twenty-one students and a don. While nominally subject to the authority of the UC Dean of Women, Miss Waddington,[27] Queen's Hall students were 'independent in our rules' and very proud of their residence, according to Professor Allin.[28] The dining room was located in No. 7 Queen's Park Crescent, and Allin remembered both the excellence of the food and that it cost $9.50 a week for her meals. Queen's Hall was presided over by Louise Livingston, an easy-going former British headmistress, who lived in No. 7. The major rule that Professor Allin recalled was the prohibition against smoking; the atmosphere she described as resembling a girls' boarding school, with its emphasis on manners and decorum. At the same time, the common room, with its piano, encouraged singing, dancing, and the entertainment of young men. And Professor Allin remembered pyjama parties in the residence, with ukulele music and 'food from home.'[29]

If residence life was cheerful and fun, so evidently was life in the undergraduate maths and physics program and, later on, in graduate physics. Presided over by Professor J.C. McLennan, who had headed it since 1907, the Department of Physics was small and vibrant and, at some level, welcoming to women students. While not consistent regarding the numbers of women in physics when she was a student, Elizabeth Allin believed that the Maths and Physics Society had no need to go outside its membership to find enough women for its parties in the early years. And university records reveal women (presumably senior undergraduate or graduate students) employed as class assistants and assistant demonstrators in physics as early as 1906 and continuously from 1909. By 1913, Vivian Ellsworth Pound had been awarded a PhD, the first woman and fourth individual to be granted a doctorate in physics at Toronto. Although Vivian Pound was teaching in Buffalo by the time Elizabeth Allin arrived at Toronto in 1922,[30] there were at least six women employed as demonstrators, assistant demonstrators, or class assistants in a department that, at the time, had only five men in the professorial ranks.[31] One of the assistant demonstrators, Florence Quinlan, had earned a master's in physics in 1921. Both Quinlan and Annie T. Reed, who had been a class assistant since 1911, and would receive the added title of departmental secretary in 1924, were on their way to becoming permanent employees in physics.[32]

By the 1920s, the physics department had not only acquired its own building and lab under Professor McLennan, but also a full-fledged graduate program in which women were encouraged to participate. It is true that the men were referred to by their last names, while the women were called 'Miss,' and that Professor McLennan was horrified at the egalitarianism implied when, at Maths and Physics Society meetings, nominees for office were referred to by their first names.[33] But Elizabeth Allin did not recall – or at least did not speak about – any serious obstacles to her presence in physics. If there were problems, they were financial ones, and Allin knew how to be frugal.[34]

A feeling for this period in the physics department emerges from the appointment diaries of Kathleen Crossley, whose employment in the department began in 1920.[35] Starting off as an assistant demonstrator, Crossley was already listed as a full-fledged demonstrator in the University of Toronto Directories for 1921–2. She was a lecturer briefly in

1935–6, and again in 1938–9, but her promotion to the professorial ranks did not come until early in the Second World War, when the department finally recognized the value of its women staff by promoting several to the rank of assistant professor.[36] Later on, Elizabeth Allin paid tribute to Crossley, noting that she 'knew elementary physics better than anyone' and that she was kindly thought of by generations of the first-year students to whom her career had been devoted.[37]

The Crossley diaries (passed on to Allin in two shoeboxes marked 'Do Not Throw Out') fascinate because of the names that keep recurring, both known and unknown. In the early years, the names of men who were graduate students or teaching assistants in physics, such as J.H. McLeod and H.J.C. Ireton, appear along with the names of women like Florence Quinlan and Annie Reed. By the late 1920s, the diaries refer increasingly to three new women physicists. One, Mattie Levi Rotenberg, earned a doctorate at Toronto in 1926, the second woman to do so in physics.[38] The second, Elizabeth Cohen, was one of two women who won doctorates in physics in 1929, a one-time majority since the total of doctorates that year was three.[39] The third name in the diaries was Elizabeth Allin.

On Monday, 17 January 1927, a tea was held in the library of the physics building 'to present [a] prize to E. Allin,' and, from then on Allin was a constant visitor to Kathleen Crossley's pages. A few entries suggest the flavour of those days. In April 1931, 'E. Allin' joined Crossley and Miss Reed at badminton, a few months before the convocation in which Elizabeth Allin received her doctoral degree. A January 1932 outing to Loew's Theatre to see Noel Coward's *Private Lives* included EA as well as FMQ; two weekends later, EJA, FMQ, ATR (Allin, Quinlan, Reed), and 'self' made up a table at a Trinity bridge party. February brought a tea at E. Allin's; March another play, *Quality Street*, with Allin and Reed. Elizabeth Cohen gave a lunch party, also in March. In May, E.J. Allin was with 'Barnes, Annie and Burton,' when they came to Oakville for tea; although not mentioned on this occasion, she was undoubtedly also part of the group that celebrated the convocation of 9 June 1932, when Florence Quinlan, along with two male students, received her doctorate in physics.

III

According to the university directories, Elizabeth Allin became involved in teaching physics at Toronto as early as 1926. But her own history of the physics department gives 1930 as the date of her formal appointment to the faculty.[40] In fact, she combined teaching duties with her course and research work as a graduate student until the granting of her doctorate, in spectroscopy and the structure of atoms, in 1931. A graduate student demonstrator typically earned \$750 for the eight-month period when classes were on, which Allin believed was excellent pay.[41] When not fulfilling their roles as class assistants or demonstrators, graduate students were expected to be in their labs working on their experiments five days a week and Saturday mornings. Most were supervised by Professor McLennan, who made his daily rounds, asking 'What's new?' and expecting an answer. As Allin put it later, 'It was unwise to have nothing to discuss since this was regarded as evidence of lack of endeavour.'[42] At the same time, graduate students were not expected to be in residence outside of term. McLennan went away to England or the continent; the labs had to be cleaned; and most students had no financial support for the summer months.[43] Like her friend Kathleen Crossley, Elizabeth Allin spent her summers at home with her family during her years of graduate study.

Allin's memories of these years in the physics department suggest a relaxed and friendly atmosphere. McLennan set long exams, but there was no time limit for them; they might take all day to write and then have to be mailed off to him in England. There were departmental seminars, at which attendance was mandatory for senior undergraduates and graduate students, every other Thursday in term. On these occasions, the wife of the department head usually poured the tea, suggesting a measure of formality. But, when Mrs McLennan, or later Mrs Burton, could not attend, a female faculty member or graduate student would pour. More informally, the graduate students got into the habit of having tea at the end of most days. The women usually prepared it (later in her life, Professor Allin wondered why), but the men took a hand, if all the women were busy. On these occasions, McLennan usually had his tea in his office, and Burton and Satterly joined the students. But Gilchrist and McTaggart, the two bachelors on the faculty, never did. The annual McLennan dance was an event to look forward to, as was what gradually became the annual spring picnic at Kathleen Crossley's family home in Oakville. At the latter event, physics staff and students played tennis and croquet – the latter with such enjoyment that the croquet games often continued past dark and had to be completed by flashlight.[44]

In the middle of all this conviviality Elizabeth Allin, both as a graduate student and a staff member, studied physics. Among the materials that Allin collected when writing her history of the department are three books in which are recorded the dates and speakers at the departmental seminars, each volume dealing with one of three periods between 1910 and 1964.[45] Frequently the speakers listed were faculty members or students, but visitors are also listed, and many came from afar. Before 1931, Allin had been exposed to the ideas of Niels Bohr of Copenhagen, as well as those of other central and northern Europeans. Seminar speakers were also recruited from the United States and Britain and, in both 1930–1 and 1931–2, there were lecturers from Cambridge University. It may have been the visits of R.H. Fowler and P.A.M. Dirac, both of Cambridge, that inspired Elizabeth Allin to plan a year of study at that university in 1933–4.[46]

Allin later said that, when she went to Cambridge, she was 'trying to learn some modern physics.'[47] Certainly, as she put it on another occasion, the mid-1930s were 'a very exciting time for any young person to be in Cambridge ... [We] got not only the latest from Rutherford and Chadwick – but we also had the advantage of [hearing] continental physicists.'[48] Among the 'first line physicists' who visited were Marie Curie, and Curie's almost equally famous daughter and son-in-law, Irène and Frédéric Joliot-Curie.[49] Max Born, then teaching at Edinburgh, also came to Cambridge the year Allin was there.

From the point of view of physics, perhaps the greatest treasures in Elizabeth Allin's papers are the volumes in which she recorded her notes from the lectures given by these luminaries, as well as by the lesser but still brilliant lights of Cambridge whose words she had come to hear. There are thirteen notebooks in all. One is a record of the theoretical colloquia and another contains notes on the constitution of matter. The remaining volumes are identified by the lecturer. These include Born on physical optics and the field theory of matter; Powell on the dynamical theory of gases; Hulme on quantum theory of dispersion; and Dirac on quantum mechanics. Allin also took lectures from Steem on functions used in mathematical physics; Fowler on statistical mechanics; Leonard Jones on quantum mechanics of atoms and molecules; and, finally, the great Rutherford himself, on ionization and radioactivity.[50] Elizabeth Allin clearly got an enormous amount out of a year that also included travel to the west of England, Scotland, and Ireland, before her return to Toronto the following September.[51]

Perhaps the best thing that Elizabeth Allin acquired during her year in England was a lifelong friendship. Pictures in the Toronto *Telegram* article detailing Royal Society fellowship awards granted to University of Toronto students in the spring of 1933 show two women, a physicist and a botanist. Elizabeth Allin was the physicist; the botanist was Dorothy Forward.[52] It was evidently Dorothy Forward who suggested that the two Toronto scholars travel together, since they were both on their way to Cambridge. They took a bedsitter together in the commercial district of Cambridge and registered as students at Newnham College.[53] This year of sharing must have been a positive experience for both women because, at some point later in their lives, they decided to live together, a happy arrangement that continued until Allin's death, late in 1993.[54]

Equally rewarding for Elizabeth Allin was the acceptance of women in science that she later recalled encountering at Cambridge. Although she volunteered nothing negative about Toronto at any point in our interviews, when comparing Toronto to Cambridge Allin did note that there was 'less difference in the way the women and men were treated' at the latter. Women had their own colleges at Cambridge, but this did not prevent them from calling on professors in the men's colleges and asking permission to attend their lectures. Coming from Toronto, Allin was surprised. She had expected more segregation between men and women. At Toronto, women had to enter the physics building by a separate door, which meant that they ended up in separate sections at the lectures. During most of her time at Toronto, women were also excluded from Hart House, the student centre where many important intellectual as well as social and athletic activities took place. Thus, despite the conviviality of dances, theatre nights, picnics, and afternoon tea, in working hours young women physicists mingled with the men only in the labs.[55]

It is interesting that it was only when talking about her year in Cambridge that Professor Allin recalled any bias against women in science at Toronto. The Cambridge experience may in fact have awakened Elizabeth Allin to disparities between the treatment of men and women that had not been so obvious to her previously. Her awakened consciousness of bias may also have been the result of the changing times. By the time Allin had received her doctorate in 1931, the Great Depression was on in earnest. The doctorates awarded to Florence Quinlan in 1932 and May Annetts in 1933 were the last granted to women for many years; after this men were clearly dominant in the Toronto graduate program in physics. Florence Quinlan and Kathleen Crossley retained their jobs in the department, as did Allin, and May Annetts managed to keep a demonstrating post until 1937; Elizabeth Cohen, Beatrice Deacon, Mattie

Rotenberg, and others would find teaching work in physics at the university both during and after the Second World War. But the encouragement of women that characterized physics at Toronto during the 1920s appears to have ceased.[56]

When queried about her return to Toronto, Allin volunteered few details. Professor Burton, who had replaced McLennan as head of the physics department in 1932, 'knew I was coming ... I think that's all the formality that was involved ... From then on I demonstrated in the lab – and, from time to time, gave lectures that I was asked to give.'[57] Allin recalled that she demonstrated in the fourth-year lab and was involved in research on spectroscopy. The records show that between 1935 and 1937, her title was 'Lecturer and Demonstrator,' after which she became a full-fledged 'Lecturer.' Florence Quinlan and Kathleen Crossley also became lecturers in the mid-1930s.[58] But there is no doubt that the men of Allin's era (some of whom, she later noted, had job offers from other universities and so could demand promotions more easily) moved ahead more quickly than she did. By 1937, a department that had numbered five in the professorial ranks throughout the 1920s had grown to eleven, all of them men. And, although Allin believed that her starting salary had been equal to that of her male colleagues, she knew that the men who were promoted faster did better financially as well.[59] Moreover, outside of the professorial ranks, no one working in the physics department in the 1930s had job security since all junior faculty appointments had to be renewed annually. Individuals in this latter category 'were ineligible for pension rights,' a fact that would eventually affect people like Kathleen Crossley very adversely.[60] Finally, married women – and there were at least three talented ones in the physics pool in Toronto during the 1930s – were not wanted on the faculty. 'That was the way they cut the staff,' Allin later recalled when referring to this problem. 'They got rid of the [married] women.'[61] Certainly, when speaking of the Burton years prior to the Second World War, there is no feeling in Allin's later commentary of the fun of the McLennan years or the excitement of her time in Cambridge.

Perhaps it is useful to turn here to Elizabeth Allin's own written summary of the Burton era. She saw this period as having three 'natural divisions': the period before World War II, the war years, and the period immediately after the war. 'The first was a time of economic depression; the second made unusual demands on the staff and the facilities of the department; the beginning of the third was marked by an influx of eager, serious students, both undergraduate and graduate, whose expectations had to be met as fully as possible.'[62] While Allin by no means gave up her sense of herself as an active researcher during this period, the enormous teaching loads of the late 1930s and the 1940s must have taken their toll. It is also possible that the increased workload fell disproportionately on the women in physics.

Their work finally began to be recognized during the Burton years, however. With war came promotions, and in 1941–2, Allin, Crossley, and Quinlan were all appointed at the rank of assistant professor. 'We felt,' Allin recalled, 'very lucky.'[63] The war also brought an enormous sense of purpose and accomplishment. In 1941, Allin's opinion was sought by the Toronto *Telegram* regarding German capabilities in the area of thermal diffusion. Could the Nazis separate Uranium 235 from Uranium 236? Allin replied that it was doubtful, disagreeing with an expert in California. It is clear from the tone of the article that her voice was accepted as authoritative.[64] Certainly, the university had no doubts about her authority when it came to teaching large courses designed for men entering or already in the armed forces. As the war progressed, the physics department was called upon to train naval, air force, and medical men who needed to know more about the physics of radar, radio, anti-submarine work, and radiation. Elizabeth Allin was among those who taught them. This sometimes meant classes of 500, but Allin rose to the occasion and made her classes memorable. Long afterwards, she continued to be invited to the reunions of those who took the special physics courses at Toronto during the war. Attending these reunions became one of the pleasures of her later life.[65]

Although the graduate program tapered off, the number of students taking physics almost tripled during the war. After a brief decrease, student numbers – both undergraduate and graduate – rose again at the war's end. By 1952 undergraduate numbers had settled at slightly more than the prewar level, but the number of doctoral students had doubled.[66] Teaching loads remained high, although graduate teaching and supervision now became an important part of the workload and was at least more compatible with research. During the war, much faculty research had been held in abeyance; now research-oriented faculty were keen to get back to it.[67]

Elizabeth Allin was part of this resurgence in research and graduate instruction, as the department expanded and the various subfields of physics competed for resources and new faculty. Although formal leadership in her area of research appears always to have been in the hands of a male physicist, most researchers saw experimental work within the subfields as collaborative endeavours. Allin was a highly valued member of the team working in 'atomic and molecular spectroscopy,' her research encompassing 'the study of solid and liquid hydrogen, deuterium, oxygen and carbon dioxide.'[68]

Engagement in research meant reporting on one's work at scholarly meetings, and Allin was among those who were keen to form a Canadian learned society so that reports and discussions could take place in Canada. The result was the founding of the Canadian Association of Professional Physicists in 1944–5, which a few years later became the Canadian Association of Physicists. The idea of a Canadian society was not popular with all Canadian physicists; nor was there easy agreement on how to proceed. Allin recalled the founding of both the CAPP and the CAP as essentially the work of the younger physicists, somewhat in rebellion against their elders.[69] Yet, to some, the move seemed urgent, given the growing visibility of the Canadian Association of Scientific Workers, an organization that Allin and her associates believed had dangerously 'international' leanings. 'At the time,' she recalled, 'the sharing of all physical knowledge did not seem like a good idea.' In short, some members of the CASW appeared to have connections to communism.[70]

The CAP began very humbly. Allin was the secretary and the convenor of the committee on the new charter, while her colleague Grayson Smith typed the bulletins. Everyone paid their own way to meetings. But the organization survived and grew. Elizabeth Allin clearly regarded her contributions to its beginnings as one of her important achievements. She wanted to meet Canadian physicists in Canada and, by the late 1940s, she could do so.[71]

IV

For Elizabeth Allin, meeting other Canadian physicists during the latter years of her career meant meeting many old friends. Grayson Smith, whose Toronto doctorate in physics was granted in 1926, taught at Toronto from 1935 to 1949, after some years at UBC. In 1949, he was appointed head of the physics department at the University of Alberta, joining many other Toronto-trained physicists whose work would take them permanently to other parts of Canada.[72] Perhaps it was thus a sense of the formative role played in Canadian physics by her fellow Toronto students of the 1920s and 1930s that prompted Elizabeth Allin to take on the history of the Toronto physics department as a project for her retirement. The result is a meticulously researched, even-handed study, which the department published in 1981. If there is any bias in *Physics at the University of Toronto*, it is the bias of the insider, a woman who felt lucky to have participated in an important period of development in Canadian physics and thought it useful to document the achievements of Toronto in her field.

Allin's history does not focus on the issue of women in physics; nor does she entirely avoid it. Indeed, she is careful to outline the achievements of the women who received their training at Toronto between 1910 and 1933. On the subject of women in physics after World War II she is silent, however. The university directories show Beatrice Deacon, Mattie Rotenberg, and Elizabeth Cohen, among others, working for the department for some years after the war. But, of Allin's women friends in physics, only Florence Quinlan and Kathleen Crossley remained with Allin as full-time faculty in the professorial ranks.

In the light of her silence on the subject of her female contemporaries after the war, it is interesting to note that in 1950 a Toronto *Telegram* columnist sought and published an interview with Elizabeth Allin, which touched on the question of women in physics. Florence Quinlan had been the subject of a similar article in the same newspaper the previous spring. Entitled 'Teaching is "Fun" for Woman Ph.D,' this earlier piece reported that Quinlan had been one of two women graduating in physics in her year, but that there were no women graduating in physics at Toronto in 1949.[73] The article on Allin, headlined 'Detective Story Fan Woman Physicist Busy in Teaching, Research,' noted her age (forty-four) and then went on to point out that with 'her soft blue eyes, fair fine skin and young smile,' Elizabeth Allin did not have to worry about looking her age – 'not that she would in any case.' In the *Telegram* interview, Allin recalled that she had been one of *four* women in physics in the class of 1926 but that, once again, few women seemed to be attracted to the field currently. At the end of the interview, Allin was asked her opinion on the vacant headship of the physics department. 'Could the new head be a woman?' the interviewer wanted to know. Professor Allin answered 'doubtfully' that she supposed it could happen – but that it wasn't 'very likely.'[74] In fact, both the previous choice (Burton's immediate successor) and the new head (W.H. Watson) were outsiders to the department and had come to Canada initially from Great Britain.

Despite her seniority in 1950, Allin knew that she was a very unlikely candidate for the headship in the climate developing not only in physics, but everywhere in the university, as Toronto's postwar quest for status as a leading research institution intensified. Physics, along with many other areas of scholarly endeavour, was developing into an increasingly male world; few young women appeared to be attracted to the field in the way that they had been attracted to it in the 1920s. That the Toronto *Telegram* felt it important to call this fact to the attention of its readers suggests that some were concerned about the way things were going. Clearly, at least one Canadian journalist was trying to show young readers that it was not unfeminine to be a physicist. One might have to work hard. But it *was* a job that an attractive, blue-eyed, forty-four-year-old woman could in fact enjoy doing.

At some level, Elizabeth Allin must also have been concerned about the status of women in physics. In 1950, she was, and would remain, the only senior woman physicist in a rapidly expanding department in which, after 1941–2, all new appointments to the professorial ranks went to men.[75] It may have been in this period that she became part of a group of University of Toronto women staff that she referred to as the Women's Faculty Union. In 1993, Professor Allin recalled the union starting as an informal luncheon group that met once a week at the University Women's Club. Occasionally there were evening meetings when one of the members gave a paper, but the essence of the group was social. Allin remembered her pleasure at meeting women from other University of Toronto departments through this association.[76]

In a letter that she wrote in 1984 to Dr Ann McMillan, the chair of the CAP's newly formed Committee to Encourage Women in Physics, Professor Allin had quite a lot to say about women in physics. Evidently responding to a query from the CAP committee, Allin focused on two obstacles to women in the field. An important one, in her view, was the continuing perception that a bachelor's degree in physics lacked professional status and was therefore not very practical. To teach secondary school one needed chemistry as well; to go into university teaching or advanced research required the doctorate, which in turn involved much sacrifice and therefore excluded all but the very dedicated. Engineering physics, in contrast, provided the built-in professional status of the engineer – and women seeking a career therefore saw in engineering physics more opportunity, both for initial employment and later advancement. Secondly, but no less importantly, Allin recognized the damaging effect of 'social pressures' on young women at all levels of their education. Told for years that they couldn't do mathematics, and encouraged, on entering university, to enrol in language courses or household science, most women saw the study of medicine or pure science as 'barely permissible,' according to Allin. Indeed, to go into maths and physics was 'to be regarded as scarcely human by many.'[77] It must have been unpleasant for Elizabeth Allin to know that women physicists were so regarded. But despite the prejudice, which she thought was declining at the time of her letter to Dr McMillan, she believed that women should be encouraged to choose physics. She herself, and other women she knew, Allin wrote, had found their work in physics both 'stimulating and satisfying.'[78]

Looking back on her life in the early 1990s, Elizabeth Allin continued to focus on the satisfactions, rather than on the obstacles. There had been outings, parties, and friends; there had been travel and stimulus; she felt lucky to have had the chance to do what she did. The main point had been the physics: doing physics, teaching it, and helping others to do the same. One cannot help but agree with her assessment in most respects. Yet, for women like myself, it is hard to view Allin's life and especially the context of that life without some regrets. Where Allin succeeded in carving out a career for herself, few others were able to follow.

Elizabeth Allin was no radical. But, given how little was possible for women in science during her time, what she accomplished was remarkable. To focus on the joys of Allin's life and career is not to deny the possible sorrows of her many women peers who perhaps found less to celebrate in the early years of Canadian physics.

NOTES

Research for this paper was supported, in part, by the Social Sciences and Humanities Research Council of Canada and by the University of Toronto Archives. My thanks to Alyson King, Susan Gelman, and Penny Stephenson, who assisted with the archival research, to Karen Fejer whose expertise in oral history created part of the record, and to Marianne Ainley, Mary Kinnear, Jim Prentice, and Ailsa Zainu'ddin, for their helpful comments on an earlier draft of the paper.

1 The history department employed three women at the instructor level in 1957–8: Mrs M.A. Bassett, MA; Miss M. (Margaret) E. Prang, MA; and Mrs M. Watson, MA. University of Toronto, Calendar, 1957–58, University of Toronto Archives (hereafter UTA), P78–0024(32)

2 The post–World War II decade has been seen as a negative period for young women, but a more accurate assessment would be to label ambigious the messages we received during this time. Recent research points to the extent to which women, especially married women, continued to increase their

numbers in the labour force during the postwar years. See Alison Prentice, Paula Bourne, Gail Cuthbert Brandt, Beth Light, Wendy Mitchinson, and Naomi Black, *Canadian Women: A History* (Toronto: Harcourt Brace Jovanovich, 1988), 291–2, 311–17, and 420–3. Also Joanne Meyerowitz, ed., *Not June Cleaver: Women in Post-War America, 1945–1960* (Philadelphia: Temple University Press, 1994). The contradictory position of the faculty wife is slowly coming under scrutiny but deserves much more study. See Marilyn Hoder-Salmon, 'Collecting Scholars' Wives,' *Feminist Studies* 4, no. 3 (Oct. 1978); Shirley Ardener, 'Incorporation and Exclusion: Oxford Academics' Wives' and Lidia Sciama, 'Ambivalence and Dedication: Academic Wives in Cambridge University, 1870–1970' in *The Incorporated Wife*, ed. Hilary Callan and Shirley Ardener (London: Croom Helm, 1984).

3 Alison Prentice, 'Bluestockings, Feminists, or Women Workers? A Preliminary Look at Women's Early Employment at the University of Toronto,' *Journal of the Canadian Historical Association* (1991)

4 Efforts were made to hire women physicists during this period, and, indeed, two women finally did agree to come to Toronto. But to summarize some troubling events very briefly, in both cases the women decided that they would be better off remaining where they were. One, Torontonian Melissa Franklin, is now Harvard's first woman full professor of physics. An account of her career and her difficulties with the hiring process at Toronto are the subjects of 'High Energy,' one of a series of six hour-long documentaries on women scientists, entitled *Discovering Women: Six Remarkable Women Scientists* (Princeton, NJ: Films for the Humanities and Sciences, 1995).

5 My interviews were conducted in May 1991 at Elizabeth Allin's home on Willowbank Boulevard in Toronto. From the very detailed notes that I made at the time of the interviews, I subsequently compiled a seven-page transcript, which will eventually be deposited at the University of Toronto Archives.

6 The Karen Fejer interviews were carried out in April and June of 1993 at Elizabeth Allin's home. Three of the Fejer tapes, dealing with Allin's years in physics, are now housed in the University of Toronto Archives, University of Toronto Oral History Program (2497). A preliminary interview, also on tape and dealing in part with Allin's early life, is in my possession. For the most part, the notes will give reference to my interviews, or Karen Fejer's, when I quote Professor Allin's exact words. Facts about Elizabeth Allin's life that are not otherwise documented come either from one interview or both.

7 Professors and others be warned! One should try to sort out one's own papers and see that they get to an archives before the opportunity to exercise some control over this process passes by.

8 Kathleen Crossley Diaries, Elizabeth Josephine Allin Papers, UTA, B93-0035

(001-004); Elizabeth J. Allin, *Physics at the University of Toronto, 1843–1980* (Department of Physics, University of Toronto, 1981)

9 Elizabeth Allin, interview with the author, 1991

10 Elizabeth Allin, preliminary interview with Karen Fejer, 1993

11 For discussion of the conflict between careers in higher education and marriage, see Prentice, 'Bluestockings,' 256–7. Studies in the history of women and higher education, and the history of women and science, note the difficulties women of this era had combining academic or scientific careers and marriage. See Barbara Miller Solomon, *In the Company of Educated Women: A History of Higher Education in America* (New Haven: Yale University Press, 1985); Margaret W. Rossiter, *Women Scientists in America: Struggles and Strategies to 1940* (Baltimore: Johns Hopkins University Press, 1982); and Marianne Gosztonyi Ainley, ed., *Despite the Odds: Essays on Canadian Women and Science* (Montreal: Véhicule Press, 1990).

12 Allin, interview with the author

13 Ibid.

14 Allin, preliminary interview with Fejer

15 Allin, interview with the author. 'Barnardo children' were British child immigrants brought to Canada without their families, under the auspices of the Dr Barnardo homes. See Joy Parr, *Labouring Children: British Immigrant Apprentices to Canada, 1869–1924* (Montreal and Kingston: McGill-Queen's University Press, 1980).

16 The 'blue books' were put out annually by the Ontario Department of Education and contained statistical information on teachers and schools. The friend was H.J.C. Ireton (PhD Toronto, 1934), who taught physics at Toronto from 1916 to 1959. Allin, interview with the author

17 Ibid.

18 Allin, preliminary interview with Fejer

19 Ibid.

20 The university calendars show an Elizabeth Allin, from Glencoe, graduating in 1898. I have not so far been able to track her subsequent career in teaching, prior to her marriage and move to the United States. Professor Allin's recollection was that she had been a secondary school principal in Bowmanville. Allin, interview with the author

21 Allin, interview with Fejer

22 For a discussion of the ambiguities of higher education for Canadian women in the last two decades of the nineteenth century, see Jo LaPierre, 'The First Generation: The Experience of Women University Students in Central Canada' (PhD thesis, University of Toronto, 1992). Also, LaPierre, 'The Academic Life of Canadian Coeds, 1880–1900,' *Historical Studies in Education/Revue*

d'histoire de l'éducation 2, no. 2 (Fall 1990), reprinted in Ruby Heap and Alison Prentice, eds., *Gender and Education in Ontario* (Toronto: Canadian Scholars Press, 1990).

23 Barry M. Moody has captured the impact of the Great War on one Canadian university in 'Acadia and the Great War' in *Youth, University and Canadian Society: Essays in the Social History of Higher Education,* ed. Paul Axelrod and John G. Reid (Montreal and Kingston: McGill-Queen's University Press, 1989). On the impact of the women's professional faculties and courses, see Margaret Gillett, *We Walked Very Warily: A History of Women at McGill* (Montreal: Eden Press, 1981), especially chap. 8; Lee Stewart, *'It's Up to You': Women at UBC in the Early Years* (Vancouver: University of British Columbia Press, 1990); and Ruby Heap, 'Training Women for a New "Woman's Profession": The Beginnings of Physiotherapy Education at the University of Toronto, 1917–1940,' *History of Education Quarterly* 35, no. 2 (Summer 1995). For an overview of the 1920s at Ontario universities, see A.B. McKillop, *Matters of Mind: The University in Ontario, 1791–1951* (Toronto: University of Toronto Press, 1994), 420–37.

24 Household science, for example, could be seen as a way of drawing women away from the other sciences. Margaret Gillett seems to dismiss this argument in the case of McGill. See *We Walked Very Warily,* 351. Kerrie Kennedy finds the argument more persuasive for the University of Toronto. See Kennedy, 'Womanly Work: The Introduction of Household Science at the University of Toronto' (MA thesis, University of Toronto, 1995).

25 Alyson King, 'The Experience of Students in the "New Era"': Discourse and Gender in *The Varsity* 1919–1929,' *Ontario Journal of Higher Education* (1994), explores the contradictory images of women in the student press at the University of Toronto. For a general American study, see Paula Fass, *The Damned and the Beautiful* (New York: Oxford University Press, 1977).

26 Nicole Neatby, 'Preparing for the Working World: Women at Queen's during the 1920's,' *Historical Studies in Education/Revue d'histoire de l'éducation* 1, no. 1 (Spring 1989), reprinted in Heap and Prentice, eds., *Gender and Education.* Also, Alison Prentice, 'Scholarly Passion: Two Women Who Caught It,' *HSE/RHE* 1, no. 1 (1989), reprinted in Alison Prentice and Marjorie R. Theobald, eds., *Women Who Taught: Perspectives on the History of Women and Teaching* (Toronto: University of Toronto Press, 1988).

27 Shortly after Elizabeth Allin's arrival at University College, Mossie May Waddington married a Trinity professor and became Mrs Kirkwood – and thus one of a tiny group of women who managed to combine marriage and university teaching. For an account of Kirkwood's life and work, see Prentice, 'Scholarly Passion.'

28 Allin, interview with Fejer

29 Ibid.

30 Vivian Pound lectured at Queen's from 1912–1917. She left the academic world for business for a few years, but from 1922 on was employed as instructor, then assistant professor and professor (from 1927) in mathematics at the State University of New York, Buffalo. She became Professor Emeritus in 1955. *American Men of Science*, 10th ed. (New York: Bowker, 1961).

31 These were J.C. McLennan, E.F. Burton, L. Gilchrist, H.A. McTaggart, and J. Satterly. They remained, throughout the 1920s, the only members of the department who had professorial rank. As Allin put it in 1981, 'all others remained lecturers, demonstrators or sessional appointees.' Allin, *Physics*, 11

32 UTA, University of Toronto Calendars, P78–0021; University of Toronto Directories of Staff and Students, P78–0171. Although Elizabeth Allin later believed that women had first achieved the rank of demonstrator towards the end of the First World War, Vivian Pound was a demonstrator, albeit sessional, in 1912–13. But Allin was probably correct to imply that change occurred as a result of the war. Prior to 1920–21, a total of twenty-five women taught for the department but, apart from Pound, all were assistants. And apart from Annie Reed, no women taught in the department prior to 1920–21 for more than four years. For Allin's discussion, see *Physics*, 10–11. Reed's secretarial work, according to Allin, had begun long before her official appointment as secretary in 1924. Her adoption of this role was also very typical – in a period when university departments first began to have secretaries, most of them chosen from the ranks of their own accomplished women graduates. Florence Quinlan eventually became known for her outstanding work teaching physics to non-physics students, particularly from the Faculties of Music and Household Science.

33 Allin, interview with the author

34 Allin, interview with Fejer. Allin recalled that she managed, 'with the help of the odd scholarship,' on about $500 a year.

35 Allin's history of the department suggests that Crossley and Kathleen Quinlan began teaching for the department in the latter years of the First World War, but, while Quinlan appears in the calendars for the first time in 1918–19, Crossley's first appointment is listed in 1920–1. UTA, University of Toronto Calendars, P78-0021

36 UTA, University of Toronto Calendars and Directories. Also, Allin, *Physics*, 34. Allin notes that several men were also promoted from junior positions to the rank of assistant professor during the war.

37 Allin, interview with the author; Allin, *Physics*, 11

38 Mattie Rotenberg (née Levi) does not appear in the university's directories as

having worked for the physics department in the 1920s and must have financed her studies in some other way. In her history of the department, Allin says that Rotenberg 'left physics for some years but returned during the war' (as was the case with another woman in physics, Beatrice Reid Deacon, who also married during the pursuit of her doctorate). Reid appears as a demonstrator for three years in the 1920s and again, as Mrs B.R. Deacon, from 1940–1 to 1947–8. Rotenberg also taught for the department beginning in 1941–2 and carried on as a demonstrator until the late 1960s. I am indebted to Penny Stephenson, Susan Gelman, and Alyson King, who helped research the career tracks of these women in the university directories.

39 The other was Beatrice (Reid) Deacon. Allin, *Physics*, 75

40 Allin, *Physics*, 70

41 Allin compared the University of Toronto rate to the $500 a year earned by a mathematical physicist she knew from McGill. 'He took what he could get.' This unnamed friend died tragically in a plane crash in the Rockies. Allin, interview with the author

42 Allin, *Physics*, 19–20

43 Ibid., 20

44 For Allin's written account of graduate student life in her era, see *Physics*, 19–23.

45 UTA, Elizabeth Josephine Allin Papers, Journal of Seminars held in the Department of Physics, B93-0036 001 (01, 02, 03). The periods are 1910–20, 1921–32, and 1940–64.

46 In addition to the volume recording seminar speakers in the period 1921–32, see the list of visiting lecturers in Allin, *Physics*, 18.

47 Allin, interview with the author

48 Allin, interview with Fejer

49 For an insightful recent analysis of Marie Curie's life and work, see Helena M. Pycior, 'Marie Curie's "Anti-natural Path": Time Only for Science and Family' in *Uneasy Careers and Intimate Lives: Women in Science, 1789–1979*, ed. Pnina G. Abir-am and Dorinda Outram (New Brunswick and London: Rutgers University Press, 1989).

50 UTA, Elizabeth Josephine Allin Papers, B93-0035 (006–008)

51 Allin, interview with Fejer

52 UTA, Newspaper Clippings Files, A73-0026/205(55)

53 Allin, interview with Fejer

54 Dorothy Forward, who completed a second doctorate at Cambridge, had a long career at Toronto, teaching in the Department of Botany. I have not been able to discover when (or where) they began living together in Toronto. At

the time of the interviews with Professor Allin, they shared a house at 36 Willowbank Boulevard.

55 Allin, interview with Fejer
56 For a fuller discussion, see Alison Prentice, 'The Early History of Women in University Physics: A Toronto Case Study,' *Physics in Canada/La Physique au Canada* 52, no. 2 (March/April 1996).
57 Allin, interview with Fejer
58 UTA, University of Toronto Directories
59 Allin, interview with the author
60 When talking about her colleague Kathleen Crossley, Allin volunteered the information that Crossley was forced to continue teaching long after the 'so-called' retirement age, because she had never had a decent salary. Interview with the author
61 Ibid. Allin made this remark in the context of a discussion of Mossie May (Waddington) Kirkwood's claim that she was forced out of her role as dean of women at University College because she was married. The three married women physicists were Mattie (Levi) Rotenberg, PhD 1926; Beatrice (Reid) Deacon, PhD 1929; and May (Annetts) Smith, PhD 1933.
62 Allin, *Physics*, 24
63 Allin, interview with Fejer. As noted above, the war also resulted in the appointment of quite a few other women in untenured positions, which must have created a sense for at least a time that women were welcome in the department once more.
64 'Doubts Nazis Can Separate Prized U-235,' *Telegram*, 24 Jan. 1941. UTA, Newspaper Clippings Files, A73-0026/005(55)
65 Allin, *Physics*, 31–4; interview with the author
66 Allin, *Physics*, 34 and 41
67 The faculty was so anxious to ensure an immediate return to fundamental research after the war, that researchers involved in teaching armed forces personnel agreed to invest a portion of the government money received to pay for this instruction in a fund earmarked for postwar research. According to Allin, this was an important factor in making a quick start-up possible, despite large student numbers. Allin, *Physics*, 35
68 'In Memoriam: Professor Helped Found Physicists Association,' *University of Toronto Bulletin* 47, no. 17 (25 April, 1994)
69 M.F. Crawford, who had 'assumed leadership of spectoscropic research' at Toronto in the 1930s, was among those who never joined the CAP. See Allin, *Physics*, 25, for the description of Crawford, and the interview with Fejer, 1993, regarding Crawford's refusal to participate. An earlier description of the founding of the CAPP and CAP, in which she leaves out much regarding

her own role and those of other university physicists, is Elizabeth Allin, 'How the C.A.P. Began,' *Physics in Canada* 26, no. 4 (1970). In this account, Allin notes that in the early 1930s physics graduate students and National Research Council employees had formed 'a loose organization' and held several meetings, but that owing to scarce resources this grouping did not continue. Two other accounts of the CAP's founding, which were written earlier than Allin's and stress other matters, are L. Kerwin, 'The Next Decade for C.A.P.,' *Physics in Canada* 11, no. 1 (Autumn 1955), and A.D. Misener, 'The Canadian Association of Physicists: A History Review,' ibid., 34, no. 5 (1978).

70 Allin mentioned two people who were involved in the CASW whose connections appeared to be a worry. One was 'Sammy' Levine (an S. Levine was granted a doctorate in physics at Toronto in 1936); the other was Levine's wife, whose name Allin could not recall. Interview with the author

71 Allin, interview with the author

72 Allin, *Physics*, 25, 38, 74–5

73 *Telegram*, 23 April 1949. UTA Newspaper Clippings Files, A73–0026/371(08)

74 Dorothy Howarth, 'Detective Story Fan ...' *Telegram*, 4 Feb. 1950. UTA, Newspaper Clippings Files, A73–0026/005(55)

75 In addition, men were promoted more rapidly than Allin. Her promotion to associate professor did not come until the early 1960s, twenty years after her appointment as an assistant professor. She was finally a full professor in 1964–5. The promotions probably only became possible when Watson relinquished the headship of the department. G. David Scott was acting head in 1961–2 and Harry Welsh was appointed in 1962–3.

76 Allin, interview with Fejer. Allin believed that when the Faculty Club moved from Hart House to Willcocks Street, the women were given a room in the building and their own secretary. It would be interesting to know more about this group of women – how long they carried on meeting and how formally they were in fact constituted as a Women's Faculty Union.

77 E.J. Allin to Ann McMillan, 26 Jan. 1984, Elizabeth Josephine Allin Papers, UTA

78 Ibid.

GIVING VOICE

'Out of a Cardboard Box beside Our Bed like a Baby': The Founders of Sister Vision Press

AFUA COOPER

THE VISION

Makeda Silvera and Stephanie Martin wanted to provide Black women and women of colour with a mechanism for the proliferation of their words. They envisioned a publishing house that would bring books by Black women and women of colour to the public.

On 10 April 1985, at the Bamboo, a popular Toronto nightclub, the vision became a reality. The club was filled with people who supported the vision. They participated in the launch of Sister Vision Press with enthusiasm and love, which were born of the hope that the project gave them. People of all races were present; the vision was important to a wide cross-section of the Ontario community.

The birth of Sister Vision Press was an act of sheer faith and enthusiasm. Its two founders, Makeda Silvera and Stephanie Martin, say in retrospect, 'We had a lot of faith and enthusiasm in those early years. But little did we know how difficult it would be.'

Faith and enthusiasm are powerful enabling mechanisms. Today, the publishing house has forty-six titles to its credit. The Canadian publishing world has the added dimension of the vibrant, powerful work that the writers produce. Issues of race, gender, and sexuality are given a new dimension by the voices of these writers – 'new' in that the Canadian reading public has not read or heard them before, but not at all 'new' for the women whose work resonates so closely with their lives and the lives of the people in their communities.

THE REALITY

Today, the co-owners of Sister Vision Press look back at *the vision* from the experience of *the reality* and assess *the journey*. They do so with much wisdom, a generosity of spirit, and a refreshing honesty about social and political issues surrounding publishing in Canada.

The mandate of the press was and still is to publish works by Black women and women of colour, voices that have traditionally been excluded from mainstream and feminist publishing houses. In 1985, armed with nothing but a dream – or rather a vision – these two women from Jamaica set out to do the impossible. Today, Sister Vision has become a respected and vibrant publishing house, breaking new ground in Canadian publishing. Sister Vision has received several awards for its work. Stephanie is the production manager while Makeda is the managing editor. Both women are artists in their own right: Makeda is a writer and Stephanie is a visual artist.

The following is a conversation with Stephanie and Makeda at their home in Toronto on 12 March 1995.

AFUA: Why did you form this press, what was the motivation behind the establishment of Sister Vision, a press specifically for Black women and women of colour?

MAKEDA: At the point we decided that there was a need for such a press, we looked around and saw that there were no presses by Black women or women of colour, or any presses catering to that particular constituency.

STEPHANIE: Up to 1984 not one individual Black woman [in Canada] had her own book published ... except for the four women who were published by Third World publisher Williams-Wallace. It's important to point out that there were alternative presses, but none of them had published a Black woman or woman of colour, except for a token one or two in collections.

One of the main reasons they gave for not doing this was that the language often used by women of colour – particularly, say, women from the Caribbean – was not accessible, not easily understood. The experience that really brought this to the fore was when Makeda tried to get *Silenced[: Caribbean Domestic Workers Talk with Makeda Silvera]* published. It was turned down by Women's Press [Toronto] and other alternative presses for that reason. They felt the language was inaccessible, and there was no market for that kind of a book. Williams-Wallace Publishers were approached. Initially, they were hesitant about publishing such a book. Their concerns were similar to those of other publishers: the

Makeda Silvera (left) and Stephanie Martin

accessibility of the language, the marketability, the financial risks, and the subject matter. The women's stories were depressing for the most part, as they focused primarily on their oppressive working conditions. After a series of discussions, they were persuaded to take the risk. For our part, to make it more appealing, we took on the editing and production of the book. Since 1983, *Silenced* has been reprinted five times. Sister Vision obtained the rights in 1989.

MAKEDA: I'm glad, Stephanie, that you mentioned there were Third World presses around like Williams-Wallace. There was Khoisan Press, headed by Harold Head, Domestic Bliss, and several other small presses, which unfortunately lasted only for three or four years. Williams-Wallace lasted for many years and made significant contributions. Our experience with the initially reluctant publishing of *Silenced* made us even more determined to develop a press for Black women and women of colour, one that addressed working-class issues and concerns, that addressed sexuality and language with an emphasis on Creole [dialect]. We can see this in the voices in *Silenced* and in the very first book Sister Vision ever published, *Speshal Rikwes* by Ahdri Zhina Mandiela, our first collection of dub poetry.

STEPHANIE: Yes. Creole was not considered publishable or of any literary value and was not used much up to that point. We have to understand what was considered to be [real] literature. Going back to *Silenced*, my sense was that the hesitation to publish was not only about the domestic workers whose stories were in dialect but about Makeda herself, who was a working-class woman, doing work that was not being done at that time – the collecting of oral testimonies of working-class women. Because she was not middle class, not part of the literary scene, her work at that time was not considered credible.

AFUA: So you both are saying that the issue of voice was an important one for you in establishing Sister Vision?

MAKEDA: Voice, most definitely. And the issue of gender – or, to be more specific, gender as it related to Black women, because race has a tremendous impact on the way our gender has been shaped and articulated.

AFUA: So let's explore further this issue of voice and how it connected to the formation of Sister Vision Press. There seemed to have been a real silencing of the voices of Black women and women of colour in both mainstream and alternative presses. Makeda, the title of your first book, *Silenced*, illustrated this point very well.

MAKEDA: Yes, there was a real silencing going on within the alternative presses that called themselves feminist and progressive. We found that as women [of colour] we could not enter that space. In terms of white women who had power and had set up presses, it was quite clear that we were not welcome. My individual experience as an artist and writer is testimony to this. As one of the earlier Black writers active in the 1970s and '80s, I speak with authority about the resistance of white publishers to take chances and publish our writings. They were often afraid of our words and our experiences. They did not identify, and for them this was a legitimate reason not to publish us. Words used to describe our creative work were 'angry,' 'depressing,' 'no humour,' or 'too autobiographical.' We decided that there was a definite need for another press that would take in these kinds of stuff that the other presses were not interested in: class, race and colour, sexuality ...

STEPHANIE: ... in relation to the other things, sexuality connected to race and class.

MAKEDA: Absolutely. In relation to all of that and the diversity in language, in voice. For example, how we talk about sexuality is different from the way white people and white women talk about it. We talk about it in relation to race and racism, class. So we decided that there was a need for a kind of press that would publish writings dealing with these things.

We went to a number of women within the Black community who were involved in literature – women writers – to try to get some kind of support to form this press. This was in 1984. And we came up against a brick wall because many of these women were saying that they couldn't subscribe to something that excluded men ...

STEPHANIE: That argument was used in the context of solidarity against racism. They said if we were going to have a Black women and women of colour press, we would be excluding men and consequently we would be splitting the Black struggle. The assumption would be made that it was a lesbian press, affirming that anything that women did that excluded men had to be lesbian.

AFUA: Oh really?

MAKEDA: The fact that the two women who were forming the press were lesbians only confirmed this assumption.

AFUA: So basically you are saying that you did not get any support from the [Black] women in the community?

BOTH: No we didn't, at least not in the beginning. We got absolutely nil support because it was going to be a women of colour press and because at that time within the women of colour community people generally feared lesbianism and feared being labelled as lesbians.

MAKEDA: I want to stress that in 1984–5 what we were doing was revolutionary. We were pioneers dealing with a lot of issues that people are now beginning to deal with. There was real hesitancy to speak out against sexism and homophobia, because it was often translated into being whitewashed and forgetting one's roots.

AFUA: Would you also say you were foolish? It's a heck of a thing to found a press.

MAKEDA: Foolish? No, we would never say that. We were pioneers. I want to give a brief history. It's important for all of us to understand – all of us in the women's community, in the women of colour community – to know this history and for us at Sister Vision to set the record straight, about who went out there, took risks, and did the groundwork to build and ensure a vibrant and growing community of women of colour writers, when others were not interested in doing this. Now some have turned big-time feminists and womanists, and some of them are lesbians, but, then, they gave us no help. I don't care if I sound bitter, but I feel it should be said.

So going back to the question of being foolish, most definitely not, because in a way, co-founding this press is my taking a personal and political responsibility in a struggle.

STEPHANIE: And you know, Afua, we did not publish a lesbian title until 1991, six years after the founding of the press. We then published *Piece of My Heart: A Lesbian of Colour Anthology*, di fuss lesbian sinting we eva do. Up until that point, the women we published were not lesbians. And if any were, they did not publicly identify themselves as such. This is not being apologetic. It took this long for women to feel relatively safe about having their stories in print. I also want to say that the women we first published have always been absolutely supportive and faithful to Sister Vision Press in a very basic, strong kind of way – in solidarity – and have kept publishing with Sister Vision knowing that the advances are either non-existent or very small. These women have also consistently helped with fund-raising events.

AFUA: How is Sister Vision perceived now in the communities to which it is connected? More specifically, the publishing, Black, women's communities?

STEPHANIE: I think that, ten years later, Sister Vision is well respected: an established, viable organization that has worked and struggled and achieved something very important in encouraging and working with many emerging writers in this country – first-time writers whom mainstream publishers would never have taken the risk in publishing.

MAKEDA: We feel we have laid the groundwork for many Black writers and writers of colour who are now being published by mainstream publishers. We have laid the groundwork in the sense that Sister Vision has put our voice on the literary agenda. We have made a difference to the face of shelves in bookstores. Ten years ago, when we took our books into these stores we were dismissed and turned away: 'Not enough room on the shelves.' 'The books won't sell.' 'Who are you?' We have worked hard over the years to ensure that our books are on those shelves.

STEPHANIE: We know that some women writers of colour have not published with us for class reasons, for reasons of prestige. They have made a political decision – like those who have chosen us. It's interesting that many of these same writers go on at length about colonialism and the colonized mind, but many of them, who are supposedly radical and spout a lot of rhetoric, would never consider publishing with us or lending their name in support of the press.

Also they are more harshly critical. So, for example, if you do something that is not as good, that has problems with mistakes, spelling errors, etc., dem quick fi criticize harshly. But they would never do it with a big press. No! I remember buying a book from the Women's Press in London [England] and there were errors in pagination, but if that had happened with us no one would be forgiving. I think it boils down to the fact that our people don't believe that their own people can do things as well, and that's a very unfortunate thing. Our minds have been terribly colonized. So some folks go to the big white presses so they can get a better deal, more recognition, more prestige. And also they feel their work would garner more respect. But that's fine, because on the other hand a lot of women come to Sister Vision, and they have made a conscious decision to work with us. Very gifted and talented women.

AFUA: Would you say that Sister Vision is an integral part of the wider community?

MAKEDA: Definitely. However, that has its down side. Because even though we are very rich in community, you also pay a price for that. Because you are so much into community and culture, less time is paid to the other, business side of publishing, because publishing is a business. A lot of time we are holding this or that event in a community centre, and the company is not making any money, when mainstream publishers don't do that. A lot of mainstream presses, for example, do not do launches. They say it costs too much. So, say, if a launch costs $400 they take that money and put a single ad in a mainstream paper or they keep that money. But here at SV we are committed to community; and we take that money, have a launch where people can come, mingle with the artists, celebrate with the artists, socialize and realize some of our dreams as writers.

AFUA: Why the name Sister Vision?

STEPHANIE: It was a collaborative thing. We were just throwing names back and forth ... maybe, Makeda, your memory is better than mine ... why did we choose that name?

MAKEDA: We saw the vision certainly of the press being one that published stuff by women of colour; so hence the name 'sister.' We also had at that point a vision of a whole group of women of colour working collectively against all odds, coming out with books, working to make a new reality. I think why we chose the name Sister Vision and not Martin-Silvera was that we felt other artists in the same kind of position as us – marginalized artists of colour – would join in and share that vision. Except we found that we had assumed a lot.

STEPHANIE: Yes, the vision was to make a publishing house for women and all the possibilities that that entailed.

AFUA: Was there also a vision to make money?

MAKEDA: We didn't think of that at the time.

STEPHANIE: When you asked the question, Afua, of being foolish; in retrospect, I think that if we had had more understanding of publishing, because our understanding was limited, of the financial difficulties of publishing, the fact that it is a virtually impossible field to make money in, and the amount of work that one had to do – as far as I am concerned up until now we have made no monetary gains – I don't know. Quite likely I would still have gone ahead. Ten years later I'm physically more tired. Were the press to have been founded now, I would have thought about it more seriously. Because it has been incredibly hard work. So people say Sister Vision has lasted this long. We have done so by sheer will-power and the fact that all our resources have gone to Sister Vision Press. And when we both had full-time jobs elsewhere, all of that resource went into the press. We borrowed money; it went into the press. We carried the press with major debts, and still do. But that is all part of the vision. People don't do anything without it costing them ...

MAKEDA: ... costing them personally, politically, and creatively. It could have been said that we were foolish when we started the press. If we had thought about it seriously we probably wouldn't have done it. But I think what drove us – I prefer the word 'crazy' to 'foolish' – what drove us was: one, that passion within us; and two, that we were artists, artists who wanted to make a difference. We did not just want to sit down and wait for the change, but we wanted to make the change and not only for our individual selves. We wanted to change that industry and how that industry perceived us as women of colour.

In retrospect, a lot of organizations – other alternative presses, for example, the Women's Press of Canada, Press Gang Publishers, and a number of others started in the '70s – developed their vision at a time of a totally different political climate. Women worked collectively, there was much more active voluntarism, and there was government seed money available to start innovative organizations. It certainly was a time of more generosity both in spirit and financially.

When Sister Vision started in the '80s, the great collective spirit of the '70s was pretty much in the past. The '80s was the Me generation; funding to start an organization like Sister Vision had dried up. In our case, Stephanie and I were asking women of colour to be involved, and there was no money that could be guaranteed. People, particularly writers, were not interested in working in collectives. However, over the years, we have had the support of a number of committed women who have worked with us until moving on to jobs that pay a reasonable wage or to pursue individual careers or interests.

In our fund-raising efforts we have always had support. When we founded the press and started the work of mobilizing support, people were excited by our vision. The women's community – Black and white – and other progressive communities inspired by change have always supported our major fund-raising efforts.

STEPHANIE: And if one were to ask about the cost of the vision, other than the fact that it had been carried by us just struggling and working with no recompense for many, many years up until now, it would be the cost to us as two individual artists. One of the things that you sacrifice is the time spent developing your own work. Because I would say that the biggest cost that I personally have paid in my relationship with Sister Vision Press has been not giving my own work full attention. I think that Makeda will say the same thing, even though she can squeeze forty-two hours out of a day.

AFUA: Yes, we'll come to that latter point later on. But what's the point of publishing books if the press is not making money? A business should be profit-oriented, shouldn't it?

STEPHANIE: It goes back to the point Makeda made earlier. When SV was first started it was not as a business to make money. We founded it because we wanted to get certain things done. We fund-raise to publish our books. The first ten books that we published, we did not go into debt to do. Both Makeda and I were working elsewhere full time, and we used our incomes to put into the press.

AFUA: At the beginning where was the press physically located?

MAKEDA: SV started out of a cardboard box, a filing box, beside our bed, like a baby. After the box we asked Fireweed, a feminist literary organization, if we could share space with them. It was an organization that I was involved with for seven years. We operated out of a small corner in their office. Then we expanded, cleared out our basement, and moved into it. Our first book launch was held here in our living room. That was for Ahdri Zhina Mandiela's book *Speshal Rikwes*. Both author and publisher fund-raised for the publication of that book. It was a real vision. So initially we never thought of the press as a money-making venture. To us it was important that we publish this voice who ordinarily would not be heard, and it was an important voice.

AFUA: How did you learn the market, say, in terms of distribution and sales?

BOTH: Trial and error. When we started out, we were going out on foot to maybe five bookstores.

STEPHANIE: The bookstore people were usually very rude, they rolled their eyes and never gave us the time of day. I tell you, the two bookstores that we were able to walk into and sell books to were the Third World Bookstore and the Women's Bookstore. That was it. The others were simply not interested in our books. We didn't have a distributor; so that made it even worse for us. The fact that we were a women of colour press interested them even less. And when we did try to get a distributor we were told we were too small. U of T Press was not interested in distributing such a small press and they also said that women of colour books have no market.

MAKEDA: Women's Press [Canada] was being distributed by U of T Press at the time; so we approached them [Women's Press] and negotiated a financial arrangement whereby under their auspices we started being distributed by U of T Press.

AFUA: So you are saying that for the press to have survived – even cut its first tooth – you had to be persistent and dogged?

BOTH: Exactly!

AFUA: What were some of your successes over the past ten years? Feel free to define 'success' in any way you choose.

STEPHANIE: Well, we have published over forty titles. The fact that we have stayed alive for ten years and are still kicking despite all kinds of problems and pressures that come with running a press with not a lot of resources and that one does get weary and tired, the fact that we have over forty titles is quite a feat.

MAKEDA: To me, our greatest success has been the many anthologies that we have published, which have given voice to a diversity of women. The mixed race anthology *Miscegenation Blues[: Voices of Mixed Race Women* (1994)] was an innovative piece of work and has been quite successful. We are the first press in Canada to publish something of that nature. For us it was a risk because we didn't know how the market would receive it.

BOTH: *Piece of My Heart: A Lesbian of Colour Anthology* was also the first book of its kind to be published in North America. It was a finalist in the American Library Association [Gay and Lesbian Book Award], the gay category.

MAKEDA: Also *The Very Inside[: An Anthology of Writings by Asian and Pacific Island Lesbians and Bisexual Women]*, edited by Sharon Lim-Hing, was nominated for a prestigious American book award. We have also worked with a number of feminist groups and organizations in the Caribbean because we understand the lack of access Third World women have in getting published. So we worked in conjunction with CAFRA [Caribbean Association for Feminist Research and Action] of Trinidad and Tobago to get *Creation Fire[: a CAFRA Anthol-*

ogy of Caribbean Women Poets (1990)], edited by Ramabai Espinet, published. *Creation Fire* brought the poetry of Caribbean women in the Caribbean and in the Diaspora together. And it was not just in English but in French, Creole, Papiemento, Dutch, Spanish, all the languages of the Caribbean region. That was absolutely a ground-breaking publication. *Lionheart Gal: Life Stories of Jamaican Women*, by Sistren Theatre Collective and Honor Ford-Smith, and *Blaze a Fire[: Significant Contributions of Caribbean Women* (1988)], by Nesha Hanif, were important and original books. One of Althea Prince's stories from her book *Ladies of the Night [and Other Stories* (1993)] was also chosen by Penguin to include in one of its short story collections. Plus the manuscript for your book, Afua, *Memories Have Tongue* [1992], was shortlisted for the Casa de las Americas Prize. One of our major successes was in discovering and working with so many talents right here in Canada.

AFUA: Do you make an effort to find writers and would-be writers from across the country, or are all your writers Toronto-based?

STEPHANIE: We do make an effort, however most of our writers, given our locale, are Ontario-based. Our anthologies do reflect the writing of women across Canada.

AFUA: Sister Vision is a feminist press, but does the fact that you both are lesbians make you take a particular approach to publishing?

MAKEDA: Definitely! It makes us so much more conscious that our publications must be more diverse and include writers with different opinions.

STEPHANIE: I would disagree with that, I don't think that every press that has a lesbian sensibility would necessarily have the same sensitivity about publishing things that are inclusive or diverse. It is the conscious thought of the publisher that would make that deduction, because if one was just to say that 'because we are a feminist, lesbian company ....' It depends on the individuals involved. There can be publishers who are lesbians but who would not think the same way as we do.

MAKEDA: I'm glad you clarified that. But I believe we are more in tune with issues around diversity not only because we are lesbians but lesbians of colour who have to deal very much with a reality of race and colour. This forces us to be much more sensitive. And I feel all the multiple realities that we deal with are pluses for us.

AFUA: Stephanie, can you describe some of your duties as production manager?

STEPHANIE: I produce the books. I work in conjunction with the editor. I get the book after it has been edited and copy edited, and I design and lay it out ... In the past year we have had someone looking after the pre-production, which is making sure that the work has been wordprocessed on disc and is pulled together as cleanly as possible. But this is not foolproof. One still ends up doing a massive amount of correction. These things take a while to sort out.

AFUA: Makeda, as managing editor what do you do?

MAKEDA: A managing editor oversees all the aspects of a manuscript even before it reaches the editor. She also solicits work (we receive a lot of unsolicited manuscripts). Thus the managing editor has to be visionary, she must have an eye and ear out in the community. So even before she starts looking at anything she has to figure out what are some of the things that the press needs to publish at the time. She has to keep the press in touch with the wider publishing community. She has to have a finger on its pulse. She has to go out there to make contacts with people. She also looks at unsolicited material and finds stuff that the press might be interested in. Once we have decided to publish a manuscript, the managing editor hooks up the writer with an editor to work with. The managing editor coordinates this. Please bear in mind that she is also working on other books at the same time. So she figures out and decides what titles the press is going to come out with within the next year or two.

AFUA: Both of you are artists in your own right. Makeda you are a writer and an anthologist and Stephanie you are a visual artist. How do you combine your creative life with publishing? What are some of the challenges that this entails?

MAKEDA: Well it's extremely difficult and at times frustrating, and many times you wonder why you are in publishing because a lot of time publishing doesn't make space for your personal work. But I think for me, what keeps me going is the passion that I have about my own work, and the tension that is created between my own work and publishing. So the tension and the passion feed me, help me to create and write. The combination keeps me going. I am committed to Sister Vision and to the growth of other writers ...

STEPHANIE: I would say that initially, of both of us, I've had the more difficult time. Possibly because my personality is quite different in the sense that I'm not able to very successfully do two things at the same time, two major things. I can do ten things which are part of the job, like in book production. But when it comes to two things that are so big in my life it's very difficult for me to do because I'm not good at dividing myself. I tend to be very intense when I'm doing my art – not to say that Mak isn't – but I'm compulsive, I'm slow, I'm a perfection- ist. I've found it hard to combine both. Compounded by the fact that when I work at my painting I become extraordinarily anti-social because I really need to be alone. I want solitude. I can't work well with people around me. I can't start a painting, then work on it for two hours, leave it, and then come back to it. It requires long periods of concentrated work.

However, in the last two years I have started to paint again after not painting for a long time. Yet I still find it difficult to make myself take the time to say that, although I need to get this done at the press, 'Hold on a minute, I have to get my own work done.' But I'm working at it. I find I'm giving my own work more time. I'm in the process of setting up a studio, and I intend to take more time to do my own work. Now I am working at figuring out how to do that. I think in the previous years I put it on hold and did other things, but it has come to the point where I am no longer prepared not to do it. I'm getting older and I don't want to reach fifty and not be painting. The thing is balance. How to balance my responsibilities at the press with my responsibility to my art.

AFUA: Both of you are involved in a relationship, you both live together. How does that affect your relationship as co-workers?

MAKEDA: Can't you see that from this interview? Ha ha ha.

STEPHANIE: I would say that many points have to be given to extreme courage and fortitude that we have remained in business together – not to mention commitment to the press – because we fight and quarrel and cuss on major issues and silly ones too. We fight like puss and dawg, but love each other dearly. We both have a great sense of humour. After our cuss we make up and laugh and continue the work. The crux of the mat- ter is that the work has to get done; so even if we cuss we know that we have to come up with an understanding of what needs to be done and do it. It's all part of the process.

MAKEDA: We have grown to be very good friends. We are extremely committed to the press and each other; we trust one another very much.

AFUA: I think it's a unique thing. Both of you being involved and successfully running a press.

STEPHANIE: It's very unique and spectacular, plus the fact that the press is still running.

MAKEDA: It can be problematic at times for individuals who become involved with the press, not only because we share a personal relationship but because we have worked together for so long and have a particular style of working. We certainly have our weaknesses, and for a new person who comes in, how does that person begin to criticize one of us? Bring in constructive criticism? How does that person discuss one of us with the other? Their views might be needed and justified but how do I take it, or how does Stephanie take it? It's difficult because we know how both of us have struggled for so long, alone, and so we are protective of each other.

AFUA: You both have run Sister Vision full time while at the same time parenting two children [who have grown up with the press]. How were you able to do both?

MAKEDA: It was difficult I must admit. Sometimes as a parent you had to make a choice of what you would do: work at the press until midnight or be here when they come home. So juggling both has been challenging. There were times when I felt extremely guilty of the time away, but I also know that I was there for them. Of course with all that said, you still pay a price for whatever decisions you've made. And it might be a cost that you are conscious of, but I must say it was my choice. I wanted to do Sister Vision and I wanted to raise my kids. Anyway we'll just wait until they write the book.

STEPHANIE: Sister Vision has never been a nine-to-five job, and because of the nature of the press and in regards to childrearing there is a price to be paid. There is the fact that we were not able to spend as much time with them. It has been an evolving kind of process for me to realize the difficulty and possibly the great adjustments they had to make as two young children growing up with having parents who were artists, living in a very unorthodox family situation, and not necessarily having a 'structured family life.' There are pros and cons for that. In one sense their lives have been enriched by the many many people – writers, artists – whom they have come to know and spend time with. And these people have been very respectful and caring toward them. A lot of young kids mightn't have had that kind of opportunity.

MAKEDA: In addition to that, the kids have had the advantage of knowing – because of who we are and our sexuality – gay and lesbian people, and have been able to break down for themselves some of the stereotypes surrounding gays.

AFUA: Finally, what kind of future do you see for Sister Vision?

MAKEDA: We certainly will continue to grow and publish original, ground-breaking, and imaginative books, to find new voices and nurture them. I also hope the future will birth other sister of colour presses to join us.

STEPHANIE: Sister Vision is here. It's an established publishing company. We don't have no where going but onward.

Evelyn Garbary:
'For Those of Us Whose Bones Are Stage Props'[1]

DONNA SMYTH

Esther Evelyn Sara Owen Bowen; Evelyn Speaight; Evelyn O'Donovan; Evelyn Garbary. I look for her in these names that mark stages in her life; I sift the details, searching for patterns, but the closer I come to her, the more the details fall away like leaves on a tree in autumn.

Cardigan, South Wales, 18 June 1911: Esther Evelyn Sara Owen Bowen is born. Welsh is her native tongue, learned from her grandmother. English is a foreign language learned from her mother, who also 'ingrains' manners in her only child: a lady never puts her spoon in the middle of the soup, a lady eats from the side of the bowl; a lady always keeps her back straight; a lady ...

Wolfville, Nova Scotia, 1993: Diminishing physical spaces in which we meet – her house (first the living room, then the bedroom), the 'guest' house (one room), the hospital (a bed). Struggling for clarity of mind, she tells me: 'Ask me more questions. I can program them in and sometimes the answer comes up.'[2]

We talk in some Other space. At play in the fields of Being – memories, jokes, gusty winds of spirit. Plans for a new children's theatre in Nova Scotia. She says she's working better than she's ever worked before – she means the writing. Her new play is a modern version of Plato's *Meno*, the dialogue that opens with Meno asking Socrates: 'Can virtue be taught?'

The question in Evelyn's mind: Can love be taught?

Owen Bowen, her father, was a doctor who died of tuberculosis of the throat when she was three years old. Her mother, Elizabeth Evans, was the daughter of the mayor of Cardigan. The young couple had run away to the next town to be married because her family considered the Bowen family lower class. The Bowen family also insisted on speaking Welsh while Elizabeth's family spoke English.

After three years of mourning for her young husband, Elizabeth married Owen Davies, a bank manager, and the family moved to Carnarvon, North Wales. The young Evelyn missed both her grandmother and the culture and language of South Wales. She felt uprooted, disconnected from a vital part of her identity.

When Evelyn was ten years old, her stepfather mocked her declared ambition to be an actress. He was not a cruel man, but he never understood the nature of his passionate and romantic foster child. He told her to forget her dreams: she had no brains, no figure, no looks, no talent.

Evelyn spent the rest of her life proving him wrong.

She was determined to become a great actress in the tradition of Mrs Siddons and Sarah Bernhardt. She took dance lessons from a teacher who, imitating Isadora Duncan, dressed the girls in Greek tunics and taught them to move rhythmically and freely. At St Winnifred's School for Girls she took voice lessons. By the time she was eighteen it was clear she could not learn to be a great actress in Wales. London was the centre of theatre and theatre training.

With the covert support of her mother, who sent money out of her housekeeping allowance, she enrolled in the London Academy of Music and Drama (LAMDA). She studied elocution and 'oral terp' (interpretation), winning a gold medal for performance. Then she was introduced to Lillian Bayliss, the owner of the Old Vic Theatre, who was determined to make the 1929–30 season both a financial and critical success. Bayliss had hired Harcourt Williams as director for the Shakespeare Company. The company's leading players were the young John Gielgud and Martita Hunt, and that season's productions included *Romeo and Juliet*, *Richard II*, *Midsummer Night's Dream*, and Bernard Shaw's *Androcles and the Lion*.

Harcourt Williams was one of the new generation of directors who undertook to modernize Shakespearean acting. He wanted 'to break down the slow deliberate method of delivering Shakespeare's verse and the absurd convention of the Shakespearean voice'[3] that had characterized earlier productions. The new, more 'natural' style of playing meant that the pace was faster and histrionic gestures, overblown theatricality, and much of the traditional stage business were gone.

Evelyn Bowen was engaged as a young apprentice with the Old Vic Company, playing small and walk-on parts and understudying Martita Hunt. She was exposed to the new acting style, but not for long. At the

Evelyn Garbary at Stonehenge in 1983

end of the season she left the Old Vic to tour in Scotland and northern England with the MacDona Players. Charles MacDona's company specialized in touring with a narrow repertoire of Bernard Shaw's plays. Evelyn loved touring but found she was learning little as an actress. Back in London, jobs were scarce; so she was delighted when she was hired by Sir John Martin-Harvey for a short London season and then a coast-to-coast farewell Canadian tour.

Martin-Harvey was one of the disappearing generation of old-style actor-managers, 'a disciple of Henry Irving and the last producer of Victorian stage romances and melodramas.'[4] He and his company had already made six trans-Canada tours, and this 1932 farewell tour was designed to showcase popular favourites such as *The Bells*, a melodrama, and *The King's Messenger*, a romantic comedy written for the aging Lady Harvey. Evelyn played the young romantic leads and learned to negotiate the personal and professional jealousy of Lady Harvey.

Despite the Depression, wherever the company played in Canada, they were fêted by well-off theatre patrons who threw lavish parties for the actors. After her relative poverty as a young actress in London, Evelyn enjoyed the high life and the adventures of touring. She had several romantic relationships and at least three proposals of marriage. However, she knew they were playing 'hack theatre'; it was great fun and a commercial success, but it lacked substance.

In Vancouver she was taken to a performance by a traditional Chinese theatre company and was excited by their 'precision, delicacy, and amount of artistry.' It took place in a shabby building with an audience of immigrant Chinese men dressed in work clothes and chewing and spitting out sunflower seed shells but completely engrossed in the play. This was both ritual and popular theatre using dance, mask, and mime to dramatize the stories of an ancient culture. It reminded Evelyn vividly of the real potential of theatre.

When she returned to London, she decided to found her own company: a Welsh version of the Abbey Theatre, Ireland's national theatre. In its golden period in the early twentieth century, the Abbey Theatre had been part of a wider movement to throw off English cultural and political dominance. Lady Gregory, W.B. Yeats, J.M. Synge, and Sean O'Casey had written plays especially for the Abbey and its players, who developed a distinctive style of acting. By the 1930s, the theatre and its players were known worldwide.

As a schoolgirl, Evelyn had read about the Abbey and been impressed by the riots that sometimes disrupted its opening nights. To her the riots were a sign that the plays touched a genuine passion in the audiences. This was infinitely preferable to the well-behaved and blasé West End London audiences clapping politely for yet another 'well-made' play or rattling their teacups at the intervals in the matinées.

Evelyn's Welsh National Theatre would feature Welsh actors in plays written for them by Welsh playwrights in both Welsh and English. This audacious move on the part of a twenty-two-year-old woman was not only inspired but shrewd. There was no modern Welsh theatre to speak of. Welsh actors in London could not hope to become stars because their Welsh lilt, the very way they spoke, was not English. Evelyn herself had already discovered she could not become an English actress in the 'grande dame' style; every time she opened her mouth her origins betrayed her. But she was already beginning to think that perhaps it was she who had betrayed her origins.

Under the sponsorship of Lord Howard de Walden, Evelyn launched her theatre with a production of *The Comedy of Good and Evil*, by Richard Hughes, at the Arts Theatre Club in London. She was advised not to take this play on tour in Wales because the people would be offended by the theme: 'a minister's wife whose wooden leg was possessed by a devil.' She persuaded a Welsh dramatist, John Francis, to write a historical play for them, *Howell of Gwent*, and also commissioned a folk play by the poet Gwyn Jones.

She took her company to Wales to rehearse their repertoire in Llangollen, home of the Welsh National Eisteddfod. She had in mind a sequestered period where they could learn to work as an ensemble company. This was following the example of Michel St Denys' Companie des Cinques, who had impressed her when they performed in London. 'I read how he had taken his companie down to a farm house outside Aix en Province [sic], how they had worked there quietly for many months and then electrified audiences all over Europe with the exquisite precision of their work.'[5]

At the same time as her company was rehearsing and preparing to go on tour in Wales, Lord Howard, their patron, was turning his attention and his money to large-scale productions such as a Welsh version of *Everyman* at the Eisteddfod. Evelyn played the role of Faith in this version of the medieval classic, but she also worried about her small, struggling company being overshadowed by these more spectacular productions. In the 1970s, looking back on this period, she wrote: 'We toured Wales twice and then died of exhaustion. I made every mistake in the book.'[6]

The next time she founded a theatre company, she threw that book away and began to write her own text. But that was years later and in another country.

Feeling she had failed in this first venture, Evelyn left the Welsh National Theatre Company and returned to London. It seemed that her theatrical career was at a dead end. Perhaps this was why she allowed herself to be persuaded by a friend that presentation at court would help her to find a niche in London society. At the age of twenty-three, she became a debutante.

Thirty years later and thousands of miles across an ocean she would tell Canadian drama students about this presentation at court. Hovering on the edge of parody, she showed them how to bow and curtsy in the proper English manner. She would draw herself erect, raise her chin and speak in her stagiest voice. She mimed the full-length white kid gloves, the gown with the train of requisite length, the ostrich feathers, the line-up of limousines at Buckingham Palace, the line to shake the royal hands. Then, with a sharp glance to see if the students got the point of the parody, she would confess, 'I'm afraid I disgraced myself dreadfully on that occasion – you see, I was so nervous and it was so stuffy that I fainted after being presented.' But the disgrace was more in recollection than in the actual event where she fainted after the royal handshake and was revived by the royal physician.

Shortly after being presented, she met and married the English actor and matinée idol, Robert Speaight. Speaight came from an upper-middle-class family, and their wedding was a London social event. Yet Evelyn was not certain about this marriage. Only the urging of her mother, who wanted to see her daughter securely established in London society, and the threatened suicide of Speaight (by throwing himself out of a taxicab) persuaded her to go through with it.

Wolfville, Nova Scotia, 1995: I find her lying on the narrow bed in her room in the guest house. She has just come from the hospital and it has been decided that she cannot manage on her own.

Her eyes are closed, sunken, deep. Her white hair wild on the pillow. As I call her name, the eyes start open. Panic, then flash of recognition. She says she's been remembering certain events in her life. There are questions she wants the answers to: 'Why did I cry all through the ceremony when I married Robert Speaight?'

London, 1934: In her new life, Evelyn played her part well, but she was not at ease in this alien disposition. She who had started life as a Welsh Methodist became a converted Catholic in deference to her husband's religion. She had a son, Patrick. She presided over her husband's gourmet dinners. When the Spanish Civil War broke out, she was appalled to find herself entertaining Catholic priests fund-raising for Franco. Speaight, along with many other upper middle-class Catholics, supported Franco in this war while Evelyn's instinctive sympathies were with the people of Spain. These tensions in their marriage must have been aggravated by the differences in their careers. Speaight was gaining acclaim for his role as Becket in T.S. Eliot's play, *Murder in the Cathedral*. Meanwhile, Evelyn was having trouble finding work.

At a party in 1936 she met the Irish writer Michael O'Donovan, who wrote under the pseudonym Frank O'Connor. O'Connor was on the Abbey's board of directors and urged Sean O'Faolian to invite Evelyn to Dublin to play the lead role in O'Faolain's play *She Had to Do Something*. Evelyn was thrilled at the thought of becoming one of the Abbey players and arrived in Dublin with her son and a nanny. Speaight had already left for New York to star in the American production of *Murder in the Cathedral*.

Instead of being welcomed, however, Evelyn found herself in the middle of a dispute. The Abbey players protested the hiring of this 'English' actress and threatened to go on strike. A compromise was reached whereby Evelyn had to audition for the part against one of the Abbey's leading ladies, Sheilagh Richards.

Evelyn got the part but continued to feel out of place at the Abbey. Not only was she not Irish, she had been trained in a different style of acting. The 'new, intimate, internal' playing of the Abbey actors seemed beyond her, and her confidence in her own talent was shaken. However, she had also 'fallen in love with Dublin' and couldn't bear the thought of returning to live in England.[7]

By this time she had no illusions about her marriage. She had heard a rumour that her husband had slept with every member of the chorus in the American production. When she wrote to ask if the gossip was true, she received the following telegram: 'Opening night great success, play well received, own performance acclaimed. Notices excellent. Sorry True. Bobbie.'[8]

Wolfville, Nova Scotia, 1994: The Speaight marriage is still very much on her mind. In retrospect, she enjoys the story of the telegram. She claims that if Bobbie had been unfaithful with only one or two women, she could have lived with it. 'But, lovey, the whole chorus! And you know what the chorus is like in that play!'

O'Connor had fallen for her and wanted to get married as soon as possible. They began an affair in the heart of Catholic Dublin in a swirl of gossip and notoriety. She applied for an annulment of her marriage but it would be a long time coming. In the end Speaight pressured her to accept guilt as the adulterous party in order to preserve his own reputation.

The situation was not made any easier by O'Connor's health problems. In 1938, he was told he had cancer of the stomach and five years to live. The couple escaped from Dublin to live in the countryside at Woodenbridge with O'Connor's mother acting as live-in chaperone. Evelyn never believed O'Connor had cancer and set out to nurse him back to health. She bought a cow, milked it herself, and made butter. She kept chickens and planted a garden. Soon O'Connor was visibly better and writing well. He had warned her that writing was the most important thing in his life, and Evelyn undertook to nurture his talent as well as his health.

They were finally married in a civil ceremony in February 1939. They had three children: Myles, Liadain (Evelyn's only daughter), and Owen.

Throughout the war years, the family was always hard-pressed for money. In 1940 O'Connor resigned from the Abbey in disgust at the internal politicking and the overt intervention of the de Valera government in the running of the theatre.[9] He was seen by the Irish establishment as a troublemaker and was blacklisted as a writer. Moreover, because of Ireland's official neutrality during the war, the overseas markets for Irish writers dwindled. He was offered work at the BBC in London, but the Irish officials took away his passport.

Evelyn continued to find occasional acting jobs, but her duties as wife and mother and her reputation as 'that Welsh woman' who 'lived in sin' with O'Connor overshadowed her artistic development. Ironically, it was the church's influence that gave her three months work with Radio Eireann. The work was intended as a bribe to break up the marriage, the idea being that the church would use its influence to see to it that Evelyn and her children didn't starve if she would agree to end the 'ungodly' marriage. Evelyn seized the opportunity and worked night and day as an actor in radio plays, as well as a broadcaster and scriptwriter.

However, she did not leave the marriage, and the three month's work came to an end. She then got a job working as a secretary for British Shipbuilder's where her salary was just enough to cover their basic living expenses.

In 1944, O'Connor obtained permission to leave Ireland and go to London to do some writing and broadcasting for the BBC. There he met a young English woman and began an affair that was to have disastrous consequences. During the next few years, Evelyn fought to save the marriage but found it hard to cope with the strain of O'Connor trying to maintain both relationships, especially after the young woman had a child. Never an easy man to live with, O'Connor turned on Evelyn and blamed her for not accommodating his other family.

Years later, Evelyn wrote to a colleague: 'I've been taught how to be bitchy by experts.'[10] She was referring, of course, to theatrical life, notorious for bitchiness. But she was surely also thinking of the dark period of the breakup when she had to fight for survival and for custody of her children. For the rest of her life she was haunted by memories of this marriage. She struggled with the ambivalence of her feelings, admiring O'Connor the writer, angry with O'Donovan the man. In 1983, when James Matthews published his biography, *Voices: A Life of Frank O'Connor*, the reliving of this period of Evelyn's life was so painful, she had a minor breakdown. Even in the last months of her life she was still fighting the ghost of Michael/Frank.

In the end, O'Connor left both his wife and his mistress to marry an American, Harriet Rich. By this time, Evelyn had met Abraham Garbary, a Polish Jew who had left Warsaw with his family in the mid-1930s. Garbary was taking his final degree in engineering at Trinity College, Dublin. He married Evelyn, and, in 1956, they emigrated to Canada where there was more work to be had. They settled first in

Toronto, which Evelyn detested, and then in Montreal where eventually she found some work as a writer/performer with the CBC. During this time she also had two more sons: David and Richard.

In 1959 the Garbarys moved to Halifax. He was teaching, and she was employed in the Arts Service, Adult Education Division of the Department of Education. When Abe Garbary decided to move back to Toronto, Evelyn refused to follow him. She loved Halifax, which she often compared to Dublin. She had a job and a house and was just beginning to establish a reputation for herself. She was forty-eight years old.

In Nova Scotia, Evelyn had found her second home. She threw herself into a variety of activities, from chairing a local school board to acting and writing for CBC radio and directing plays. In 1963 she directed the Travelling Players of Halifax in *Look Back in Anger*, a production that won first place at the National Dominion Drama Festival. She gave playwriting workshops to encourage local writers to explore the rich cultural background of the Atlantic region and use the speech/dialects of the people. As she often said, it was not her job to impose classic English standards on these Maritimers. It *was* her job to teach them skills so they could write and perform for local, national, and international audiences. She told one young playwright: 'Work is the only way to deal with depression. And SKILL is the only means whereby you can achieve freedom.'[11]

In the midst of this whirlwind of activity, she fell in love with two very different people. One was the novelist Ernest Buckler, whom she met in December 1964. *The Mountain and the Valley* (1952) and *The Cruelest Month* (1963) had already established Buckler's reputation as a writer. At this period he was living in relative seclusion in the country, just outside Bridgetown in the Annapolis Valley. Lonely and shy, he was dazzled by Evelyn's theatrical past and her present energy and enthusiasm. For her part, Evelyn loved the true writer in him and enjoyed the creative sparks that flew whenever they were together.[12]

The other person was Tessie Gillis. Where others might have dismissed Tess's pleas for help with her writing as simply the daydreams of an isolated Cape Breton housewife, Evelyn saw in her a rare, raw talent. She made the five-hour journey by car from Halifax to Cape Breton with the two small Garbary boys to try to find her. It took two days but finally she located the small farmhouse on the side of a hill, high up in beautiful Glencoe. Evelyn described Tess at their first meeting: 'She was a frail woman in her early fifties. She told me she had had a heart attack three years ago in the middle of winter and due to the delay in getting her into hospital a part of her heart had atrophied. There was an oxygen tank beside her bed.'[13]

Compared to the poverty of some of their neighbours, the Gillis farm was relatively comfortable. Tess had two children but felt isolated as a writer. She opened her heart to Evelyn and the two became loyal friends. Evelyn made Tess promise to send her writing down to Halifax and thus took on the job of editor and mentor.

Wolfville, Nova Scotia, 1985: Having returned from the hospital and still recovering from the effects of pneumonia, Evelyn begins to reread Buckler's novel *The Cruelest Month* and a sentence leaps out at her. The narrator is describing a woman: 'her gaunt face ... like a talent, when there is no one to love it alive.' Evelyn immediately thinks of Tessie and writes: 'These words explain why for nearly three years I did not behave like a rational human being with frightening responsibilities; who in their right mind would take on the care of an invalid woman, who lived hundreds of miles away ... to care for Tess and *"love her talent alive"*?'[14]

In a 1990 interview, she dwelt again on this relationship: 'I loved Tess ... [S]he was as astonishing and wonderful to me as if someone had said Moses was coming down the Valley.' She spoke of Tess's great love of life and declared, 'I'd never met a human being with so much that was noble and wonderful.' Evelyn thought Tess was driven to write by the creative spirit that runs through the universe. Both she and Tess had to serve that spirit.[15]

Determined to see some of Tessie's work published, Evelyn persuaded Buckler to read many of the stories and offer his professional advice. But Tess didn't live to see her stories published; she died in 1972. Evelyn continued to try to persuade someone to publish the manuscript they (and Buckler) had worked on together. Finally, in 1992, a small press in Nova Scotia brought out a selection of Tessie's stories under the title *The Promised Land*.[16]

Buckler also read Evelyn's own writing, mainly stories and plays, with a critical eye. Evelyn always said that Frank O'Connor had taught her how to write but there was only room for one author in that family and, of course, it had to be O'Connor. Now she was gaining confidence in her own talent and in Buckler had found a mentor who, like O'Connor, was a perfectionist and valued craft above all else. She later wrote to another aspiring writer, 'Ernest Buckler taught me how to edit my own work over many years, and that, let me tell you, was a shattering experience, but – of incredible value.'[17]

In 1967 Evelyn was appointed Artistic Adviser for the Performing and Visual Arts for the Centennial Celebration in the Province of Nova Scotia. She commissioned a young playwright, David Giffin, to write a pageant play, *Coming Here to Stay*, about the arrival of the Black Loyalists in Nova Scotia. She then worked as Artistic Director with the Inglewood Community Players to produce the play with an all-Black cast. It opened in March 1967 at the Dominion Drama Festival in Halifax and was a great success. It toured the province and was even performed at the First Baptist Church in Toronto. Evelyn was thrilled to direct the 'first all-Negro Drama group in the entire country' but also confessed to a friend that 'the pressure is very great and I'm exhausted.'[18]

In the fall of that same year, she was hired to teach theatre and creative writing at Acadia University in Wolfville, Nova Scotia. Her students adored her; she was unpredictable, compelling, and exciting to work with. She taught them the power of imagination: whatever you imagine on that stage will be there; the audience will see it and so will you. She taught them artistic economy: on the stage, less is more; often a whisper is more dramatic than a scream. She showed them where the real dramatic action is, not in the twists and turns of a plot, but in the tension between characters, in the subtext, in the mind and spirit. She would quote O'Connor who once told her, 'Stop listening to what I'm saying and listen to what I'm thinking.'[19] She used her own experience to inspire her students to act and speak and write as themselves. 'Look at what happened to me,' she would say, 'I thought I had to become English to be an actress.'

She discovered that many students came to university never having seen live theatre, and this troubled her greatly. By 1971, she and her students had formed the Acadia Child Drama and Puppet Theatre to take plays out into the schools. They were so enthusiastically received that Evelyn was convinced there was a need for a professional theatre for young audiences in the Atlantic region. Around this time she met two dynamic people who were also interested in theatre for children: Tom Miller, a visual artist and gifted maker of puppets, and Sara Lee Lewis, a superb arts administrator from Montreal.

In 1973, these three founded the Mermaid Theatre for Young Audiences. Based in Wolfville, they hired local actors and trained them carefully. Evelyn's own training, mainly in the 'grand style' of acting, had given her an unforgettable voice and stage presence but had also limited what she could do as an actor. Now she wanted an ensemble company with the actors trained to be more flexible and visceral: 'only a group of players who can measure each other's breathing is of use to me. Until I can reach this point I don't even begin to work as I want to.'[20]

Mermaid's early reputation was founded on their playing of Mi'kmaw[21] legends, many adapted for the stage by Evelyn herself who became fascinated with these stories. In 1974, she wrote to a friend: 'the quality of the material has blown my mind – I think – I'm sure that we have here legends that can be compared with the Norse legends and the Irish Red Branch Sagas.'[22] At this time nothing of the Mi'kmaw heritage was being taught in the schools. She consulted Native leaders on details of the culture and language and made sure that Mi'kmaw children were bussed to performances of the plays.

In order to dramatize these myths, she and Tom Miller worked out the conventions of a stylized theatre combining narration, mime, dance, mask, and puppets. This style allowed human, animal, and supernatural characters to play on the same stage, 'making the invisible visible.' Excited by the connections they were making between the artistic and spiritual worlds, Evelyn wrote: 'we are working in an art form that is more closely associated with the Japanese theatre and W.B. Yeats' plays for dancers.'[23] A kind of artistic innocence informed her vision: 'to both Tom and I the spirit world is as real as what they are pleased to call the real world.'[24]

Mermaid quickly gained a national and international reputation. The company toured across Canada and played in London's West End, in Dublin, in Wales, and at international theatre conferences in Europe and the United States. Evelyn was writing and directing plays, hiring actors, sewing costumes, and teaching classes. The pressure on her was intense, but she thrived on it.

In 1976 she wrote to a relative in Wales: 'It took me 10 years to become established in Canada and obtain a measure of security. The last ten years have been the happiest of my life.'[25] She had refused to marry Buckler, and their relationship had become more distant. Her home in Wolfville was a drop-in centre for actors, writers, artists, and local people. If she wasn't writing or directing or travelling, she was sewing costumes in her kitchen or in putting down vegetables from her garden. She loved practical tasks and enjoyed doing them well.

In 1979 she returned to Ireland on a Canada Council grant to research the life of St Brendan who, according to medieval legend, sailed with a band of brothers in a small boat to the New World. She turned this research into a play, *The Navigator*, which became a Mermaid production directed by Felix Mirbt, well-known for his work in adult puppet theatre.

Her next play, *The Promised Land*, was a dramatization of the Tessie Gillis stories. Convinced that young audiences' tastes had shifted because of television, she was becoming interested in more realistic theatre. Tensions developed between her and her Mermaid partners, who wanted to retain Mermaid's distinctive style with its emphasis on puppets. In 1981, feeling she had no other option, Evelyn resigned as Mermaid's Artistic Director. She felt betrayed and bereft. It was like the breakup of the O'Connor marriage and it took her a long time to recover.

She did not, however, retire to lick her wounds in private. She ran as an NDP candidate in the 1981 provincial elections and, although she lost, she doubled the local popular vote and felt she had done her civic duty. She also broadcast on CBC radio the first series of her memoirs, *Letters from a Grandmother*. The series proved very popular and was repeated the following year. She continued to write plays and stories and even played a bit role in the Nova Scotia film *Life Classes* (1987).

Although she never stopped working, the rheumatoid arthritis that had troubled her for years began to slow her down. When she could no longer type, she continued to write even though her fingers were so crippled she could scarcely hold a pen. She worked on a more extended version of her memoirs and wrote a poetic epigraph for the project:

Great Spirit
let your winds
blow me out of the water,
out of the dark and stagnant water.
Do not look with pity
on my bowed head,
my crippled body.
Lift me out of the water
and I will be your messenger.[26]

Her motto was the Welsh saying 'O hyu allan,' which she translated as 'now is the beginning.'[27] She insisted that there is 'no limit to the excitement of living, even if it's death around the corner ... [I]t's an adventure to be prepared for ... [O]ne doesn't really know one's limits.'[28]

Evelyn did not acknowledge any limits. She continued to work on her adaptation of Plato's *Meno*. The other major project was a comedy. She said she was dragging the comic lines out from the very mouth of Hell. She meant it both theatrically and spiritually. On the medieval stage,

Hell's Mouth was the visible entrance to the underworld. Great comedy, Evelyn insisted, can only come from great suffering.

She was never reconciled to the diminishing physical space of her life. She talked about her dream of a new children's theatre and arts centre in Nova Scotia, her dream of Crystal Cliffs. In her vision, art was a healing and transforming power. Crystal Cliffs was a real place and project but also a metaphor. Earlier, in the 1960s, she had talked about setting Nova Scotia on fire dramatically and explained it this way: 'The fire that I wanted to see burning was the spiritualizing of the natural elements of the earth.'[29]

Wolfville, Nova Scotia, September 1994: Her memories of childhood and young adulthood are very strong, and she feels an urgent need to return to Wales where she says she has 'unfinished business.' One day, when she is looking particularly small and fragile, she tells me: 'I am dazzled at being on the cusp of the old world dying and the new one being born. It's so exciting to see that happening.'

I stare at her in awe, wondering: Who is this who speaks to me?

4 November 1994: She dies on a golden autumnal day. Four of her six children are with her and one grandchild. Much to the disapproval of the hospital staff, they hold an Irish wake at their mother's bedside, celebrating her person even as they grieve their loss.

7 November: Her memorial service. All night and day a big wind is blowing. Blowing away cobwebs and dead leaves to reveal the stark forms of the trees. As we sit in the small Acadia chapel, we know the big wind is no coincidence.

Each speaker brings a different Evelyn alive. Fran Gallagher-Shuebrook, who has been making a film of Evelyn's life, talks about her early years and her great capacity for love. Bill Carr, an ex-student and now a well-known comic actor, reminds us: 'It has to be said: she was a mad woman!' And, unscripted, a long-time friend, Joy Cooper, stands up in the balcony and speaks her heart: 'She was the kindest woman I ever knew!'

I come forward to invoke the wind and to quote some lines from W.B. Yeats's play, *Purgatory* where one of the characters points to a naked tree bathed in light on the stage and says:

> Study that tree!
> It stands there like a purified soul,
> All cold, sweet, glistening light.[30]

I know now that she is the tree and the leaves and the light. Evelyn, herself. Like no other.

NOTES

1 Evelyn Garbary, letter, July 1974. Garbary Collection, Acadia University Archives, Wolfville, NS. Unless otherwise indicated, all quotations from E.G.'s correspondence are taken from this collection. I wish to thank the Acadia archivist, Patricia Townsend, for her generous help.

2 Personal communication, Winter 1994. I met Evelyn in 1974 at Acadia and worked with her as a colleague in the English department and as a playwright for two Mermaid productions in the late 1970s, *Susanna Moodie* and *Giant Anna*. I interviewed her about her life several times between Fall 1993 and Fall 1994. Her health was failing and so was her memory for dates.

3 Harcourt Williams, *Four Years at the Old Vic, 1929–1933* (London: Putnam, 1935), 17

4 Robert Lawrence, 'John Martin-Harvey in Canada,' *Association for Canadian Theatre History Newsletter* 2, no. 1 (Sept. 1978): 6

5 Garbary Collection, draft fragment, box 1 of estate papers, file marked Part 3

6 Garbary Collection, undated letter, envelope 15

7 Evelyn Garbary, interview with Marjorie Whitlaw for the NS Women's Oral History Project, Public Archives of Nova Scotia (hereinafter PANS), tape 3, side B (1990)

8 Quoted verbatim from E.G.'s letter, 21 April 1979, in James Matthews, *Voices: A Life of Frank O'Connor* (New York: Atheneum, 1983), 139–40

9 See Frank O'Connor, *My Father's Son* (London: Macmillan, 1968), for a full account of this period of the Abbey's history from O'Connor's point of view.

10 Garbary Collection, letter, Oct. 1974

11 Ibid., letter, Feb. 1974

12 Claude Bissell describes their relationship in *Ernest Buckler Remembered* (Toronto: University of Toronto Press, 1979)

13 Note by E.G., p. 15 of an unpublished manuscript by Tessie Gillis and Evelyn Garbary (with letters from Ernest Buckler), *A Woman from Away*. I wish to thank Leo Deveau who first drew my attention to this collection of Tess's unpublished stories and the letters between the three writers about the stories.

14 Garbary Collection, box 1 of estate papers, unfiled draft fragment dated 15 Jan. 1985

15 Garbary interview, PANS, tape 5, side 1

16 *The Promised Land: Stories of Cape Breton* (West Bay, NS: Medicine Label Press, 1992) contains a tribute and introduction by James O. Taylor that documents the relationship between the two women.
17 Garbary Collection, letter, Feb. 1975
18 Ibid., letter, July 1967
19 Garbary Collection, box 1 of estate papers, file labelled Canadian Nationalism, is just one of many places throughout her papers where E.G. notes this directive from O'Connor.
20 Garbary Collection, letter, Feb. 1974
21 Instead of Micmac, which was the accepted English transliteration of this period, I have used the adjectival form preferred today. The Mi'kmaw people are indigenous to the Atlantic region.
22 Garbary Collection, letter, Aug. 1974
23 Ibid., letter, June 1973
24 Ibid., letter, Oct. 1975
25 Ibid., letter, June 1976
26 Garbary, Collection, box 1 of estate papers, unfiled draft
27 Ibid.
28 Garbary interview, PANS, tape 5, side 1
29 Garbary Collection, box 1 of estate papers, in file labelled Talk to Atlantic Institute PEI Charlottetown, Aug. 1982, draft fragment of earlier talk
30 In *The Collected Plays of W.B. Yeats* (London: Macmillan, 1966), 688

Contributors

Marianne Gosztonyi Ainley is the president of the Canadian Science and Technology Historical Association and chair of women's studies at the University of Northern British Columbia. Her publications include more than half a dozen book chapters and over twenty articles on Canadian women and science, as well as *Despite the Odds: Essays on Canadian Women and Science* (1990) and *Restless Energy: A Biography of William Rowan, 1891–1957* (1993). She is working on three other books.

Helen Buss is associate professor of English at the University of Calgary, where she teaches life writing and Canadian literature. Her most recent book, *Mapping Our Selves: Canadian Women's Autobiography*, won the Gabrielle Roy Prize in 1993. Under her other name, Margaret Clarke, she has published two novels, *The Cutting Season* (1994) and *Healing Song* (1988), and a play, *Gertrude and Ophelia* (1994). She has recently edited a special issue of Life Writing for *Prairie Fire Magazine* (Fall 1995). At present she is researching and writing about women's uses of the memoir form and is writing a memoir of her own childhood with the working title 'A New Found Land Childhood.'

Elspeth Cameron is a professor of English at the University of Toronto, where she currently directs the Canadian studies program at University College. She has written three literary biographies: *Hugh MacLennan: A Writer's Life* (1981), *Irving Layton: A Portrait* (1985), and *Earle Birney: A Life* (1994). She has won several literary awards, including the UBC Medal for Biography in 1982, and National Newspaper Awards for her biographical profiles in Canadian magazines.

Sally Cole is an associate professor in the Department of Sociology and Anthropology at Concordia University. Her publications include *Women of the Praia: Work and Lives in a Portuguese Coastal Community* (1991) and *Ethnographic Femi-*

nisms: Essays in Anthropology (1995) (co-edited with Lynne Philips). She is currently writing a biography of anthropologist Ruth Landes.

Afua Cooper is a Jamaican-born poet of African descent living in Toronto. She has published three books of poetry, including *The Red Caterpillar on College Street* (1989) and *Memories Have Tongue*, which was the runner-up for the 1992 Casa de las Americas Prize in the English-language category. Her poetry has been recorded on the album *Womanspeak* and on several cassettes. Afua is now working on a collection of short stories, *Waiting for the Moon*, a children's story, *Fatima's Nightgown*, and a novel, *The Rowing*. She is also pursuing a doctorate in history at the University of Toronto. Drawing on her background in history, she has co-authored *'We're Rooted Here and They Can't Pull Us Up': Essays in African Canadian Women's History* (1994).

Janice Dickin is director of the law and society program at the University of Calgary. She has recently edited *Suitable for the Wilds* (1995) and is completing a biography of the evangelist Aimee Semple McPherson. She and Elspeth Cameron are collaborating on *Echo*, a series of reclaimed women's writing for a new series for the University of Toronto Press.

Marlene Epp completed a doctorate in Canadian history at the University of Toronto in 1996, specializing in the history of immigrant women. She has published a variety of articles on themes related to Mennonite women and currently teaches courses in Canadian studies and Mennonite history at the University of Waterloo.

Marlene Kadar teaches women's studies and life writing in the Humanities Division at York University. Her publications include the editing of *Essays on Life Writing*, which won the Gabrielle Roy Prize (English) for 1992. She is currently researching explicit and metaphoric representations of genocidal policies among survivors of the Jewish and Romani holocausts. She is the editor of the Life Writing Series for Wilfrid Laurier University Press.

Wendy Mitchinson is a professor of history at the University of Waterloo. She has published widely on the topic of women and health in Canada. Her works include *Essays in Canadian Medical History* (1988) (co-edited with Janice Dickin McGinnis) and *The Nature of Their Bodies: Women and Their Doctors in Victorian Canada* (1991).

Alison Prentice is a professor in the Department of History and Philosophy of Education at the Ontario Institute for Studies in Education. She has published books and articles in the fields of women's and educational history and has been an active member of the Canadian Historical Association, the Canadian Committee on Women's History, the Canadian History of Education Association, and the Ontario Women's History Network, which she helped found.

Beverly J. Rasporich is associate dean and professor in the Faculty of General Studies at the University of Calgary. Her publications on Canadian arts and culture include *Dance of the Sexes: Art and Gender in the Fiction of Alice Munro* and the co-edited Canadian studies and women's studies texts, *A Passion for Identity* and *Woman as Artist: Papers in Honour of Marsha Hanen*.

Patricia Smart is a professor of French at Carleton University in Ottawa. Her books include *Hubert Aquin agent double* (1973) and *Écrire dans la maison du Père: l'émergence du féminin dans la tradition littéraire du Québec* (1988), for which she won the Governor General's Award for non-fiction in French. Her translation of this book, *Writing in the Father's House: The Emergence of the Feminine in the Quebec Literary Tradition*, was published by University of Toronto Press in 1991. She is currently working on a study of the women in the *Refus global* movement.

Donna E. Smyth has published numerous short stories, poems, and articles as well as two adult novels, *Quilt* (second edition, 1994) and *Subversive Elements* (1986), a novel for young adults, *Loyalist Runaway* (1992), and a play, *Giant Anna*. She is the co-author of *No Place Like Home: Diaries and Letters of Nova Scotia Women, 1771–1938* (1988). She teaches English and creative writing at Acadia University, Wolfville, Nova Scotia.

Carolyn Strange is a historian who has written about the history of gender, crime, and justice. In *Toronto's Girl Problem: The Perils and Pleasures of the City, 1880–1930* (1995), she explores the material circumstances and discursive construction of urban working girls. She is the editor of *Qualities of Mercy: Justice, Punishment, and Discretion* (1996), a collection of historical essays on Canada, Australia, and England. With Tina Loo, she is preparing a textbook tentatively titled *Making Good: Law and Moral Regulation in Canada, 1867–1939*.

Aritha van Herk is a professor of English and creative writing at the University of Calgary. Her first novel, *Judith* (1978), won the Seal First Novel Award. She has since published two other novels, *The Tent Peg* (1981) and *No Fixed Address* (1986). She has also published experimental and critical prose works, including the *geografictione, Places Far from Ellesmere* (1990), *In visible Ink* (1991), and *A Frozen Tongue* (1992). She has edited or co-edited various collections of Western Canadian short fiction. Her work has been widely translated.

Illustration Credits

Doris McCarthy. Photo by Fred Langer
Mrs Ibolya Grossman. Photo by Jason Schwartz
Exodus II. Courtesy of Conrad Grebel College Archives and Central Photographic Services, University of Waterloo
Mrs Florence Lassandro. Glenbow Archives, NA-3282-2.
Ruth Landes. Courtesy the estate of Ruth Landes
Maggie Wilson. Photo by Ruth Landes, courtesy the estate of Ruth Landes
'Domesticity was the antidote ...' Ontario 'Report of the Inspector of Prisons and Public Charities,' volume 35 (1903), 87
Thérèse Renaud. Photo by J.A. Renaud, courtesy Thérèse Renaud
Gwethalyn Graham. Courtesy Earle Birney fonds, Special Collections Division, University of Calgary Library
Pioneer woman washing. Glenbow Archives, NA-2041-1
Anna Koivu and her children. Courtesy of Aili G. Lehto
Mabel McIntosh. Photo courtesy of Ms Shane Kelly
Dr Marion Hilliard. Photo courtesy of Ashley and Crippen, Toronto
Henrietta Ball Banting. Courtesy COMSTOCK/Yousuf Karsh
Elizabeth Allin. Photo courtesy of the Department of Physics, University of Toronto
Makeda Silvera and Stephanie Martin. Photo by Alviro Gozeia
Evelyn Garbary. Photo by Fran Gallagher-Shuebroook

Index

Prepared by Joan Eadie

sexual assault, 45, 99, 111. *See also* rape
sexual equality, 160
sexual harassment, 45–6, 248
sexual immorality, 103
sexuality, 128, 291, 295, 302
silence, code of, 167
Silenced (Silvera), 292–4
silenced women, 141–2
silencing, 294
Silvera, Makeda, 8, 14–15, 291–306
Sister Vision Press, 10, 14, 291–306; distribution and sales, 300–1; mandate, 292; parenting and, 305
sisu, 193–5
Smart, Elizabeth, 147
Smart, Patricia, 10, 13–14, 325
Smith, Grayson, 277
Smith College, 141, 264
Smyth, Donna, 10, 14, 325
Social and Economic Change among the Northern Ojibwa (Dunning), 79
socialism, Finnish, 194, 204n. 23
Speaight, Evelyn. *See* Garbary, Evelyn
Speaight, Robert, 312
Spector, Maurice, 155
Steeves, Jack, 216, 219
Steeves, Marion, 216, 219
Strange, Carolyn, 10, 13, 15, 325
Strong-Boag, Veronica, 11–12
Student Christian Movement, 269
Subterfuge et sortilege (Renaud), 140
Sub/version, 10
suffrage, 97, 197, 200
suicide, 44, 110, 116, 122
Sullivan, Françoise, 122–3, 125, 134–5
Surpassing the Love of Men (Faderman), 15
surrealism, 122, 135
Sweet, Annie, 111–15

Swiss Sonata (Graham), 148, 153–5, 161
syndicalists, 194

temperance, 57
Third World presses, 292–3
Thormin, Terry, 212, 216
Tit-Coq (Gélinas), 122
Total Refusal. *See Refus global*
Trial of Steven Truscott, The (Lebourdais), 153
Troeger, Annemarie, 43
Trofimenkoff, Susan Mann, 4
truth, 7, 10, 13, 93, 136; different versions of, 177; fiction and, 147
Two Solitudes (MacLennan), 157–9
Types of Canadian Women and of Women Who Are or Have Been Connected with Canada (Morgan), 6

United Student Christian Movement, 231
University Women's Club, 152, 269

vagrancy, 103, 105, 115
van Herk, Aritha, 10, 13–14, 325; identification with subject, 8
Van Kirk, Sylvia, 80
Vertical Mosaic, The (Porter), 161
Very Inside, The, 301
victimization, 101, 115
victimless crimes, 103
victims, 98, 103; of crime, 100; criminalization of, 104; of illegal abortion, 99; sexual history of, 109; status as, 100, 115; of violence, deprivation, 35
violence, 35, 39, 79, 106, 150, 161, 249–50. *See also* domestic abuse
violent offenders, 116